P9-CQD-045

CREATING CONTEXTS
FOR
SECOND
LANGUAGE
ACQUISITION

CREATING CONTEXTS
FOR
SECOND
LANGUAGE
ACQUISITION

Theory and Methods

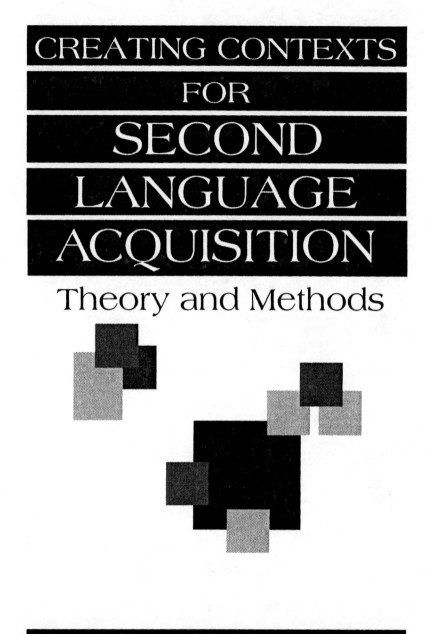

Arnulfo G. Ramírez

Louisiana State University, Baton Rouge

Longman *Publishers USA*

**Creating Contexts for Second Language
Acquisition: Theory and Methods**

Longman, 10 Bank Street, White Plains, N.Y. 10606

Associated companies:
Longman Group Ltd., London
Longman Cheshire Pty., Melbourne
Longman Paul Pty., Auckland
Copp Clark Longman Ltd., Toronto

Senior acquisitions editor: Laura McKenna
Production editors: Victoria Mifsud and Halley Gatenby
Cover design: Bob Crimi
Text art: Fine Line, Inc.
Production supervisor: Richard C. Bretan

Library of Congress Cataloging-in-Publication Data

Ramírez, Arnulfo G. Date.
    Creating contexts for second language acquisition : theory and
methods / Arnulfo G. Ramírez.
      p. cm.
    Includes bibliographical references and index.
    ISBN 0-8013-0480-6
    1. Language and languages—Study and teaching.   I. Title.
P51.R26   1995
418'.007—dc20   94-6628
                                         CIP

3 4 5 6 7 8 9 10-CRS-98

To my mentor, Robert L. Politzer,
who taught me how to apply linguistics
to classroom contexts

Contents

CHAPTER 11   **LANGUAGE TESTING FOR THE
                         CLASSROOM   304**

CHAPTER 12   **TEACHING FOR LEARNING   358**

Preface

How does one create effective learning contexts in second language classrooms? What kinds of knowledge, skills, and attitudes do teachers need to have in order to develop a language pedagogy that promotes second language (L2) acquisition? What role do learners play in the acquisition process? What strategies do students use to learn the linguistic content presented to them in specific language lessons? What teaching insights can be derived from an examination of L2 acquisition research? These are some of the fundamental questions that this book attempts to answer by linking teaching acts with learning behaviors, instructional activities with learning tasks, and research findings with classroom applications.

ORGANIZING PRINCIPLES

This book is designed to help language teachers construct their own frameworks of knowledge, which can be used as guides for establishing effective learning environments. this orientation views teaching as a dynamic process, shaped by such factors as program goals, teaching philosophies, and student characteristics. Teachers ultimately construct their own theories about language learning and establish their own sets of actions to meet particular classroom demands.

Knowledge about a broad range of topics and issues related to language learning and teaching principles is essential for enabling teachers to view their own actions from a variety of positions. Teachers need to develop a critical understanding of such areas as current teaching approaches, the dimensions of language proficiency, the connections between language and culture, learning strategies, and the interrelationships between oral and written language development. Lesson planning entails an awareness of the components of language and the ways they are combined to create a text—a unit of language with structure and meaning. Teachers can facilitate language learning by suggesting strategies for acquisition, by designing appropriate language tasks, and by translating important research findings into classroom practice. In a dramatic way, teachers must come to view themselves as learners. They need to learn, among other things, how to reflect on their own classroom practices, how to identify student approaches to learning different tasks, and how to utilize authentic language input. Throughout the book an attempt is made to present information heuristically rather than algorithmically. Teaching is situated as action, rather than sets of formulas to be followed without concern for the learner, program goals, or classroom routines.

PURPOSE AND SCOPE

The aim of this book is to provide prospective and practicing L2 teachers with an understanding of language teaching and learning principles that are essential for creating effective learning contexts. The term *L2* is used here to refer not only to foreign language (FL) learning in terms of languages such as French, German, and Spanish in the United States and elsewhere, but also to English as a second/foreign language (ESL/EFL). The interconnections between the fields of second language acquisition and foreign language learning are numerous and should be seen as mutually useful in contributing to the development of a language pedagogy that promotes L2 acquisition. In FL situations, the social context plays a lesser, supporting role with respect to natural language use in different settings (e.g., business, government, media, workplace, education). The L2 classroom tends to be the only source of language and cultural input. In ESL situations, the structured language input is enhanced with authentic language use in different situations. The new FL paradigm recognizes this important aspect of L2 acquisition and advocates curricular goals that incorporate authentic input through cultural materials created and used by native speakers.

The examples provided in English, French, German, and Spanish are intended for L2 learners in the middle grades, high school, and university language classes. Some of the examples might be more appropriate for the lower grades, while others might be more relevant for students in higher levels. Two important features are used in all of the examples: the notion of *text type* or *genre* (e.g., conversation, announcement, TV commercial, list, letter, story) and *learning tasks* (e.g., identify and classify information presented orally, create a dialogue based on functions requested, analyze a written text and respond orally). By highlighting text type or genre as the unit of language input, one is able to expose learners to language as it naturally occurs. Another unique feature of this book is the inclusion of many types of questionnaires teachers can use to assess how they teach and how their students learn. Understanding how students learn language ultimately contributes to how they should be taught. By connecting learning to the teaching process, teachers will be able to create a classroom environment that enhances the students' own language learning capacity.

CONTENT AND SEQUENCE

The twelve chapters in the book are sequenced in a way that will enable L2 teachers to approach teaching/learning processes in a comprehensive manner. The book begins with the language classroom as an instructional setting and ends with reflections on the components of effective teaching practice. Each chapter contains an explanatory part and an exploratory segment. The explanatory part includes an overview, a set of questions with answers that highlight the chapter's major issues, and a summary. The exploratory segment consists of a set of teacher activities designed to relate the chapter's major concepts and issues in terms of concrete problems or situations. This latter aspect allows for a critical examination of the ideas presented in the chapter. The assumption here is that teachers need to examine their own modes of thinking and acting in relation to their knowledge about L2 teaching/learning processes.

The first three chapters focus on three important aspects in language teaching: current teaching approaches, concepts of language proficiency, and the relationship between language and culture. Chapter 1 examines the nature of classroom activities when instruction is organized to promote communication abilities focused on how language is used, proficiency-oriented teaching centered on performance goals, and student-centered interactive language learning. The uses of technology and the media are also considered as ways of taking the students "beyond the classroom" into the target culture.

Chapter 2 discusses what it means to "know" a language, in terms of a broad range of linguistic competencies, skills, and abilities. Different concepts of communicative competence are described, along with various systems of knowledge that constitute language proficiency within sociocultural situations. The development of L2 proficiency is a complex process requiring time, interactional opportunities, and learner commitment.

Chapter 3 considers the issue associated with the integration of language with culture, the presentation of culture as "information" and "process," the connection between cultural competence and language proficiency, and techniques for developing cultural competence.

The next two chapters explore a number of aspects associated with curriculum design and the use of teaching strategies to accomplish specific learning goals. Chapter 4 presents various models for organizing language content, procedures for adapting textbooks, ways to plan lessons, procedures for involving students in content selection, and approaches for incorporating content areas into lessons. Chapter 5 analyzes different teaching methods and describes specific techniques that can result in meaningful learning experiences. The development of grammatical and phonological accuracy is discussed. Error correction techniques are also proposed.

Chapter 6 directs attention to the role of the learner in the process of second language acquisition. Students approach the learning task with different personality characteristics, strategies, attitudes, and learning preferences. The effective teacher needs to consider ways of assessing learner differences as a part of the instructional process.

Chapters 7, 8, 9, and 10 address the development of language proficiency in relation to the four major language skills where most communication and interaction tends to occur. Learners will find themselves in listening, reading, speaking, and writing situations. Each situation can be seen in terms of a specific set of circumstances involving particular genres, topics, participants, and communicative uses of language. Research findings can provide many insights about effective teaching techniques designed to promote language learning. Specific learning tasks are offered for listening, reading, speaking, and writing situations.

Chapter 11 offers a number of procedures for testing language abilities within the classroom contest. Language abilities can be assessed through various stimuli-and-response formats, productive and receptive means, and simple and complex tasks. Numerous examples for preparing test items are provided, along with actual tests in English, French, German, and Spanish prepared by classroom teachers.

Chapter 12 examines issues related to teacher effectiveness in the language classroom. Successful language instruction entails a critical understanding of the dynamics of the teaching process as well as of the paths that learners follow in developing their language proficiency. Concerns about creating an effective classroom climate, evaluating lessons, and analyzing textbooks are addressed. Reflective teaching enables teachers to consider the consequences their actions have in creating contexts for language learning.

ACKNOWLEDGMENTS

This book evolved with the help of many persons. In New York, I had the opportunity to learn from my students while teaching courses at SUNY-Albany (1985-1989) on foreign language methodology, second language learning, and instructional materials and their design, I am particularly grateful to those students whose materials I have incorporated throughout the chapters. These contributions are from Yukiko Amemiya, Amy Arnold, Marilyn Bien, Moira Buhr, Isabel Chevillard, Walter Cichacki, Elmire Figliuolo, Anne Garber, Nancy Herman, David Jones, Carol Rayder, Maureen Shiland, and Denise Thompson.

My involvement with NYSAFLT (New York State Association of Foreign Language Teachers) afforded me the unique opportunity to participate in a statewide effort to implement a communicative curriculum. As the editor of three NYSAFLT annual-meeting yearbooks (1987-1989) and a member of the editorial board of the *Language Association Bulletin*, I gained knowledge and insights about the many problems faced daily by classroom teachers. I am particularly indebted to NYSAFLT members Robert Ludwig, John Webb, and the late Anthony Papalia, who all involved me with confidence in the many tasks of the association. Members of the Foreign Language Bureau of the New York State Education Department also involved me in many of their activities. From Paul Dammer, bureau chief, and his associates Dolores Mita and Alain Blanchet, I learned to view language teaching and testing efforts at the district, regional, and state levels.

At Louisiana State University, I have been able to bring this project to completion with the help of José Luis Montiel, director of the Audio and Computer Laboratory for Foreign Languages, Chetan Thakker, computer specialist and master of text processing problems, and others. Brien Louque provided valuable assistance by incorporating the final corrections and changes into the text, tables, and figures. I wish to thank Holly Sessions for proofreading the manuscript and offering valuable editorial suggestions. I am also appreciative of the help provided by a number of persons who reviewed the materials written in German (Evelyn Meyer, Kurt Goblirsch, and John Pizer), French (Dela Frazier), and Spanish (María Esther Ramírez, and, again, José Luis Montiel).

I would also like to thank the following reviewers for their contributions:

Theresa Austin, New York University

Marva A. Barnett, University of Virginia

Joan Kelly Hall, University of Georgia

L. Kathy Heilenman, University of Iowa

Elaine Horwitz, University of Texas at Austin

Randall J. Lund, Brigham Young University

Corinne Mantle-Bromley, Colorado State University

Paul Markham, University of Kansas

Mary E. McGroarty, North Arizona University

Theresa Pica, University of Pennsylvania

Monserrat Villarrubla, Illinois State University

Finally, to my family—my wife, María Esther, and daughters Cristina and Dominica—I extend a special thanks for their understanding and kindness.

CREATING CONTEXTS
FOR
SECOND
LANGUAGE
ACQUISITION

chapter 1

Language Learning Contexts

The classroom lesson is an event of several different kinds. It is a unit in a planned curricular sequence, an instance of a teaching method in operation, a patterned social activity, and an encounter between human personalities. Much of what happens in any given classroom represents a stable routine which best reconciles the varied demands of these different dimensions for the particular teacher and learners in question.

N. S. Prabhu, 1992

Second language classrooms are structured in ways that provide students with varied opportunities for interacting and learning language. Teachers and students interact in a number of language activities that can range from mechanical language drills to authentic communication situations. The particular methodology utilized in a classroom makes specific assumptions about (1) the nature of language, (2) second language learning, (3) learner and teacher roles, and (4) learning activities and instructional materials (Richards, 1990).

This chapter examines the language classroom from three current instructional approaches: *communicative-based, proficiency-oriented* and *interactive-based* instruction. The principal features associated with each teaching approach are described. Further, specific procedures for utilizing authentic materials are outlined so that students can be provided with opportunities to engage in a broad range of intercultural experiences within the classroom setting. Some of the characteristics of effective learning environments are also identified.

This chapter addresses a number of questions associated with creating different types of learning contexts that will promote second language acquisition. Among the issues raised are the following concerns:

1. What is the nature of verbal interaction in second language classrooms?
2. What are the features of communicative-based instruction?
3. What are the features of proficiency-oriented instruction?
4. What are the features of interactive-based language instruction?
5. How can authentic materials be utilized in the classroom to promote intercultural experiences?
6. What are the characteristics of effective learning contexts?

CLASSROOM INTERACTIONAL PATTERNS

In many classroom situations the verbal interaction between teachers and students has been described as an exceedingly constrained form of communication, often distinct from conversation between social equals (Stubbs, 1976). Pupils, for example, learn to give expected replies to teachers' questions:

TEACHER: Where do you live, Steve?

STUDENT: 35 Lexington Avenue.

TEACHER: Answer in a complete sentence.

STUDENT: I live at 35 Lexington Avenue.

TEACHER: Good.

This example also serves to illustrate the artificial nature of classroom dialogue, especially when questions are asked by the teacher not as requests for information but as opportunities to check for the mastery of particular linguistic structures or vocabulary (e.g., "I live _____" or "I like to eat _____").

In many classroom situations students play a passive role, never initiating a discussion and usually speaking only when addressed by the teacher. Students may spend a considerable amount of time learning words and grammatical structures that correspond to a range of *communicative situations* pertaining to a distinct culture (e.g., ordering a meal in a German restaurant, buying food in open markets in Spain, asking directions from a police officer in Paris). Authentic discourse among students is frequently reduced to a rehearsal role (e.g., practicing greetings or farewells, asking for information, or praising others) that might become real at a later date when they interact with native speakers in the target country (Kramsch, 1985). In second language situations (e.g., English as a second language—ESL—in the United States), on the other hand, students have the opportunity to participate in authentic communicative situations outside the classroom, negotiating meaning as they engage in real conversation with native speakers, taking turns at speaking, and using different communication strategies to maintain the discussion. ESL students relate classroom activities to the natural uses of language outside the classroom. For example, they can interview native speakers and report the results to the class. They can be asked to bring in authentic cultural materials (e.g., newspapers, magazines, labels, advertisements) and react to information individually or in groups.

The nature of the verbal exchanges between teachers and pupils is influenced by such factors as lesson content and classroom activities (Green, 1983). The language used to greet pupils is different from that required to present a new grammatical point or communicative function. From a sociolinguistic perspective, each language lesson can be seen as consisting of a series of speech events (e.g., greetings, lecture, review, question-and-answer drills, and role-playing situations) with a specific set or range of language functions (e.g., apologies, directives, informatives, requests, leave-taking). To accomplish a lesson, various interactional structures (student groupings—teacher with whole class, teacher with small group, pupils in small groups, pupils in pairs, pupils working individually) are used. Table 1.1 illustrates the nature of classroom discourse with respect to events, interactional sequences, and communicative acts. These events are based on a series of classroom routines that might occur in a typical lesson (Finocchiaro & Brumfit, 1983).

Much of the communicative activity in this lesson is teacher directed and language centered. Of the 10 lesson events, students interact with students in only two activities (events 6 and 7), and only in one event (7) do students engage in free fluency practice. The type of language that is used can be classified according to McTear's (1975) four basic categories:

1. *Mechanical*, where no exchange of meaning is involved (event 3)
2. *Meaningful*, where language usage is contextualized but no real information is conveyed (events 4 and 6)
3. *Pseudocommunicative*, where information is exchanged but in ways that would not likely occur outside the classroom (event 7)
4. *Real communication*, which consists of spontaneous natural speech

The extent to which one will find examples of "real communication" in the classroom might be conditioned by such factors as the lesson's goals, the students' proficiency level, and the type of activity—role-playing, paired interview, surveys/polls, or problem-solving simulations. The presence of "mechanical" or "pseudocommunicative" language could depend on the features—grammar, vocabulary, functions—that are being introduced and the aspects of language that are being reviewed or practiced for different situations.

An important aspect of classroom language is the "tension" that exists between classroom management and target language discourse. Teachers use directives, ask questions, and correct their students in order to accomplish their lessons. At the time, students are asked to engage in so-called authentic language functions such as greetings, asking for directions, providing information, or expressing personal feelings in various social situations such as checking in at a hotel, ordering a meal at a restaurant, or getting directions from a police officer—all in the distant target culture. Thus, the foreign language classroom can be seen as "coexisting discourse worlds" (Edmonson, 1985) where the target language may

TABLE 1.1   Classroom discourse during a second language lesson

Lesson Events	Interactional Structures	Language Functions
1. Greetings and warm-up activity	Teacher interacts with whole class, nominates some students to speak; pupils directed to initiate dialogue with others	Greetings, requests for information, reports, descriptions, expressing emotions
2. Correction of homework	Teacher interacts with whole class, nominates students individually or in groups/rows	Pseudoquestions and replies, corrections, inquiries about possible answers to questions
3. Pronunciation practice	Teacher interacts with whole class, nominates students individually or in groups/rows	Modeling, repetitions, pseudoquestions and replies, correction of errors
4. Discussion to introduce new material—narrative dialogue, cultural situation	Teacher interacts with whole class, nominates students to answer questions; pupils can ask teacher questions about topic	Requests for information about topic, explanations, descriptions, reports, expressing opinions and attitudes
5. Presentation of new material (language functions, vocabulary, grammatical structures)	Teacher presents to the whole class (recorded dialogue, reading of text, use of visual representations); students listen and observe, taking notes at times	Explanations, descriptions, narration, translating
6. Practice of new material	Students work individually, sometimes in groups or pairs; students can solicit help from the teacher	Pseudoquestions and replies, directives, suggestions, inquiries about possible answers to questions/exercises
7. Free fluency activity	Students engage in group activities (role-playing) or work in pair situations	Interpersonal (greeting, introduction, praising, advising, apologizing, offers), personal (opinions, attitudes, concerns), and imaginative (creating stories, dialogues) use of language
8. Summary of lesson	Teacher presents to whole class the major linguistic/cultural points, questions for clarification	Explanations, narration, question/answers about lesson content
9. Homework assignment and references to next lesson	Teacher explains to the whole class; students listen and can ask questions for clarification	Directives, information about assignment (suggestions, requests, advice)
10. Dismissal and leave-taking	Teacher explains to the whole class; students respond; some students may address each other	Leave-taking/farewell formulas, expressions of personal feeling/emotions

SOURCE: From "Assessing the Communicativeness of Language Lessons," by Arnulfo G. Ramírez, in P. W. Wood (Ed.), *Creating an Environment for Second Language Acquisition* (p. 32). ©1987, New York State Association of Foreign Language Teachers, Schenectady, NY. Reprinted with permission.

serve multiple functions and purposes. The language used might be the content of instruction, the goal of instruction, the medium for presenting new language items, the medium to manage classroom behavior, the medium for nonpedagogical talk, and the medium for practicing authentic language use in specific target culture situations.

THE COMMUNICATIVE-BASED PERSPECTIVE

Language teaching approaches can differ in a number of ways: theories of language and language learning, language goals, organization of the syllabus/lessons, role of teachers and students, classroom instructional techniques, and the use of materials and media. In community language learning (Curran, 1976), for example, students pass through five stages of growth, from dependence on the teacher to independence from the teacher. In the first stage, the teacher translates in "chunks" what the students want to say in the target language. The students then tape-record the chunks, the conversation is transcribed, and the transcript becomes the text for several lessons. Classroom language tends to be student centered, based on the needs and interests of the students with the teacher serving as the language counselor. With methodologies such as total physical response (Asher, 1982) and the comprehension approach (Winitz, 1978), students are silent for an extended period of time. Teachers do most of the talking in the form of commands: "Stand up," "Go to the blackboard and write your name," "Draw a picture of a tree next to a house." Students act out the commands, and eventually roles can be reversed. With this approach the use of directives, particularly the imperative form, tends to be the basic discourse feature.

The communicative-teaching orientation tends to stress the uses of language (greetings, suggestions, apologies, directives, and informatives) within social situations (a friend's home, the doctor's office, the train station). Students receive practice by interacting with their teacher and peers. Class activities are usually characterized by interactive situations where there is an information gap (one of the speakers knows something the listener does not know—"Where do you live?" "What are your plans for the summer?"). The speaker who wants to obtain this information needs to use the appropriate linguistic forms (grammatical structures and vocabulary) to convey the meaning to the listener. Based on the feedback received from the listener, the speaker may have to negotiate the meaning of the message by paraphrasing, restating, or using nonlinguistic resources.

Specific procedures for developing communicative ability among second language learners in the ESL classroom have been formulated by Littlewood (1981). Classroom activities are organized so that there are both precommunicative (structural practice of linguistic forms and their meanings) and communicative activities (functional language use and social interaction practice). As can be seen in Figure 1.1, during the precommunicative phase the focus initially is on the linguistic forms/structures of the target language, emphasizing acceptability and/or accuracy. Later, an attempt is made to relate the language forms to their potential functional

Precommunicative Activities

Structural practice

Language features: singular/plural forms of nouns

I have three dollars.
She has one sister.
My brother has a new car.
He needs to buy sugar, eggs, and flour.

Quasi-communicative practice

Relate language forms to specific meanings (answer written questions)

Q: How many dollars do you have now?
A: I have five dollars.
Q: How many brothers and sisters do you have?
A: I have one brother and two sisters.
Q: What do you need to buy at the grocery store?
A: I need to buy bread, some sugar, and one dozen eggs.

Relate language forms to a social context (prepare a conversation based on cues)
Persons/situation: a brother (B) and his sister (S) at home
Shopping: B will go to a mall and S will go to a grocery store.
Things to buy: pants, sweater, shoes, coffee, oranges, sugar, bread

B: Mary, where are you going?
S: I have to go to the grocery store.
B: What are you going to buy?
S: I need to buy one pound of coffee, five oranges, two pounds of sugar, and one loaf of bread. What are you going to do?
B: I need to go the mall.
S: What are you going to buy?
B: I have to buy a pair of pants, a brown sweater, and a pair of shoes.
S: I'll see you later. Have fun shopping.
B: Bye.

Communicative Activities

Functional practice

Sharing information with other students

This afternoon, I have to go to the grocery store to buy some food for a neighbor. I need to get two pounds of flour, one dozen eggs, one can of beans, one bag of onions, and two loaves of bread. On Saturday I have to take my younger brother shopping for clothes. He needs two shirts, one pair of boots, and a raincoat. Next week I will buy something for myself.

Social activities

Simulation: You are a reporter. Interview four classmates to find out about their buying habits.

Some questions to ask:
Who buys what in each family?
In what type of stores do they shop?
What things do they buy daily, weekly, or monthly?
What types of things do they like/dislike to buy?

FIGURE 1.1 Communicative language activities from structural practice to social interaction

Based on concepts and categories from Littlewood, 1981

meanings (e.g., "Shall we go. . . ," "Oh, no, I don't feel like. . . ," or ways of making and rejecting suggestions). During the communicative phase, the learner is initially placed in a cultural situation, which requires various uses of language:

1. Sharing information with restricted cooperation (e.g., yes/no questions)
2. Sharing information with unrestricted cooperation (e.g., information gap activities—discovering differences)
3. Sharing and processing the information (e.g., discuss or evaluate information—pooling information to solve a problem)
4. Processing information (e.g., discuss and evaluate facts in order to solve a problem or reach a decision)

The last phase involves social interaction activities, which require the learner to pay close attention to the social as well as the functional meanings that language conveys. Communicative activities might involve role-playing situations through cued dialogues, role playing cued by information for participating in a social situation, debate, and improvisation. Some of the activities call for language use in the context of a classroom setting, while others use simulation as a means to place the learner in target culture situations. Thus, sequences of language activities range from the use of mechanical drills in the precommunicative phase to the practice of authentic language use in specific sociolinguistic situations included during the communicative phase.

What conditions must be met to create a learning environment that promotes communication? Vogel, Brassard, Parks, Thibaudeau, and White (1983), for example, characterize the communicative classroom in terms of six major components:

1. Language input that focuses on ideas and information
2. Interaction that determines the dynamics of classroom discourse
3. Demands of the task that meet real-world criteria
4. Materials that are interesting, intellectually stimulating, and challenging
5. Methodology that promotes interaction through student-centered activities
6. Language tasks that stress information-gathering activities, create information-gap situations, and promote development of skills and strategies

Authentic communication in the classroom results from the input of ideas and information (including reading and listening sources) that students exchange and discuss because they find the materials interesting and intellectually stimulating. Because language learning is an interactive process, students must have opportunities to express personal feelings, provide and obtain information, and get others to adopt a course of action, thereby allowing the learners to formulate, confirm, and disconfirm hypotheses about the grammatical structures and meaning of the language they are trying to learn. Teachers can plan language activities so that students can participate in various interactive situations, carrying out a range of language functions reflecting both instructional and natural communication. Van Lier (1982) has noted four major types of interactional situations in the classroom, all of which reflect different degrees of teacher- or group-controlled activities with respect to a particular topic and the linguistic rules that may vary with the activity. For example, students can engage in private conversations in pairs without the teacher monitoring the way interaction is organized or the level of accuracy. In another situation, the teacher might assign a topic to a group, enabling the students to work on a text, participate in a role-playing situation, or take part in a problem-solving activity. The teacher can direct the whole class by choosing the topic, by controlling and managing the course of the conversation, or by directing communicative exercises to illustrate a grammar point. The teacher can also control the interaction during a mechanical drill (e.g., pronunciation exercise, transformation/substitution drill) where students are asked to respond on cue without regard to specific conversational topic.

The nature of the learning task is particularly critical, since some activities are more appropriate for intermediate or advanced levels of language study than beginning or novice levels (Bragger, 1985). Still, it is possible for students at different levels of language proficiency to respond to a particular task (e.g., retelling a story describing a street scene) in ways appropriate to the particular proficiency level. Beginning students can identify the main elements (topic, situation, and participants). Intermediate students can describe (e.g., actions, sequences, and personal opinions), while advanced students can change the elements of the story (e.g., situation, characters, and ending) and write directions or a script for the situation depicted in the street scene. Throughout the process, students would have opportunities to interact in structured situations involving small groups and pairs of students, as well as in exchanges with the teacher.

Savignon (1987, p. 20) argues that communicative classrooms must involve "learners in the *dynamic* and *interactive* process of communication" and offer them the opportunity "to experience language as well as to analyze it." The learning experience should involve the whole learner—the cognitive and physical dimensions as well as the affective. In order to engage the three facets that characterize the communication goals of second language learners, Savignon (1983) suggests the inclusion of five components in the curriculum. Each component consists of a series of activities and experiences that correspond to a particular facet of the learning process:

1. *Language arts*: includes many of the exercises used in first-language instructional programs where the focus is on formal accuracy. Among the activities included are the use of vocabulary-expansion exercises through definitions, descriptions, synonyms, and cognates; pronunciation exercises that stress the contrast of second language (L2) sounds with those of the learner's native language (L1); substitution drills requiring a change such as from one aspect to another, statement to question, present tense to past tense, or indicative to subjunctive.
2. *Language for a purpose*: involves the use of language for a real and im-

mediate communicative purpose. The most important examples of this feature are the immersion-bilingual programs at the elementary school level in which the L2 (French, Spanish, or German) is used as the medium of communication to teach content in subjects such as math, science, social studies, and art. At the secondary level, minicourses on diverse topics such as cooking, art, cinema, etc., allow learners to use language in a natural, interactive manner by focusing on content. Crafts and motor activities of various kinds can provide opportunities for authentic language use. Recipes can be prepared for an international fair or holiday, and students can learn to dance or play soccer or chess in the target language. Directions can be given in the L2 so that students can construct model airplanes and masks, draw pictures and maps, and carry out requests from the teacher and fellow classmates.

3. *My language is me*: implies respect for all learners as they use the L2 for self-expression. Personalized language activities provide learners with opportunities for expressing and exploring their values and attitudes. Students should have opportunities to share their feelings, thus contributing to the creation of a community of learners able to work together toward common linguistic goals.

4. *You be, I'll be: Theater arts*: offers learners the opportunity to make believe, experiment, try out hats and wigs, moods, gestures, accents, and ways of relating. Play production, role playing, pantomime, simulations, and the interpretation of characters in a dialogue or story are some of the few activities that should be included in the theater arts component of an L2 curriculum.

5. *Beyond the classroom*: activities to prepare the learner for the real world beyond the school setting. Learners may have the possibility of interacting systematically with an adjacent L2 community. They may be able to bring ads from local newspapers, compare the prices of different products, go shopping, and then report to the class. Native speakers can be invited to visit the class and talk about native cultural experiences or cross-cultural problems. Media such as newspapers, magazines, radio, and television may be available as means for developing functional language use. Learners may respond as individuals, or as a group by preparing a class newspaper that can be exchanged with another class in a different school, region, or country. The preparation of a newspaper would involve almost everyone in the class in some capacity—as reporters on sports, important academic or social events, food, and fashion; as cartoonists, crossword puzzle and other word gamemasters, layout artists; and as commercial copy writers.

The language arts component may be particularly useful for those analytical activities associated with sentence-level grammatical forms. Experiential activities such as personal language use, theater arts, and beyond the classroom will enhance the development of functional language proficiency. The appropriate balance between analytical and experiential activities will depend on learner factors (age, interests, motivation), the learning context (type of school, language goals, proximity to L2 cultural group), and the program resources (financial support, curriculum materials, and technological means).

More specifically, Enright and McCloskey (1985) offer seven criteria for organizing the classroom to promote communication and language acquisition, particularly among younger children in elementary schools. The criteria call for classroom activities that promote:

1. *Collaboration*: Students need to have opportunities to interact with other students to solve problems and find solutions cooperatively.
2. *Purpose*: Activities should be organized so that they can be accomplished or completed with active pupil participation (e.g., play performance, science projects, or measurement problems).
3. *Student interest*: Students' interests with respect to topics and goals need to be considered in curriculum planning.
4. *Students' previous experience*: Learners should have opportunities to share their sociocultural experiences with each other in the class (e.g., maps and drawings of their homes, vacations, and drawings of family or friends).
5. *Holism*: Curricular and learning activities should integrate various skills (e.g., reading a story about measuring could be followed by measurement activities—teacher demonstration and student projects—and then additional reading and oral reports).
6. *Support*: Students' efforts at communication need to take place in a pleasant and comfortable atmosphere with multiple options available (e.g., small groups, dialogue with the teacher, in front of the whole class).
7. *Variety*: The teacher must utilize a variety of materials, purposes, topics, activities, and ways of interacting.

This section has presented various interpretations associated with the concept of communicative-based teaching. On the basis of this discussion, a number of classroom principles can be established. The communicative-based perspective:

- Stresses the functional uses of language in different social settings
- Organizes classroom activities that relate language forms with functions and offer functional practice within social situations
- Uses materials that are interesting, intellectually stimulating, and challenging to learners
- Incorporates language tasks that involve information gathering, collaboration, and purposeful interaction
- Focuses on the whole learner—the cognitive, physical, and affective qualities

- Provides learners with opportunities to share and explore their attitudes, feelings, and opinions
- Offers learners opportunities to integrate different sets of language skills to complete language tasks

THE PROFICIENCY-BASED PERSPECTIVE

The concept of proficiency as reflected in the American Council on the Teaching of Foreign Languages (ACTFL) proficiency guidelines (1986) presents language in terms of four performance levels (novice, intermediate, advanced, and superior) for each of the four language skill areas (listening, speaking, reading, and writing). Each proficiency level comprises integrated descriptions of linguistic abilities according to function, context, and accuracy. Proficiency guidelines were established initially (1982) for cultural competence but were not retained in the revised guidelines published in 1986. A more detailed description of the problems associated with the definition and measurement of cultural proficiency is presented in Chapter 3.

Table 1.2 presents the ACTFL descriptions for the assessment of oral proficiency levels according to various components of language: functions/global tasks (the uses of language, such as questioning, reporting, giving instructions), context/content (the topics or content of the communication, such as clothing, family, travel, current events), accuracy (the overall quality of the message, both in terms of linguistic criteria and sociolinguistic appropriateness), and text type (words, sentences, paragraph discourse).

The proficiency guidelines, which were designed as rating scales for individual performance, have been characterized as the "organizing principle" for curriculum planning and course development (Higgs, 1984). Teachers can use the ACTFL guidelines to specify learning goals for their students. Figure 1.2 presents a set of goal statements for four semesters of college French, prepared by faculty at the University of South Carolina. These statements illustrate possible use of the ACTFL guidelines in setting specific performance levels for the four language skill areas along with a concern for cultural awareness.

In order to develop high levels of language proficiency in the classroom, several hypotheses need to be followed with classroom practice (Omaggio, 1986):

Hypothesis 1. Opportunities must be provided for students to practice using language in a range of contexts likely to be encountered in the target culture.

Corollary 1. Students should be encouraged to express their own meaning as early as possible after productive skills have been introduced in the course of instruction.

Corollary 2. A proficiency-oriented approach promotes active communicative interaction among students.

TABLE 1.2 Assessment criteria for speaking proficiency

Global Tasks/Functions	Context	Content	Accuracy	Text Type
Superior				
Can discuss extensively by supporting opinions, abstracting and hypothe-sizing	Most formal and informal settings	Wide range of general topics and some special fields of interest and expertise; concrete, abstract and unfamiliar topics	Errors virtually never inter-fere with communication or disturb the native speaker	Extended discourse
Advanced				
Can describe and narrate in major time/aspect frames	Most informal and some formal settings	Concrete and factual topics of personal and public interest	Can be understood without difficulty by speakers unaccustomed to non-native speakers	Paragraph discourse
Intermediate				
Can maintain simple face-to-face conversation by ask-ing and responding to simple questions	Some informal settings and a limited number of transactional situations	Topics related primarily to self and immediate envi-ronment	Can be understood, with some repetition, by speak-ers accustomed to non-native speakers	Discrete sentences and strings of sentences
Novice				
Can produce only formulaic utterances, lists and enu-merations	Highly predictable common daily settings	Common discrete elements of daily life	May be difficult to under-stand, even for those accustomed to non-native speakers	Discrete words and phrases

SOURCE: From "Assessment Criteria: Speaking Proficiency," by Heidi Byrnes and Irene Thompson, contributing editors, and Kathryn Buck (Ed.), *The ACTFL Oral Proficiency Interview Tester Training Manual,* ©1989, The American Council on the Teaching of Foreign Languages, Yonkers, NY. Reprinted with permission.

Semester 1

1. Speak the language well enough to satisfy immediate needs using learned utterances, and with a pronunciation that is intelligible to native speakers used to dealing with foreigners;
2. Comprehend some non-memorized, spoken language in areas of immediate need or on very familiar topics provided that such topics are supported by context; comprehension is reasonably accurate if utterances are short and contain redundant elements;
3. Read simple, connected discourse, either authentic material or specially prepared recombinations of known and unknown material; accuracy in comprehension depends on high-frequency and highly contextualized vocabulary and syntax that parallel the native language;
4. Write, from dictation or memory, simple, fixed expressions, and short sentences based on very familiar sentence patterns; spelling errors do not interfere with comprehension of such writing;
5. Display limited awareness in basic, culturally specific verbal and non-verbal behavior, does not offend a native of the culture used to dealing with North Americans.

Semester 2

1. Speak the language well enough to satisfy basic survival needs and minimum courtesy requirements; engage in spontaneous, short conversations on familiar topics; understood by native speakers used to dealing with foreigners;
2. Comprehend the spoken language well enough to participate in simple conversations about some survival needs, familiar topics, and limited social conventions; restatement (simplification or elaboration) may be necessary;
3. Read for information simple printed and/or illustrated discourse on familiar and unfamiliar topics; locating main idea depends on repeated readings and overtly structured texts with high degree of predictability;
4. Write short messages, paragraphs, short compositions on familiar, personal, or survival topics, evidence of good control of basic constructions but lack of basic cohesive elements of discourse;
5. Display limited awareness in basic, culturally specific verbal and non-verbal behavior, does not offend a native of the culture used to dealing with North Americans.

Semester 3

1. Speak the language well enough to satisfy most routine travel and survival needs and some limited social demands; understood by persons used to dealing with foreigners;
2. Comprehend the language well enough to participate in short conversations about most survival needs and limited social conventions; comprehend main ideas and some details in non-face-to-face situations;
3. Read the language accurately enough to interpret connected discourse with simple cohesive elements for personal communication, information or recreational purposes;
4. Write with sufficient control to create paragraphs relating to some survival needs; some limited social demands, and some familiar topics grounded in personal experience;
5. Understand basic cultural differences and begin to recognize and practice correct social conventions.

(continued)

FIGURE 1.2 Goal statements for four semesters of French

SOURCE: From "Designing the Proficiency-Based Curriculum," by Frank W. Medley, in A. C. Omaggio (Ed.), *Proficiency, curriculum, articulation: The ties that bind.* pp. 27–29. Middlebury, VT: Northeast Conference on the Teaching of Foreign Languages, copyright 1985. Reprinted with permission.

Semester 4

1. Speak the language well enough to initiate and sustain general conversation on some factual topics beyond basic survival needs in a manner comprehensible to native speakers used to dealing with foreigners;
2. Comprehend the language well enough to participate in conversations about routine social conventions and limited school and work requirements; understand standard French spoken at a normal rate with some repetition and rewording, by a native speaker not used to dealing with foreigners; comprehend main ideas and some details in some non-face-to-face, authentic situations;
3. Read uncomplicated, extended discourse on familiar topics and unfamiliar topics that are not highly specialized; read a variety of authentic prose texts including carefully chosen literary selections;
4. Write well enough to create sentences and paragraphs relating to most survival needs and limited social demands; take notes in some detail on familiar topics and express fairly accurately present and future time;
5. Understand basic cultural differences and begin to recognize and practice correct social conventions.

FIGURE 1.2 (continued)

Corollary 3. Creative language practice (as opposed to exclusively manipulative or convergent practice) must be encouraged in a proficiency-oriented classroom.

Corollary 4. Authentic language should be used in instruction wherever and whenever possible.

Hypothesis 2. Opportunities should be provided for students to practice carrying out a range of functions (task universals) likely to be necessary in dealing with others in the target culture.

Hypothesis 3. There should be concern for the development of linguistic accuracy from the beginning of instruction in a proficiency-oriented approach.

Hypothesis 4. Proficiency-oriented approach should respond to the affective needs of students as well as their cognitive needs. Students should feel motivated to learn and must be given opportunities to express their own meanings in a non-threatening environment.

Hypothesis 5. Cultural understanding must be promoted in various ways so that students are prepared to live more harmoniously in the target-language community. (pp. 45-53)

From a teaching perspective, the classroom procedures necessary to implement this type of proficiency-oriented learning should call for more-student-centered activities. Students should interact with other students, engaging in creative language use related to their affective needs and interests. Authentic language and cultural situations should be used as much as possible, creating many opportunities for students to carry out a range of communicative functions. The teacher should correct those errors that affect linguistic accuracy (phonology and grammar) along with errors of meaning and information.

In order to achieve specific performance levels, teachers need to utilize certain instructional techniques. Figure 1.3 specifies the instructional content and

FIGURE 1.3 Curricular guide for listening: Intermediate level

SOURCE: From *Teaching Language in Context* (p. 130) by Alice C. Omaggio. Boston, MA: Heinle & Heinle Publishers, copyright 1986. Reprinted with permission.

Content

Text types:
Narrative on familiar topics
Simple face-to-face conversation
Radio/television broadcasts
Announcements
Simple instruction

Everyday survival topics such as:
Personal biographical information
Restaurants/foods
Asking/giving directions
Activities/hobbies
Transportation
Talking on phone
Lodging
Money matters
Health matters
Post Office
Numbers 1–1000
Customs
Shopping/making purchases

Courtesy/social situations such as:
Greetings/introduction
Making appointments
Accepting/refusing invitations
Polite formulaic expressions

Functions

Can understand simple questions and answers, simple statements, and simple face-to-face conversations in standard dialect
With authentic materials, can understand main gist, main ideas, some supporting detail
Can detect mood of message, determine to limited degree attitudes, feelings, of speakers, urgency, etc.

Techniques
Listening for the gist
Listening with visuals
Graphic fill-ins
Selective listening
Comprehension checks
Dictation and variations
Clue searching
Kinesics/physical response
Paraphrase in native language
Note taking
Selective listening
Story rebuilding
Logical continuation
Identifying sociolinguistic factors
Remembering responses of others
Prelistening activities
SAADs (Simple active, affirmative, declarative sentences)

Accuracy

In conversational exchanges may need some repetition; more deliberate speech; difficulty understanding speech delivered at normal rate; cannot generally understand vocabulary beyond most elementary needs teaching techniques essential to the development of intermediate-level listening comprehension skills.

According to Omaggio (1986), at the novice level the general text types should focus on short utterances drawn from familiar materials (time, dates, weather, numbers, clothing). Through various instructional techniques (listening for gist, graphic fill-ins, selective listening), students learn to identify main ideas and key words in familiar materials. At the intermediate level, attention should center on simple, narrative texts and brief face-to-face conversations in the standard dialect. The range of topics should include food, transportation, health, custom, shopping, and lodging concerns. Students are expected to identify main ideas with supporting details. Clue searching, paraphrasing in the native language, note taking, and listening for the gist are some of the strategies used to help students develop their abilities to comprehend oral texts.

At the advanced level, content widens to include topics of a factual nature (current events, politics, education, economics, academic lectures, reports, and descriptions). The topics are instructive and require understanding of facts and literal information. Through the use of clue searching, getting the gist, paraphrasing, comprehension checks, and inferential listening, students learn to decode and classify information that corresponds to the four main language functions. At the superior level, comprehension tasks include grasping the implications of the main ideas. The texts now range from telephone communications to technical reports, instructions, radio and television broadcasts, movies and plays, and abstract and professional topics. The students must be able to infer, guess, hypothesize, and interpret the meaning of authentic, sometimes unfamiliar topics. The listening guidelines assume that all listening tasks take place in an authentic environment at a normal rate of speech using standard or nearly-standard language norms.

The ACTFL guidelines might be seen as useful generic statements about general goals for language instruction. The concept of proficiency provides direction for language-teaching professionals in charge of curriculum planning, teacher preparation, materials development, and classroom instruction. Language teachers and school personnel can discuss specific learning goals and achievement levels. Nevertheless, the guidelines do not address specific language issues (e.g., case-ending problems in learning German). At the same time, the 1986 guidelines are not definitive and may have to be refined and updated on the basis of the performance levels or authentic linguistic needs of actual learners, as well as advances in the profession (Hipple, 1987). More importantly, using the suggested proficiency levels as "blueprints for syllabus and curriculum design" has been called into question by many language teaching professionals (Dodds, 1992).

One of the major problems is that "to date the profession has no acceptable definition of proficiency, and the validity of the tests has not been established" (Chastain, 1989, p. 49). Language abilities can vary depending on social factors (e.g., formal vs. informal situations) and linguistic considerations (e.g., unplanned face-to-face conversations vs. planned written communication). Not a single proficiency, language competence is typically "heterogeneous, rather than homogeneous" (Ellis, 1985, p. 71). And aside from these theoretical concerns, there are the practical issues of implementing proficiency-oriented testing procedures. It may be both costly and difficult to train large groups of teachers to administer individual oral interviews to all their students. (See Chapter 2 for a description of the ACTFL oral interview.)

This section has presented the proficiency-based perspective. From this discussion, a number of classroom principles can be established. The proficiency-based perspective:

- Describes language abilities in terms of four performance levels for each of the four language skill areas
- Specifies the language functions/tasks, content/topics, accuracy, and text types that characterize performance levels for each language skill area
- Proposes that the guidelines can be used as the "organizing principle" for course design, curriculum planning, and evaluation
- Encourages active communication and interaction among learners
- Provides opportunity for creative language use and practice in carrying out a range of language functions likely to be encountered in the target culture
- Focuses on the cognitive as well as affective needs of learners
- Incorporates authentic language texts or materials whenever possible

THE INTERACTIVE-BASED PERSPECTIVE

Interactive language teaching focuses on creating communicative situations that enable students to convey and receive authentic messages containing information that appeals to both sender and receiver. According to Rivers (1987, pp. 10–15), among other things an interactive classroom:

1. Encourages listening to authentic materials (e.g., teacher talk, audio and videotapes, and native speakers where available)
2. Uses newspapers, magazines, cartoons, books, letters, instructions for products, menus, and maps as reading materials
3. Stresses that from the beginning students listen and speak while reacting to pictures and objects in role-playing situations and discussions (pairs, small groups, and whole class)
4. Involves students in joint tasks that require different language functions (e.g., suggesting, requesting, directing, convincing, praising, explaining, and informing)
5. Exposes students to films and videotapes of native speakers interacting in different situations, thus promoting an awareness of nonverbal behaviors, conversational strategies (e.g., exclamations, turn-taking strategies, topic changes), and ways by which meaning is negotiated
6. Uses reading activities that are made interactive by asking the reader to respond creatively (e.g., discussing alternative possibilities, or writing a short play from the narrative)

7. Uses writing activities that include personal communication exchanges between students (pairs and/or groups) or between the students and teacher (dialogue journals, where the teacher can comment on the content and rephrase awkward expressions or structures)
8. Promotes grammatical and pronunciation accuracy by incorporating various language activities (e.g., poetry reading and creation for pronunciation practice, practice of the imperative by giving directions, practice of hypothetical expression or conditions by asking students to inform others what they would do if they had a lot of money: "If I had a million dollars, I. . . .")

Through interaction "students achieve facility in using a language" as they participate in situations that call for collaboration and the negotiation of meaning in a shared context (Rivers, 1987, p. 4). Interactive teaching starts not with the communicative functions of language or functional proficiency levels but with the characteristics of the learners (age, needs, cultural background, and reasons for language study). After this is established, it is then possible to plan the course and determine appropriate ways of selecting and presenting material. Information about learner needs is usually established on the basis of three general categories: (1) background information (age, educational level, previous language learning experience, proficiency level in the target language, learning goals and expectations), (2) language needs (settings where the language will be used, topics, tasks, communicative acts), and (3) learning styles and preferences (Yalden, 1987). Figure 1.4 is a sample questionnaire illustrating the types of information that can be obtained through students' self-reporting. Some sections of the questionnaire may have to be administered on different occasions, given the number of sections in the survey. Teachers may find it necessary to obtain additional information about their learners' needs through such means as observation, interviews, and discussions.

Keeping interaction central means that teachers need to plan language activities so that students can participate in various interactive situations, carrying out a range of language functions that reflect both instructional and natural communication. *Linguistic interaction* involves establishing a relationship between the sender, the receiver, and the context of the situation (Wells, 1981). It involves a broad range of collaborative and group activities to promote interaction. This can include group investigations and discussions, role-playing situations, skits, and dialogue journals between various participants, and games. Cohen (1986) suggests that to be successful interactive activities must:

1. Have more than one answer or more than one way to solve the problem
2. Be intrinsically interesting and rewarding to most students
3. Allow different students to make different contributions
4. Involve multimedia sources
5. Involve sight, sound, and touch
6. Require a variety of skills and behaviors
7. Require some reading and writing
8. Represent a challenge

Examples of possible interactive tasks having some of these characteristics are presented in Figure 1.5.

The tasks outlined in Figure 1.5 interrelate the oral (listening and speaking) and written (reading and writing) language modalities in different sequences. At the same time, they place specific linguistic demands on the participants. Task 3, for example, involves knowledge of grammatical features (prepositions of place) and the creation of descriptive sentences based on a picture. Tasks such as 1, 4, and 8 require group collaboration and encompass both reading and writing abilities.

Long and Porter (1985) argue for the use of group work based on sound pedagogical arguments as well as psycholinguistic concerns. They suggest that teachers should consider including as many two-way tasks (e.g., question-and-answer situations, problem-solving tasks) as possible among those activities students can carry out successfully in small groups or pairs. Enright and McCloskey (1985) provide criteria for organizing the classroom to promote second language acquisition, especially among ESL learners in elementary schools. They point out the need to consider such structural aspects as the arrangement of materials and the physical environment. Pica and Doughty (1988) have found that the nature of the task in group work appears to be a particularly critical factor affecting the type of discourse patterns among pupils. This suggests that group work activities need to be examined in relation to the nature of the task itself, which requires the exchange of different types of information among the participants.

Di Pietro (1987) uses the strategic interactive technique as a means of developing oral language proficiency through the use of scenarios. Students are placed in situations or scenarios that follow three phases of strategic interaction (Di Pietro, 1987, p. 2):

> Preclass preparation: Teacher selects or creates appropriate scenarios and prepares the necessary role cards.
>
> Phase 1 (rehearsal): Students form groups and prepare agendas to fulfill the roles assigned to them. Teacher acts as advisor and guide to student groups as needed.
>
> Phase 2 (performance): Students perform their roles with support of their respective groups, while teacher and remainder of class look on.
>
> Phase 3 (debriefing): Teacher leads the entire class in a discussion of the students' performance.

The scenario can involve socially determined roles, such as vendor-customer, ticket-agent-traveler, doctor-patient, and can include different psychological dispositions (friend-stranger, adult-child, newlyweds-mother-in-law). The scenario can consist of two principal roles, multiple roles for different students, open-ended situations allowing for diverse episodes based on new circumstances, and data-based situations that relate to factual information or props to which each participant must react. Because the scenarios focus on prototypical encounters with an often unexpected twist, learners leave the classroom with meaningful and significant lan-

Background Information

Name _____ Age _____ Sex _____

Birthplace _____ Educational Level _____

Language(s) spoken at home _____

Indicate what other languages you   Circle one

Understand _____   F   W   L

Speak _____   F   W   L

Read _____   F   W   L

Write _____   F   W   L

and specify whether *fluently* (F), *well* (W) or in a *limited way* (L).

Indicate with an X your reason(s) for studying this language:

_____ To fulfill the foreign language requirement

_____ To learn about other peoples and cultures

_____ To gain a better understanding about my cultural-linguistic heritage

_____ To be able to communicate with my relatives

_____ To prepare for study abroad

_____ To enhance future career opportunities

_____ To interact more closely with friends from the target culture

_____ To obtain a well-rounded education

_____ Other _____

How long have you been studying this language?   _____ (years/months)

Language Needs

Indicate with an X those settings/ tasks where the target language will be used:

_____ Arriving at the airport

_____ Checking in/out at a hotel

_____ Eating at a restaurant

_____ Conducting business at a bank

_____ Sending letters/packages at a post office

_____ Making telephone calls

_____ Visiting a family

_____ Taking a taxi

_____ Arranging a trip

_____ Asking directions on the street

_____ Shopping in a store/market

_____ Going to the movies/theatre/museum

_____ Participating in a meeting

_____ Other _____

FIGURE 1.4 Learner needs analysis: A sample questionnaire

Based on Yalden (1987), New York State Syllabus (1986), Nunan (1989), and Richards (1990).

Indicate with an X those language contexts in which you will engage with respect to listening, speaking, reading, and writing situations:

Listening Contexts

_____ Information and announcements from providers of common public services (sales personnel, bank tellers, ticket agents, police, hotel personnel, etc.) in face-to-face communications

_____ Information (bulletins/announcements) provided over loudspeakers, radio, and television

_____ Short presentations of interest to the general public given in person, on radio, or on television

_____ Songs, live and recorded

_____ Feature programs on television, in the movies, and on the radio

_____ Other _____

Listening/Speaking Contexts

_____ Interaction with providers of common public services in face-to-face communications

_____ Informal everyday conversations with individual peers and adults

_____ Informal conversations with peers and familiar adults

_____ Interaction with providers of common public services by telephone

_____ Group conversations among peers and familiar adults

_____ Group discussions with peers

_____ Informal presentations to groups of peers and familiar adults

_____ Other _____

Reading Contexts

_____ Information provided to the general public on forms, signs, billboards and posters, labels, programs, timetables, maps, plans, menus, etc.

_____ Announcements, ads, and short reports of general interest in newspapers, magazines, and other publications; short, informal notes

_____ Simple business correspondence and pamphlets

_____ Facts, opinions, feelings, and attitudes in correspondence from acquaintances and friends (peers and adults)

_____ Letters to the editor and feature articles from general-interest publications

_____ Excerpts from poetry and prose for cultural appreciation

_____ Other _____

Writing Contexts

_____ Forms to be filled out for the use of common public services

_____ Informal notes for communications in everyday life situations

_____ Brief reports describing simple situations and sequences of events

_____ Personal letters to acquaintances and friends (peers and adults)

_____ Formal letters to agencies, institutions, and businesses on topics of personal needs

_____ Short samples of expository or creative writing

_____ Other _____   *(continued)*

FIGURE 1.4   (continued)

Classroom Learning Preferences

Indicate with an X your preferences on how you like to learn:

In class I like to learn:

_____ Individually

_____ In pairs

_____ In small groups

_____ In one large group

I enjoy classroom activities that involve:

_____ Learning grammatical rules

_____ Listening and taking notes

_____ Reading passages and texts

_____ Participating in speaking situations

_____ Learning new words

_____ Pronunciation practice

_____ Memorizing dialogs

_____ Completing textbook exercises

_____ Writing compositions

_____ Other _____

I like to learn the language and cultural content found in:

_____ Textbooks

_____ Videos/films

_____ Audio recordings

_____ Printed media (newspapers and magazines)

_____ Pictures and captioned visuals

_____ Cultural materials (labels, menus, maps, timetables, receipts)

FIGURE 1.4 (continued)

guage experiences. As Di Pietro (1987, p. 10) explains it, "learners are placed in situations where the motivation to think is translated into the challenge to reach goals through verbal exchanges with others" as the classroom is turned "into a proving ground where such challenges are faced and overcome with the aid of the teacher and the cooperation of other learners."

This section has presented various interpretations associated with the concept of interactive-based teaching. Based on the discussion, a number of classroom principles can be established. The interactive-based perspective:

- Stresses the role of learner characteristics—age, needs, reasons for language study—in curriculum planning and course design
- Emphasizes collaborative and group work as a means to promote both instructional and natural communication

Task 1: *Listen, discuss, and write*
Students listen to a brief story and discuss ways of writing a different ending. They then write a different ending and read it to the class.

Task 2: *Read, note, and discuss*
Students read a short text and carry out several activities, including creating a visual to accompany the text.

Task 3: *See, discuss, and write*
Students study a picture, make a list of prepositions of place, and use these in writing four descriptive sentences.

Task 4: *Read, discuss, write, and dramatize*
Students read a story, discuss ways of dramatizing a scene, and then write a script to be enacted before the group/class

Task 5: *Discuss, interview, and write*
Students decide on a group project (e.g., opinions adults have about other languages and clutures, music, the environment) and they develop a questionnaire to interview various persons. Then they tally the results and write a brief summary.

Task 6: *Read, discuss, and write*
Students read and discuss the contents of an advertisement. Then they prepare a similar text with accompanying visuals.

Task 7: *See, discuss, write, and dramatize*
Students watch a TV commercial and discuss their impressions. Afterwards they write a script to be enacted along with accompanying props and costumes.

Task 8: *See, discuss, and write*
Students examine a set of pictures and discuss the contents. Later they write a story based on the set of pictures.

Task 9: *Read, discuss, and write*
Students read and discuss a set of sentences. Then they write a paragraph based on the sentences.

Task 10: *Discuss and list*
Students examine maps, brochures, and travel guides. Then they prepare a written itinerary: Where/when to go? How to get to the different cities within a two-week period?

FIGURE 1.5 Interactive language tasks

Based on Nunan (1989).

- Incorporates language tasks that require a variety of language skills and behaviors
- Uses activities that are interesting, rewarding, and challenging to learners
- Provides opportunities for different learners to make different contributions
- Focuses on the different learning modalities: sight, sound, touch, and multimedia sources
- Places learners in specific problem-solving situations having various solutions

CONTRASTING THE THREE APPROACHES

The three classroom approaches described above have a number of similarities and differences. All three stress functional uses of language over grammatical forms. They place the functions in the context of specific social situations. Some of the important differences between them are presented in Table 1.3.

The communicative classroom organizes teaching activities on the basis of the functions of language in various social situations, which can involve different locations, participants, and topics. The particular grammatical constructions, vocabulary items, and verbal routines needed to perform the specific language function(s) are also presented and practiced through a range of learning tasks. The proficiency-based classroom specifies levels of linguistic performance in regard to the four language modalities (listening, speaking, reading, and writing). Specific instructional techniques appropriate to the different proficiency levels (novice, intermediate, advanced, and superior) relate language functions to content or topics and performance criteria. Proficiency-level specifications serve as the organizing principle for all classroom instruction and assessment procedures. Moreover, the proficiency-based approach presupposes that there are developmental sequences for acquiring linguistic features within specified topic areas.

The interactive classroom emphasizes language tasks that enable learners to carry out a broad range of functions related to both instructional and natural communication. The exchange, rather than the function, is the basic discourse unit. The exchange serves to establish a relationship between a sender and a receiver within a situation. It can involve more than one language function (Speaker A: "How are you today?" Speaker B: "Not too well today."). Interactive tasks take into account learner needs, realistic social situations, and authentic cultural materials. Language subskills, in turn, form the basis for planning activities that promote student collaboration and personal reaction to both oral and written texts. Interactive lessons promote language development as a result of task completion. Language is used as a means to accomplish tasks, not primarily to demonstrate fluency. Task completion will obligate students to integrate various language subskills and to engage in the negotiation of meaning. Sustained interactional lessons in a foreign language may contribute to the development of proficiency as well as other types of language abilities such as strategic competence (see Chapter 2).

All things being equal, each approach may have different linguistic consequences. A communicative orientation enables learners to perform a range of language functions, especially in face-to-face speaking situations. Proficiency-based teaching prepares learners to perform a number of functions related to specific topics according to performance-level criteria for each of the four language modalities. Interactive-based classrooms stress the language goals of learners rather than place emphasis on the teaching of a preestablished linguistic content or performance levels. The development of language abilities "proceeds through creativity, which is nurtured by interactive, participatory activities" (Rivers, 1992, p. 381). All three orientations share a number of features, such as the use of authentic materials and group activities.

TABLE 1.3   The Three Perspectives Contrasted

Communicative	Proficiency	Interactive
Major Learning Goals		
Develop communicative language abilities in relation to specific social contexts	Develop the ability to perform language tasks according to proficiency levels and modalities	Develop the ability to send/receive authentic messages (interactive competence)
Language Categories		
Language functions Grammatical structures Vocabulary Verbal formulas Communicative situations	Language functions Topics/content Language modalties Proficiency levels Accuracy of the message Authentic texts	Interactional exchanges Language tasks Language modalties Authentic texts Language skills
Learning Assumptions		
Focus on language functions incorporating appropriate grammatical, lexical, and verbal formulas and relate to social contexts (generally a parts-to-whole language sequence)	Use a specific set of teaching techniques to develop appropriate proficiency levels in terms of the four modalities (both parts-to-whole and whole-to-parts sequences)	Identify learner needs and develop appropriate language tasks that involve both oral and written modalities React to authentic texts and develop specific language subskills (a whole-to-parts sequence pattern)
Typical Teaching Techniques		
Pair activities, role plays, information gaps	Various techniques appropriate for proficiency levels and four modalities, including those used in the other two approaches	Group/pair work, collaborative activities, problem-solving tasks
Problematic Concerns		
Coordination of grammatical forms with communicative uses of language Listening and speaking skills tend to be emphasized over written language	Development of preestablished proficiency levels not based on empirical findings of actual learners' abilities or authentic linguistic needs Particular language and cultural features are not specified	Coordination of instructional sequences on the basis of learners' needs Language subskills (grammar and vocabulary) tend not to be developed systematically

The appropriateness of one approach over another depends on many factors: local situation (language attitudes, language policy, economic considerations), educational concerns (instructional objectives, resources, class size, administrative commitment), teacher-related issues (preparation, language proficiency, beliefs, autonomy, skills), and learner-related matters (age, language goals, attitudes toward learning). As Prabhu (1990, p. 162) notes, "there is no best method of language teaching"; . . . it all depends on the teaching context." The communicative approach highlights the functional uses of language as the "organizing principle" for classroom activities. The proficiency-oriented approach specifies performance levels according to the four language modalities. Communicative uses of language are developed in relation to content/topics and accuracy criteria. The interactive classroom, on the other hand, focuses more on the learners' linguistic needs.

The interactive-based perspective can be seen in terms of a learner-centered syllabus. This type of syllabus focuses on the process of learning language rather than on the linguistic units that have been learned. While it can be difficult to structure a learner-centered syllabus, this orientation might prove to be a pathway to true educational innovation (Breen, 1987). It should be noted that each approach brings to the foreground an important aspect of the teaching/learning process: (1) the linguistic content of instruction, (2) the learner's language needs, and (3) the performance levels in different language tasks. By taking into account these three important concerns, a teacher might be able to develop an appropriate classroom environment that "is motivated and sustained by conceptual exploration" (Prabhu, 1992, p. 225). This means that teachers themselves need to become investigators in order to determine how their classroom routines are governed by concerns for language content, the learner, and proficiency levels.

AUTHENTIC MATERIALS IN THE CLASSROOM

Authentic materials are varied cultural forms of communication used by native speakers. They come in many shapes and sizes and can be classified according to the means of communication: audio, visual, video, and printed (Lopez, 1986). The audio category includes radio programs, announcements made through loudspeakers in public places such as train stations, airports, bus stations, and department stores; and recorded songs, stories, and plays, as well as telephone communication and taped face-to-face conversations. The visual category is comprised of such media as posters, notices, public displays, signs, advertisements, and billboards. Video materials might include soap operas, commercials, musical shows, interviews, news, and public-service programs. Many current motion pictures are also available in videocassette formats. The printed media category includes such obvious forms as the newspaper and magazines, but there are also pamphlets, leaflets, brochures, flyers, manuals, telephone directories, menus, and maps.

These tools for communication can be used in relation to different cultural topics (food, travel, entertainment, current events, ecology, and shopping). At the same time, different forms of media can be used to develop a range of communicative abilities, along the lines of Canale and Swain's (1980) fourfold communicative framework: grammatical, discourse, sociolinguistic, and strategic competence, as noted in Chapter 2. Penfield (1987) presents a series of activities for English language development that involve the utilization of different types of media within the classroom setting. He notes that media can serve as "catalysts for communicative language learning" by presenting language holistically, as an instrument for communication and as means for learning cultural information. Nuessel (1989) offers a systematic plan for the introduction of selected "enrichment techniques" into the L2 classroom. Wine labels, postage stamps, menus, weather maps, crossword puzzles, songs, and games can be used to develop specific language skills (reading, writing, listening comprehension), grammatical competence, and cultural knowledge. Students can interact with the cultural materials individually or in small groups as they engage in problem-solving activities and use language "as a tool of communication and knowledge acquisition" (Penfield, 1987, p. 6). According to Swaffar (1989, p. 33), authentic materials provide the learner with numerous opportunities to experience language within a broad range of cultural situations. Moreover, this attention to authentic cultural/linguistic input represents the emergence of a new paradigm in language instruction: second language learning "as the ability to perceive and operate within real-world situations, in order to perform real-world tasks."

Specific procedures for utilizing authentic materials in the classroom have been developed by the New York State Education Department's Bureau of Foreign Languages. The French specialist for the bureau offers (Blanchet, 1986) guidelines for using television commercials (Figure 1.6), captioned visuals (Figure 1.7), printed materials (Figure 1.8), and periodicals (Figure 1.9). Authentic materials are incorporated into later chapters of this book devoted to the development of listening (Chapter 7), reading (Chapter 8), speaking (Chapter 9), and writing competencies (Chapter 10).

EFFECTIVE LEARNING CONTEXTS

Effective classroom environments encompass a number of issues beyond the selection of a particular teaching approach. Addressed in the chapters that follow, these issues have to do with a broad range of topics, such as (1) the nature of language proficiency, (2) the incorporation of culture into instruction, (3) the planning of instructional sequences, (4) the use of techniques for promoting language acquisition, (5) the significance of learner characteristics, (6) the development of oral and written language abilities, (7) procedures for assessing language learning, and (8) reflective methods for increasing teaching competencies.

At this point, it is important to start identifying some of the characteristics of effective language classrooms. A list of 20 features specified by the National Association of District Supervisors of Foreign Languages (NADSFL) provides an extensive framework for describing effective classroom environments. The NADSFL's instructional guidelines, presented in Figure 1.10, offer evaluators, observers, trainers, and practitioners a common set of criteria for delineating language learning contexts. The multiple dimensions involving teaching objectives, classroom climate,

Level: *Beginners*

1. Select TV ad (either 30 or 60 second) for appropriate content.
2. Instruct pupils to jot down any words they recognize as the ad is played.
3. Play the ad uninterrupted. (Pupils jot down whatever words they recognize.)
4. Ask one pupil to report the words he or she has recognized verbally.
5. Teacher writes those words on the board.
6. Teacher plays the ad a second time. . . .
   - Pupil raises hand whenever listed, recognized word is heard.
   - Teacher backs up tape and replays that segment to confirm the word for the whole class. (choral repetition optional)
7. Entire class reports verbally any additional words it may have recognized.
8. Teacher writes those words on the board.
9. Then repeat step 6 above.
10. Teacher adds to the list other words the class might have recognized, cognates, etc.
11. Repeat step 6 again.
12. Play the whole ad uninterrupted for general comprehension.
13. Discuss the whole ad with a focus on the following points:
    - What product does the ad promote?*
    - What main characteristic of the product does the ad emphasize?
    - How is that emphasis carried out? (words, intonation, repetition, visual cues, etc.)
    - In what way is that ad different from or similar to an American ad for a similar product?

* Can be done in the target language even in a level I class.

FIGURE 1.6   Use of television commercials

SOURCE: From Utilizing Authentic Cultural Materials with Special Reference to French (workshop materials prepared by Alain Blanchet), 1986. Albany, NY: New York State Education Department, Foreign Language Bureau. Reprinted with permission.

FIGURE 1.7   Use of captioned visuals

SOURCE: From Utilizing Authentic Cultural Materials with Special Reference to French (workshop materials prepared by Alain Blanchet), 1986. Albany, NY: New York State Education Department, Foreign Language Bureau. Reprinted with permission.

Level: *Intermediate*

1. Select captioned photos or cartoons from newspapers or magazines.
2. Cut captions off visuals.
3. Mount individual captions and individual visuals on separate pieces of construction paper.
4. Distribute scrambled captions and visuals to students individually or in teams (at least one caption and one visual to each individual or team).
5. Have each individual or team read the received caption aloud to all others.
6. Set time limit for individuals or teams to negotiate in the target language* in order to obtain a matching set of caption and visual.
7. Ask individual pupils or teams to justify in the target language* their choice of a match.
8. Ask pupils to prepare, individually or in teams, their own captions for the visual they have been issued.
9. Ask pupils to share verbally and/or in writing the captions they have developed on their own for the visual they have been assigned.

* Depending on level

Level: *Any*

1. Select newspaper or magazine column of appropriate length and content.
2. Remove one, two, three, four, five, or more letters from either the beginning or the end of each line by cutting the document.*
3. Make xerox copies for all pupils in the class.
4. Instruct pupils to supply the missing letters individually or in teams.
5. A) Have pupils turn in their completed columns as an exercise, or
   B) Ask pupils to report individually, by teams, or as a class which letters they have supplied for each line, or
   C) Ask pupils to read the column aloud with the letters they have supplied.*
6. Ask pupils to justify their choice of the letters they have supplied.
7. Provide the letters pupils were not able to supply and their justification.
8. A) Terminate exercise.
   B) Proceed to analysis/discussion of the content of the column:
   • Who?   • What?   • Where?
   • When?   • How?   • Why?
   • Personal comments, reactions, opinions.

* Depending on level

FIGURE 1.8 Use of print media

SOURCE: From Utilizing Authentic Cultural Materials with Special Reference to French (workshop materials prepared by Alain Blanchet), 1986. Albany, NY: New York State Education Department, Foreign Language Bureau. Reprinted with permission.

and learning strategies constitute some of the many considerations required for creating effective language learning contexts.

SUMMARY

Second language classrooms are special linguistic settings with specific rules for talking and interacting. The verbal exchanges between teachers and students involve various types of classroom activities, ranging from mechanical drills to meaningful, authentic use of language.

In communicative-based classrooms, activities are usually organized to promote the functional uses of language in different social situations. Students learn to perform such functions as greetings, requests, informatives, and expressions of personal feelings. Activities such as interviews, role-playing, skits, and problem-solving situations are typically used to enable learners to share and process information. The concern for authentic communication requires an analysis of the demands of learning tasks in terms of such aspects as student-centered interaction, the use of intellectually stimulating materials, self-expression of learners' values and attitudes, real-world situations, and the integration of various language subskills.

Proficiency-oriented instruction emphasizes such categories as language functions, content or topics, accuracy levels, and text types, all in terms of a hierarchical scale for each of the four language skill areas. Omaggio, for example, offers spe-

Level: *Intermediate/Advanced*

Preparation:

- As soon as periodical is available, teacher passes to one pupil for overnight perusal and choice of one article of stated minimum length on which the pupil will report.
- On the next day, pupil indicates his/her choice to the teacher.
- Teacher photocopies the selected article for that pupil and passes the periodical to the next pupil for his/her perusal and selection.
- Pupil reads the photo copy of the selected article in depth with the aid of all available resources.*
- Pupil reads additional background information documents if necessary with the aid of all available resources.*
- Pupil prepares written report on the article with the aid of all available resources.* This report includes a factual description of the content of the article and the pupil's own reactions, comments, and opinions on the content of the article.
- On scheduled day, pupil makes a verbal presentation of his/her report to the class.
- The class discusses the pupil's report, focusing on the content of the article and on the reporting pupil's own reactions.

Comments and opinions on the article. This discussion should be encouraged to include at least the following:

1. Clarification and elaboration of the content of the article and of the reporting pupil's reactions, comments, and opinions.
2. Questioning of and/or disagreement with the content of the article and dissenting as well as converging reactions, comments, and opinions.
3. Submission of additional pertinent information.

NOTE: At each stage of development of the activity, the teacher's role is twofold:

1. To support the pupils' use of the language;
2. To diagnostically identify the pupils' most pressing needs in their efforts to achieve comprehension and comprehensibility so that those needs may be addressed later in a strictly instructional setting.

In an effort to support the pupils' verbal use of the language, the teacher:

1. Refrains from interrupting the pupils' use of the language by correcting errors unless comprehensibility is seriously jeopardized
2. Seeks clarification in the target language if comprehensibility is threatened
3. Supplies missing or incorrect elements of language with no or minimal explanation if comprehensibility is not achieved

   * Depending on level

FIGURE 1.9 Use of periodicals

SOURCE: From Utilizing Authentic Cultural Materials with Special Reference to French (workshop materials prepared by Alain Blanchet), 1986. Albany, NY: New York State Education Department, Foreign Language Bureau. Reprinted with permission.

cific classroom techniques for each of the four proficiency levels: novice, intermediate, advanced, and superior. In order for learners to achieve high-level proficiency, they need opportunities to practice, express their own meanings, interact, use language creatively, and carry out a broad range of functions related to a number of topics.

1. The teacher uses the target language extensively, encouraging the students to do so.
2. The teacher provides opportunities to communicate in the target language in meaningful, purposeful activities that simulate real-life situations.*
3. Skill-getting activities enable students to participate successfully in skill-using activities. Skill-using activities predominate.
4. Time devoted to listening, speaking, reading, and writing is appropriate to course objectives and to the language skills of students.*
5. Culture is systematically incorporated into instruction.
6. The teacher uses a variety of student groupings.
7. Most activities are student-centered.
8. The teacher uses explicit error correction in activities which focus on accuracy, and implicit or no error correction in activities which focus on communication.
9. Assessment, both formal and informal, reflects the way students are taught.
10. Student tasks and teacher questions reflect a range of thinking skills.
11. Instruction addresses student learning styles.
12. Students are explicitly taught foreign language learning strategies and are encouraged to assess their own progress.
13. The teacher enables all students to be successful.
14. The teacher establishes an affective climate in which students feel comfortable taking risks.
15. Students are enabled to develop positive attitudes towards cultural diversity.
16. The physical environment reflects the target language and culture.
17. The teacher uses the textbook as a tool, not as curriculum.
18. The teacher uses a variety of print and non-print materials, including authentic materials.*
19. Technology, as available, is used to facilitate teaching and learning.
20. The teacher engages in continued professional development in the areas of language skills, cultural knowlege, and current methodology.

FIGURE 1.10 Characteristics of effective foreign language instruction: Guidelines

SOURCE: From "Characteristics of Effective Foreign Language Instruction Guidelines." NADSFL Newsletter, Spring 1992. Reprinted with permission.

* Listening, speaking, and authentic non-print materials are emphasized, but to a lesser degree, in Latin and Greek language classrooms.

The interactive-based classroom focuses on the needs and characteristics of the learners. Tasks that promote collaboration and personal reaction to oral and written texts form the basis for curriculum planning. Specific activities such as group investigations, role-playing situations, problem-solving tasks, and sociodramas offer learners opportunities to use language interactively.

Deciding which perspective to emphasize in a particular teaching situation is not a simple matter. Each perspective highlights an important aspect of the teaching/learning process. The communicative perspective stresses the functional uses of language in different social situations. The proficiency-oriented approach organizes instructional activities on the basis of preestablished performance levels. The interactive-based perspective focuses on learner language needs as the means to formulate most learning tasks. All three approaches share a number of features, and each can contribute to the formulation of an appropriate classroom environment that is the result of conceptual exploration and reflective teaching. Teachers must ultimately develop the ability to view their own teaching from a variety of perspectives. This enables them to determine how their classroom routines are governed by concerns for learner needs, proficiency-oriented goals, and the communicative uses of language.

The use of authentic materials in audio, visual, video, and printed forms offers students a wide range of cross-cultural experiences within the classroom. Cultural materials provide learners with the real-world situations available to native speakers performing their daily routines. Television commercials, captioned visuals, and printed media present interactive occasions with authentic linguistic input and genuine cultural scenarios.

The creation of effective language learning contexts involves a number of considerations beyond implementating a particular instructional approach. The NADSFL (1992) guidelines for identifying the characteristics of effective foreign language classrooms enumerate 20 critical classroom features. The chapters that follow examine these features along with other aspects of the language learning/teaching process.

ACTIVITIES

1. Observe an L2 classroom and characterize it in terms of the framework suggested by Table 1.1.
2. Prepare language activities according to McTear's four basic categories: mechanical, meaningful, pseudocommunicative, and real communication.
3. Prepare a set of questions that can be used to ask pseudoquestions (answers already known or obvious) and real questions. Discuss your types of questions in relation to Littlewood's precommunicative and communicative phases of a lesson.
4. List some specific examples of classroom activities and instructional materials that would correspond to Vogel's major components of a communicative classroom.
5. List some specific examples of classroom activities that could be included in Savignon's five communicative components for pupils at the novice, intermediate, and advanced levels of proficiency.
6. Write your opinions about Omaggio's five instructional hypotheses for proficiency-oriented classrooms. Compare your comments with those of other students. Determine the level of agreement or disagreement for each hypothesis.
7. Analyze the goal statements for the four semesters of French prepared by a group of college teachers (Figure 1.2). What language functions and content/topics are developed during each semester? What are your opinions about the development of cultural competence (goal 5, for each semester)?
8. Discuss the curricular implications of Rivers's approach of planning interactive teaching activities starting with the learner.
9. Review the learner needs analysis questionnaire (Figure 1.4). Discuss it with a language learner to determine communicative needs and instructional preferences.
10. Study the 10 examples of interactive tasks, and prepare two activities for a particular group of learners.
11. Design a scenario that could be used in an L2 classroom following the phases outline by Di Pietro.

12. Read the guidelines prepared by Blanchet for utilizing television commercials, captioned visuals, and printed materials in the classroom. Select one type of media and follow the procedure in a peer-teaching situation, or in a real L2 classroom, if possible.

REFERENCES

American Council on the Teaching of Foreign Languages [ACTFL]. (1986). *ACTFL provisional proficiency guidelines.* Hastings-on-Hudson, NY: ACTFL Materials Center.

Asher, J. (1982) *Learning another language through actions: The complete teacher's guidebook* (2nd ed.). Los Gatos, CA: Sky Oaks Productions.

Blanchet A. (1986). *Utilizing authentic cultural materials with special reference to French.* Materials distributed at the Upper Hudson Foreign Language Consortium, Albany, NY.

Bragger, J. D. (1985). Materials development for the proficiency oriented classroom. In C. J. James (Ed.), *Foreign language proficiency in the classroom and beyond. ACTFL foreign language series* (pp. 79-115). Lincolnwood, IL: National Textbook.

Breen, M. P. (1987). Contemporary paradigms in syllabus design, Part I and Part II. *Language Teaching, 20,* 81-174.

Byrnes, H., & Thompson, I., contributing editors, Buck, K. (Ed.). (1989). *The ACTFL oral proficiency interview tester training manual.* Yonkers, NY: ACTFL.

Canale, M., & Swain, M. (1980). Theoretical bases of communicative approaches to second language teaching and testing. *Applied Linguistics, 1,* 1-47.

Chastain, K. (1989). The ACTFL proficiency guidelines: A selected sample of opinions. *ADFL Bulletin, 20,* 47-51.

Cohen, E. G. (1986). *Designing groupwork: Strategies for the heterogeneous classroom.* New York: Teachers College Press.

Curran, C. (1976). *Counseling-learning in second languages.* East Dubuque, IL: Counseling-Learning Publications.

Di Pietro, R. J. (1987). *Strategic interaction: Learning languages through scenarios.* Cambridge, England: Cambridge University Press.

Dodds, D. (1992). Using proficiency as the organizing principle in an advanced speaking course for majors. *Foreign Languages Annals, 25,* 497-506.

Edmonson, W. J. (1985). Discourse worlds in the classroom and in foreign language learning. *Studies in second language acquisition, 1,* 159-168.

Ellis, R. (1985). *Understanding second language acquisition.* Oxford: Oxford University Press.

Enright, D. S., & McCloskey, M. L. (1985). Yes, talking: Organizing the classroom to promote second language acquisition. *TESOL Quarterly, 19,* 431-453.

Finocchiaro, M., & Brumfit, C. (1983). *The functional-notional approach: From theory to practice.* Oxford: Oxford University Press.

Green, J. (1983). Exploring classroom discourse: Linguistics perspectives on teaching learning processes. *Educational Psychologist, 18,* 180-199.

Higgs, T. V. (Ed.). (1984). *Teaching for proficiency: The organizing principle.* Lincolnwood, IL: National Textbook.

Hipple, D. (1987). A progress report on the ACTFL proficiency guidelines, 1982-1986. In H. Byrnes & M. Canale (Eds.), *Defining and developing proficiency* (pp. 5-14). Lincolnwood, IL: National Textbook.

Kramsch, C. J. (1985). Classroom interaction and discourse options. *Studies in second language acquisition, 1,* 169-183.

Littlewood, W. (1981). *Foreign and second language learning: Language acquisition research and its implications for the classroom.* Cambridge, England: Cambridge University Press.

Long, M. H., & Porter, P. (1985). Group interlanguage talk and second language acquisition. *TESOL Quarterly, 19,* 207-228.

López, J. (1986). Authentic materials in second language instruction. *Language Association Bulletin, 37*(5), 1-5.

McTear, M. (1975). Structure and categories of foreign language teaching sequences. In R. Allwright (Ed.), *Working paper: Language teaching classroom research.* University of Essex, England, Department of Languages and Linguistics.

Medley, F. W., Jr. (1985). Designing the proficiency-based curriculum. In A. C. Omaggio (Ed.), *Proficiency, curriculum, articulation: The ties that bind* (pp. 13-40). Middlebury, VT: Northeast Conference on the Teaching of Foreign Languages.

National Association of District Supervisors of Foreign Languages. (1992, Spring). Characteristics of effective foreign language instruction guidelines. *NADSFL Newsletter.*

Nuessel, F. (1989). Selected enrichment techniques for the second language classroom. *The Canadian Modern Language Review, 45*(2), 294-317.

Nunan, D. (1989). *Designing tasks for the communicative classroom.* Cambridge, England: Cambridge University Press.

Omaggio, A. C. (1986). *Teaching language in context.* Boston, MA: Heinle & Heinle.

Penfield, J. (1987). *The media: Catalysts for communicative language learning.* Reading, MA: Addison-Wesley.

Pica, T., & Doughty, C. (1988). Variation in classroom interaction as a function of participation pattern and task. In J. Fine (Ed.), *Second language discourse: A textbook of current research* (pp. 41-55). Norwood, NJ: Ablex.

Prabhu, N. S. (1990). There is no best method—Why? *TESOL Quarterly, 24*(2), 161-176.

Prabhu, N. S. (1992). The dynamics of the language lesson. *TESOL Quarterly, 26*(2), 225-241.

Ramirez, A. G. (1987). Assessing the communicativeness of language lessons. In P. W. Wood (Ed.), *Creating an environment for second language acquisition* (pp. 31-39). Schenectady, NY: New York State Association of Foreign Language Teachers.

Richards, J. C. (1990). *The language teaching matrix.* Cambridge, England: Cambridge University Press.

Rivers, W. M. (Ed.). (1987). *Interactive language teaching.* Cambridge, England: Cambridge University Press.

Rivers, W. M. (1992). Ten principles of interactive language learning and teaching. In W. M. Rivers (Ed.), *Teaching languages in college: Curriculum and content* (pp. 373-392). Lincolnwood, IL: National textbook.

Savignon, S. J. (1983). *Communicative competence: Theory and classroom practice.* Reading, MA: Addison-Wesley.

Savignon, S. J. (1987). What's in communicative language teaching? *Forum, 25*(4), 16-21.

Stubbs, M. (1976). *Languages, schools, and classrooms.* London: Methuen & Co.

Swaffar, J. (1989). Curricular issues and language research: The shifting interaction. *Profession, 89* (Modern Language Association), 32-38.

Van Lier, L. A. (1982). *Analyzing interaction in second language classrooms.* Unpublished doctoral dissertation, University of Lancaster, England.

Vogel, P., Brassard, M. L., Parks, S., Thibaudeau, S., & White, J. (1983). The communicative classroom: Tasks, materials, methodology. In M. A. Clarke & J. Handscombe (Eds.), *On TESOL '82* (pp. 243-252). Washington, DC: TESOL.

Wells, G. (Ed.). (1981). *Learning through interaction: The study of language development.* Cambridge, England: Cambridge University Press.

Winitz, H. (Ed.). (1978). *The comprehension approach to foreign language instruction.* New York: Newbury House.

Yalden, J. (1987). *Principles of course design for language teaching.* Cambridge, England: Cambridge University Press.

chapter 2

Concepts of Language Proficiency

Proficiency can be looked at as a goal *and thus be defined in terms of objectives or standards. These can then serve as criteria by which to assess proficiency as an empirical* fact, *that is the actual performance of given individual learners or groups of learners. Once proficiency has been established it can be related to the other variables in the model: context, learner characteristics, learning conditions, and learning process. The conceptualization and description of proficiency is therefore an important step in the study of second language learning.*

H. H. Stern, 1983

Knowing a language involves a broad range of linguistic competencies, skills, and abilities. Terms like *linguistic, communicative, interactional,* and *sociolinguistic competence* have been used to describe the multitude of abilities or skills that constitute the mastery of a language. The concept of language proficiency has been depicted in relation to the components of language itself, face-to-face communication, and comprehension of written texts. Notions of communicative abilities can involve various systems of knowledge and skills, including grammatical, sociolinguistic, discourse, and strategic competence.

Recent developments in foreign language teaching have introduced the categories of language functions, content/topics, and levels of linguistic accuracy. These categories, in turn, are depicted in terms of specific performance levels and behaviors, within the modalities of listening, speaking, reading, and writing. This conception of proficiency includes various systems of knowledge that go beyond the specific elements of language; it includes an understanding of sociocultural conventions along with the use of different cognitive strategies for processing information. The development of L2 proficiency is influenced by such factors as program goals, L2 language complexity, and oral versus written language abilities.

This chapter reviews different notions of second language proficiency. It addresses a number of issues associated with the concept of proficiency. Some of the issues raised are seen in the following questions:

1. What does it mean to know a language?
2. How is communicative competence characterized?
3. How is functional language proficiency depicted?
4. What types of skills, knowledge, and behaviors are associated with functional language proficiency?
5. What major factors influence the development of L2 proficiency?

KNOWING A LANGUAGE

The notion of language "competence" has been used to characterize a speaker's underlying knowledge of the system of a language, including the rules for generating grammatical sentences (Chomsky, 1965). *Linguistic competence* has been viewed as the native speaker's internalized grammar, consisting of a complex system of rules and operating at different levels—syntactic, lexical, phonological, semantic—to determine the organization of grammatical structures. This type of competence cannot be observed directly and is likened to an idealized speaker-hearer who does not display any overt errors associated with memory limitations, distractions, shifts of attention, and hesitation phenomena such as repetition, false starts, pauses, or omissions.

The term *communicative competence* has been used by a number of persons since the 1970s to depict a range of ability wider than the one associated with a grammatical knowledge of language (Hymes, 1985). This broader notion of competence involves such aspects as the social and functional rules of language use along with the skills needed to negotiate meanings interpersonally within specific sociocultural situations (Hymes, 1972). Paulston (1974), for example, has distinguished between linguistic competence and communicative competence to underscore the essential difference between (1) knowledge of language rules and structures and (2) the knowledge that enables a person to communicate effectively in face-to-face interactions.

Other terms associated with a broader view of grammatical competence have been proposed. Scholars concerned with literary (verbal art) styles conceive of "rhetorical" competence (Steinmann, 1982) and "narrative" competence (McLendon, 1977). Those concerned with the interactive uses of language identify "conversational" competence (Kennan, 1974), "interactional" competence (Erickson & Schultz, 1981), "social" competence (Cicourel, 1981), and "sociolinguistic" competence (Troike, 1970). These kinds of competencies suggest that a multitude of abilities or skills constitute knowledge or mastery of a language.

COMPONENTS OF COMMUNICATIVE COMPETENCE

The notion of communicative competence has been characterized in a number of ways. The depiction of linguistic abilities according to a structural view segments language elements into discrete, independently measurable components. Hernández-Chávez, Burt, and Dulay (1978), for example, characterize language in terms of a three-dimensional matrix consisting of 64 possible separate abilities. One of the dimensions consists of the aspects of language associated with vocabulary, grammatical structures, pronunciation, and semantics. The second dimension includes the oral and written modalities of language, with comprehension and production abilities related to the oral channel and reading and writing abilities associated with the written mode. The third dimension brings in sociolinguistic performance with respect to usage area (range of speech styles and the functions of language) and the types of language varieties (knowledge and use of standard and nonstandard dialects and sociolinguistic contexts, e.g., home, school, work, and neighborhood).

Oller (1978, 1979), on the other hand, argues for the existence of a global language factor that accounts for most of the performance differences in a wide variety of language proficiency measures. This single-concept expression of proficiency, described as "expectancy grammar," is strongly related to cognitive variables and academic achievement, and it appears to exist across all four language skills (listening, speaking, reading, and writing). Global ability is attributed to the belief that "in the meaningful use of language, some sort of pragmatic expectancy grammar must function in all cases" (1979, p. 25), and that this perceptual ability is "a psychologically real system that sequentially orders linguistic elements in time and in relation to extralinguistic elements in meaningful ways" (1979, p. 25). This position emphasizes the central role of expectation and prediction across language tasks, and that language itself cannot be meaningfully segmented into separate, discrete components.

Cummins (1980, 1981) has proposed a twofold approach to characterizing language proficiency. Initially, he distinguished between basic interpersonal communicative skills (BICS) and cognitive/academic language proficiency (CALP). The BICS dimension of proficiency is the communicative capacity of language that all children acquire so as to function in daily face-to-face exchanges. CALP involves the ability to manipulate or reflect upon the features of language (reading a text, writing an essay), independently of extralinguistic supports such as the use of gestures or situational cues. The initial BICS-CALP distinction has been modified to include a developmental perspective for describing relationships between academic performance and language proficiency.

Thus, this framework conceptualizes language proficiency along two continua. The horizontal continuum distinguishes between context-embedded (face-to-face) communication and context-reduced communication (interaction with written texts). In context-embedded communication the participants negotiate meaning through the use of gestures and feedback to indicate that the message has or has not been understood. This type of language is supported by a wide range of situational cues. Context-reduced communication, in contrast, relies primarily on linguistic cues to establish meaning; in some cases this may involve suspending knowledge of the real world so as to interpret or manipulate the logic of communication correctly. A good amount of classroom language is context-reduced, requiring linguistic messages to be elaborated precisely and explicitly so that misunderstanding is minimized, as in writing a letter, answering an essay question, or reading an article. Context-embedded communication, on the other hand, is more typical of interactive situations outside the classroom. This form of communication derives part of its meaning from interpersonal involvement in a shared reality, which makes it unnecessary to elaborate explicitly the entire linguistic message.

The vertical continuum addresses the developmental aspect of communicative proficiency in relation to the degree of active cognitive involvement in the task or activity. Cognitively demanding tasks, such as persuading another person or writing a composition to explain a complicated process, require the individual to process a considerable amount of information (e.g., knowledge of the topic and audience, ways of organizing the message) in order to complete the activity. Cognitively undemanding tasks consist of communicative activities that require little cognitive involvement. The linguistic requirements for these tasks have become automatized, as in greetings, asking for permission, filling out a form with personal information, or locating the title of a story or chapter.

A fourfold concept of communicative competence has been advanced by Canale (1983), based on a framework by Canale and Swain (1980), specifying three interacting factors. According to Canale (1984a), linguistic communication can be characterized in terms of various systems of knowledge and skills noted in four areas:

1. *Grammatical competence*: mastery of the language code (verbal or nonverbal), thus concerned with such features as lexical items, and rules of sentence formation, pronunciation, and literal meaning
2. *Sociolinguistic competence*: mastery of appropriate language use in different sociolinguistic contexts, with emphasis on appropriateness of meanings (e.g., attitudes, speech acts, and propositions) and appropriateness of forms (e.g., register, non-verbal expression, and intonation)
3. *Discourse competence*: mastery of how to combine and interpret forms and meanings to achieve a unified spoken or written text in different genres by using (a) cohesion devices to relate utterance forms (e.g., pronouns, transition words, and parallel structures) and (b) coherence rules to organize meanings (e.g., repetition, progression, consistency, and relevance of ideas)
4. *Strategic competence*: mastery of verbal and nonverbal strategies (a) to compensate for breakdowns in communication due to insufficient competence or to performance limitations (e.g., strategies such as use of dictionaries, paraphrase, and gestures) and (b) to enhance the effectiveness of communication (e.g., deliberately slow and soft speech for rhetorical effect) (p. 112)

It is important to note that communicative competence here is used to refer to both knowledge and skill in using language. Actual communication involves the realization of various underlying systems of knowledge (linguistic and nonlinguistic–knowledge of the world) and skills (using the sociolinguistic conventions of a given language) under limiting psychological and environmental conditions such as perceptual and memory constraints, fatigue, or nervousness (Canale, 1983, p. 5). This framework of four subsystems does not describe how these factors interact with one another and how they develop among learners and users.

Attempts by Bachman and Palmer (1982) to validate Canale and Swain's (1980) hypothesized components of communicative competence resulted in their identifying three distinct traits: linguistic competence, pragmatic competence, and sociolinguistic competence. Grammatical competence includes morphology and syntax, both of which can vary in range and accuracy. Phonology and orthography are excluded since they are viewed as channels rather than components of communication. Pragmatic competence is associated with the ability to express and comprehend messages; it includes as subtraits vocabulary, cohesion, and text coherence. Cohesive devices such as "first," "later," and "finally" are used in English to relate sentences to one another by connecting temporal events in a sequential order. A text, as in the case of an oral narrative, is said to be coherent if such aspects as the organization, purpose, and goals for the audience are consistent with story-telling notions. Sociolinguistic competence incorporates the ability to distinguish registers, nativeness, and control of nonliteral, figurative language and relevant cultural allusions.

This framework appears to have the status of a model, in that through statistical procedures it establishes the independence of the various components or traits. However, Cummins and Swain (1986) note that Bachman and Palmer have been unable to distinguish grammatical competence from pragmatic competence among a group of ESL students at the university level. Similarly, among sixth-grade French-language immersion students, results of the factor analysis have failed to show the validity of three postulated traits: grammatical, sociolinguistic, and discourse competence. Only grammar and discourse competence seem to emerge as distinct traits among this group of language learners, and only when they are considered in the wider context of immersion students along with native speakers of French.

Other frameworks for depicting communicative competence have been proposed. Faerch, Haastrup, and Phillipson (1984), for example, argue that communicative competence consists of phonology/orthography, grammar, vocabulary, pragmatics, discourse, communication strategies, and fluency. Bachman's (1990) model incorporates two major components, organizational and pragmatic competence. Organizational competence, in turn, consists of grammatical and textual competence. Grammatical competence includes those competencies associated with the features of language use (knowledge of vocabulary, morphology, syntax, and phonology/graphology). Textual competence includes knowledge of the conventions for connecting utterances or sentences to form a text. From this perspective a text is defined as a unit of spoken or written language consisting of two or more utterances or sentences joined together according to rules of cohesion and rhetorical organization. By Bachman's model, pragmatic competence consists of two components, illocutionary and sociolinguistic competence. Illocutionary competence involves knowledge of the pragmatic conventions for performing acceptable language functions (e.g., using different strategies for requesting: "Hey, open the door"; "Please open the door"; "Would you mind opening the door?"; "I need someone to open the door"; "Can you help me with the door?"). Sociolinguistic competence includes knowledge of the conventions for performing language functions appropriately in a given sociocultural context. This type of competence reflects a sensitivity to differences such as dialects or language varieties, levels of discourse (e.g., formal, informal, literary, scientific language styles), cultural references, and figures of speech. Strategic competence is seen as a general set of abilities that utilize all of the components of language competence in addition to psychomotor skills (e.g., gestures and facial expressions) in the process of negotiating meaning. Bachman notes that his hierarchical "tree" framework representing various relationships among the components of language should be seen as a metaphor rather than a theoretical model of communicative language ability. During actual language use, all of the components interact with each other as well as with the language use situation.

Conceptions of communicative competence have important implications for how language is tested and how language is taught within a communicative perspective. Determining the validity of the various components that make up the different models noted above may be a difficult task in terms of producing an absolute model of communicative competence. Cummins and Swain (1986) argue for the need to test how the various components or traits of communicative competence become differentiated from each other for particular groups of students in specific learning situations.

To summarize, communicative competence has been characterized according to different linguistic categories. These categories include such components of language as knowledge of vocabulary, grammar, phonology, and uses of language with respect to aspects such as functions, situations, and oral or written texts. Other categories involve nonverbal strategies such as the use of gestures, reference materials, negotiation skills, and the knowledge of cultural and social rules. Communicative competence can be illustrated in terms of various components or traits, as presented in Figure 2.1. The depiction of communicative competence ranges from the relatively abstract, single-concept notion of Oller's "expectancy grammar" to the more differentiated model of Hernández-Chávez et al. that shows more specifically the actual features of language involved.

FUNCTIONAL LANGUAGE PROFICIENCY

The concept of *proficiency*, as reflected in the ACTFL guidelines (1986), organizes the characteristics of speakers at various performance levels according to function, context, and accuracy. *Function* refers to the communicative acts that the student

Relatively Abstract ——————————————▶			Relatively Concrete
Single concept	Twofold concept	Fourfold concept	Multiple categories
• Linguistic competence (Chomsky)	• Linguistic and • communicative competence (Paulston)	• Grammatical • Sociolinguistic • Discourse • Strategic (Canale)	*Levels of language* • Pronunciation • Vocabulary • Grammar • Semantics
			Language modalities
• Expectancy grammar (Oller)	• BICS and • CALP (Cummins)	• Listening • Speaking • Reading • Writing (levels of performance on language tests)	• Listening • Speaking • Reading • Writing
			Sociolinguistic aspects • Functions • Speech styles • Dialects • Domains (Hernández-Chávez, Burt and Dulay)
			Language aspects/skills • Phonology/orthography • Grammar • Vocabulary • Pragmatics • Discourse • Communication strategies • Fluency (Faerch, Haastrup, and Phillipson)

FIGURE 2.1   Components of communicative competence

SOURCE: Adapted from Stern, 1983, p. 356.

must be able to accomplish, such as enumerating events, asking questions, and narrating past or future activities. *Context* refers to the topics or content—everyday survival situations, travel, professional interests—in which the functions are realized. *Accuracy* relates to how well the functions are performed or to what extent the message is found acceptable among native speakers. This tripartite description of proficiency is used to characterize hierarchical performance levels in the areas of speaking, listening, reading, and writing. Ratings of an individual's proficiency are made by comparing performance levels with integrated descriptions of linguistic abilities, taking all three factors into account. Table 1.2 in Chapter 1 provides an example of the functional trisection of oral proficiency levels according to various components of language (function, context, accuracy, and text type).

As seen in Table 1.2, students at the novice level are expected to be able to communicate minimally with memorized material. They have the ability to list and respond briefly to questions with words and phrases that have been memorized in first-year textbooks: colors, numbers, foods, days of the week, and names of family members. These speakers function primarily at the vocabulary level. They experience great difficulties in producing sentence-type utterances and encounter numerous difficulties in being understood by native speakers. Students at the intermediate level are able to create language by combining or recombining learned elements. They are able to ask and answer questions as well as initiate and minimally sustain conversations about familiar topics: home, school, friends, personal history, and family members. They can be understood by sympathetic interlocutors even though they are likely to have problems with grammatical accuracy and strong interference from their first tongue. Advanced-level speakers have moved from sentence-level utterances to paragraph-length connected discourse. These speakers can narrate and describe present, past, and future activities. They can talk about a variety of concrete topics: personal background, family, work, travel, interests, and events they have experienced or read about. They are able to express facts, report incidents, and make comparisons, but they are not able to support an opinion with examples or argue against an opposing viewpoint. Speakers at the superior level are able to participate effectively in most formal and informal conversations on topics connected to practical, social, professional, and abstract concerns. They can support their opinions and hypothesize about abstract topics, offering detailed narration and description with nativelike discourse strategies. These speakers, while not nativelike in their linguistic abilities, are able to function effectively with most native speakers.

Novice-level speaking performance is characterized in terms of three specific categories (novice-low, novice-mid, and novice-high). The intermediate speaker is also classified according to three levels, intermediate-low, intermediate-mid, and intermediate-high. The advanced learner is either advanced or advanced-plus, followed by the superior-level speaker, who can interact successfully with native speakers on a variety of topics but is still unable to tailor language to fit the audience or discuss in depth a highly abstract subject. Writing performance levels are characterized similarly. Listening and reading proficiency levels include a 10th category, "distinguished," the ability to understand or read accurately most linguistic styles and forms within the cultural framework of the language.

Along similar lines, the New York State syllabus *Modern Languages for Communication* (1986) characterizes language competence in terms of achievement rather than proficiency levels. Communicative ability is conceptualized according to language functions, situations, and topics placed in relation to listening, speaking, reading, and writing modalities. Functions, situations, and topics are listed under three levels of achievement, checkpoints A, B, and C, which correspond to three different instructional intervals. Functions are defined according to communicative intent and are identified under four major headings: socializing (greetings, leave-taking, introducing, thanking, and apologizing); providing and obtaining information about facts, events, needs, opinions, attitudes, and feelings; expressing personal feelings about facts, events, opinions, and attitudes; and getting others to adopt a course of action by suggesting, requesting, directing, advising, warning, convincing, and praising. Situations are used to indicate the contexts in which communication occurs. They define the role the participants assume, what the individuals talk about, the settings, the channels of communication (oral or written), and the purpose of communicating (functions). They also establish the parameters for the negotiation of meaning between two or more persons or between the listener or reader and the type of text.

The New York syllabus places situations at the center of the communicative framework and distinguishes among them by language modality and proficiency levels, as can be seen in Figure 2.2. Separate proficiency statements are offered for each modality, and three achievement levels are noted (Table 2.1, on p. 46). Functions are not differentiated across the three levels of proficiency, and the fifteen major topics, ranging from personal identification to current events, are not significantly varied across the three checkpoints. The proficiency levels are the standards of competence that students are expected to achieve at each checkpoint and for each modality. The use of the term *proficiency* here is more analogous to the *accuracy* component of ACTFL's functional trisection construct. The checkpoints are seen as a component of the achievement appropriate for a given level, incorporating functions, situations, and topics as indicators of how well students are expected to communicate.

FACTORS ASSOCIATED WITH LANGUAGE PROFICIENCY

Functional language proficiency is currently being depicted with reference to particular performance skills and behaviors within the language modalities of listening, speaking, reading, and writing. It also seems to involve skills and behaviors that go beyond the purely linguistic elements of a language. Papalia (1983) points out that communicative proficiency depends on:

1. Interactional use of the language in the social context (roles of the participants, purpose for interacting, and appropriateness of utterances)
2. Linguistic competence (lexical, morphological, syntactic, and phonological features of the language)
3. Discourse and cultural inference (appropriate interpretation of connected sentences leading to a coherent, global and meaningful whole, and appropriate interpretation of cultural manifestations and values)
4. Strategic functions (manifestations for coping with a variety of factors dealing with misunderstanding, clarifying, pausing, taking time to collect one's thoughts, reactive listening, etc.) (p. 11)

Modality	Checkpoint		
	A	B	C
Listening			
Information and announcements from providers of common public services** in face-to-face communications	●	●	●*
Information (bulletins/announcements) provided over loudspeakers, radio, and television	●	●	●
Short presentations of interest to the general public given in person, on radio, or on television		●	●
Songs, live and recorded			●
Feature programs on television, in the movies, and on the radio			●
Listening/speaking			
Interaction with providers of common public services** in face-to-face communications	●	●	●
Informal everyday conversations with individual peers and adults	●	●	●
Informal conversations with peers and familiar adults	●	●	●
Interactions with providers of common public services** by telephone		●	●
Group conversations among peers and familiar adults		●	●
Group discussions with peers		●	●
Informal presentations to groups of peers and familiar adults		●	●
Reading			
Information provided to the general public on forms, signs, billboards and posters, labels, programs, timetables, maps, plans, menus, etc.	●	●	●
Announcements, ads, and short reports of general interest in newspapers, magazines, and other publications; short, informal notes	●	●	●*
Simple business correspondence and pamphlets		●	●
Facts, opinions, feelings, and attitudes in correspondence from acquaintances and friends (peers and adults)		●	●
Letters to the editor and feature articles from general-interest publications		●	●
Excerpts from poetry and prose for cultural appreciation		●	●
Writing			
Forms to be filled out for the use of common public services**	●	●	●
Informal notes for communications in everyday life situations	●	●	●
Brief reports describing simple situations and sequences of events		●	●
Personal letters to acquaintances and friends (peers and adults)		●	●
Formal letters to agencies, institutions, and businesses on topics of personal needs		●	●
Short samples of expository or creative writing			●

 * Dot indicates that the communicative situation should be included at the particular checkpoint.
 ** Sales personnel, bank tellers, ticket agents, police, hotel personnel, etc.

FIGURE 2.2 Communicative situations where interaction occurs

SOURCE: From *Modern Languages for Communication*, p. 11. 1986. Albany, NY: University of the State of New York, copyright 1986. Reprinted with permission.

These elements can be observed operating concurrently by studying two examples of an integrated curriculum, one in French (Table 2.2) and the other in Spanish (Table 2.3). Both examples begin with cultural topics (greeting, personal qualities, the classroom, and numbers and time in French; children and recreation, courtship, weddings, occupations, possessions, and entertainment in Spanish), fol-

TABLE 2.1 Proficiency levels by modality and achievement level

Listening	Speaking	Reading	Writing
		Checkpoint A	
Can comprehend simple statements and questions. Usually comprehends the main idea of extended but simple messages and conversations. Often requires repetition for comprehension even when listening to persons who are used to speaking with non-natives.	Can initiate and respond to simple statements and engage in simple face-to-face conversation within the vocabulary, structure, and phonology appropriate to the communicative situations and functions of this level. Can be understood, with some repetitions and circumlocutions, by native speakers used to foreigners attempting to speak their language.	Can understand simple material for informative or social purposes. Can understand the essential content of short, general, public statements and standardized messages. Can comprehend the main ideas of materials containing simple structure and syntax when relying on visual cues and prior familiarity with the topic. Understanding is limited to simple language containing only the highest frequency grammatical patterns and vocabulary items. Can sometimes guess at cognates and highly contextualized unfamiliar vocabulary. May have to read the material several times in order to achieve understanding.	Can express basic personal needs and compose short messages on very familiar topics based on personal experience. Writing consists mostly of mastered vocabulary and structures in simple sentences and phrases. Although errors in spelling and grammar are frequent, writing can be understood by native speakers used to dealing with foreigners.
		Checkpoint B	
Can comprehend short conversations on simple topics in everyday situations. Limited vocabulary range necessitates repetitions and/or circumlocutions for understanding. Can understand frequently used tense forms and word-order patterns in simple sen-	Can initiate and sustain a conversation, but limited vocabulary range necessitates hesitation and circumlocution. Can use the more common verb tense forms, but still makes many errors in formation and selection. Can use word order accurately in simple sentences,	Can understand simple narrative and descriptive authentic materials and edited texts within a familiar context. Has specific comprehension of selected passages in familiar sentence patterns. Can follow essential points and some details of expository writing when dealing	Can write simple notes, letters, and short reports using elementary vocabulary and commonly encountered structures. Can express present, future, and past ideas comprehensibly. Major errors still occur when expressing more complex thoughts. Begins to

tences. Has both general and detailed understanding of short, discrete expressions but has only general understanding of longer conversations and messages within familiar communicative situations. Can sustain comprehension through contextual inferences in short communications on familiar topics with native speakers who are aware of the non-native status of the listener.

but still makes errors in more complex patterns. Can sustain coherent structures in short and familiar communicative situations. Can employ selectively basic cohesive features such as pronouns and verb inflections. Extended communication is largely a series of short, discrete utterances. Can articulate comprehensibly but has difficulty in producing certain sounds in certain positions or combinations. Speech is usually labored. Has to repeat to be understood by the general public.

with areas of special interest and is able to guess meaning from the context.

develop sequential relationships. Writing is comprehensible to native speakers used to dealing with foreigners.

Checkpoint C

Can understand standard speech delivered with some repetition and rewording by a native speaker not used to dealing with foreigners. Can understand the essential points of discussions or presentations on familiar topics. Tension, pressure, emotional stress, and unfavorable listening conditions as well as vocabulary and complex utterances may hinder comprehension. Can sometimes detect emotional overtones and understand inferences.

Can handle most communicative situations with confidence but may need help with a complication or difficulty. Vocabulary, with some circumlocutions, is sufficient to communicate. Can handle elementary constructions accurately. Limited control of more complex structures may interfere with communication.

Can understand most factual information in nontechnical prose as well as some expository texts on topics related to areas of special interst. Can read excerpts from literature for pleasure. Is able to separate main ideas from lesser ones and thus begins to analyze materials written for the general public. Is able to use linguistic context and prior knowledge to increase comprehension. Can detect the overall tone or intent of the text.

Can compose unified and organized texts on everyday topics with sufficient vocabulary to express oneself simply with some circumlocution. Is able to show good control of the morphology of the language and of the most frequently used syntactic structures, but errors may still occur. Can express complex ideas sequentially with simple language. Writing is comprehensible to a native speaker not used to reading the writing of foreigners.

SOURCE: From *Modern Languages for Communication*, pp. 19–20. Albany, NY: University of the State of New York, copyright 1986. Reprinted with permission.

TABLE 2.2 An integrated French curriculum

Topics	Natural Interactional Use of Language	Possible Grammatical Structures or Features	Cultural Considerations
Greetings	Greet people Give thanks Seek information Take leave Ask about others *Other*	Verb *aller* (pres. ind.); question formation; inversion; personal pronouns; negation; use of verb *aller* such as in *Bonjour, comment allez-vous?, Bonjour, comment vas-tu?;* use of the subject pronouns *vous* and *tu* *Other*	Use of *vous* and *tu;* difference between *Comment allez-vous?* and *Ça va?;* customs (shaking hands or kissing) accompanying greetings; greetings; removing hat, handshake, kissing on both cheeks; French very seldom use first names in greetings
Personal qualities	Seek information Express curiosity Give information Be positive Pay a compliment Describe what a person looks like Describe what a person is like	Verb *être* (pres. ind.); question word order; *est-ce que;* agreement of adjectives; common adjectives that precede substantive; irregular forms of some adjectives; descriptive adjectives; use of familiar and formal means of addressing each other *Other*	In the target culture strangers use formal forms; friends and peers use familiar forms
The classroom	Name objects in classroom Tell about the classroom Ask assistance Ask permission	Name things around the room; definite/indefinite articles; *Il y a; avoir:* descriptive adjectives (*grande classe/petite classe*); use of the following expressions: *Qu'est-ce que c'est? Montrez-moi un crayon. Voici un crayon* or *Voilà un crayon. Où est . . .? J'ai une règle.* *Other*	The various names of schools; setup of French classroom; how this reflects the student/teacher relationship; what French children take to school
Number and times	Count Ask the time Tell the time Add and subtract	Expressions: *Quelle heure est-il? Il est _____ ; demi (e), quart . . .;* adding and subtracting; years; *Il y a* with time expression *Other* Need for contextual cultural manifestations to explore value systems	Special way of stating time; difference between *temps* and *heure;* measurements—metric; use of 24-hour system; school times; play times; different setup of math operations

SOURCE: From *Developing Communicative Proficiency and Cultural Understanding in Secondary School Language Programs* (p. 87) by Anthony Papalia. Schenectady, NY: New York State Association of Foreign Language Teachers, copyright 1983. Reprinted with permission.

TABLE 2.3 An integrated Spanish curriculum

Topics	Natural Interactional Use of Language	Possible Grammatical Structures or Features	Cultural Considerations
Children/ recreation	Name games that children play Tell what you do for recreation Ask about leisure-time activities *Other*	Interjections; nouns, verbs; adjectives, adverbs *Other*	Children's responsibilities; types of recreation
Courtship	Name where you go on dates Pay a compliment *Other*	*Ir; gustar;* progressive tenses; *salir;* *Other*	Dating customs; at what age does dating start?; chaperone; marriage; family; where do you go on a date?
Weddings	Tell who is going to get married Seek information Give information Name some of the gifts given Say when a person gets married *Other*	*Casarse* *Other*	Size of weddings; clothing; receptions; religious vs. civil ceremony; *luna de miel;* age at marriage
Occupations	Name occupations Name what you want to be Tell which occupation you like/dislike *Other*	Ommission of article with professions, i.e., *Es profesor; ser; ser* vs. *estar;* *Other*	Most common occupations; work hours; wages; prestige; dual role of education
Possessions	Name some of your possessions Tell what you would like to have Tell to whom certain things belong *Other*	*tener;* demonstratives; possessives *Other*	Social classes; types of possessions; family; importance of personal possessions; wages; cost of living
Entertainment	Name your favorite forms of entertainment and what you do in your leisure time	*Gustar; ir; venir; llegar; volver;* *Other*	Where people go; when; who goes; sports; *la corrida*

SOURCE: From *Developing Communicative Proficiency and Cultural Understanding in Secondary School Language Programs* (p. 97) by Anthony Papalia. Schenectady, NY: New York State Association of Foreign Language Teachers, copyright 1983. Reprinted with permission.

lowed by communicative uses of language, grammatical structures and expressions, and the cultural concepts that serve to illuminate the ideas, message, and social context.

Greetings in French, for example, involve considerations beyond when to use *tu* and *vous* forms. One needs to know social conventions such as when to shake hands or kiss, when to use first names, and what to say after the greetings. In Spanish, appropriate cultural scripts (typical pattern of behavior for different situations) may be essential for going on a date, attending a wedding reception, or renting an apartment. What are the dating customs (cultural information)? What can one say on a date (topics and functions)? Where does one go (settings)? What is the sequence of events: meeting, invitation, date, departure? How does one ask for the time in French when speaking to a friend, stranger, teenager, or adult? Is there a particular interactional sequence that should be followed? In American English, one might observe the following sequence:

A: Excuse me. (apology)
B: It's 2:30 P.M. (informative)
A: Thank you. (thanking)

Along with an understanding of social conventions and the cultural context of language use, there are cognitive considerations. Current research efforts in the area of the receptive skills suggest that reading and listening comprehension involve different types of cognitive processes (modes for processing information—scanning, interpreting) associated with particular types of texts (Canale, 1984b; Dandonoli, 1987; Child, 1987). Lee and Musumeci (1988), for instance, have established parallel hierarchies of text types along with the cognitive tasks associated with specific reading skills (Table 2.4).

Students at the 0/0+ level (novice) are expected to read signs, addresses, numbers, and names, processes that involve the ability to recognize memorized elements. Students at level 1 (intermediate) skim and scan orientational types of text such as travel forms and schedules, menus, and newspapers. At level 2 (advanced), students need to engage in decoding and classifying tasks as they read factual reports, short narratives, labels, and invitations. At the superior levels, students must employ numerous cognitive processes such as the ability to infer, hypothesize, interpret, analyze, and verify while reading editorials, literary texts, critiques, technical papers, and argumentative prose.

It is also important to note that oral proficiency assessment using ACTFL/ETS interview procedures (1982) follows a particular conversation sequence. The student must assume various communicative roles in the face-to-face oral interview. An oral interview lasting 10 to 30 minutes must be structured around four phases, each with a psychological, linguistic, and evaluative purpose. The student generally plays "follow the leader," responding to questions and talking about topics posed by the interviewer and asking the interviewer a series of questions in a structured role-playing situation:

TABLE 2.4 Parallel hierarchies of text types and reading skills defining levels of foreign language reading proficiency

Level	Text Type	Sample Texts	Reading Skills
0/0+	Enumerative	Numbers, names, street signs, money denominations, office/shop designations, addresses	Recognize memorized elements
1	Orientational	Travel and registration forms, plane and train schedules, TV/radio program guides, menus, memos, newspaper headlines, tables of contents, messages	Skim, scan
2	Instructive	Ads and labels, newspaper accounts, instructions and directions, short narratives and descriptions, factual reports, formulaic requests on forms, invitations, introductory and concluding paragraphs	Decode, classify
3	Evaluative	Editorials, analyses, apologia, certain literary texts, biography with critical interpretation	Infer, guess, hypothesize, interpret
4	Projective	Critiques of art or theater performances, literary texts, philosophical discourse, technical papers, argumentation	Analyze, verify, extend hypotheses

SOURCE: From "On Hierarchies of Reading Skills and Text Types" by James F. Lee and Diane Musumeci, 1988, *Modern Language Journal, 72*, p. 174. Reprinted with permission.

1. *Warm-up.* During this phase the examiner attempts to put the candidate at ease, reacquainting the candidate with the language if necessary. The examiner can also obtain a preliminary indication of the candidate's speaking and comprehension ability.

2. *Level check.* The purpose of this phase is to determine the highest level at which the candidate can most comfortably and consistently sustain a speaking performance. This involves establishing a "floor" or a base-line level to judge subsequent performance.

3. *Probes.* This phase provides the opportunity to establish the "ceiling" beyond which the candidate's language performance breaks down. There should be several probes using different questions and topics. The level check and probe phases can be repeated. If the candidate is able to perform at the probe level, the process starts again until a ceiling is established.

4. *Wind-down.* The purpose of this phase is to allow the candidate to leave the interview with a sense of accomplishment, usually by returning to the level of difficulty that the candidate can sustain comfortably.

Freed (1989) raises a few concerns regarding the use of the oral proficiency interview. It has been criticized on the basis that it is too teacher- or test-centered rather than stressing a more student-centered assessment approach. There is also the problem of a single holistic or global score (e.g., proficiency levels—novice high, intermediate low, advanced plus), which is confounded by the language features tested and the method used to elicit the oral language samples. Furthermore, the performance of an educated native speaker is the norm against which all levels have been established. There may be considerable differences among educated native speakers with respect to their performance on a structured oral interview. Variation must exist among different types of educated native speakers on the basis of their professional training (elementary school teachers, college professors, lawyers, actors, accountants).

DEVELOPMENT OF L2 PROFICIENCY

The development of L2 proficiency has been examined from various perspectives. The data collected and analyzed by the School of Languages of the Foreign Service Institute indicate the amount of time (hours of instruction) needed to attain certain oral proficiency levels in different languages, grouped according to difficulty for English speakers. Students with an average aptitude for language learning, for example, would need at least eight weeks (240 hours) of instruction to attain level 1 or 1+ on the governmental rating scale (intermediate mid/high on the basis of the ACTFL guidelines) in group I languages such as Danish, French, Italian, Portuguese, Spanish, Swahili, and Swedish. Students with a similar aptitude would require at least 16 weeks (480 hours) of training to reach a comparable level in a group II language such as Bulgarian, Farsi, German, Greek, and Hindi. For group III languages such as Amharic, Czech, Finnish, Hebrew, Polish, Russian, Turkish, and Vietnamese, students with a superior language aptitude could attain level 1 or 1+ with 16 weeks of instruction, while students with a minimum aptitude would require at least 24 weeks (720 hours) to attain similar levels. For group IV languages such as Arabic, Chinese, Japanese, and Korean, students with an average aptitude might reach level 1 (intermediate low to mid) with 16 weeks of training and level 1+ (intermediate high) with 24 weeks of instruction. It would take superior students approximately 44 weeks of training (1,320 hours) to reach levels 3 or 3+ (superior on the ACTFL scale) for group II, III, and IV languages. Similar types of students could attain the same proficiency level in about 24 weeks with group I languages (Liskin-Gasparro, 1982).

The development of L2 proficiency has also been described in terms of models that identify such factors as the social context, individual characteristics (age, personality, motivation, cognitive abilities), L2 acquisition contexts, and linguistic outcomes. The framework by Stern and Cummins (1981) identifies three types of variables: social context, learning conditions, and learner characteristics that affect the learning process and the linguistic outcomes (Figure 2.3).

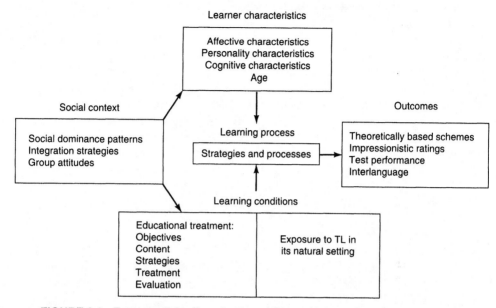

FIGURE 2.3 Framework for Examination of Second Language Learning

SOURCE: From "Language Teaching/Learning Research: A Canadian Perspective on Status and Direction" by H. H. Stern & Jim Cummins, in J. K. Phillips (Ed.), Action for the '80s: A Political, Professional, and Public Program for Foreign Language Education (p. 200) 1981, Lincolnwood, IL: National Textbook Company. Reprinted with permission.

The characteristics of the learner and the context for learning (e.g., language learning time and objectives, instructional procedures, testing methods) are influenced by the wider social context, for example, group attitudes about L2, interethnic contacts, and the like. The learning process consists of the conscious use of strategies and techniques employed by the student along with the conscious and unconscious mental processes (e.g., deductive and inductive reasoning, verbal association, transfer) that the student brings to a learning task. The linguistic outcomes can be evaluated on the basis of proficiency levels and performance of language tests that assess particular language areas (grammatical competence, appropriate use of language forms according to the social situation, answers on reading comprehension questions).

With respect to the acquisition of different aspects of language proficiency, Cummins (1980) cites Canadian research from a study of immigrant children who mastered oral communication skills in approximately two years of schooling. It took the children five to seven years to master the cognitive (context-reduced) language skills associated with academic tasks. The acquisition of discourse competence and the written aspects of proficiency among these students seems to be strongly associated with cognitive abilities (Harley, Allen, Cummins, & Swain, 1990).

Among language-majority pupils, the type of language program (language as subject, language plus content, immersion education) is critical to the development of high levels of proficiency. The Canadian experience provides clear evidence that it takes time—years of language study plus learning content via the language—to develop functional proficiency. English-speaking students who attended early total-immersion programs, beginning in kindergarten, were the most successful in acquiring a nativelike command of French. The other programs (early partial immersion or late immersion, starting in the middle grades) were less successful in producing bilingual students, but they were superior to the typical model of language learning as a subject (Swain & Lapkin, 1982).

SUMMARY

Knowing a language and being able to use it as a native speaker does encompasses many linguistic competencies, verbal skills, and systems of knowledge. For the language teacher, an understanding of the concept of proficiency is an important consideration for establishing program goals, designing learning tasks, and assessing student linguistic development.

The term communicative competence points to the dynamic nature of language involving various linguistic components and skills: grammatical, sociolinguistic, discourse, and strategic competence. Different language tasks (face-to-face communicative versus interaction with written texts) require the use of different language abilities. Conversation can take place with the aid of gestures, facial expressions, and feedback. Writing a letter requires knowledge of content and topics, language abilities, genre conventions, purpose, and audience.

The ACTFL proficiency guidelines describe language abilities in terms of four performance levels for each of the four language skill areas. Language functions/global tasks, content/topics, accuracy, and text types are the categories used to characterize proficiency levels. The various performance levels established for each of the four language skill areas involve extralinguistic knowledge, as in the case of social conventions, cultural patterns of behaviors, and norms for appropriate language use in different situations. With reading levels, for example, cognitive strategies such as scanning, decoding, classifying, inferring, and hypothesizing are utilized to process different text types. The ACTFL oral interview requires students to follow a particular conversational sequence including a question-and-answer phase along with a structured role-play situation.

The development of L2 proficiency is a relative process requiring time, interactional opportunities, and collaboration among learners and the teacher. The developmental patterns across the four language skill areas tend not to be uniform. The development of different aspects of proficiency (oral communication skills versus reading and writing abilities) require varying amounts of instruction for mastery. The type of language program (e.g., language immersion versus language as subject) influences the ultimate L2 attainment levels. At the same time, because of their complexity (case endings in German, the Cyrillic alphabet of Russian, the tones of Chinese, etc.) some languages require longer periods of training for attainment of proficiency levels comparable to those in other languages.

ACTIVITIES

1. What is your definition of "knowing a language?" What components of language do you include? Why?
2. Compare Oller's definition of global language proficiency with Cummins's twofold approach. How does your definition of knowing a language compare with Oller's or Cummins's conception of communicative competence?
3. In a dictionary look up *competence, skill, ability,* and *knowledge.* What do Canale and Swain mean when they say that communicative competence is used to refer to both knowledge and skill in using language?
4. Interview a second language learner, asking him or her to select the ACTFL description that best describes his or her oral proficiency level in terms of function, context, and accuracy. How would you rate your own proficiency level?
5. Examine the communicative situations included in the New York State syllabus for checkpoints A, B, and C. What functions and topics would likely occur with some of the listening situations? What functions and topics would be associated with some of the listening and speaking situations?
6. What types of cognitive tasks are associated with the different reading situations included in the New York State syllabus?
7. Read the New York State syllabus descriptions for proficiency levels by modalities for checkpoints A, B, and C. Examine the descriptions according to functions, topics, and linguistic considerations. To what extent are the three factors treated similarly or differently across the four modalities? What are some of the problems encountered in writing proficiency statements by level and modality?
8. To what extent does the "integrated" French or Spanish curriculum proposed by Papalia correspond to some of the components of communicative competence? What additional components need to be added, and why?
9. Consider the conversation structure used as part of the ACTFL/ETS oral interview process. Can the structure influence the performance level of some students? What competencies, skills, or abilities are also being tested as a result of the format with its four phases?
10. Examine some of the reading passages used in a second language textbook. What is the range of text types included in two or three of the lessons? Evaluate the kinds of comprehension questions that are asked for the various text types. What cognitive demands are associated with the different kinds of comprehension questions?

REFERENCES

American Council on the Teaching of Foreign Languages [ACTFL]. (1982, 1986). *ACTFL provisional proficiency guidelines.* Hastings-on-Hudson, NY: ACTFL Materials Center.

Bachman, L. (1990). *Fundamental considerations in language testing.* Oxford: Oxford University Press.

Bachman, L., & Palmer, A. (1982). The construct validation of some components of communicative proficiency. *TESOL Quarterly, 16,* 449-465.

Canale, M. (1983). From communicative competence to communicative language pedagogy. in J. Richards & R. Schmidt (Eds.), *Language and communication* (pp. 2-25). New York: Longman.

Canale, M. (1984a). A communicative approach to language proficiency assessment in a minority setting. In C. Rivera (Ed.), *Communicative competence approaches to language proficiency assessment: Research and application* (pp. 107-122). Avon, England: Multilingual Matters.

Canale, M. (1984b). Considerations in the testing of reading and listening proficiency. *Foreign Language Annals, 4,* 349-357.

Canale, M., & Swain, M. (1980). Theoretical bases of communicative approaches to second language teaching and testing. *Applied Linguistics, 1*(1), 1-47.

Child, J. R. (1987). Language proficiency levels and the typology of texts. In H. Byrnes & M. Canale (Eds.), *Defining and developing proficiency: Guidelines, implementation, and concepts* (pp. 97-106). Lincolnwood, Il: National Textbook.

Chomsky, N. (1965). *Aspects of the theory of syntax.* Cambridge, MA: MIT Press.

Cicourel, A. (1981). Notes on the integration of micro and macro levels of analysis. In K. Knorr-Cetina & A. V. Cicourel (Eds.), *Advances in social theory and methodology* (pp. 51-80). London: Routledge and Kegan Paul.

Cummins, J. (1980). The cross-lingual dimensions of language proficiency: Implications for bilingual education and the optimal age issue. *TESOL Quarterly, 14,* 175-187.

Cummins, J. (1981). The role of primary language development in promoting educational success for language minority students. In *Schooling and language minority students: A theoretical framework* (pp. 3-49). Los Angeles: California State University, Evaluation, Dissemination, and Assessment Center.

Cummins, J., & Swain, M. (1986). *Bilingualism in education.* New York: Longman.

Dandonoli, P. (1987). ACTFL's current research in proficiency testing. In H. Byrnes & M. Canale (Eds.), *Defining and developing proficiency: Guidelines, implementations, and concepts* (pp. 75-96). Lincolnwood, Il: National Textbook.

Erickson, F., & Shultz, J. (1981). When is a context? Some issues and methods in the analysis of social competence. In J. Green & C. Wallat (Eds.), *Ethnography and language in educational settings.* Advances in discourse processes, V (pp. 147-160). Norwood, NJ: Ablex.

Faerch, C., Haastrup, K., & Phillipson, R. (1984). *Learner language and language learning.* Copenhagen: Gyldendals Sprogbibliotek.

Freed, B. F. (1989). Perspectives on the future of proficiency based teaching and testing. *ADFL Bulletin, 20*(2), 52-57.

Harley, B., Cummins, J., Swain, M., & Allen, P. (1990). The nature of language proficiency. In B. Harley, P. Allen, J. Cummins, & M. Swain (Eds.), *The development of second language proficiency* (pp. 7-25). Cambridge, England: Cambridge University Press.

Hernández-Chávez, E., Burt, M. K., & Dulay, H. C. (1978). Language dominance and proficiency testing: Some general considerations. *NABE Journal, 3,* 41-54.

Hymes, D. (1972). On communicative competence. In J. B. Pride & J. Holmes (Eds.), *Sociolinguistics* (pp. 269-293). London: Penguin.

Hymes, D. (1985). Toward linguistic competence. *Revue de L'AILA, 2,* 9-23.

Kennan, E. O. (1974). Conversational competence in children. *Journal of Child Language, 1,* 163-185.

Lee, J. F., & Musumeci, D. (1988). On hierarchies of reading skills and text types. *Modern Language Journal, 72*(2), 173-187.

Liskin-Gasparro, J. (1982). *The ETS oral proficiency interview manual.* Princeton, NJ: Educational Testing Service.

Liskin-Gasparro, J. (1986). Teaching and testing for oral proficiency: Some applications for the classroom. In A. Papalia (Ed.), *Teaching our students a second language in a proficiency-based classroom* (pp. 91-99). Schenectady, NY: New York State Association of Foreign Language Teachers.

McLendon, S. (1977). Cultural presupposition and discourse analysis. Patterns of presupposition and assertion of information in Eastern Pomo and Russian narrative. In M. Saville-Troike (Ed.), *Linguistics and anthropology* (pp. 153-189). Washington, DC: Georgetown University Press.

Modern languages for communication. (1986). Albany, NY: State Education Department.

Oller, J. W., Jr. (1978). The language factor in the evaluation of bilingual education. In J. E. Alatis (Ed.), *Georgetown University round table on languages and linguistics* (pp. 410-422). Washington, DC: Georgetown University Press.

Oller, J. N., Jr. (1979). *Language tests at school: A pragmatic approach.* New York: Longman.

Papalia, A. (1983). *Developing communicative proficiency and cultural understanding in secondary school language programs.* Schenectady, NY: New York State Association of Foreign Language Teachers.

Paulston, C. B. (1974). Linguistics and communicative competence. *TESOL Quarterly, 8,* 347-362.

Steinmann, M. (1982). Speech act theory and writing. In M. Nystrand (Ed.), *What writers know: The language process and structure of written discourse* (pp. 291-324). New York: Academic Press.

Stern, H. H. (1983). *Fundamental concepts of language teaching.* Oxford: Oxford University Press.

Stern, H. H., & Cummins, J. (1981). Language teaching/learning research: A Canadian perspective on status and direction. In J. K. Phillips (Ed.), *Action for the '80s: A political, professional, and public program for foreign language education* (pp. 195-248). Lincolnwood, IL: National Textbook.

Swain, M. K., & Lapkin, S. (1982). *Evaluating bilingual education: A Canadian case study.* Clevedon, England: Multilingual Matters.

Troike, R. C. (1970). Receptive competence, productive competence, and performance. In J. Alatis (Ed.), *Linguistics and the teaching of standard English to speakers of other languages and dialects* (pp. 63-74). Washington, DC: Georgetown University, Round Table on Languages and Linguistics.

chapter 3

Culture in the Language Classroom

Every word, every expression we use has a cultural dimension. Culture is the means by which a community communicates. If people were not referring to a commonly agreed upon set of meanings in their interactions with each other, no communication would take place. Speakers of a language share not only the vocabulary and structure of the language; they share the perceptions of reality represented by that vocabulary and structure. And because speakers of different languages have different perceptions of reality, no two languages show a one-to-one correspondence between vocabulary items or grammatical structures. It stands to reason, then, that learning a second (or additional) language, without learning about and understanding the culture(s) in which it is used, will not enable an individual to communicate effectively with speakers of that language.

R. Steele, 1990

It is commonly accepted that culture is reflected in language and encompasses such aspects as materials, customs, values, and ways of using language. Speakers of a particular culture share similar perceptions of reality that are represented by the vocabulary and linguistic structures of their language. Establishing a direct link between language and culture is not often a central concern in many language textbooks, nor in usual classroom practice. Setting goals for cultural awareness and understanding in addition to language proficiency entails designing instructional activities that also promote sociocultural awareness. Incorporating specific cultural situations, teaching the features of language within a social context, and using authentic materials for cross-cultural analysis are some of the strategies that can be used in the classroom to integrate culture and language learning.

This chapter considers specific ways of integrating cultural elements and language study. A number of issues are examined:

1. What are the definitions of culture?
2. How are language and culture integrated in textbooks?
3. What types of knowledge, skills, and behaviors are associated with the concept of cultural proficiency?
4. What teaching techniques can be used to promote cultural learning?

DEFINITIONS OF CULTURE

The term *culture* carries many different meanings. Culture has been defined in distinct ways and from different academic perspectives:

1. "Culture is a way of thinking, feeling, believing. It is the group's knowledge stored up (in memories of people; in books and objects) for future use. A culture constitutes a storehouse of the pooled learning of the group." (Kluckholn, 1944, pp. 24–25)
2. "Culture is communication and communication is culture." (Hall, 1959, p. 169)
3. "Culture is the unique life style of a particular group of people. Culture is also communicable knowledge, learned behavioral traits that are shared by participants in a social group and manifested in their institutions and artifacts." (Harris & Moran, 1979, p. 57)
4. "Culture . . . provide[s] . . . a set of principles for map-making and navigation. Different cultures are like schools of navigation designed to cope with different terrains and seas." (Frake, 1981, pp. 375–376)
5. "Culture refers to that relatively unified set of shared symbolic ideas associated with societal patterns of cultural ordering." (Gudykunst & Kim, 1984, p. 11)

The concept of culture reflected in definitions 1 and 3 highlights that fact that "cultures provide sets of unique and interrelated selected blueprints for living and accompanying sets of values and beliefs to support these blueprints" (Damen, 1987, p. 88). Definition 2 makes the connection between language and culture. Culture is embedded in language, and language is one of the means by which culture is transmitted. Art, dance, music, and nonverbal behaviors are other means by which culture is conveyed and represented. Definitions 4 and 5 suggest that culture "structures how we actually *experience* reality" (Mukhopadhyay, 1985, p. 19). A culture "functions as a filtering device between its bearers and the great range of stimuli presented by the environment" (Damen, 1987, p. 89). Culture is created collectively by members of a given society and consists of interrelated elements: material objects and artifacts (dress, types of shelter, tools for working), social patterns for living (kinship arrangements, educational systems, governmental structures, and economic organization), and mental patterns (ways of thinking, beliefs, values, and rules for actions).

LANGUAGE AND CULTURE IN TEXTBOOKS

Language textbooks are written to provide students with a knowledge of the language and culture of the target group. Language lessons are usually arranged so that students are presented with linguistic forms (e.g., grammatical structures, vocabulary, verb morphology) and communicative functions (asking for directions, greetings, apologizing, expressing personal opinions) in an organized manner. Specific aspects of language are often placed in the context of social situations, such as shopping in a market, visiting a family, or going on a trip. Culture is sometimes presented within the framework of themes illustrating what and how the natives eat, dress, work, play, and live their daily lives. In some instances, examples of conventional behaviors are included to show the way some members of the target culture complain, console each other, celebrate joyful events, and resolve real-life situations.

Kramsch (1987) suggests that we should conceive of foreign language textbooks as a "construction of foreign reality," as well as a "culturally coded educational construct," representing "a complex nexus of various forces, requiring the collaboration of a variety of people: linguists and educators, authors, reviewers, publishers, school boards, teachers and students" (1988, p. 65). Teachers need to reflect on how their textbooks develop cultural literacy through the use of exercises that promote higher levels of abstraction and critical modes of thinking.

Since the 1970s, considerable scholarly attention has been paid to foreign language textbook description and evaluation. Checklists (like one prepared to analyze German language texts, in Engel 1977, 1979) include such categories as the structure of the textbook, language exercises, grammar study, vocabulary items, language functions, thematic goals, and cultural details. Comparative studies of textbooks in French, German, English, Dutch, and Spanish have been completed to determine the relative emphasis on aspects such as vocabulary, grammar, pronunciation, exercises, audiovisual methods, and culture (Van Els, Bongaerts, Extra, Van Os, & Janssen-van Dieten, 1984). One publisher concerned with the opinions of Spanish and French teachers recently conducted a survey involving more than 200 secondary schools in the United States (Brown, 1984). Questions were directed at teachers' preferences regarding the presentation of vocabulary, grammar, readings, use of English, and culture material. The cultural content and the manner of presentation of first-year college French textbooks have been examined by Levno and Pfister (1980). Walz (1980) has also considered the colonial attitude towards the French-speaking world as reflected in American textbooks.

Spanish textbooks, in particular, have been analyzed to determine the specific cultural content, especially as it pertains to the portrayal of Hispanic ethnic groups in the United States. Williams (1978), for example, has focused on the connection of Spanish cultural materials to Chicanos, Cubans, and Puerto Ricans in secondary school texts. Arizpe and Aguirre (1987) have evaluated the level of accuracy in the depictions of Mexican, Puerto Rican, and Cuban ethnic groups living in the United States as presented in first-year, college-level texts.

More recently, Ramirez and Hall (1990) have studied the cultural perspectives and linguistic content presented to high school students in various Spanish textbooks presently in use. They investigated first-level books from a series of secondary textbooks focusing on a sociocultural analysis of major social themes using the five broad cultural topics proposed by Pfister and Borzilleri (1977):

   I. The family unit and the personal sphere
      A. Family relationships
      B. Eating and shopping
      C. Housing
  II. The social sphere
      A. Class structure
      B. Work
      C. Leisure
      D. Attitudes toward sex
      E. Population
 III. Political systems and institutions
      A. Government
      B. Education
      C. Law and justice
  IV. The environmental sphere
      A. Geography
      B. Economic development
      C. Urban versus rural
      D. Natural resources and the environment
      E. Weather
   V. Religion, the arts, and the humanities
      A. Role of churches
      B. Folklore and history
      C. Literature, music, creative arts

The relative emphasis on major cultural themes for chapters selected from the beginning, middle, and end of each book (approximately 60% of the total number of chapters or units) yielded an interesting pattern. Activities associated with the social sphere accounted for one-third (34%) of the topics presented, followed by personal needs (25%) and humanistic concerns (25%) associated with religion, the arts, folklore, and history. The two spheres given the least amount of representation were those dealing with political and institutional issues and environmental concern (8% respectively).

Within the social sphere, leisure (15%) and population and nationality (10%) were given more emphasis. Leisure activities were presented within the domain of sports, particularly those of soccer and snow skiing. References to South American countries were usually made in this context, noting seasonal differences that make skiing possible in July or August. The topic of population and nationality was most frequently depicted by a photograph of a person or a picture with a caption describing the person's nationality. People in photographs were generally well-dressed, appearing to come from middle- to upper-middle-class backgrounds. In addition, the social places most frequently highlighted were those attended most often by the small segment of the population who are considered highly educated and/or wealthy: museums, ultramodern shops, sports resorts, and universities. Few explicit references were given to the notion of social class (3%). In fact, only two books referred to a social class other than those of the middle to upper-middle classes within any of the Spanish-speaking countries or groups.

Within the personal sphere, eating and shopping received most mention (17%), usually through photographs of families eating, people shopping, and foods typical of those found in Spain or Mexico. As in the social sphere, the families and foods depicted were generally those found within the middle to upper-middle classes.

In the humanities, literature, music, and the arts (14%) accounted for most of the references, depicted most frequently through pictures. One of the books adapted reading selections from some of Spain's most noted authors. Although the Roman Catholic Church plays a major cultural role in most Spanish-speaking countries, it was rarely presented as a cultural theme (1%). References to the political sphere were usually associated with the monetary and transportation systems within various countries. Politics, law and justice, and governmental institutions received no mention whatsoever. Generally, across all five spheres and within four of the five books, the information given was culture-general rather than culture specific. Specific references to countries were used as examples of general cultural information presented as applicable to all Spanish-speaking peoples—be they from Spain, Puerto Rico, or Mexico.

Cultural information was presented through various visual and written modalities. Photographs (48%) were the principal means of depicting cultural situations. The photographs were often accompanied by a brief caption (15%) in an effort to highlight a particular feature or establish a context. In many instances, no explanations were given along with the pictures, making it difficult to judge the cultural content. Snow-covered mountains, rolling hills, traffic situations, and crowds of people could be scenes from any number of countries. One book in particular tended to use many ambiguous photos interspersed throughout the text, with little reference given to the figures. Two books did provide colorful photographs, most of which were referenced by either a brief narrative or a picture caption. Short narratives, ranging from one sentence to several paragraphs, were the second most frequently used means (31%). Maps, charts, and drawings were used infrequently (5% combined) for this purpose.

Analysis of the relationship between the linguistic and cultural elements in specific lessons yielded two basic curricular patterns: (1) language and culture presented in a linear, nonintegrated manner, and (2) an integrated model of language/culture developed around a main topic (Crawford-Lange & Lange, 1984). For instance, in a lesson that sequences linguistic and cultural activities in an alternating manner (Table 3.1), the learner starts at an outdoor cafe in Spain, learns some conventional expressions, useful words, and grammatical features, and then practices pronunciation of various sounds. Later, he or she reads about playing tennis in Cuernavaca, Mexico, and then celebrates a fifteenth birthday (quinceañera) in Mexico City, followed by a grammar review and a "brief" English description of Puerto Rico. Participation in the lesson centers on the interaction between the teacher and students. The students are asked to read, answer questions, in turn, about the texts, and complete grammatical exercises. Here, emphasis is on development of linguistic accuracy, as reflected in the various pronunciation and grammatical exercises. Students read and answer questions about Mona and Paco's discussion at an outdoor cafe in Spain. They also learn about the food typically served in Spanish cafes. Yet there is no attempt made to develop the theme of food, ordering a meal, or social functions of a cafe. Playing tennis and celebrating a fifteenth birthday in Mexico are treated primarily as reading comprehension activities instead of sociocultural contexts.

The lesson that integrates language with culture is centered around the lottery as a major cultural phenomenon (Table 3.2). Four of the five activities are devoted to the lottery; the student learns about buying tickets and the importance of the lottery in various Spanish-speaking countries. Pictures of authentic lottery tickets are presented, along with numerous questions related to the topic. The subjunctive mood is included in its various forms, and attempts are made to contextualize grammar to various cultural themes: going to the theater, a telephone conversation, and traveling. This lesson represents a thematic approach for relating language to culture. Vocabulary and grammar exercises are planned around the topic of the lottery. Students learn how to purchase tickets for different social events and daily activities while gaining an understanding, through a cultural reading, of the role that the lottery plays in places such as Madrid, Mexico City, and San Juan. Photographs of authentic materials are also used to provide a visual representation of cultural artifacts.

Analysis of language lessons according to the categories of component or activity, topic, situation, participants, and learner roles allows examining the interconnection between the linguistic and cultural content. Teachers may then decide on the extent to which features of language need to be linked to cultural situations and the activities required to accomplish the instructional goals. Steele (1990) points out that the development of a culturally based curriculum rests on a flexible, task-oriented methodology and testing of both linguistic and cultural competence. Teachers can supplement the cultural content of their lessons through the use of authentic documents such as magazines, newspapers, advertisements, travel timetables, and catalogues. These materials can become the basis for learning tasks that in turn are utilized for the presentation of linguistic content. Authentic materials are incorporated in later chapters of this book devoted to the development of listening (Chapter 7), reading (Chapter 8), speaking (Chapter 9), and writing skills (Chapter 10).

TABLE 3.1 An example of a nonintegrated sequence of linguistic and cultural activities in a Spanish lesson

Component	Topic	Situation	Participants	Learner Activity
1. Dialog	Talk about cafes and personal topics	Outdoor cafe in Spain	Mona and Paco, two young persons	Reading and answering questions about dialog
2. Conventional expressions and useful words	Verbal routines and formulas	Based on outdoor cafe dialog plus situation in photograph	Teacher, students	Reviewing popular expressions and grammatical constructions
3. Proverb	"Reading and eating should be done slowly"	Classroom	Teacher, students	Reading and interpreting proverb
4. Supplemental grammar and vocabulary	Related to cafe scene	Food typically found in Spanish cafe plus visuals	Teacher, students	Reading and answering questions about activities at an outdoor cafe
5. Pronunciation exercises	Sound and word stress with written accent	Classroom	Teacher, students	Practicing sounds and word stress along with recognizing written accent
6. Tongue twisters	/r/ and /n/ sounds	Classroom	Teacher, students	Reading and pronouncing sounds at natural rate of speed
7. Questions and answers	Typical foods; eating habits/preferences	Visuals representing foods; classroom	Teacher, students	Expressing personal interests, preferences, and habits regarding foods
8. Dialog	Eating at a restaurant	Restaurant menu and dialog	Role-playing waiter/waitress and customers	Reading a menu and ordering a meal
9. Grammar features and practice drills	Imperfect tense, singular and plural forms	Classroom	Teacher, students	Cued responses
10. Dialog and comprehension questions	Family reunion	The apartment of the Sender family	Various family members	Reading and answering questions about dialog
11. Vocabulary and questions	Nouns, verbs, adjectives, and grammatical constructions	Visuals representing various scenes (family, church, food, cleaning)	Teacher, students	Cued responses agreeing and disagreeing with common expressions
12. Cultural corner	A visit to Puerto Rico (English text)	Tourist description of the island plus three photographs of various scenes	Teacher, students	Reading narrative for cultural information

64

Component	Topic	Situation	Participants	Learner Activity
13. Grammatical rules and examples of the features	Present perfect, indirect object, pronouns, word order, written accent marks	Classroom	Teacher, students	Reviewing grammatical rules in English with Spanish examples
14. Bilingual vocabulary list	Words included in the lesson	Classroom	Teacher, students	Reviewing words included in the lesson

SOURCE: From "Language and Culture in Secondary Spanish Textbooks" by Arnulfo G. Ramírez and Joan Kelly Hall, 1990, *Modern Language Journal, 74,* pp. 61–62. Reprinted with permission.

TABLE 3.2 An example of an integrated sequence of linguistic and cultural activities in a Spanish lesson

Component	Topic	Situation	Participants	Learner Activity
1. Vocabulary and useful expressions	Lottery Reflexive verbs	Visuals representing persons, lottery tickets, and various situations	Teacher, students	Completing grammatical exercises
2. Grammatical features and practice drills	Subjunctive forms in noun clauses and in impersonal expressions	Some items related to theatre, telephone conversation, hotel, and travel topics	Teacher, students	Completing grammatical exercises
3. Conversation	Luck with the lottery	Visual representing sale of lottery tickets	Ana and Fernando	Reading and completing questions based on dialog
4. Cultural reading	Role of lottery in society	Visual and photographs representing sale of lettery tickets	Teacher, students	Reading narrative and answering questions related to the text
5. Examination of authentic documents	Lottery tickets	Lottery tickets from Mexico, Spain, Puerto Rico, and photographs of persons buying tickets	Teacher, students	Reading authentic texts and answering questions related to topic

SOURCE: From "Language and Culture in Secondary Spanish Textbooks" by Arnulfo G. Ramírez and Joan Kelly Hall, 1990, *Modern Language Journal, 74,* p. 62. Reprinted with permission.

DIMENSIONS OF CULTURAL PROFICIENCY

Culture in the L2 classroom can be characterized as "information acquisition" (i.e., knowledge about a set of identifiable facts) and as a "process of becoming" (i.e. discovering and examining another culture for the purpose of hypothesis refinement). The notion of *culture as information* can be observed in terms of learning goals such as the following, by which students should be able to:

1. Recognize/explain major geographical monuments
2. Recognize/explain major historical events
3. Recognize/explain major institutions (administrative, political, religious, educational, etc.)
4. Recognize/explain major "artistic" monuments (architecture, arts, literature)
5. Recognize/explain "active" everyday cultural patterns (eating, shopping, greeting people, etc.)
6. Recognize/explain "passive" everyday cultural patterns (social stratification, marriage, work, etc.)
7. Act appropriately in common everyday situations
8. Use common gestures appropriately (Lafayette, 1988, p. 49)

Students learning *culture as process* engage in different types of performance behaviors. Through a set of cognitive and affective learning activities, they should be able to:

1. Recognize/explain similarities and differences between L1 and L2 cultures
2. Recognize/explain the changing nature of culture, the inaccuracy of stereotypes, and the sources of culturally conditioned behavior
3. Examine cultural information and sources, and describe, report, and analyze findings
4. Value cultural contributions and accept cultural uniqueness through cross-cultural analysis
5. Engage in hypothesis refinement by following a step-by-step process starting with perceiving a cultural aspect, make a statement, gathering information, and contrasting with native culture, leading to a modification/refinement of the initial cultural perception
6. Participate successfully in novel cultural situations (Crawford-Lange & Lange, 1984, pp. 143–146)

Some of the learning outcomes for learning culture as "information" and "process" are reflected in the inventories or frameworks proposed by Nostrand (1967) and Seelye (1984). Nostrand's emergent model classifies 30 different aspects of human behavior into four major subsystems: cultural, social, ecological, and personal. The cultural category includes national character, values, beliefs, art forms, and kinesics, for example. Society covers 13 areas, from family life to interpersonal and intergroup conflicts. Ecology contains six topics, ranging from attitudes toward nature to transportation and travel. The fourth subsystem, the individual, incorporates status, age, sex, and personality characteristics.

Seelye modified Nostrand's conceptual structure for approaching culture themes by organizing cultural content into seven instructional goals. The student should be able to:

1. Understand how culture conditions behavior
2. Understand how social variables—age, sex, social class, and place of residence—affect the way people speak and behave
3. Understand the conventional behavior of people in ordinary and crisis situations
4. Indicate an awareness that culturally conditioned images are associated with many common target words and phrases
5. Demonstrate the ability to evaluate statements about a society
6. Demonstrate the ability to locate and organize information about the target culture from the library, mass media, people, and personal observation
7. Demonstrate intellectual curiosity about the target culture and empathy its people

The *ACTFL Provisional Proficiency Guidelines* (1982) initially established cultural proficiency levels for novice, intermediate, advanced, superior, near-native competence, and native competence along the lines of the trisectional framework of function-content-accuracy. The novice student, for example, should demonstrate the following characteristics:

Limited interaction. Behaves with consideration. Is resourceful in nonverbal communication, but is unreliable in interpretation of nonverbal cues. Is limited in language, as indicated under the listening and speaking skills. Generally lacks the knowledge of culture patterns requisite for survival situations.

The advanced student, on the other hand, should display the following behaviors:

Limited social competence. Handles routine social situations successfully with a culture-bearer accustomed to foreigners. Shows comprehension of common rules of etiquette, taboos, and sensitivities, although home culture predominates. Can make polite requests, accept and refuse invitations, offer and receive gifts, apologize, make introductions, telephone, purchase and bargain, do routine banking. Can discuss a few aspects of the home and the foreign country, such as general current events and policies, as well as a field of personal interest. Does not offend the culture-bearer, but some important misunderstandings and miscommunications occur in interaction with one unaccustomed to foreigners. Is not competent to take part in a formal meeting or in a group situation where several persons are speaking informally at the same time.

The cultural guidelines have been criticized on the grounds that they do not follow any inherent hierarchical pattern of "cultural proficiency" (Galloway, 1985). Allen (1985) has suggested reconceptualizing the trisectional scheme of function-content-accuracy with a more culturally relevant tripartite framework consisting of:

1. *Information:* data about the particular culture and the organization of that information into a coherent whole, divided according to successive stages
2. *Experience:* cognitive processes by which the learner approaches the information and emerges with an understanding of the particular culture
3. *Authenticity:* affective reactions of the learner in terms of socioeconomic behavior and attitudes that result from an empathetic understanding of the culture

Nevertheless, Allen's reformation of the cultural component has not been incorporated into the revised ACTFL *Proficiency Guidelines* (1986). What constitutes cultural competence remains elusive, and ways of integrating culture effectively into an instructional scheme need to be reconsidered. As Galloway (1985, p. 11) points out, our goal should be "to increase the students' cognitive abilities to process and understand cultural phenomena in an active, analytical way."

One approach might be to arrange instructional sequences according to Hanvey's (1979) four-level schema for measuring cross-cultural awareness (Table 3.3). At levels I and II, the learner's knowledge about the culture is based on isolated facts and visible, superficial cultural traits. Comments about the culture are expressed in terms of what the culture lacks, how it differs from the native culture. The behavior of the culture-bearer is regarded as unbelievable, exotic, frustrating, and, at times, irritating. When individuals reach Level III, they began to develop a sense of cultural relativism. They began to accept cultural differences on intellectual terms. Cultural traits become believable because they can be explained. At Level IV the individual begins to see the culture as an insider. By living in the cultural setting and interacting with members of the group, it is now possible to understand the feelings and behaviors of the culture-bearers.

Papalia (1983) offers a sequential mode of instruction for developing cultural understanding by involving students in observation, reflection, and valuing. He argues that "developing cultural empathy and understanding depends largely on the learner's emotional state, feelings, personality, and moral development" (p. 68). The instructional sequence consists of four steps, based on Krathwohl, Bloom, and Massi's (1964) taxonomy of the affective domain. It involves receiving, responding, valuing, organizing, and characterizing by a value:

TABLE 3.3 Stages of cross-cultural awareness

Level	Information	Mode	Interpretation
I	Awareness of superficial or very visible cultural traits; stereotypes	Tourism, textbooks, *National Geographic*	Unbelievable (i.e., exotic, bizarre)
II	Awareness of significant and subtle cultural traits that contrast markedly with one's own	Culture conflict situations	Unbelievable (i.e., frustrating, irrational)
III	Awareness of significant and subtle cultural traits that contrast markedly with one's own	Intellectual analysis	Believable cognitively
IV	Awareness of how another culture feels from the standpoint of the insider	Cultural immersion; living the culture	Believable because of subjective familiarity

SOURCE: From *An Attainable Global Perspective* by Robert G. Hanvey, 1976, New York, NY: Center for Global Perspectives. Reprinted with permission.

1. Sensation

Students are introduced to the linguistic and cultural items through the senses (what I see, hear, and touch). During this phase teachers should provide an environment for spontaneous reactions so that students feel free to indicate what the stimulus has evoked. Knowledge, beliefs, customs, skills, behaviors, lifestyles, and other cultural manifestations are presented through sensory modalities.

2. Perception

Students are asked to interpret the linguistic and cultural phenomena (what do I make of it?). Here teachers "debug" the minds to find out what students' beliefs, knowledge, attitudes, and feelings are. They must identify how the cultural items that have been presented affected the individual, how the learner organized the new knowledge, and what conclusion he or she has drawn.

3. Concept

Students are asked to formulate the linguistic and cultural concepts (what is the code, message, belief, custom, value?). Teachers help in organizing new knowledge and in developing an awareness and identification of values. They help in analyzing facts and behaviors as a manifestation of that culture by discovering causal relationships and value systems.

4. Principle

Students are asked to develop a guide to action (why do people have certain beliefs, customs, and values and how are they guided applying them?). Through rational thinking and emotional acceptance, teachers develop an analysis and commitment to relativism. They develop situations or simulations in which students apply the new knowledge and predict ways of valuing and behaving that are proper to the people whose language they are studying. In addition, they promote an analysis of the learner's value system and an ability to analyze a given culture from within (-emic) rather than from without (-etic).

The selection of specific cultural concepts and topics depends on such factors as the students' age, cognitive abilities, and interests. According to Papalia, it is possible to teach students how to approach cultural differences and to think about the world in terms of cultural relativism by comparing, analyzing, and assessing their value systems.

STRATEGIES FOR TEACHING CULTURE

Culture is learned behavior. As such it can be taught in a classroom setting (Damen, 1987). Cultural content can be presented in various formats and used to accomplish different instructional goals. A lesson on the purchasing of an item of clothing in a department store in Germany, for example, encompasses both linguistic and cultural elements. The linguistic features might include (1) communicative functions of language such as asking and giving information about sizes, colors, fabrics, prices; expressing personal feelings about the different aspects associated with the clothing item, greetings, leave-taking, etc.; (2) specific grammatical forms that correspond to those functions; and (3) vocabulary items such as nouns, adjectives, verbs, and prepositions, needed to express notions related to the topic of buying clothes. The cultural content can comprise such elements as European clothing sizes, the monetary unit, borrowed English words (e.g., jeans), a shopping script (procedures for getting service, trying out clothes, and paying for the item), and an understanding of department stores (when and where to shop for what items).

What techniques can be used to teach about European sizes, the monetary system, and special expressions for shopping? What teaching strategies are needed to present information on shopping, the types of stores, their location, and ways of buying? The answers to these questions suggest that different types of activities might be needed for teaching "culture as information" versus "culture as process."

The most familiar strategies for presenting culture include the culture capsule, culture assimilator, culture cluster, minidrama, audio-motor unit, role playing, critical incident, and simulation. These techniques have been described and exemplified in numerous publications (Jarvis, 1977; Lafayette, 1978; Morain, 1978; Nostrand, 1967; Seelye, 1984; Strasheim, 1981).

Examples of Cultural Activities

Culture Capsule.   The culture capsule is designed to explain a specific cultural difference between an American and a target-culture custom. Using a variety of visual aids and realia, the teacher provides a brief oral explanation of the foreign custom and contrasts it with the related American custom. This is followed by a series of content-related questions and appropriate student activities. The capsule can be written by teachers or students and can be used in small groups or with the entire class. A capsule in French may discuss the difference between setting the table in French and American homes.

Culture Cluster. This consists of a series or cluster of related culture capsules, used to develop a central theme such as a dinner party, a wedding, a shopping trip, or eating at a restaurant. With this approach, the teacher usually develops three separate, 10-minute capsules plus one 30-minute segment of class time devoted to a dramatization or role playing of the information presented in the capsules. Thus, going out to eat in a Spanish restaurant might involve (1) taking a taxi, (2) reading a Spanish menu, and (3) ordering the meal.

Culture Assimilator. The culture assimilator incorporates three basic parts: (1) a brief episode in narrative or dramatic form that documents an intercultural exchange involving a misunderstanding, (2) four possible interpretations of the incident, and (3) feedback to the students as to the appropriate interpretation. Garber (1986) provides an example of this technique with "handshaking in France":

> Sarah Fish was living with her parents and her two younger brothers in Paris. The Fish family planned to live there for one year while Mr. Fish completed a research project for the chemical firm he worked for.
>
> During their year in Paris, Mr. and Mrs. Fish entertained Mr. Fish's colleagues from work. Since Sarah was 14, her mother usually asked her to help in preparing dinner for the guests. Oftentimes Sarah would answer the door and show the guests to the living room.
>
> After several occasions when Mr. and Mrs. Fish invited their colleagues to their apartment, Sarah saw that part of the meeting seemed to be a custom that she had never noticed at home in the United States. Each time these people greeted her parents, everyone took the time to shake each other's hands. This same ritual took place even after their first meeting. Sarah seemed to remember that in the United States her father usually shook hands with someone he was meeting for the first time. After the first meeting, Sarah's father greeted his friends by simply saying hello without shaking hands.

Why did Mr. Fish and his French colleagues shake hands every single time they met?

    A. Mr. Fish's friends wanted to show a great deal of respect for their American colleague.

    B. Mr. Fish's colleagues were a little intimidated by him so they shook hands in order to help create a more friendly relationship.

C. It is normal for French people who are business associates or colleagues in work to greet each other with a handshake at each meeting.
D. French people like to shake hands with foreigners as often as possible in order to make them feel more at home in a foreign country.

If you chose A:
It might be true that Mr. Fish's colleagues wanted to treat him with respect; however, it isn't likely that they would do so simply by shaking hands with him.
Reread the episode and choose a more likely answer.

If you chose B:
This is not the correct answer. No information was given in the episode to lead you to believe that Mr. Fish's colleagues were intimidated by him.
Reread the episode and select another answer.

If you chose C:
This is the correct answer. Although it may seem strange to Sarah to see her father's colleagues shake hands with him at every meeting, this is the normal custom of French business associates.

If you chose D:
This is not the correct answer. It contradicts information you have already learned. French people tend to behave in a reserved manner in their dealings with people they don't know well.
Reread the episode and choose another answer.

Cultural Minidrama.   A cultural minidrama presents three to five brief episodes each of which may contain one or more examples of miscommunication, as in the cultural assimilator. Information is provided to students at the end of each episode, but the information is not sufficient to make the miscommunication obvious until the last scene. Students are led into an open-ended discussion after each episode, permitting an examination of cultural assumptions and bias perceptions.

Audio-Motor Unit.   The audio-motor unit is designed primarily to teach listening comprehension as students are instructed to react physically to a series of oral commands given by the teacher. When the commands contain culturally related material, the cultural phenomena are demonstrated through the physical response. Students might be told that they are at a restaurant and that they are to do the following:

1. Take their napkins, unfold them, and put them on their laps
2. Take their forks with their left hands
3. Take their knives with their right hands
4. Cut a piece of meat and put it in their mouths
5. Place their knives and forks back on the table (Based on Chastain, 1988, p. 311)

Stereotype Perceptions. Perceived stereotypes can be examined through a number of techniques. Semantic differential scales can be used to assess cultural stereotypes through a series of bipolar traits: In general, Chinese people tend to be:

happy	—	—	—	—	—	—	—	—	—	sad
honest	—	—	—	—	—	—	—	—	—	dishonest
kind	—	—	—	—	—	—	—	—	—	cruel
clean	—	—	—	—	—	—	—	—	—	dirty
rich	—	—	—	—	—	—	—	—	—	poor
educated	—	—	—	—	—	—	—	—	—	uneducated

(Based on Seelye, 1984, p. 168)

Statements about cultural groups can be evaluated with respect to the truth value and/or the frequency of occurrence.

	True/ False	Always	Usually	Seldom	Never
1. Hispanics are not concerned about being late.	—	—	—	—	—
2. Hispanic women like to stay at home.	—	—	—	—	—
3. Hispanics are fascinated by death.	—	—	—	—	—
4. Bullfights are cruel and barbaric.	—	—	—	—	—
5. Hispanics are dark-skinned people.	—	—	—	—	—

(Based on Heusinkveld, 1985, p. 322)

Respondents can be asked to agree or select a series of statements that are appropriate for the group:

Following is a list of statements about the people of Neverlandia. Place a check before each statement with which you agree, or disagree, or have no opinion.

	Agree	Disagree	No opinion
1. Show a high rate of efficiency in anything they attempt	—	—	—

2. Can be depended upon as
   being honest   _____   _____   _____

3. Are noted for their industry   _____   _____   _____

4. Are envious of others   _____   _____   _____

5. Are highly emotional   _____   _____   _____

6. Are tactless   _____   _____   _____

7. Are a God-fearing group   _____   _____   _____

8. Are self-indulgent   _____   _____   _____

9. Are quick to understand   _____   _____   _____

10. Have an ideal home life   _____   _____   _____

(Adapted from Seelye, 1984, p. 169).

Artifact Study.   Students are helped to study the cultural significance of unfamiliar artifacts from the target group. Students provide descriptions and form hypotheses about the purpose and social meaning of the artifact. They can engage in small-group discussion, answer questions like the ones listed below, and report to the whole class, confirming their hypotheses with the teacher's explanations:

1. What are the physical qualities of the object?
2. Was it made by hand or machine?
3. What are its uses?
4. Where can you find one?
5. What role does it play in society?
6. What is its social meaning, if any? (Is it associated with status, wealth, power, prestige?)
7. What does the object tell us about the culture?
8. If this object were yours, what would you do with it? (Based on Omaggio, 1986, p. 393)

Nonverbal Cultural Awareness.   Cultural awareness can also be developed in class nonverbally through a series of activities based on Morain (1978):

I. To help students understand postural differences across cultures:
   Ask for two volunteers to come to the front of the class to demonstrate the postures used in different cultures to represent, for example, the emotion of humility. Then ask them to demonstrate the postures of other cultures. In the discussion that follows, ask the students who participated how they felt when assuming the positions: Were some postures more awkward or embarrassing than others? Ask the other students how they felt watching the demonstration.

II. To make students aware of cultural differences in gestures:
Have several students demonstrate the American gestures for the following list of emotions or directions: Yes, no; come, go; start, stop; that's good, bad; I'm happy, sad; it's over here, there; go up, down; I like, dislike you; bring it here, take it away; a little bit, a lot; short, long; stand up, be seated; up, down; be quiet, make more noise.
Take about five minutes to conduct the class without words, using the gestures demonstrated. Then ask the class to imagine that they are in a culture where the meaning of each gesture is exactly reversed: a head nod means "no," a smile means "I'm sad," etc. Conduct the class for another 5-10 minutes using the new gestural code, or divide the class into small groups to prepare skits showing a segment of social interaction with the new code. Discuss the possibilities for cross-cultural misunderstandings.

III. To sensitize students to their own communicative patterns:
A. Do you ever avoid talking to someone because he or she speaks too slowly or too loudly?
B. What are the three most common gestures you make while you speak? Do these gestures say anything about your personality?
C. How do you know that someone is interested in talking with you when that interest is not verbalized?
D. Under what circumstances do you say what you don't mean? When you do, have you ever noticed yourself telling a lie with your face?
E. Why do you act differently when you are in your own house than when you are in the house of a friend?
F. At what distance does a good friend get "too close"? At what distance does a fellow student, whom you don't know well, get "too close"? Why is there a difference?
G. Have you ever felt hostile or friendly toward someone just because of his or her appearance?

Cultural Content in Relation to Language Study

Cultural content can also be highlighted in relation to language study. This can be accomplished at the levels of vocabulary, grammar, listening comprehension, and oral communication. The activities listed below are based on the procedures outlined by Lafayette (1978):

Integrating Culture and Vocabulary. Vocabulary should be taught integrally, in a meaningful language context; attention should be paid to cultural connotation within that context. Accompany introduction and drill of vocabulary items with appropriate visuals from target language sources. For example, the word *bread* might conjure up the idea of a loaf of sliced bread to Americans, whereas it does not necessarily have an identical cultural referent in other cultures. A French person would think of a *baguette*.

Group vocabulary items in culture-related clusters. Provide an opportunity to discuss a culture point. Instead of grouping all food vocabulary together, items might be separated into subgroups that would reveal cultural differences. For example, "At breakfast I eat cereal (eggs, toast, nothing). At lunch I eat a sandwich (Big Mac, main meal). At supper. . . ."

Integrating Culture and Grammar.   Grammatical drills can be integrated into cultural context. For example, as an addition to the usual visual clock drills used in teaching time, drills could be constructed in which the students indicate the normal time of daily events (perhaps revealing cultural differences), as in:

Normally, we have lunch (breakfast, snack, dinner) at noon (7:30, 3:30, 6:30). Dad gets home from work at _____.
We usually get up at _____. But on Sundays we get up at _____, go to church at _____, and usually have brunch at _____ with family or friends.

Integrating Culture with Listening.   To integrate culture with listening, have students carry out a series of commands or follow a set of directions, as in the case of "Making a Salade Niçoise," designed by Thompson and Figliuolo (1985):

Making a Salade Niçoise
Purpose:
To acquaint students with a French food
To use the vocabulary needed for this food
To teach commands using direct object pronouns

Matériaux nécessaires:

un grand bol	une boîte d'olives noirs
de la laitue	un poivron
2 oeufs durs	de l'huile et du vinaigre
un couteau	du sel, et du poivre
2 tomates	un ail
une boîte de thon	une recette pour la vinaigrette

Directions:
1. D'abord, sortez un grand bol pour la salade.
2. Lavez la laitue et mettez-la dans le bol.
3. Coupez les oeufs et ajoutez à la laitue.
4. Coupez ensuite deux tomates en huit. Ajoutez-les.
5. Ouvrez le thon et mettez-le dans le bol.
6. Maintenant, ajoutez les olives et un poivron coupé.
7. Preparez la vinaigrette avec la recette donnée.
8. Versez la vinaigrette sur la salade et mélangez-la.   Bon appétit!

Follow-up Ideas:
1. Combine this with the table setting exercise and enjoy a meal.
2. Students can do a cultural project on Nice or the Côte d'Azur.
3. Students can write directions for the recipe given for the vinaigrette dressing.
4. Discuss different types of salads familiar to the students. Then, discuss the order of courses in a meal in France.
5. Change each direction to a negative command.
6. Write directions for making French onion soup (or any other French food).
7. Ask the students questions about salads, service in restaurants, what they did, and the different ingredients in the recipe.

Integrating Culture and Communication. To integrate culture and communication, have students conduct interviews with native informants, or have them question you or other students playing the role of natives. Sets of questions could be prepared for various cultural points. For instance, an interview with questions designed to discover the characteristics of a home or apartment could bring out important differences between the native and target cultures.

Create role-playing situations in the classroom where students assume different roles (buyer and seller, guest and host, traveler and agent) associated with different cultural situations (buying a book, attending a dinner party, planning a trip) and involving numerous language functions (greeting, thanking, requesting, informing, suggesting) and special verbal formulae and cultural scripts.

Authentic Materials in a Cultural Context. Advertisements, movies, television, magazines, radio, mail-order catalogs, telephone directories, comic strips, newspapers, and other authentic materials all place language in a cultural context (Berwald, 1988). Photographs and illustrations can serve as the basis for integrating language and culture. Lafayette (1988, pp. 53–54) suggests that a basic set of questions can be formulated for each illustration to elicit descriptive language, information gathering through observations, and a higher level of cognitive processing as a result of cross-cultural comparisons. Sample questions for each category could be as follows:

Description
1. What do you see in this picture/illustration?
2. Can you describe some of the items you see?
3. What are the people doing?
4. How are they dressed?

Information Gathering
1. Can you tell where or when this picture was taken?
2. Do some of the objects or people in this picture tell you something about life in that country?

3. Does the picture portray a certain segment of society in that country?
4. Is the picture of a general or specific nature?
5. Could a similar picture have been taken in other parts of the target country?

Cultural Comparisons
1. What makes this picture French, German, or Spanish, if anything?
2. Could a similar picture have been taken in the United States? Where? If not, why not?
3. Where would you go in the United States to take a picture of contrasting cultural elements?

Films and televised materials can also be exploited for linguistic and cultural content. Drawing from a list of cultural characteristics initially proposed by Morain (1972) for examining a series of commercials, Berwald (1988, pp. 93–94) offers a list of categories that are applicable to any film or videocassette release. The cultural categories may consist of such elements as:

1. *Art:* Examine the materials for artistic use of language as well as for artistic use of form and design.
2. *Artifacts:* What physical objects of the culture are visible (household appliances, automobiles, fashion accessories, etc.)? Are they used differently? Do their characteristics in any way reflect the culture of the country?
3. *Attitudes:* How are cultural attitudes shown in the material (i.e., the French concern with the liver; the American concern with getting fat)?
4. *Background setting:* Does the setting depict locations of geographic or historical interest?
5. *Clothing:* What conclusions can the viewer draw, as to social level, occupation, and geographic region, from the clothing worn in the film?
6. *Gestures:* Note examples of gestures, posture, and facial meaning that convey cultural meaning. Are there equivalents in American culture?
7. *Humor:* What type of humor is shown in the film? Is it slapstick or sophisticated? Is it possible to make generalizations about a "national humor"?
8. *Interpersonal relationships:* Note significant relationships between parent and child, between teenagers, between men and women, between members of one occupation interacting with members of another.
9. *Onomatopoeia:* Does the foreign culture use the same or different sounds to portray a yawn, a sneeze, a sob? How does the culture express pleasure in taste, fragrance, and sight?
10. *Proverbs and sayings:* Examine the script for examples of proverbs or proverbial similes and metaphors.
11. *Social customs:* Do the films present examples of table manners? Of greetings? Of techniques for such social amenities as lighting cigarettes,

entering rooms, holding chairs, opening doors, and proposing toasts? What traditional customs are revealed (birthday and anniversary celebrations, holiday observations, etc.)?

12. *Stereotypes:* Do the materials illustrate stereotypes held by the foreign culture? How are doctors, athletes, clergy, and in-laws characterized? Be alert for foreign equivalents of "the dumb blonde," "the old maid librarian," "the hayseed," "the used car salesman," and other stereotypes.

The categories listed above enable teachers to identify specific cultural features that can form the basis for intensive analysis and discussion. The categories of "clothing," "gestures," and "social customs" could be highlighted when viewing a film or videotape. Advertisements in magazines might be examined for their "artistic content," depiction of "interpersonal relationships," and the use of "stereotypes."

Cultural learning, like language learning, is a complex process. Cultural teaching strategies such as the ones outlined above provide numerous opportunities for the exploration of human values and patterns of behavior. At the same time, it is important to recognize that cultural learning consists of a series of stages often accompanied by feeling discomfort, seeing the logic (or illogic) of one's own native culture, and not always being willing to accept the ways of others (Damen, 1987).

SUMMARY

The term *culture* carries many different meanings and can be used to refer to such aspects as material objects, patterns of behavior, beliefs, and rules for acting. Language and culture are closely linked with each other, language being, of course, one of the principal means by which persons express and interpret their way of life. The connection between language and culture is especially significant for teachers because cultural learning should be considered an important feature of language study. The examples provided in Chapter 2 (an integrated French curriculum in Table 2.2 and an integrated Spanish curriculum in Table 2.3) illustrate how cultural topics can be related with language functions, grammatical features, patterns of behavior, and human values.

The connection between language and culture can also form the basis for examining how linguistic and cultural content are depicted in textbooks. Specific language lessons often consist of a series of learning activities, cultural topics or situations, and language skill areas. By reviewing the cultural topics and their connection to the linguistic content, teachers might be able to devise learning activities that integrate both features.

The distinction between culture as information and culture as process is a useful contrast to keep in mind when planning cultural activities. Activities related to culture as information involve the presentation of knowledge about a set of identifiable facts. Learning tasks associated with culture as process encompass such exercises as making cross-cultural comparisons, examining values and attitudes, and exploring the sources of culturally conditioned behavior.

The development of cultural proficiency is a relative process as well as a complex phenomenon. The ACTFL proficiency guidelines initially included a cultural component but later abandoned the effort because cultural learning could not be framed in terms of the trisectional schema of function-content-accuracy. Hanvey's framework for assessing cross-cultural development classifies learners according to four levels on the basis of their knowledge of cultural traits and experiences in the cultural setting. Papalia's four-step instructional sequence allows students the opportunity to compare, analyze, and evaluate value systems. Teachers can use a broad range of cultural activities to promote cultural awareness among their students. Such activities include the use of the culture capsule, culture cluster, culture assimilator, cultural minidrama, audio-motor unit, analysis of stereotypes with the use of questionnaires, examination of artifacts, and exploration of nonverbal behavior. It is also possible to highlight cultural concepts during study of language skill areas (vocabulary, grammar, listening comprehension, and conversational routines). Authentic materials such as newspapers, photographs, commercials, films, and songs can be used to develop language skills within culturally appropriate contexts.

ACTIVITIES

1. Interview two people and ask them for a definition of *culture*. Compare their definitions with those listed in the beginning of the chapter.
2. Examine a language textbook by comparing the table of contents with the five major cultural themes proposed by Pfister and Borzilleri. Which themes are omitted? Why?
3. Examine a language textbook by considering the types of pictures and illustrations used in two lessons. What aspects of the culture are revealed through the pictures? To what extent is the cultural content of the pictures related to the linguistic features presented in the lessons?
4. Review the list of learning goals proposed by Lafayette that approach culture as "information." Rank the goals from easiest to most difficult. Compare your ranking order with that of a fellow classmate.
5. What are some of the problems associated with teaching culture as "process"? How can one assess student learning goals that include such words as "examine," "value," "participate," and "engage in hypothesis refinement"?
6. Compare Seelye's seven instructional goals with ACTFL's cultural proficiency statements for the novice and advanced levels. To what extent do the proficiency statements reflect cultural competencies in terms of function, content, and accuracy? Try to write your own statements for novice and advanced cultural proficiency levels.
7. Prepare a culture assimilator for a specific social situation in the target culture.
8. Design a questionnaire for eliciting cultural stereotypes of a particular target group or nationality. Try to use different formats and techniques, like the ones illustrated in this chapter. Consider some of the problems associated with changing stereotype perceptions among L2 learners.
9. Prepare a series of language activities that integrate L2 culture with vocabulary and grammar, following a set of directions.
10. Analyze a foreign film or videotape using the cultural categories suggested by Berwald.

Then write 20 statements to characterize the culture depicted in the movie. Consider the following questions, adapted from Lafayette, to make some cultural comparisons:

a. What makes the film French, German, Spanish, etc.?
b. Could a similar film be produced in the United States?
c. Where would you go in the United States to make a movie of contrasting cultural elements?

REFERENCES

Allen, W. W. (1985). Toward cultural proficiency. In A. C. Omaggio (Ed.), *Proficiency, curriculum, articulation: The ties that bind.* Middlebury, VT: Northeast Conference on the Teaching of Foreign Languages.

American Council on the Teaching of Foreign Languages (ACTFL). (1982, 1986). *ACTFL provisional proficiency guidelines* Hastings-on-Hudson, NY: ACTFL Materials Center.

Arizpe, V., & Aguirre, B. E. (1987). Mexican, Puerto Rican, and Cuban ethnic groups in first-year college level Spanish textbooks. *Modern Language Journal*, 71: 125-37.

Berwald, J. P. (1988). Mass media and authentic documents: Language in cultural context. In A. J. Singerman (Ed.), *Toward a new integration of language and culture* (pp. 89-102). Middlebury, VT: Northeast Conference.

Brown, C. L. (1984). The challenge for excellence in curriculum and materials development. In G. A. Garvis (Ed.), *The challenge for excellence in foreign language education* (pp. 107-133). Middlebury, VT: Northeast Conference.

Burstall, C., Jamieson, M., Cohen, S., & Hargreaves, M. (1974). *Primary French in the balance.* Windsor: NFER Publishing.

Chastain, K. (1988). *Developing second-language skills: Theory and practice.* San Diego: Harcourt Brace Jovanovich.

Crawford-Lange, L., & Lange, D. L. (1984). Doing the unthinkable in the second language classroom: A process for the integration of language and culture. In T. V. Higgs (Ed.), *Teaching for proficiency: The organizing principle* (pp. 128-177). Lincolnwood, Il: National Textbook.

Damen, L. (1987). *Culture learning: The fifth dimension in the language classroom.* Reading, MA: Addison-Wesley.

Di Pietro, R. J. (1987). *Strategic interaction: Learning languages through scenarios.* Cambridge, England: Cambridge University Press.

Engel, U., Krumm, H., & Wierlacker, A. (1977). *Mannheimer gutachten zu ausgewählten lehrwerken Deutsch als fremdsprache.* Heidelberg: Quelle & Mayer.

Engel, U., Krumm, H., & Wierlacker, A. (1979). *Mannheimer gutachten zu ausgewählten lehrwerken Deutsch als fremdsprache. Band 2.* Heidelberg: Quelle & Mayer.

Finocchiaro, M., & Brumfit, C. (1983). *The functional-notional approach: From theory to practice.* Oxford: Oxford University Press.

Frake, C. (1981). Plying frames can be dangerous: Some reflections on methodology in cognitive anthropology. In Casson, R. (Ed.), *Language, culture, and cognition: Anthropological perspectives* (pp. 366-377). New York: Macmillan.

Galloway, V. B. (1985). A design for the improvement of the teaching of culture in foreign language classrooms. Hastings-on-Hudson, NY: ACTFL Project Proposal.

Garber, A. (1986). Cultural materials for teaching French. Materials prepared for a class project. Albany: State University of New York, School of Education.

Gudykunst, W., & Kim, Y. (1984). *Communicating with strangers: An approach to intercultural communication*. Reading, MA: Addison-Wesley.

Hall, E. (1959). *The silent language*. New York: Doubleday.

Hanvey, R. G. (1976). *An attainable global perspective*. New York: Center for Global Perspectives.

Hanvey, R. G. (1979). Cross-cultural awareness. In E. C. Smith & L. F. Luce (Eds.), *Toward internationalism* (pp. 46-56). New York: Newbury House.

Harris, P., & Moran, R. (1979). *Managing cultural differences*. Houston: Gulf Publishing.

Heusinkveld, P. R. (1985). The foreign language classroom: A forum for understanding cultural stereotypes. *Foreign Language Annals, 18*, 321-325.

Higgs, T. V. (Ed.). (1984). *Teaching for proficiency: The organizing principle*. Lincolnwood, IL: National Textbook.

Jarvis, D. K. (1977). Making cross-cultural connections. In J. K. Phillips (Ed.), *The language connection ACTFL foreign language education series* (Vol. 9). Lincolnwood, IL: National Textbook.

Kluckhohn, C. (1944). *Mirror for man*. New York: McGraw-Hill.

Kramsch, C. J. (1987). Foreign language textbooks' construction of foreign reality. *Canadian Modern Language Review, 44*, 95-119.

Kramsch, C. J. (1988). The cultural discourse of foreign language textbooks. In Singerman, A. J. (Ed.), *Toward a new integration of language and culture* (pp. 63-88) Middlebury, VT: Northeast Conference.

Krathwohl, D., Bloom, B., & Massi, B. (1964). *Taxonomy of educational objectives: The affective domain*. White Plains, NY: Longman.

Lafayette, R. C. (1978). *Teaching culture: Strategies and techniques*. Washington, DC: Center for Applied Linguistics.

Lafayette, R. C. (1988). Integrating the teaching of culture into the foreign language classroom. In A. J. Singerman (Ed.), *Toward a new integration of language and culture* (pp. 47-62). Middlebury, VT: Northeast Conference.

Levno, A. W., & Pfister, G. G. (1980). An analysis of surface culture and its manner of presentation in first-year college French textbooks. *Foreign Language Annals, 13*, 47-52.

Littlewood, W. (1981). *Foreign and second language learning: Learning acquisition research and its implications for the classroom*. Cambridge, England: Cambridge University Press.

Morain, G. (1972). *Language in the marketplace: A cultural analysis*. Publication for American/Swiss Foundation at ACTFL meeting in Atlanta.

Morain, G. (1978). *Kinesics and cross-cultural understanding*. Arlington, VA: Center for Applied Linguistics.

Mukhopadhyay, C. C. (1985). Teaching cultural awareness through simulations: Bafa Bafa. In H. Hernández & C. C. Mukhopadhyay, *Integrating multicultural perspectives into teacher education* (pp. 100-104). Chico, CA: California State University.

Nostrand, H. L. (Ed.). (1967). *Background data for the teaching of French. Part A, La culture et la société françaises au XXe siècle*. Seattle: University of Washington.

Omaggio, A. C. (1986). *Teaching language in context*. Boston: Heinle & Heinle.

Papalia, A. (1983). *Developing communicative proficiency and cultural understanding in secondary school language programs*. Schenectady, NY: New York State Association of Foreign Language Teachers.

Penfield, J. (1987). *The Media: Catalysts for communicative language learning*. Reading, MA: Addison-Wesley.

Pfister, G. G., & Borzilleri, P. (1977). Surface culture concepts: A design for the evaluation of cultural materials in textbooks. *Unterrichtspraxis, 10,* 102-108.

Ramírez, A. G., & Hall, J. K. (1990). Language and culture in secondary Spanish textbooks. *Modern Language Journal, 74* (1), 48-65.

Rivers, W. M. (Ed.). (1987). *Interactive language teaching.* Cambridge, England: Cambridge University Press.

Savignon, S. J. (1983). *Communicative competence: Theory and classroom practice.* Reading, MA: Addison-Wesley.

Seelye, H. N. (1984). *Teaching culture: Strategies for intercultural communication.* Lincolnwood, IL: National Textbook.

Steele, R. (1990). Culture in the foreign language classroom. *ERIC/CLL News Bulletin, 14,* 4-5.

Strasheim, L. A. (1981). Establishing a professional agenda for integrating culture into K-12 foreign languages: An editorial. *Modern Language Journal, 65,* 67-69.

Thompson, D., & Figliuolo, E. (1985). Learning French through communicative activities. Course materials prepared for class project. Albany: State University of New York, School of Education.

Van Els, T., Bongaerts, T., Extra, G., Van Os, C., & Janssen-van Dieten, A. M. (1984). *Applied linguistics and the learning and teaching of foreign languages.* London: Arnold.

Walz, J. (1980). Colonialistic attitudes toward the French-speaking world in American textbooks. *Contemporary French Civilization, 5,* 87-104.

Williams, S. A. (1978). Spanish cultural materials with a local focus: The Chicano, Cuban, and Puerto Rican connection. *Foreign Language Annals, 11,* 375-380.

chapter 4

Designs for Language Teaching

It is possible to study 'the curriculum' of an educational institution from a number of different perspectives. In the first instance we can look at curriculum planning, that is, at decision making, in relation to identifying learners' needs and purposes; establishing goals and objectives; selecting and grading content; organizing appropriate learning arrangements and learner groupings; selecting, adapting, or developing appropriate materials, learning tasks, and assessment and evaluation tools.

Alternatively, we can study the curriculum 'in action' as it were. This second perspective takes us into the classroom itself. Here we can observe the teaching/learning process and study the ways in which the intentions of the curriculum planners, which were developed during the planning phase, are translated into action.

D. Nunan, 1988

Deciding what to teach, how to sequence language content, what teaching techniques to use, and how to evaluate learning outcomes are some of the major issues associated with curriculum planning. Curriculum development involves making decisions about learning goals and objectives; determining the content, sequence, methods, and teaching strategies to be used; and specifying the evaluation procedures. Language curricula have tended to organize linguistic content on the basis of grammatical structures, communicative uses of language, proficiency levels, and language situations such as shopping, eating, and checking in at a hotel. More recently, there has been increased concern about learner needs and the incorporation of subject-matter content.

This chapter surveys some of the issues associated with curriculum planning and addresses the following topics:

1. What are the different types of language curricular models?
2. How are the various components of language organized within different curricular designs?
3. What procedures can be used to adapt textbooks and plan curriculum units?
4. What considerations should be taken into account in curriculum planning?

TYPES OF LANGUAGE CURRICULA

Questions about aspects of language content (grammar, functions, oral and written discourse, situations) and the way the linguistic context should be sequenced are generally addressed in terms of a syllabus or a curriculum. *Syllabus* is often used to refer to the subject-matter content of a given course or a series of courses (first, second, third semesters or years). A well-designed course syllabus maps language content to be covered over a time period. It usually outlines the linguistic goals, assessment procedures, the number and types of tests and quizzes, homework assignments, laboratory requirements, classroom tasks, and grading system. The term *curriculum* also refers to course content, but it incorporates goal statements for different language skill areas (listening, reading, speaking, and writing) and learning outcomes for a prescribed sequence of instruction (e.g., four-year high school program, four-semester college program). Goals statements for four semesters of college French were presented in Figure 1.2.

A curriculum is both content and process. The linguistic content equals the competency specifications that students are expected to demonstrate with respect to areas such as the four language modalities (listening, reading, speaking, and writing). Process can involve a series of steps followed in an effort to organize and sequence the content according to general goals: specific learning objectives, performance outcomes, learning tasks, and teaching approaches (Lange, 1987). Curriculum statements often relate philosophical assumptions about language, learning processes, and educational goals. Learning outcomes demonstrate a particular view about the structure of language as it relates to the four language modalities and the processes required to master the different domains.

Grammar-based views of language have resulted in *structural syllabi* organized principally around sentence patterns and grammatical features. *Communicative-based syllabi* have organized and sequenced instructional content around such language functions as identifying, reporting, requesting, and apologizing. A *proficiency-based curriculum* presents language content in relation to linguistic levels (novice, intermediate, advanced, and superior levels) according to language functions, content, and accuracy. A *task-based curriculum* organized language content on the basis of learner activities such as using the telephone, reading for information, answering inquiries, and following instructions. *Situational-based* frameworks sequence language content around social settings and the activities associated with these settings, such as shopping at a supermarket, eating at a restaurant or friend's home, and visiting a hospital due to an emergency.

Richards (1990) points out that "there is little empirical evidence to warrant commitment to any particular approach to syllabus development" (p. 9). The reality is that a combination of approaches is often used under such headings as "a functional-notional approach," "a communicative syllabus," "a communicative proficiency approach," and "an interactional curriculum." Yalden (1987) illustrates the possibility of mixing various types of syllabi (e.g., situational, task-based, and linguistic essentials). A situational sequence such as airport $\longrightarrow$ hotel $\longrightarrow$ post office $\longrightarrow$ store $\longrightarrow$ restaurant can involve various tasks: making inquiries, negotiating, asking for assistance, and reading for information. To accomplish these tasks, basic vocabulary and grammatical forms would be required to express concepts of time, money, dates, location, and direction. The particular combinations of situations, tasks, and linguistic essentials can be assembled according to the needs of the learners.

As noted in Chapter 1, instructional approaches correspond to particular views of language that are organized on the basis of specific curriculum models. The communicative-oriented classroom organizes language content and sequences instruction in relation to language functions usually within social situations (see Table 4.1). This perspective incorporates elements of both the communicative-based syllabus and the situationally based framework. The proficiency-oriented classroom sequences language content in relation to preestablished hierarchical performance levels for the four language skill areas. The proficiency-based syllabus outlines the content, functions, accuracy levels, and relevant teaching techniques for each level and skill area. See Figure 1.3 for an example of a curricular guide for listening—intermediate level and Table 8.1 for recommended reading techniques appropriate for novice, intermediate, and advanced levels. Table 1.2 illustrates the assessment criteria for speaking proficiency, which is compatible with a proficiency-oriented curriculum. The interactive approach follows a task-based curriculum and may combine situationally based features with communicative-based notions.

LANGUAGE COMPONENTS AND CURRICULUM DESIGNS

Curriculum models establish overall program goals and course-level objectives, enabling teachers to construct unified and articulated instructional plans. A *functional-notional curriculum* unit such as the one outlined by Finocchiaro and Brumfit (1983) organizes language content in relation to language functions, situations, grammatical content, and classroom activities (see Table 4.1). The functions of apologizing, requesting directions, and asking for information are related to specific social situations requiring a specific set of communicative formulas and grammatical forms. Instructional activities such as dialogue study, role-playing, reading exercises, and sociolinguistic considerations (e.g., use of indirect speech and register shift) are recommended as appropriate learning tasks. The functions of language serve as the basic organizing principle.

TABLE 4.1 A functional-notional minicurriculum

Unit	Date	Title and Function	Situation	Communicative Expressions or Formulas	Structures	Nouns	Verbs	Adj.	Adv.	Structure Words	Misc.	Activities
X	2/4	Apologizing	Theater (asking someone to change seats)	Excuse me. Would you mind . . .? I'm very grateful.	Verb + *ing*	seat place friend	move change					Dialog study Role play Expanding sentences Paired practice
XI	2/11	Apologizing	Department store (returning something)	I'm sorry. Would it be possible . . .?	Simple past Present Perfect	shirt wear	buy	small	too	you	dates	Aural comprehension Indirect speech Changing register
XIV	3/15	Requesting directions	At the bus stop	I beg your pardon. Could you tell me . . .?	Interrogatives (simple, of present) places Modal *must*	names	must get to get off take		how where	us	numbers	Reading questions and answers Cloze procedures Dictation
XVI	3/25	Asking for information	In a post office	Excuse me. Where should I find . . .?	Modal *can*	stamps savings account	sell buy open					Expanding sentences of previous dialogs Role playing with these

SOURCE: *The Functional-Notional Approach: From Theory to Practice* by Mary Finocchiaro and Christopher Brumfit, Oxford: Oxford University Press. Copyright ©1983 by Oxford University Press. Reprinted by permission.

In a *task-based curriculum*, instructional units are organized not in terms of notions of language features but in relation to language required for performing specific activities. These tasks can involve reading maps, interpreting timetables, solving word problems, comprehending stories and dialogues, asking for information or opinions, and completing forms and reports. This organizational approach, also known as a procedural syllabus, stresses what is to be learned (Nunan, 1988b). Each task "will require learners to arrive at an outcome from given information through some process of thought, and . . . [will enable] teachers to control and regulate that process" (Prabhu, 1987, p. 24). A task is solved through language, making communicative competence a means to an end rather than a linguistic goal. An example of a task-based unit on buying and selling tickets is presented in Table 4.2. The assumption here is that grammatical features can best be learned if the focus is on meaning instead of language forms.

There are a number of important questions that need to be addressed during the planning phase of task-based units. Breen (1987, p. 25) specifies four major questions to take into account in a work plan:

1. Why is the task being undertaken? (To practice a grammatical feature, to deduce the main ideas from a written text. to share information, or to solve a problem with the use of a chart)
2. What is the content of the task? (Grammatical features; functions of language, vocabulary, and concepts related to a cultural topic; information about language use in particular social settings; or skills and abilities needed for shopping in an outdoor market)
3. How is the task to be done? (Through recall/transfer of previously learned information or skills, by a problem-solving process, by analyzing data, by using various language skills)
4. Where is the task to be performed? (In pairs or groups in a classroom, in class with teacher guidance, individually with resources such as reference materials or dictionaries, outside the classroom using native informants, as homework assignment for skills reinforcement)

Learners are likely to interpret the teacher's work plan in their own ways. They answer each of the four questions and, in turn, recreate the plan during the actual task-in-progress phase. The task generates diverse learning outcomes that can be used as the basis for assessing the quality and efficacy of the task itself (Breen, 1987). Ideally, tasks should be selected on the basis of students' interests and the level of conceptual difficulty. However, as Long and Crookes (1992) point out, there is presently no rationale for determining the content of such a syllabus for any given group of learners. There are also problems associated with grading task difficulty and sequencing tasks that call for specific linguistic features (vocabulary or grammatical forms) and communicative functions (requesting, answering, commanding, insisting, suggesting). Furthermore, there is the important issue of language input. Research findings on the effects of classroom instruction on L2 acquisition support the need for a focus on language forms in language teaching

TABLE 4.2 Task-based unit on buying/selling tickets

Learner Tasks	Task Type	Activities
Buying/selling bus, train, airline and theater tickets	Buying/selling tickets	Matching dialog Requesting ticket availability Informing customer of ticket availability Role playing

Adapted from *The Learner-Centered Curriculum* (p. 86) by David Nunan, 1988, Cambridge, England: Cambridge University Press. Copyright 1988a, Cambridge University Press. Used with permission.

(Long, 1988). Learners derive explicit knowledge of language largely from form-focused instruction, and this knowledge can, in turn, serve to make the learner aware of the existence of nongrammatical forms in the developing target language (Ellis, 1990).

Lund (1988) suggests using the notion of tasks to bring together elements of communication and language for a given instructional unit. The task would link the components of communication (functions, context, and modalities) with the corresponding aspects of language (structures, vocabulary, and cultural notions). A series of tasks derived from a unit on shopping for clothes in Germany, for example, would be based on the communicative and linguistic specifications noted in Table 4.3.

TABLE 4.3 Communicative and linguistic context of a unit

Communicative Elements	Aspects of Language

Functions
  Getting and giving information about facts
  Expressing personal feeling about facts
Content
  Shopping
  Clothes
  Sizes
  Prices
	Structures
	  Long and short *u*
	  Verbs w/ vowel change
	  Articles
	  Negation in noun phrases
	  Pronoun use
	Vocabulary
	  Clothes
	  Currencies
	  Colors
	  Adjectives
	Cultural Notions
	  European sizes
	  Money
	  Borrowed English words

SOURCE: From "Planning Communicative Units and Lessons" by Randall J. Lund, in A. G. Ramírez (Ed.), *Spotlight on Teaching* (p. 14). Schenectady, NY: New York State Association of Foreign Language Teachers. Copyright 1988. Reprinted with permission.

Students could engage in a number of tasks:

1. Purchase an item of clothing. Tell the clerk what you want to buy. Ask what it costs, and pay the correct amount. Check your change.
2. Return an item of clothing and tell what is wrong with it.
3. Exchange an item of clothing and ask for a different size and color.
4. Advise a friend who is purchasing clothing. Ask the size. Comment on the looks and quality of the clothing. Suggest alternatives.
5. Discuss what clothing to buy for a brother or sister.
6. In preparation for a shopping trip, consult a chart and write down your sizes for all types of clothing.
7. Describe a new student at school, including what the person is wearing.
8. Describe what you will be wearing to an activity, or to meet someone who doesn't know you.
9. Ask what others are wearing to an activity.
10. You share clothes with a sibling or friend. You both want to wear the same thing. Suggest alternatives for the other person and come to an agreement.
11. You have an amount of money to spend on new clothes. Look through advertisements and determine how many different articles you can buy.
12. You have an amount of money to spend on clothes. Look through a mail-order catalog and fill out an order.
13. Prepare and give the commentary for modeling an outfit.
14. Write your own clothing ad.
15. Write and produce a clothing commercial.

In designing a specific unit based on one of the tasks noted above, a teacher has to follow a series of steps:

1. Select a primary objective for the unit; it should correspond to the learner task itself.
2. Specify the enabling objectives or the learning steps that are necessary to achieve the primary objective. This may involve prerequisite communicative or linguistic knowledge from other units or new language content that needs to be taught.
3. Determine the classroom activities (e.g., reading a dialogue, pair practice, role playing, writing a script) that are essential for accomplishing particular enabling objectives in relation to the primary objective of the unit.

A unit planned according to a proficiency-based curriculum focuses on a specific language modality (listening, speaking, reading, and writing) and relates language functions, context, and linguistic forms according to the learners' language abilities (novice, intermediate, advanced, and superior levels). A given lesson would include both communicative and linguistic considerations. Porter (1987) illustrates the application of the ACTFL proficiency guidelines for an elementary French course to specific activities for the development of listening, speaking and listening, reading, and writing skills. An example of an interactive activity and the linguistic and cultural content necessary for expressing and recognizing food and drink items at a French restaurant is presented in Table 4.4.

CURRICULUM PLANNING AND ADAPTATION

With respect to the availability of communicative-oriented textbooks and teaching materials, the gap between theory and practice represents a long-term challenge to second language professionals. Textbooks may be organized around situations, grammatical/functional considerations, or proficiency-based units. Many of them may claim to promote communicative competence or functional proficiency, but in reality, categories such as "functions," "language situations," and "topics" are not addressed systematically. Procedures for adapting a textbook that is grammar-based into a more communicative-oriented approach have been delineated by Guntermann and Phillips (1982). The adaptation process is described in four stages:

1. Select from the text materials the essential grammar and vocabulary that are to be emphasized in the intensive communication practice.
2. Select and sequence the meanings (semantic-grammatical notions, e.g., time, space, quantity; modal meanings, e.g., probability, doubt, disbelief, intentions; communicative functions, e.g., argument, personal emotions, opinions) that are expressed through the forms chosen in stage 1.
3. Select and sequence the common purposes for language use for speaking and listening situations (socializing, arguing, giving and responding to feedback) and reading and writing situations (giving directions, seeking and sharing information, establishing and maintaining relationships).
4. Select appropriate classroom activities (role playing, listening to a tape recording of a native speaker, following instructions) to use the grammar and vocabulary in stage 1 to express meanings in stage 2.

Application of this model is presented in Figure 4.1.

Mita (1987) suggests the use of a worksheet as a means to determine the functions, topics, and language situations that should be taught during a week of instruction. Based on the New York State syllabus, *Modern Languages for Communication*, four major language functions are detailed along with specific listening, speaking, reading, and writing situations. Teachers can identify a topic such as home life, sports, meal taking, or travel, and select those functions and language situations that reflect both the students' communicative needs and their interests. Linguistic content from a textbook and some of the suggested lesson activities could be incorporated into the unit, forming the basis for particular learning ac-

TABLE 4.4 Components of a proficiency-oriented activity and the linguistic content

Speaking and Listening	Function	Context	Vocabulary	Grammar (Lexical)	Phonology	Culture
Title: Expressing and recognizing food/drink items	Say food/drink items	Food/drink	meat ham beef	I would like . . . (*Je voudrais . . .*)	Intelligible to native used to foreigners	Some table manners
Objective: Students will express what they would like for lunch. Students will recognize what others have expressed.	Order food/drink		steak chicken fish	Partitive Definite article		Tipping Eating patterns
Functions: Express, recognize (aurally) food/drink items *Linguistic elements:* Vocabulary as listed on unit cards for food/drink	Express one's desire to eat		vegetables carrots peas	I would like to eat. (*Je voudrais manger.*) I like . . . (*J'aime . . .*)		Breakfast/lunch/dinner—typical menus, time spent, places
Je voudrais (I would like) Partitive	Express one's likes and dislikes		green beans potatoes fruits apples	I don't like . . . (*Je n'aime pas . . .*) I hate . . .		
Pronunciation of foods/drinks	Express appreciation		pears peaches wine	Thank you very much. (*Merci beaucoup.*)		
Activity: Three members of the class state consecutively what they would like for lunch, while classmates listen. After three have spoken, others report what each has said. The activity then continues with another group of three speakers.	Refuse		bread cheese tea coffee milk soup	No, thank you. (*Non, merci.*) A lot, very much. (*Beaucoup.*) Not at all. (*Pas du tout.*)		
Example: Je voudrais du fromage, du pain, et de la glace. (I would like cheese, bread, and ice cream.)						

This activity may be varied by giving a list of unavailable items to some students who play waiters. As customer-students place orders, waiter-students may respond using such lexical expressions as *Bien sûr* (certainly) or *Je suis désolé (e) mais il n'y en a pas* (I am sorry but there is none). Students may reverse roles and continue the activity. Following these preceding activities, students may compare what the French people have ordered for lunch (types and amount of food) to what they have ordered. Typical cultural differences may be noted.

Title: Writing a menu for a French restaurant	List food/drink desired	Food/drink	Name of special foods and dishes	Written forms of expressions listed under listening and speaking	Menu formats and dishes/special foods
Objective: Students will design and write a menu typical of a French restaurant	Write a food shopping list				*Prix fixe*
Functions: Write (list) food/drink for menu	List favorite foods		Any vocabulary peculiar to a menu, such as *à la carte*		*Service compris*
Linguistic elements: Vocabulary as listed on cards for food/drink	Write menu for restaurant				*Service non-compris*
Optional, personalized vocabulary	Write ad for restaurant				*Unit of money (franc)*
Specific expressions pertaining to menu as listed on reading unit card					*À la carte*
Material: Paper/pencil					

The student is told his or her family has just purchased a French restaurant. They want to create a new yet truly French menu. He or she has been assigned the task of creating and writing an appropriate menu. He or she is to be sure to include the various categories of the menu such as *légumes* (vegetables) and *viandes* (meats).

SOURCE: Adapted from "Using the ACTFL Proficiency Guidelines to Achieve Goals of Exploratory Language Courses" by Lewis P. Porter, 1987, *Foreign Language Annals, 20,* pp. 326–329. Used with permission.

Grammar point: Contrary-to-Fact Constructions (Si-Clauses)

Meaning: Supposition about illusory conditions

Skills/functions/activities:

A. Listening/interpreting warnings/communication about topics of interest.

Students pretend to receive a list of warnings, which they must translate into direct commands or an explanation of the meaning to show they have comprehended. (Examples: If I were you, I would be very careful about cheating. If you were smart, you would do the assignment on time.)

B. Speaking/empathizing/role-playing

Students pretend to be a series of other people, and each states a wish that those people might have made. (For example, Jack Benny: If I were young, I would study the violin better. Your mother: If I were single, I would take a long vacation.)

C. Reading/contemplating world events/making generalizations/communication about topics of interest

Students read a paragraph entitled "What if . . .?" Suppositions are made in it such as "If the British had colonized South America and the Spanish had come to New England . . .," "If Detroit had produced a good small car in 1975 . . .", "If France had not aided the American Colonies during the Revolution . . .". A true/false comprehension exercise follows with suggested results. (Examples for above: We would speak Spanish. The Japanese would have produced a cheaper one. We would belong to England today).

D. Writing/making polite suggestions/classroom/school exchanges

Students write notes to school authorities for the suggestion box. (Examples: To the teacher: "If you spoke in a louder voice, we could hear you better." To the principal: "If you let us have a recreation room, we would not get into trouble during free time." To the cafeteria staff: "If you prepared what we like, less food would be wasted.")

FIGURE 4.1 Function aligning grammatical forms

SOURCE: From *Functional Notional Concepts: Adapting the Foreign Language Textbook* (Language in Education: Theory and Practice, vol. 44) (pp. 55–56) by Gail Guntermann and June K. Phillips, 1982, Washington, DC: Center for Applied Linguistics. Reprinted with permission.

tivities designed to practice essential vocabulary and grammatical structures needed for the communicative tasks (Figure 4.2).

Arnold (1989) extends the application of this approach by first preparing an inventory of the communicative components and the respective linguistic content for a unit in German on "Guten Appetit!" from a school textbook (Table 4.5). Then she outlines a two-week curriculum that links the communicative components, lesson objectives, materials, student groupings, and evaluation procedures (Table 4.6).

Most teachers have been trained to plan instruction on the basis of thematic, situational, grammatical, and functional syllabi. This emphasis has resulted in a language-centered approach, reflected in the teaching of certain linguistic content and the use of instructional procedures designed for selecting and sequencing classroom activities to accomplish learning objectives. However, in some cases teachers can negotiate a curriculum with their learners. Learners, for example, could be consulted to indicate their preferences with regard to communicative sit-

The purpose of this week's lessons is to perform the following language functions. Identify the specific functions to be developed: macro and micro.

Provide/Obtain Information About:	Socializing:	Expressing Personal Feelings About:	Get Others to Adopt a Course of Action by:
_____ facts	_____ greeting	_____ facts	_____ suggesting
_____ events	_____ leave taking	_____ events	_____ requesting
_____ needs	_____ introducing	_____ opinions	_____ directing
_____ opinions	_____ thanking	_____ attitudes	_____ advising
_____ attitudes	_____ apologizing		_____ warning
_____ feelings			_____ convincing
			_____ praising

All the above functions are to be performed within the theme (topic) of: _____

	Language situations	Cultural contexts	Grammar	Vocabulary
Listening comprehension	Informational bulletins Announcements over radio, TV, loud-speakers			
Listening/ speaking	Interaction with sales, police, hotel personnel, etc. Conversations with peers and familiar adults			
Reading	Information on signs, billboards, programs, maps, timetables, etc. Announcements, ads, and reports in magazines and newspapers			
Writing	Forms to fill out for use of common services Informal notes for communications in everyday life			

FIGURE 4.2 Worksheet for instructional planning

SOURCE: From workshop materials prepared by Dolores Mita, 1987, Albany, NY: New York State Education Department, Foreign Language Bureau. Reprinted with permission.

TABLE 4.5 Unit 20 "Guten Appetit!" (German II), inventory for communication and linguistic content

Functions	Situations	Topics	Grammar	Vocabulary	Formulas

Socializing
• Inviting to dinner
• Accepting or declining a dinner invitation
Getting others to adopt a course of action by
• Ordering food in a restaurant
• Requesting the bill
Providing and obtaining information about
• Facts
• Plans
Expressing personal feelings about
• Cultural differences
• Preferences
	Listening
	• Feature program on television
	Listening/speaking
	• Interaction with providers of common public services in face-to-face communications (simulated restaurant experience)
	• Informal everyday conversations with individual peers and adults
	Reading
	• Authentic menu; McDonald's advertisements in German
	• Information for appreciation of cultural differences
	Writing
	• Informal notes for communications in everyday life situations
	• Personal letter of declination to peer for dinner invitation
		Meal taking/food/drink
		• German regional and national specialities
		• Daily meals
		Table manners and customs
		• Joining strangers
		• Toasting
		• Paying bill
		• Tipping
		• Table settings
		• European style of eating
		German money
		• Coins and bills
			Narrative past forms of *haben, sein, werden,* and modals	General restaurant related vocabulary
				• Waiter/waitress
				• Common food items and beverages
				• Place settings
				• Verbs expressing:
				  • To order, pay,
				  • Request check
				Names of daily meals in Germany and verbs to express partaking of meals
				• Breakfast, late breakfast, lunch, Kaffeestunde, dinner
				Vocabulary related to money
				  • Change
				  • Coin, check
				  • Verbs to express paying, returning change
					• die Speisekarte, bitte
					• den Tisch decken
					• Selbstverständlich
					• ich möchte . . .
					• Zahlen, bitte!
					• guten Appetit!
					• gleichfalls!
					• Mahlzeit!
					• prost!
					• zum Wohl(e)!
					• mach dir keine Sorgen!

SOURCE: From "A German Unit on 'Guten Appetit!' (German II)" by Amy Arnold, 1989, materials prepared for a course assignment, Albany: State University of New York, School of Education. Used with permission.

TABLE 4.6 Two-week curriculum unit for "Guten Appetit!"

Communicative Components

Function(s)	Situation(s)	Topic(s)	Objectives (Ss will be able to:)	Materials	Activities/ Groupings	Evaluation
Providing and obtaining information about: • Facts • Plans	Listening/ speaking Interactive discourse	Meal taking/ food and drink	Recall and identify new vocabulary	*Day 1* Physical objects: plate, silverware, glass, cup, napkin Overhead of place setting Kaufhof advertisement	T. holds up object, Ss respond chorally T. uses overhead to illustrate location of objects Use group and pair work	T. corrects pronunciation of objects learned, questions Ss to monitor performance
Providing and obtaining information about: • Facts • Plans	Listening/ speaking Informal conversations with peers	German money	Use new structures in conversations to answer and pose questions	*Day 2* German money Café menu, McDonald's ads (copies of menus, ad)	T. helps Ss create a typical café, fast food scenario Ss practice ordering 1) from café menu 2) as if at McDonald's Ss role play in pairs Pretend to pay with play money	T. asks Ss "Are you with me? Do you follow?" T. helps Ss working in pairs T. evaluates progress
Expressing personal feelings about: • Preferences	Writing/ speaking	Meal taking/ food and drink	Recognize usage of narrative past (inductively) and begin to manipulate successfully			
Getting others to adopt a course of action by: • Ordering • Reqesting	Writing/ reading	Script for dinner at restaurant (for fast food)	Compose a restaurant-scenario dialogue Read authentic menu	*Day 3* Teacher-generated overhead	T. tells Ss a story using a narrative past about herself . . . "But I had to . . ." "I couldn't . . ." Ask Ss: What do you notice—what tense was I using? T. uses all overheads to explain narrative past forms Ss use forms in conversations	T. gives Ss three sentences that they must put in the narrative past T. monitors Ss' ability: "How many got one wrong, two wrong, three wrong?"
Expressing personal feelings about: • Cultural differences	Listening/ speaking feature TV program	German table manners and customs Specialties	Analyze video and acquire an awareness of cultural differences			

(continued)

TABLE 4.6 (continued)

Communicative Components

Function(s)	Situation(s)	Topic(s)	Objectives (Ss will be able to:)	Materials	Activities/ Groupings	Evaluation
Getting others to adopt a course of action by • Ordering & requesting	Listening/ speaking	Simulated restaurant scenario Manners	Physically act out restaurant scenario Demonstrate cultural differences			
Providing requested information	Reading/listening Speaking Writing	All of the above	Accomplish objectives days 1–6			
Providing and obtaining information about: • Facts • Plans	Listening/ speaking Interactive discourse	Meal taking/ food and drink	Recall and identify new vocabulary	*Day 4* Blank overhead Overhead pens Copies of dinner menu textbook	T. helps Ss compose a typical scenario for a restaurant Ss will create dialogues in pairs T.-guided	T. circulates as Ss work in pairs Helps with questions T. asks class, "Who knows the answer . . . ?"
Providing and obtaining information about: • Facts • Plans	Listening/ speaking Informal conversations with peers	German use of money	New structures in conversation to answer and pose questions	*Day 5* Props for restaurant setting: plate, silverware, candle, menu, glasses	T. has three pairs of Ss act out their written restaurant dialogues for the class Ss act out cultural differences as teacher	T. monitors by notes during Ss' performance, comments after, advises
Expressing personal feelings about: • Preferences	Writing/ speaking	Meal taking/ food and drink	Recognize usage of narrative past (inductively) and begin to use in context	*Day 6* Video machine Copy of video, "Montags Erste Stunde Dennoch" Copies of article	T. introduces video, directs Ss to look for cultural differences Group discussion follows film	T. makes sure Ss take notes during video Helps Ss find details in film

Day	Function	Skill	Context/Content	Task	Materials	Procedure	Evaluation
Day 7	Getting others to adopt a course of action by: • Ordering • Requesting; Expressing personal feelings about: • Cultural differences	Writing/reading; Listening/speaking Feature TV program	Script for dinner at restaurant (or fast food); German table manners and customs	Compose a restaurant scenario dialogue; React to authentic materials; Analyze video and acquire an awareness of cultural differences	Teacher-produced quiz	T. proctors quiz for Ss testing all four language components	Summative evaluation by percentage correct on quiz
Day 8	Getting others to adopt a course of action by: • Ordering • Requesting	Listening/speaking	Simulated restaurant scenario • Manners	Act out restaurant scenario; Demonstrate cultural differences	Index cards: Each card has a different A/B role scenario involving excusing one-self	T. helps Ss generate a list of possible excuses; Ss divided into pairs; One S. is A, the other B; Role play based on index card	T. guides Ss' generating of list; T. helps Ss with role plays; T. monitors performance
Day 9	Providing and requesting information	Reading all; Listening/speaking; Writing	Same as above	Accomplish objectives days 1–6	Overhead: give Ss idea how to write a letter to decline/accept invitation	T. asks Ss randomly, "Could you come to dinner tonight?"; Ss verbally decline or accept invitation; Pairs work on letter of declination	T. asks Ss directly, monitors pronunciation, usage
Day 10	Providing and obtaining information about: • Plans; Socializing • Inviting to dinner • Accepting/declining invitation	Reading/speaking	Setting the table; Cooking dinner	Provide excuses for not following a particular course of action	T. provides Ss with copies of a model letter	Ss works in pairs on a letter declining invitation and provide written excuses	T. circulates and helps Ss on project; Letter collected at end of class
Day 11		Speaking/listening	Going to a German restaurant (invitation)	Verbally decline or accept a dinner invitation	Flowers (what you would bring to a dinner?) to be used as prop	T. tells Ss about customers and dinner manners; Ss act out appropriate behaviors	T. watches as Ss demonstrate, corrects any behavioral errors
Day 12	Providing information about plans/needs	Writing personal letter of dec-	Dinner invitation	Written declination of a dinner invitation (excuses)	Authentic German foods: bratwurst, etc.	T. brings in sample German foods; Ss are questioned about their attitudes and opinions concerning German culture	Ss answer personal questions

(continued)

TABLE 4.6 (continued)

Communicative Components

Function(s)	Situation(s)	Topic(s)	Objectives (Ss will be able to:)	Materials	Activities/ Groupings	Evaluation
	lination to peer			*Day 13* (Text p. 206)	Ss will read passage in text regarding why someone couldn't go to the restaurant (car breakdown)	T. monitors Ss pronunciation in reading of dialogue
Socializing simulated behaviors	Speaking/ listening	German manners and customs	Act out appropriate behaviors and customs at simulated dinner		In pairs, Ss create their own scenario (writing)	T. circulates and helps Ss write their own scenario
Expressing personal feelings about: • Cultural differences	Speaking	German regional and national specialities	Sample authentic German foods Acquire cultural appreciation	*Day 14* Teacher-prepared test (days 1–13)	Individual effort Teacher proctors	Summative evaluation based on percentage correct (of 100)
				End of Unit Plan		
Providing information about: • A course of action	Speaking/ listening	Simulated scenario: why we had to go to the restaurant	Synthesize textbook scenario and create personal scenarios			
All previous functions days 1–13	Reading/listening Speaking Writing	All of the above	Accomplish objectives days 1–13			

SOURCE: From "A Two-Week Curriculum Unit for 'Guten Appetit!'" by Amy Arnold, 1989, materials prepared for a course assignment, Albany: State University of New York, School of Education. Used with permission.

uations, learning activities, and classroom groupings. In the area of ESL, learner-centered curriculum is seen as the most appropriate curricular approach, particularly among adult learners who have clear learning goals and needs (Nunan, 1988a). In foreign language classroom situations, the learner is less likely to be an active participant in the selection process. Nevertheless, Doctor (1989) argues that the selection and ordering of linguistic context can be done as a collaborative process between teachers and learners. Negotiation between teacher and learners emphasizes the process of learning rather than the linguistic content. Learners play a role establishing their own criteria for assessing language outcomes (Long & Crookes, 1992). Teachers can involve their students in a more learner-centered curriculum by following a series of basic steps:

1. Discuss with students themes and topics of interest to them.
2. List and prioritize the topics, using the students' native language, if necessary.
3. Start with the theme or topic that is most appealing, and select a specific situation that is considered most relevant.
4. Determine what functions are needed to perform the given situation. For each function, identify the possible meanings appropriate to the context.

After this process the teacher has the content necessary for developing an instructional unit. Decisions can then be made about how to select and order general and specific semantic-grammatical notions (e.g., concepts for expressing time, location, quantity, causality) for precommunicative activities. After the students have participated in pre-communicative activities, they have the opportunity to engage in communicative activities (e.g., working in small groups to develop real-world scenarios) that relate both communicative and linguistic aspects of language. Doctor (1989) offers an example to illustrate the various functions, meanings, and notions associated with purchasing a car, planned for a particular group of English-speaking adolescents learning French (Figure 4.3).

Specific language forms (verbal formulas, sentence types, words) are identified along with the corresponding language functions (requesting a service, expressing a want, inquiring about product availability and product quality). Then the teacher indicates the meanings already mastered ($\sqrt{}$), the ones requiring practice for productive use (*) or comprehension only (/), those that are seldom used or too difficult for the students (X), and the ones containing similar linguistic elements (C) in the prescribed curriculum. The existential (availability/nonavailability of product) and qualitative (age, value and price, physical condition, adequacy of product) notions of language are central in this unit. Verb constructions with *vouloir, pouvoir,* and *devoir* are essential, along with expressions to indicate likes and dislikes (*j'adore, je déteste*) and demonstrative adjectives (*ce, cet, cette, ces*).

Another important development in curriculum design has been the inclusion of content material usually found in other subject areas: as science, geography, social studies, art, mathematics, and history. Such books as *Language and Content* (Mohan, 1986), *Content-Area Language Instruction: Approaches and Strategies*

Language activities _____ Listening, speaking _____

Topic _____ Purchasing a car _____

Situation(s) _____ Young client at a used car dealer _____

Function 1 *To request or accept service*

Meanings	General notions	Specific notions
Pardon, Mme./M.		
Pouvez-vous m'aider, s'il vous plaît?		
Excusez-moi, Mme./M.		
Pour vous, Mme./M?		
Est-ce que je peux vous aider?		

Code   √   Already mastered by most students

        *   Requires mastery for active use

      ( )   Requires mastery for comprehension only

       x   Omit

       c   Required in the curriculum

Function 2 *To state what you want*

Meanings	General notions	Specific notions
Je cherche une auto de sport d'occasion.		
Est-ce que vous avez une Corvette de 1978?		
Je voudrais acheter une auto de sport pour moins de 3,000,00$.		
Avez-vous une belle auto de sport pas trop chère?		
Pourriez-vous me la montrer?		

Function 3 *To understand whether the product is available*

Meanings	General notions	Specific notions
Bien sûr, Monsieur.		
Suivez-moi		
On ne vend pas les autos de sport.		
Je n'en ai pas au présent.		

FIGURE 4.3 Relating functions, meanings, and notions to a topic

SOURCE: "C'est en forgeant qu'on devient forgeron or Towards a Communicative Pedagogy" by Eleanor Doctor, 1989, *Canadian Modern Language Review/La Revue canadienne des langues vivantes*, pp. 322–324. Reprinted with permission.

Nous en avons plusieurs. _____   _____   _____

Combien voulez-vous payer? _____   _____   _____

Function 4 ·*To ask questions about quality of the car and understand the responses*

Meanings	*General notions*	*Specific notions*
C'est de quelle année?		
Quel est le kilométrage?		
Est-ce que les freins sont en bon état?		
Et les pneus?		
Le kilométrage a été fait sur l'autoroute.		
Puis-je faire un petit tour avec la Corvette '78?		
Ça donne combien de kilomètres par litre d'essence?		
Une auto qui a très peu roulé.		

FIGURE 4.3   (continued)

(Cantoni-Harvey, 1987), and *Content-Based Second Language Instruction* (Brinton, Snow, & Wesche, 1989) advocate use of the language as the vehicle to convey informational content that is both interesting and relevant to the learner. The argument is that "teaching language as communication" or "teaching language for proficiency" focuses on language as the subject matter, whether the emphasis is on functions, grammar, meanings, topics, or situations. By relating language to content, a number of concerns on language teaching and student learning can be addressed. Brinton et al. offer the following justification for content-based instruction:

1. Content-based language curriculum takes into account the interests and needs of the learners.
2. The curricular approach incorporates the eventual uses the learner will make of the target language, particular in ESL contexts.
3. It builds on the students' previous learning experiences in different subject areas.
4. It allows teachers to focus on language use as well as language forms.
5. It offers learners the necessary conditions for authentic language use by providing meaningful learning experiences.

Learners can "learn by doing" math problems, science experiments, art projects, and historical reenactments as they participate in content-based instruction. While commercially prepared materials in the area are limited, teachers could pre-

Content Area: Geography (map distortion)

Objectives:

1. To draw attention to the phenomenon of map distortion
2. To orient students to the relative location of bodies of land and water
3. To teach and reinforce select comparative and superlative adjectives

Language Teaching points: Imperative, comparative, superlative

Vocabulary:

Nouns	Verbs	Adjectives
distortion	change	round
map	distort	flat/flatten
land	peel	bigger
globe		most
earth		smaller
shape		least
peel		
water		

Procedures:

1. Using the target language, examine a flat map of the world. Pay particular attention to the size and shape of bodies of land and water.
2. Now examine a globe, Compare the size and shape of bodies of land and water on the globe with the same bodies on the map. Note that the map makes the bodies look bigger. Which is accurate: the map or the globe? Why does the map distort the shapes and sizes?
3. *Activity:* Give each student an orange. Instruct them to peel the orange as carefully as possible so the peel is left in one piece. Next, tell students to try to flatten the peel out. What happens? How does this activity relate to the map and globe? Where is there the most distortion? The least distortion?
4. *Activity:* Find Greenland on the map. Now find Mexico on the map. Which is bigger? Now find Greenland on the globe, Find Mexico on the globe. Which is bigger now?

Content Area: Creative arts (the making of clay)

Objectives:

1. To familiarize students with the properties of various basic ingredients when combined
2. To promote creativity with a pliable substance
3. To familiarize students with select vocabulary
4. To reinforce the learning of imperatives, infinitives, adverb clauses

FIGURE 4.4 Sample Lessons Relating Linguistic Features and Content

SOURCE: From "Teaching Foreign Language through Content" by Jeffra Flaitz, in A. G. Ramírez (Ed.), *Spotlight on Teaching* (pp. 59–61), Schenectady, NY: New York State Association of Foreign Language Teachers, copyright 1988. Reprinted with permission.

Language Teaching Points: Select vocabulary, infinitives, conjunctions, time clauses

Nouns	Verbs	Adjectives
cup	mix	cool
teaspoon	boil	hot
clay	stir	
cornstarch	cook	
baking soda	remove	
dough	knead	
food coloring		
water		

Procedures:

1. Ask students to guess what kinds of ingredients may be used to make clay. Allow them to guess the procedure.
2. Distribute the following directions (written in target language) on recipe cards:

   To mix clay, mix 1 cup of cornstarch, 2 cups of baking soda, and 1-1/4 cups of water together in a pan. Boil the mixture, stirring constantly. Continue to cook the mixture until it looks like dough. Remove it from the hot stove, and when it is cool enough to touch, knead it a little. Add a few drops of food coloring.

A discussion of the ingredients of several common foods—pancakes, pudding, syrup, rice, bread, etc.—may be useful here. The use of adverb clauses in the target language would be well suited to the discussion (e.g.: "When you heat flour and water, you get a thick mixture"). Students may enjoy and would benefit from a discussion of the properties of basic ingredients such as eggs, flour, cornstarch, salt, and so forth when combined with heat. And, or course, students should subsequently be allowed to take the clay home or fashion a sculpture in class.

Content Area: Science/health (caloric value of foods); mathematics (addition)

Objectives:

1. To increase students' knowledge and awareness of the energy value of food
2. To increase students' awareness of their own caloric intake
3. To heighten students' awareness and sensitivity to problems related to hunger
4. To strengthen math skills
5. To reinforce the learning of the names of foods in the target language
6. To reinforce the learning of the names of large numbers in the target language

Language Teaching Points: food vocabulary, large numbers

Procedures:

1. Present a chart indicating the desired caloric intake for children of various age groups:

Females			Males		
age 6–9	50 lbs.	2100	age 6–9	50 lbs.	2100
9–12	70 lbs.	2200	9–12	70 lbs.	2400
12–15	100 lbs.	2500	12–15	100 lbs.	3000
15–18	115 lbs.	2300	15–18	135 lbs.	3400

(continued)

FIGURE 4.4 (continued)

2. Present another chart indicating the caloric value of various foods:

Food	Calories	Portion
apple	47	1
banana	100	1
green beans	27	1 cup
beef	214	1 serving
bread	63	1 slice
milk	124	1 8 oz. glass

3. Have students keep track of their daily caloric intake on a large wall chart in the target language. Have them report orally to the class the foods they consumed on the previous day and the total number of calories they consumed. The reports should be followed by a discussion of how closely the students' caloric intake corresponds to the ideal figures presented in the first calorie chart. There may also be discussion around the topic of what constitutes a healthy diet, which foods belong to which basic food groups, and the effect of a poor diet on one's health. This is a good opportunity to begin discussion of world famine. A map of the world indicating areas of widespread famine may be drawn or shown, or students may locate on the classroom map or globe the following countries in which hunger is a serious problem:

Guinea	Ivory Coast	Ghana	Somalia	Bangladesh	Central
India	Nepal	Burma	Sierra Leone	Mauritania	African
Laos	Kampuchea	Thailand	Bhutan	Liberia	Republic
Togo	Benin	Cameroon	Senegal	Guinea-Bissau	
Chad	Ethiopia	Mali	Nigeria	Gambia	

FIGURE 4.4   (continued)

pare their own lessons to integrate certain linguistic features with appropriate content matter. Flaitz (1988) cautions that a great deal of time is needed to prepare these materials, and that one might have to introduce this approach on a gradual basis, starting with perhaps one or two tasks per week and then increasing the number as time permits. She provides sample lessons in the areas of geography, science and health, and creative arts that serve to illustrate the possible connections between language features and subject matter content (Figure 4.4).

CONSIDERATIONS IN CURRICULUM PLANNING

Instructional planning involves making decisions about (1) the content to be taught, (2) the unit goals and learning objectives to be accomplished, (3) the techniques, methods, and strategies to achieve the goals and objectives, and (4) the evaluation of student performance and learning progress (Kindsvatter, Wilen, & Ishler, 1988). The functional-notional minicurriculum for ESL presented in Table 4.1, for example, specifies the linguistic content to be taught in terms of function, situation, verbal expressions, grammatical structures, and vocabulary categories. Classroom activities such as dialogue study, role playing, reading, and writing tasks are some of the means used to accomplish the unit goals. Specific unit goals (broad and general objectives stating intended learning outcomes, usually with the verbs "understand," "produce," "recognize," "create," etc.) are not formulated.

In the two-week unit curriculum unit plan in German for "Guten Appetit!" seen in Table 4.6, the linguistic content is given along with the specific lesson objectives and evaluation techniques. The lesson objectives are stated in relation to student performance behaviors. For example, students will be able to:

1. Recall and identify the new vocabulary items
2. Use the new grammatical structures in conversation
3. Compose a restaurant dialogue
4. Read an authentic menu
5. Analyze a video to acquire an awareness of cultural differences
6. Recognize the use of the narrative past
7. Provide excuses for not following a course of action
8. Decline or accept orally a dinner invitation
9. Act out appropriate behaviors and customs during a simulated dinner situation
10. Acquire cultural appreciation by sampling German food

All of the performance objectives specify the audience (Who will perform the task?) and the behavior (What is the task to be accomplished?). Objectives 5 and 10 are related to affective considerations in learning (Krathwohl et al., 1964) such as "attitudes" toward cultural differences and "appreciating" German foods. The other objectives are linguistic in nature and correspond to Bloom's (1956) taxonomy for classifying behaviors within the cognitive domain. Objectives 1 and 6 correspond to the "knowledge" level, emphasizing the recall of information; objectives 2, 7, and 8 involve the "application" of information in a particular situation; objectives 3 and 9 require a "synthesis" of information for the student to produce appropriate written and oral texts; and objective 4 emphasizes the "comprehension" of previously learned content.

The evaluation techniques used to assess student learning incorporate both the formative (daily assessment) and the summative (unit testing). Daily evaluation is used as the basis for determining whether particular student objectives have been accomplished. Some student objectives can be assessed through formal means (written tests or quizzes scored to determine the number and types of errors or the types of reactions) and informal means (observation of student behavior, as in how they respond to teacher questions and the degree to which they participate in group or class activities). Most of the evaluation procedures used in this unit are formative in nature. Written tests are planned for days 7 and 14. These involve items that can be judged right or wrong to determine a score.

Designing a language curriculum entails a number of considerations, ranging from linguistic goals and content to the specification of instruction and evaluative techniques. A syllabus could be organized using any number of formats (Dubin & Olshtain, 1986):

1. Linear format (discrete linguistic elements, particularly grammatical structures and features graded on the simple to complex criteria)

2. Modular format (integration of linguistic features and language skills in terms of topics or social situations)
3. Cyclical format (reintroduction of the same linguistic features or content in subsequent lessons, but, each time the concepts reappear, at a more complex or difficult level)
4. Matrix format (linguistic content can be presented in any number of situations; format is particularly useful in relating communicative tasks to various social settings)
5. Story-line format (use the same story line across lessons to maintain coherence among notions and functions)

A modular format, particularly suitable for elementary and middle school grades, could be organized in relation to the theme of "I with others in the world." Papalia and Wallace (1983) suggest a sequence of five major units using various topics related to different content areas. The first unit includes the student as a person, his or her family, and certain socializing behaviors. The second unit consists of topics related to basic needs, food, clothing, and home. The third module is devoted to concerns about time (days, months, seasons, holidays), classroom activities, and schooling matters. The fourth unit deals with leisure-time activities such as sports, hobbies, amusements, and vacations. The final unit encompasses transportation, travel, and places in the community, such as stores, services, and recreational facilities. Each topic allows the use of interactional language (greetings, asking for information, directing others to do something, reporting, expressing opinions) and makes it possible to highlight certain cultural points (use of gestures, family activities and celebrations, types of home furnishings, eating habits). It also calls for the inclusion of verbal formulas (typical expressions for greeting, expressing pleasure, paying a compliment, expressing surprise, apologizing, blaming, making an offer) and a number of grammatical features. This design can promote functional communication by integrating linguistic and cultural skills within a broad range of topics, starting with the learner at the center of the curriculum spiral and radiating beyond to the family, classroom, school, and wider community. This design also offers the teacher numerous opportunities to integrate concepts from such subjects as social studies, language arts, science, and mathematics.

In the case of ESL instruction, Finocchiaro and Brumfit (1983) suggest the following procedures for designing a curriculum:

1. Analyze learners' target language proficiency and actual communicative needs;
2. Survey language resources in the school and community (materials available, places to visit, people to involve as types of native speakers).
3. Specify language content (functions, situations, topics, linguistic features).
4. Gather or prepare audiovisual materials.
5. Specify involvement of school and community resources to ensure an interdisciplinary approach.

6. Prepare or adapt dialogues and situations for presentation of linguistic content.
7. Identify tasks and activities for student participation in class.
8. Determine evaluation techniques for assessing student language development.

The New York State foreign language syllabus, *Modern Languages for Communication*, (1986) offers the following steps in planning a unit of instruction:

1. Specify the functions, situation, and topics to be covered.
2. Enumerate the learning outcomes in terms of specific communicative tasks that the students will be able to perform as the result of instruction. The learning outcomes should be realistic and reflect students' communicative needs and their interests.
3. Identify the cultural contexts in which the communication can take place (eating at a restaurant, mailing a letter at the post office, taking a taxi) and provide opportunities for presentation and analysis of the cultural characteristics inherent in those contexts.
4. Prepare an inventory of the basic vocabulary and useful grammatical structures.
5. Select the appropriate teaching strategies to be employed to achieve the learning outcomes.
6. Select the instructional materials to be used (commercially prepared, teacher-made, derived from other sources, with special attention to the use of authentic cultural materials).
7. Prepare the format for assessment and the schedule for evaluating student proficiency.

At the level of a specific lesson, students might engage in several short tasks that can contribute to the learning of different objectives during one class period. The California *Foreign Language Framework* (1989) suggests that one class period might include several tasks:

1. Working on the "input" phase of new linguistic content
2. Working on the "practice" stage of previously introduced material
3. Discussing a reading assignment given as homework
4. Presenting or practicing a cultural feature
5. Practicing conversations in small groups
6. Preparing for a writing assignment as homework

By participating in various activities, students can work toward several objectives during the same class period and complete the different stages of the learning sequence for each objective. The variety of activities and the change of pace should stimulate greater student interest and attention in the learning process.

Overall proficiency is enhanced by recycling previously learned material and communication skills and integrating their use in different language situations. Learning a language is a cumulative, spiraling process requiring practice, recycling, interactive activities, and meaningful input (Schulz, 1991).

With respect to inclusion of authentic texts, Lopez (1987) provides a format for planning daily lessons to utilize cultural materials as a means for presenting vocabulary, grammar, language functions, and topics. In addition to outlining the linguistic content, the format includes the essential components: (1) specific lesson objectives, (2) the specification of instructional procedures (including a closure activity to allow for a summary, integration, or application of content) and (3) an evaluation of the learning objectives (Figure 4.5).

The use of cultural materials appears to be a powerful catalyst for communicative language learning. Students are surrounded by media (television, radio, newspapers, magazines, movies) in their everyday life. By integrating authentic materials into the language classroom, students can engage with language as a personal, holistic, and social experience (Penfield, 1987).

SUMMARY

There are a number of curriculum frameworks that can be used to structure and sequence language content. The selection of one model over another (e.g., communicative-based vs. proficiency-oriented syllabus) might be influenced by such factors as program goals, student characteristics, and teacher-related issues. As noted earlier in Chapter 1, it is possible to combine elements from different approaches since many of the basic categories are similar: topics, text types, language functions, social situations, grammatical structures, vocabulary, and language modalities.

The textbook often determines the particular curricular framework used to present language. Teachers need to examine their class texts critically to establish how language elements and skills are sequenced across lessons. A worksheet might prove to be a useful tool for planning week-long units of instruction to include categories such as functions, topics, language areas (listening, speaking, reading, and writing situations), grammatical features, and cultural elements.

Curriculum planning involves making decisions about (1) the linguistic content, (2) the learning goals and objectives, (3) the use of specific techniques, strategies, and methods, and (4) the evaluation procedures to assess learning. A specific lesson plan should include several essential components: (1) specification of linguistic content, (2) learning objectives, (3) teaching procedures, and (4) an evaluation plan. In planning curricular units, it is important to remember the learner, who has needs, interests, and ways of learning. The ordering and selection of some of the language content can be accomplished as a collaborative effort between teacher and students.

Proficiency Level: *Novice/intermediate*	Date:

Topic: *Personal identification: name, address, occupation, age*

Situation: *Reading: advertisement, form   Writing: form to fill out*

Function: *To obtain and to provide information*

Cultural Content: *Forms in Spanish*

Major Concept: *Last names in Spanish*

Objectives: *Students will be able to say in Spanish:*

• *Name*	• *State/province*	• *Issue*
• *Address*	• *Country*	*In English:*
• *City*	• *Occupation*	• *Por talon bancario*
• *Age*	• *Postal code*	• *Giro postal no.*
• *Surname*	• *Year, months*	• *Firma (la misma de la tarjeta)*

Instructional procedures

Anticipatory (Problem-Solving) Activity:
- *Have students work on their own to fill out the form.*
- *Have them write down what they think* acorte las distancias *means.*
- *Have them translate all vital questions (nombre, etc.) on a sheet of paper.*

Presentation/Discussion of New Material:
- *After they have figured out as much information as possible on their own:*
- *Answer questions.*
- *Fill out a form on overhead projector.*
- *Focus on c. postal, apellidos, edad, provincia, acorte las distancias*

Oral Drill:
Questions: *¿Cuál es tu apellido?*
¿Cuál es tu edad?
¿Cuál es tu dirección?
¿Dónde vives?
¿Cuál es tu profesión?

Reinforcement Activity:
Have students in groups of two or three create a form of their own for a different purpose

Closure:
Give a similar form to be filled out.

Evaluation:
Have students write down answers to teacher's oral questions related to the objectives.

Key Vocabulary

código postal
nombre
appellidos
dirección
cuidad
provincia
departamento
edad
profesión
país
estado
año
mes
número
tijeras
edición
internacional
talón bancario
firma

FIGURE 4.5   Authentic Material Lesson Plan

SOURCE: Adapted from workshop materials prepared by Jesús López, 1987, Albany: State University of New York. Used with permission.

ACTIVITIES

1. Examine a language textbook by considering its introduction and table of contents to determine: (1) the type of language syllabus (grammatical, communicative and/or situational), (2) the assumptions about language learning, and (3) the interrelationship among the four language skill areas (listening, reading, speaking, and writing).
2. Choose one of the lessons from a language textbook and list (1) the types of grammatical structures, (2) the number of communicative functions, and (3) the social situations that are included. To what extent are grammatical structures related to the communicative functions of a language? Are the communicative uses of language placed within specific sociocultural situations?
3. Review the curriculum unit outlined by Finocchiaro and Brumfit in Table 4.1. What are some of the advantages and disadvantages in presenting language within this framework?
4. Consider a task-based curriculum unit, as proposed by Nunan in Table 4.2. What are some of the advantages and disadvantages in organizing language content on the basis of learner needs for the real world?
5. Prepare a communicative unit based on the framework suggested by Lund in Table 4.3. List some classroom activities that a particular group of students could engage in with respect to the various language functions.
6. Examine the components of the proficiency-oriented lessons related to the linguistic and cultural context necessary for expressing and recognizing food/drink items at a French restaurant in Table 4.4. Interview a teacher and/or fellow students to explore how the different features of these lessons would be used in planning instruction. Compare and contrast the differences in the teaching implementation plans.
7. Suggest ways of adapting a particular lesson from a language textbook based on the procedures outlined by Guntermann and Phillip. What additional features or issues do you consider important?
8. What role should students play in curriculum planning? To what extent are the steps noted by Doctor for curriculum development useful in different teaching situations?
9. Develop a language lesson that relates content to specific linguistic features, as in the examples provided by Flaitz.
10. What are some of the curriculum problems associated with relating content to linguistic features? Compare your answer with those of other students. Interview a teacher in order to explore beliefs about this topic.
11. Consider the suggestion from the California *Foreign Language Framework* to include several tasks or activities during one class period. What are some of the problems and benefits?
12. Prepare a lesson plan based on the format offered by López for using authentic materials.

REFERENCES

Arnold, A. (1989). A German unit on 'Guten appetit.' Materials prepared for a course. Albany: State University of New York, School of Education.

Bloom, B. (Ed.). (1956). *A taxonomy of educational objectives. Handbook I: Cognitive domain.* White Plains, NY: Longman.

Breen, M. P. (1987). Learner contributions to task design. In C. N. Candlin & D. F. Murphy (Eds.), *Language learning tasks* (pp. 23-46). London: Prentice-Hall International.

Brinton, D. M., Snow, M. A., & Wesche, M. B. (1989). *Content-based second language instruction*. New York: Newbury House.

Candlin, C., & Nunan, D. (1987). *Revised syllabus specifications for the Omani school English language curriculum*. Muscat, Oman: Ministry of Education and Youth.

Cantoni-Harvey, G. (1987). *Content-area language instruction: Approaches and strategies*. Reading, MA: Addison-Wesley.

Doctor, E. (1989). C'est en forgeant qu' on devient forgeron or towards a communicative pedagogy. *Canadian Modern Language Review*, *45*(2), 318-328.

Dubin, F., & Olshtain, E. (1986). *Course design*. Cambridge, England: Cambridge University Press.

Ellis, R. (1990). *Instructed second language acquisition*. Oxford: Basil Blackwell.

Finocchiaro, M., & Brumfit, C. (1983). *The functional-notional approach: From theory to practice*. Oxford: Oxford University Press.

Flaitz, J. (1988). Teaching foreign language through content. In A. G. Ramírez (Ed.), *Spotlight on teaching* (pp. 57-62). Schenectady, NY: New York State Association of Foreign Language Teachers.

Foreign language framework for California public schools, K-12 (1989). Sacramento: California State Board of Education.

Guntermann, G., & Phillips, J. K. (1982). *Language in education: Theory and practice: Vol. 44. Functional notional concepts: Adapting the foreign language textbook*. Washington, DC: Center for Applied Linguistics.

Kindsvatter, R., Wilen, W., & Ishler, M. (1988). *Dynamics of effective teaching*. New York: Longman.

Krathwohl, D. R., Bloom, B. S., & Massi, B. (1964). *A taxonomy of educational objectives: The Affective domain*. White Plains, NY: Longman.

Lange, D. L. (1987). The language teaching curriculum and a national agenda. In R. C. Lambert (Ed.), *The annals of the American academy of political and social sciences: Vol. 490. Foreign language instruction: A national agenda* (pp. 70-96). Newbury Park, CA: Sage Publications.

Long, M. H. (1988). Instructed interlanguage development. In L. M. Beebe (Ed.), *Issues in second language acquisition: Multiple perspectives* (pp. 115-141). New York: Harper & Row.

Long, M. H., & Crookes, G. (1992). Three approaches to task-based syllabus design. *TESOL Quarterly*, *26* (1), 27-56.

López, J. (1987). *Authentic materials for the classroom*. Materials distributed at teachers' workshop. Albany: State University of New York.

Lund, R. J. (1988). Planning communicative units and lessons. In A. G. Ramírez (Ed.), *Spotlight on teaching* (pp. 9-16). Schenectady, NY: New York State Association of Foreign Language Teachers.

Mita, D. (1987). Material and procedures for instructional planning based on the New York state syllabus, *Modern languages for communication*. Albany, NY: State Education Department.

Modern languages for communication (1986). Albany, NY: State Education Department.

Mohan, B. A. (1986). *Language and content*. Reading, MA: Addison-Wesley.

Nunan, D. (1988a). *The learner-centered curriculum*. Cambridge, England: Cambridge University Press.

Nunan, D. (1988b). *Syllabus design*. Oxford: Oxford University Press.

Papalia, A., & Wallace, N. (1983). *Developing communicative proficiency and cultural understanding in early second language programs.* Schenectady, NY: New York State Association of Foreign Language Teachers.

Penfield, J. (1987). *The media: Catalysts for communicative language learning.* Reading, MA: Addison-Wesley.

Porter, L. P. (1987). Using the ACTFL proficiency guidelines to achieve goals of exploratory language courses. *Foreign Language Annals, 20*(4), 323-330.

Prabhu, N. S. (1987). *Second language pedagogy.* Oxford: Oxford University Press.

Richards, J. C. (1990). *The language teaching matrix.* Cambridge, England: Cambridge University Press.

Schulz, R. A. (1991). Bridging the gap between teaching and learning: A critical look at foreign language textbooks. In S. S. Magnan (Ed.), *Challenges in the 1990s for college foreign language programs* (pp. 167-181). Boston: Heinle & Heinle.

Yalden, J. (1987). *Principles of course design for language teaching.* Cambridge, England: Cambridge University Press.

chapter 5

Stimulating Language Acquisition

Many methods have been proposed for the teaching of foreign languages. Different approaches have fallen in and out of fashion along with associated psychological or linguistic theories as well as dynamic individuals representing the different points of view. An eclectic approach has also been suggested, but there has been no principled basis for a decision on which aspect of which method one should choose in a particular circumstance. These different methodologies for language teaching have met with varying degrees of success and failure. What is amazing is that there are some examples of successful language learners for different and even contradictory methods . . . , and the question of which overall method is superior remains to be answered.

M. R. Eisenstein, 1987

Teaching methods represent patterns of teaching actions designed to achieve certain learning outcomes. Different teaching methods make particular assumptions about the nature of language, learning processes, the roles of teachers and learners, and the kinds of learning activities and instructional materials. Terms like "approach," "method," "model," and "syllabus" have been used to describe some current methodologies, for example, Comprehension Approach, Natural Approach, Functional-Notional Syllabus, Total Physical Response, and Proficiency-Oriented Approach. Teaching techniques and learning activities are the specific means by which methods are implemented into actual classroom practice. A number of considerations need to be kept in mind in deciding the appropriateness of certain teaching strategies for accomplishing specific learning goals. Linguistic accuracy is an important issue that needs to be addressed along with methodological questions. The development of grammatical and phonological accuracy needs to be approached in terms of other language subskills as well as learner characteristics.

This chapter addresses a number of questions related to teaching methods and instructions. Among the topics discussed are the following concerns:

1. What are the major characteristics of some of the common teaching methods?
2. What considerations need to be kept in mind in designing learning tasks?
3. What role should grammar play in a language syllabus?
4. What procedures are appropriate for developing grammatical accuracy?
5. What procedures are appropriate for developing pronunciation accuracy?
6. What correction strategies are appropriate for error correction in oral communication?

LANGUAGE TEACHING METHODS

Teaching methodology, according to Richards (1990), encompasses "the activities, tasks, and learning experiences used by the teacher within the teaching and learning process" (p. 35). It is not necessarily a set of fixed principles or teaching procedures but a dynamic, creative process reflecting assumptions about language (How do we describe or talk about language?), proficiency (What does it mean to know a language?), and learning (How should we teach language?). Descriptions and analysis of the numerous methods have appeared in such books as *Twenty-five Centuries of Language Teaching* (Kelly, 1969), *Methods that Work: A Smorgasbord of Ideas for Language Teachers* (Oller & Richard-Amato, 1983), *Approaches and Methods in Language Teaching* (Richards & Rodgers, 1986), *Techniques and Principles in Language Teaching* (Larsen-Freeman, 1986), and *Developing Second Language Skills: Theory and Practice* (Chastain, 1988).

Discussions about teaching methods have often been confusing and misleading since the terms *method*, *approach*, and *procedure* are used along with curriculum models. Finocchiaro and Brumfit (1983) for example, discuss language learning and teaching during the last century according to the following methods:

1. Grammar-Translation Method
2. Direct Method
3. Reading Method
4. Structural Approach
5. Audio-Lingual Method
6. Situational Method
7. Functional-Notional Approach

The *Grammar-Translation Method*, inherited from the teaching of Latin, focused on learning the rules of grammar and vocabulary from bilingual lists of words that pertain to a written text or reading selections in a lesson. Grammar rules were learned deductively by means of explanations. Students engaged in translating passages from the target language to the native language, and vice versa. Listening and speaking abilities were not developed. With the exception of reading sentences and passages aloud on certain occasions, most of the class time was devoted to reading and translation activities. The *Direct Method*, on the other hand, stressed listening and speaking. Language learning activities emphasized the direct association of words and phrases with objects and actions, without the use of the students' native language. Oral communication skills were developed in a carefully graded progression organized around question-and-answer exchanges between teachers and students in small, intensive classes. Grammar was taught inductively, and new linguistic content was first introduced orally. The ability to interact with written text was not developed as in the *Reading Method*, which advocated a reading knowledge of a foreign language, to be achieved through the gradual introduction of vocabulary and grammatical structures in simplified reading selections.

The *Structural Approach*, known variously as the oral approach and the aural-oral approach, organized the presentation of language in terms of basic linguistic patterns (subject-verb-object, question forms, simple and complex sentences). It advocated the development of language skills in a particular sequence: (1) listening, (2) speaking, (3) reading, and (4) writing. Language was identified with speech, and written language was seen as an extension of the oral modality.

The *Audio-Lingual Method*, an extension of the structural approach, was also concerned about language patterns and the primacy of speech. Principles based on behavioral psychology led to extensive use of techniques such as dialogue memorization, choral repetition, and pattern drills. Through repetition drills (exercises requiring no change from the teachers' model) and transformation drills (exercises requiring some change such as replacement, restatement, completion, expansion, contraction, and integration), students learned language as a "set of habits" by engaging in pattern practice.

The *Situational Method* linked the structural patterns of language to the situations or context of occurrence. Language activities were to be seen as part of a whole complex of events involving participants, objects, and actual situations. Language learning was seen as habit formation involving linguistic input, repetition, and practice (Frisby, 1957). Grammar was to be taught inductively, and classroom activities were to move from controlled (repetition, mechanical drills) to freer practice (more authentic, question-and-answer sequences) and from oral use of sentence patterns to their use in speech, reading, and writing contexts.

The *Functional-Notional Approach*, described previously in Chapter 4, serves more like a syllabus or curriculum model for sequencing language functions in relation to situations, grammatical features, vocabulary, and classroom activities. The approach links language functions (thanking, directing, apologizing, suggesting) with grammatical notions (meaning expressed through linguistic forms such as time, quantity, space, and relations between entities). The approach places an emphasis on communicative rather than grammatical competence. Questions related to the role of practice, the grammatical sequence, and the integration of functions with grammar remain unresolved (Guntermann & Phillips, 1982).

Some of the more recent approaches to reflect a communicative orientation and incorporate various insights from second language research include:

1. Dartmouth (Rassias) Intensive Language Model
2. Comprehension Approach
3. Total Physical Response (TPR)
4. Natural Approach
5. Silent Way
6. Community Language Learning
7. Suggestopedia

The *Dartmouth Intensive Language Model* retains many of the tenets of the audio-lingual approach from the 1950s. The approach places considerable attention on the use of pattern drill practice. The intensive course requirements instituted by Rassias (1983) involve a three-hour class period per day for five days a week during a 10-week period. The first hour of class is spent with the master teacher, who presents and explains the language content; the second hour is devoted to intensive drill practice with an apprentice teacher, and the third hour involves additional practice in the language laboratory with a person monitoring the students' performance. Grammar, vocabulary, listening comprehension, fluency, and pronunciation accuracy are the five aspects of language highlighted. The teachers' concern for grammatical competence is matched with a sincere interest in making the class interesting, dynamic, and dramatic. Any type of classroom behavior is considered acceptable if it evokes student interest and participation. Props, make-believe, press conferences, screams, and heart attack victims on the floor are part of the arsenal of techniques used to encourage speaking.

The *Comprehension Approach* is based on the premise that students must first develop the ability to comprehend and process language before they can speak it. This approach stresses activating the individual's internal mental processes as the basic component in second language learning. In order to develop listening comprehension skills, teachers should (1) present the material in ways that can be understood by the students, (2) verify that students have understood what has been presented, and (3) prepare students to infer meaning from context (Postovsky, 1982). Speaking is delayed to the point where students choose to speak, as in the case of the preproduction period that children pass through when acquiring their native language.

Two of the best methods associated with the comprehension approach are the *Total Physical Response (TPR)* (Asher, 1982) and the *Natural Approach* (Krashen & Terrell, 1983). The TPR approach utilizes oral commands that students act out to show their understanding. Through mime and example, teachers expose students to a broad range of grammatical structures and vocabulary items in the target language. During the listening training period, students respond to teacher commands (Stand up! Go to the chalkboard and write your name.). After a period of approximately 10 hours of training, students reverse roles with the instructor and begin the production phase by giving their own commands to fellow students and the teacher. Reading and writing skills are used to support aural/oral components. Students record in their notebooks at the end of each session the vocabulary and structures presented in class.

The Natural Approach recognizes comprehension as the basic skill that promotes language acquisition and should therefore precede speech production. Speech emerges in stages, moving from responses to commands to producing connected discourse. Comprehension and production abilities are developed through a series of affective language activities designed to (1) provide comprehensible input, (2) lower student anxiety, and (3) create opportunities to convey messages. Three stages of language acquisition are proposed in the Natural Approach, along with its various techniques.

I. Comprehension (preproduction)
   A. TPR activities
   B. Answers with names: objects, students, pictures (students respond to descriptions based on hair color, clothing, physical attributes)
II. Early speech production
   A. Yes-no questions (Are you tired, John? Yes.)
   B. Either-or questions (Do you prefer ice cream or cake? Ice cream.)
   C. Single- or two-word answer (Where do you work? At home.)
   D. Open-ended sentences (What kind of movies do you like?)
   E. Open dialogue (question-and-answer sequence about various topics: family, sports, cars)
   F. Interviews (Tell me about your summer plans.)
III. Speech emerges
   A. Games and recreational activities (Guess who?)
   B. Content activities (reports, slide presentations)
   C. Humanistic-affective activities (opinions, feelings)
   D. Information and problem solving (planning a trip) (Adapted from Terrell, 1982, p. 129)

The emphasis on the learner as an active agent in the acquisition process is associated with the cognitive-code approach to language teaching. Rather than simply responding to the stimuli in the environment, as with the audio-lingual orientation, the *Silent Way* is based on the philosophy that learners "silently" use their own inner criteria (i.e., learning strategies, cognitive processes, experiences, knowledge of the world), and the teacher needs to guide students as they engage in their own hypothesis-testing process (Gattegno, 1976). Through the use of colored rods, referred to as Cuisenaire rods, teachers present the basic vocabulary and grammatical features. Students learn to say the noun "rod", the numeral adjectives (one, two, three, etc.), the adjectives (blue, red, yellow, long, short), verbs (take, place, give me, put), conjunctions (take a green rod and a blue one), personal pronouns (me, him, her, them), and adverbs (here, there). With around 27 words, many sentences can be produced. A set of wall charts is used to reinforce learning by relating the oral presentation of vocabulary to the visual modality. The words are color-coded and make it possible for the teacher to conduct visual dictation exercises by pointing to the words and having the students read them individually, in phrases, or as sentences.

The *Counseling-Learning Approach*, alternatively referred to as Community Language Learning, is based on therapeutic techniques borrowed from psychological counseling. The approach developed by Curran (1976) stresses the need to see learners as "whole persons," not just "cognitive beings." Teachers need to be concerned about their students' individual needs and their fears about learning. By fostering a sense of community, teachers can establish a secure learning environment so that students will be able to direct their positive energies to the task of language learning. The teacher acts as a "counselor," enabling the students to express whatever they want to say in the target language. Thus, the syllabus is learner-generated and corresponds to five learning stages.

1. Each student expresses in English only to the counselor what he or she would like to say to the others in the group. The teacher translates the utterance for the student, who, in turn, repeats the teachers' model and records it on tape. Students desiring to make a response will request the counselor to provide a target-language equivalent. Again, the student repeats the expression, and the response is recorded on tape so that by the end of the session the entire dialogue is recorded. The tape recording is subsequently used as the script for a later class session, making it a source of language input that can serve for linguistic analysis and practice. (Maximum security stage)
2. Students try to speak more directly to the group with less teacher assistance. The counselor aids only if a student hesitates or turns for help. (Self-assertive stage)
3. Students speak directly to the group in the target language. At this stage, the learners have greater confidence, independence, and linguistic insights (i.e., vocabulary, grammar, functions). Translation is given only when a group member desires it. (Birth stage)
4. Students speak freely in the group using more complex structures and are secure enough to accept teacher's correction of grammatical errors and mispronunciations. (Adolescent stage)
5. Students interact with each other and the teacher freely. Corrective feedback is offered to add idioms and improve stylistic matters. No individual feels threatened within the group. The atmosphere is one of trust, acceptance, and understanding. Some students can become counselors to those in Stages 1, 2, or 3. (Independent stage)

Suggestopedia, also known as the Lozanov method, centers on the use of relaxation and concentration techniques designed to help learners tap their subconscious mental powers in order to increase the retention of greater amounts of vocabulary and structures (Lozanov, 1982). The main feature of the approach requires the creation of a "suggestive" learning atmosphere through the use of soft light, baroque music, comfortable seating, and dramatic techniques used by the teacher to present language content. The Lozanov method, which originated in Bulgaria, calls for a three-part "suggestopedic" cycle:

1. First, students review the material from the previous day's lesson, mainly through conversations, games, and skits. Mechanistic repetition of language patterns is avoided. To help overcome inhibitions, each member of the class is given a new name and a new role to play. By learning a biography that corresponds to the new role, students are able to practice difficult sounds in the target language.

2. Then, new material is presented through lengthy dialogues based on real-life situations. The techniques are traditional, with the necessary grammatical analysis and translation activities. The dialogues are constructed to have continuity in plot, characters, and situations. Students listen to music as the teacher reads the dialogue, usually one line at a time. The teacher's tone of voice and the music change during the course of the oral reading, while the students, with their books, follow the text in the target language, along with translation into their native language.

   Students also practice controlled breathing techniques to improve their concentration as they listen to the dialogue. This represents the "active concert" of learning. Later, students listen to the reading of the dialogue for a second time, this time with their eyes closed and accompanied by more baroque music. This is the "passive concert." The two concert phases are designed to activate learning at the unconscious level by allowing relaxation and presenting material that is emotionally relevant and interesting to students.

3. The third session, or activation phase, provides for reinforcement opportunities for the new material learned in the second part. Students engage in role-playing situations and practice activities. Grammatical explanations are provided, if necessary in the native language.

All of the methods described above have their practitioners. One method may be preferred over another on the basis of language teaching goals, learner needs, or educational realities. It is safe to say that none of the methods dominates classroom practice to the same degree as the audio-lingual approach once did, with its emphasis on pattern practice drills so that students would learn the language through habit formation (Larsen-Freeman, 1987). Teachers who are knowledgeable with some of the innovative methods—Natural Approach, Silent Way, Community Language Learning, or Suggestopedia—may actually follow an *eclectic approach*, combining techniques and principles from different methods. Some techniques may be particularly suited for teaching particular aspects of language. The Total Physical Response approach, with teachers commanding their students to "stand up, walk to the door, turn around, and walk back to your desk and sit down" may

TABLE 5.1 Teaching approaches and learner roles

Approach	Roles
1. Oral/Situational	learner listens to teacher and repeats; no control over content or methods
2. Audiolingual	learner has little control; reacts to teacher direction; passive, reactive role
3. Communicative	learner has an active, negotiative role; should contribute as well as receive
4. Total Physical Response	learner is a listener and performer, little influence over content and none over methodology
5. The Silent Way	learner learns through systematic analysis; must become independent and autonomous
6. Community Language Learning	learners are members of a social group or community; move from dependence to autonomy as learning progresses
7. The Natural Approach	learners play an active role and have relatively high degree of control over content language production
8. Suggestopedia	learners are passive, have little control over content or methods

SOURCE: From *Designing Tasks for the Communicative Classroom* (p. 80) by David Nunan, 1989, Cambridge, England: Cambridge University Press: ©1989, Cambridge University Press. Reprinted with permission.

be especially appropriate during the initial level of language learning. The Dartmouth Intensive Language Model may be unsuitable with some high school classes, while Suggestopedia techniques may be appropriate for small groups of college students who want to combine relaxation techniques with language learning.

It is important to understand the role that students play with a particular teaching method or approach. Nunan (1989) offers an analysis of student roles with respect to eight different teaching approaches (Table 5.1). The roles that learners and teachers are expected to play in carrying out a method have both learning and interpersonal consequences. Learners can be treated as passive recipients of information, listeners and performers, or active agents responsible for their own learning.

TEACHING TECHNIQUES

Teaching techniques are the principal means by which specific methods are implemented in language classrooms. To avoid some of the confusion that exists in using the concepts of approach, model, method, and technique, Richards and Rodgers (1986) advocate using a three-part distinction—approach, design, and procedure—to label the three interrelated elements that constitute a method. *Approach* is the first level, which defines the assumptions, beliefs, or theories about the nature of language and language learning, usually presented in the form of axioms (e.g., language consists of a set of patterns that can be learned through memorization, repetition, and practice; or, language is a series of communicative acts that can be learned incrementally through exercises, practice, and role-playing situations). *Design* is the second level of analysis; it specifies the syllabus model (selection and sequencing of linguistic content) and types of learning and teaching activities (kinds of language drills, student groupings, uses of oral and written language, communicative tasks). At this level the form and function of instructional materials and classroom activities are enumerated in relation to the approach being followed regarding theories of language and learning. *Procedure* is the third level of distinction. It consists of the teaching techniques and practices that can be observed when the method is being utilized. The use of certain teaching behaviors (question-and-answer sequences, error correction strategies, the amount of time devoted to different aspects of language), the kinds of audiovisual materials, and the interactional patterns between teachers and learners all mirror to varying degrees the consequences of a particular approach and design for language teaching.

Some methods exist in the form of textbooks (e.g., a functional-notional approach, a communicative approach, or a proficiency-oriented approach) that organize language in a particular sequence and present content in ways that support the basic axioms of the approach. Audio-lingual and communicative-oriented textbooks usually provide numerous learning activities, tasks, and experiences to promote learning consistent with the method's goals. At the same time, numerous books have been published that present teachers with a broad range of learning activities suitable for different methods, language learning objectives, and learner interests. Such books as the ones listed below offer many different kinds of techniques to fulfill different instructional objectives:

> *Caring and Sharing in the Foreign Language Class: A Sourcebook for Teachers* (Moskowitz, 1978)
>
> *ESL Operations: Techniques for Learning While Doing* (Nelson & Winters, 1980)
>
> *Creative Activities for the Second Language Classroom* (Birckbichler, 1982)
>
> *Idea Bank: Creative Activities for the Language Class* (Sadow, 1982)
>
> *Games for Language Learning* (Wright, Betteridge, & Buckby, 1984)
>
> *Action Plans: Eighty Student-Centered Language Activities* (Macdonald & Rogers-Gordon, 1984)
>
> *Developing Communication Skills: A Practical Handbook for Language Teachers with Examples in English, French, and German* (Pattison, 1987)
>
> *The Media: Catalysts for Communicative Language Learning* (Penfield, 1987)
>
> *Pictures for Language Learning* (Wright, 1989)

The selection of particular kinds of learning activities should be based on a series of considerations. Richards (1990) points out that it is important to establish

Title of materials: _____

Cost of materials: _____

Date acquired: _____

Dates used: This allows the instructor to determine the frequency and success of a given activity.

Place acquired: This permits the instructor to add additional materials, update materials, and provide proper citation.

Linguistic structures: This includes a wide array of possibilities, e.g., vocabulary building, or notional tasks—questioning, informing, arguing, etc.

Language skills: Understanding, speaking, writing, reading, culture.

Course level: Specify appropriate achievement level for a given activity, e.g., beginner, advanced beginner, intermediate, advanced. This determination will require appropriate testing.

Time required: Specify length of time for each activity. This may require in-class experience.

Participants: Indicate if the activity is designed for individuals, pairs, small groups or the entire class.

Materials: Specify the materials that will be needed prior to class presentation. What will the teacher provide? What will the student provide?
                        Examples of materials include equipment (overhead or slide projector, audio or video recorder/player), copies of handouts, colored chalk. etc.

Preparation: What type of intellectual or material preparation is required prior to the class-room activity?

Procedure: What instructions are necessary to allow the student to be successful?

FIGURE 5.1   Sample form for the introduction of new techniques into L2 curriculum

SOURCE: From "Selected Enrichment Techniques for the Second Language Classroom" by Frank Nuessel, 1989, *Canadian Modern Language Review/La Revue canadienne des langues vivantes.* pp. 295–296. Reprinted with permission.

a set of criteria for selecting learning activities and deciding how much time to al-locate to each activity type per lesson or unit. Nuessel (1989) provides a frame-work for supplementing the use of teaching techniques in a meaningful, organized manner. The sample form in Figure 5.1 enables teachers to develop a file of in-structional materials over a period of time. A separate file folder can be kept for each activity, permitting the teacher to integrate multiple activities into an organic, meaningful learning experience.

Learning activities can fulfill a number of functions. According to Nunan (1989, pp. 139-140), they can, for example:

1. Enable learners to manipulate and practice specific features of language.
2. Allow learners to rehearse, in class, communicative skills they will need in the real world.
3. Activate psychological/psycholinguistic processes of learning.

4. Involve learners in solving a problem, coming to a conclusion.
5. Involve learners in sharing information with others.
6. Allow learners to think and talk about language and learning.
7. Promote the integration of various language subskills.
8. Involve learners in risk-taking.
9. Require learners to rehearse, rewrite, and polish initial efforts.
10. Require learners to relate learned material to new content.

Deciding *which* techniques to use *when* and *why* brings us back to many issues related to program goals, learner characteristics, teaching philosophies, and local resources. The use of particular techniques might be seen more clearly in relation to language learning tasks. A task-oriented perspective identifies (1) the learning objective, (2) language content (e.g., genre, topic, functions, linguistic elements), (3) types of student responses, and (4) teaching techniques. This perspective is illustrated by the examples offered for listening situations (Chapter 7), reading contexts (Chapter 8), speaking activities (Chapter 9), and writing tasks (Chapter 10). The teaching techniques are listed as the procedures or steps to be followed to accomplish each task.

METHODOLOGY AND THE ACCURACY ISSUE

The teaching of grammar has been a central issue in language instruction. The Grammar-Translation Method devoted a considerable amount of class time to explaining grammatical rules. Audio-lingual teachers drilled their students on grammatical patterns, using repetition and choral practice as the means to promote rule learning, mainly through an inductive process. Conscious manipulation of grammatical structures through a variety of language drills and exercises did result in some students' acquiring grammatical accuracy, but not necessarily communicative competence. Rivers (1986) provides anecdotal evidence to support the claim that students who are grammar-trained can become fluent communicators once they are placed in the language-rich environment of the target country. However, she notes that the reverse does not seem to be true, since learners who have interacted with native speakers and acquired communicative competence are not always capable of developing grammatical accuracy. Higgs and Clifford (1982) argue along with others that a teaching methodology that stresses communicative activities before students have learned the relevant grammatical features will foster fossilization of learner errors.

The questions regarding the role of grammatical explanations, drills, and exercises needs to be addressed with respect to their pedagogical value (Chastain, 1987). Krashen and Terrell (1983), proponents of the Natural Approach, claim that students should focus on meaning rather than grammatical forms in order to develop language competence. Conscious understanding of grammar does not seem to be a prerequisite to developing communicative competence. A study by

Hammond (1988) examining the acquisition of accuracy versus communicative competence among first-year university students indicates that learners who learned grammar through inductive means (a series of examples leading to a generalization or rule) performed on tests and exams as well as or better than students who learned grammar through a deductive approach (rule explanation followed by exercises and drills). Moreover, students of the communicative approach were as "accurate" as the students taught by the grammar-based methodology. Still, grammatical accuracy is a major consideration of the proficiency approach. Omaggio (1986) stresses the importance of linguistic accuracy from the beginning of language instruction, since it is one of the three components of proficiency-based instruction. Magnan (1988) further claims that grammar plays a central role in the ACTFL oral proficiency interview. She notes at least seven different kinds of grammatical errors in the areas of morphology and syntax that were found to have a significant association with proficiency levels among learners of French.

To be sure, grammar is an essential feature of language instruction. It seems that the place of grammar in language teaching needs to be reformulated. Grammar might be approached in terms that link language forms and meaning. Adjectives like "this," "that," "there," and "those" can also be used to designate location, differentiation, and identification. Question forms ("What do you think you're doing?") may be used not as interrogatives but as indirect commands ("Why don't you stop doing that?"). Grammar can be regarded as a "system for converting meaning into language" (Higgs, 1985, p. 285). It can be seen as the means by which native speakers combine different elements of language (vocabulary, morphology, and syntax) to express meanings. The teaching of grammar as processing rules for expressing communicative intent with particular language forms is likely to play an important role in the development of communicative competence (Garrett, 1986). Learners need to be made aware of the major organizing principles of language in such areas as the kinds of grammatical marking devices (use of affixes, word order, stress); means for connecting sentences to differentiate between main, coordinating, and subordinate clauses; and the use of discourse markers (pronoun reference, substitution, ellipses, and conjunction) to achieve a unified text.

More importantly, grammar needs to be seen as a component of listening, speaking, reading, and writing tasks rather than as a separate skill. This means that the use of particular grammatical structures should be presented in the context of authentic, communicative tasks such as giving or requesting information, telling a personal story, writing an invitation, and following a set of directions. Each language learning task presented in Chapters 7 (listening), 8 (reading), 9 (speaking), and 10 (writing) provides an opportunity to examine how grammatical forms are used in purposeful communication. In other words, language tasks determine the presence of certain grammatical features. Scarcella and Oxford (1992) recommend that teachers integrate grammar instruction throughout their lessons. Such factors as pupils' language levels (novice, intermediate, advanced), communicative value, frequency and salience of the grammar forms, and importance of grammatical errors to native speakers should be taken into account.

DEVELOPING GRAMMATICAL ACCURACY

There are a number of issues associated with the teaching of grammar. Some have to do with the teaching procedures that should be used, while others have to do with the relationship between language forms used to express meanings. Eisenstein (1987) argues that it is important to consider the backgrounds and needs of the learners when making pedagogical decisions about grammar instruction. The age of learners, their learning experiences, their cognitive style, the type of language program, and the kind of grammatical rule being taught should be taken into account. These factors determine whether to use a deductive or an inductive approach, whether to include grammatical terminology, and whether to provide both oral and written forms of explanations. Eisenstein offers the following list of critical variables and their applications in ESL lessons:

1. *Explicit grammatical explanations.* No conscious explanations seem necessary with children. Conscious grammatical explanations may be useful with adults, taking into consideration their literacy levels in L1 and previous educational experiences.
2. *Isolation of grammatical rules.* Many adult learners may find conscious statements of grammar rules and structures useful, especially those who have a learning style that is analytical, form-focused.

   Form-focused instruction, according to Ellis (1990), results in explicit language knowledge that serves to sensitize learners to the existence of nonstandard usage in their emerging L2. This type of knowledge, in turn, enables learners to attend to specific linguistic features in the instructional input and then incorporates these elements into the developing L2. At the same time, learners need to be exposed to meaning-focused instruction since this type of input leads to implicit language knowledge. Both types of knowledge appear to be interdependent because control over linguistic knowledge is achieved by means of performing under real communicative conditions in meaning-focused activities. Children, on the other hand, tend to be "data gathers" and do not seem to respond to explicit grammar presentations.
3. *Inductive-deductive presentations.* Grammar presentations in the middle of a lesson allow for both inductive and deductive experiences for different types of learners. Certain grammatical structures are more suitable for deductive presentation, while others can be taught through an inductive approach.
4. *The rule explainer.* Teachers should consider giving their students the opportunity to state the rule when possible. Because of personality characteristics or cultural factors, some learners may be reluctant to do this and may use avoidance or guessing strategies.
5. *Use of grammatical terms.* Teachers should consider using grammatical terms if students are familiar with them or if it makes a concept easier to explain or use appropriately.

6. *The medium of explanation.* Both oral and written explanations should be offered to learners since different learners favor one or the other modality for language learning.

As a way to focus on the presentation of a particular grammatical feature, Ur (1988, pp. 6-10) offers an instructional sequence of four steps:

I. *Presentation.* The purpose here is to present the grammatical structure within the context of written and spoken texts. The aim is to enable the learners to perceive the structure—its form and meaning—in both speech and writing. The text can be a section from a story or a short dialogue that appears in written form and can also be read aloud by the teacher and students. Students may be asked to read aloud, repeat, reproduce from memory, or write down its use within the text.

II. *Isolation and Explanation.* This stage focuses on the grammatical items themselves. The objective here is to move away from the context and concentrate on the rules that govern the various aspects of the structure. This may require the use of the students' native language to explain, translate, or draw generalizations.

III. *Practice.* This stage might consist of a number of exercises or drills done both in the classroom and as homework assignments. This enables students to learn the structure and transfer this knowledge from short-term to long-term memory. The exercises can range from slot fillers to more-communicative drills:

    A. Slot-fillers

        The book is _____ the table. (in/on)

        He is going to eat _____ apple. (a/an)

    B. Transformation

        Singular to plural

        This is a book ⟶ These are books.

        He is a student ⟶ They are students.

    C. Integration

        This is a book. The book is red. The book is on the desk. The book is mine ⟶ The red book that is on the desk is mine.

    D. Completion (personalized)

        I like to eat _____ , _____ , and _____ .

        Mary is wearing _____ .

        This weekend I am going _____ , and _____ .

    E. Matching (form and function)

        _____ Don't be late.   a. question

        _____ I'm sorry for being late.   b. order

        _____ Why are you so late?   c. threat

        _____ I'm very sorry to be late.   d. apology

        _____ If you are late, you're going to be punished.

IV. *Assessment.* This phase can provide feedback to both student and teacher and indicate whether the structures have been mastered. The testing can include both informal (i.e., performance on practice exercises) and formal written means. To test grammatical competence, students can:

A. Select the appropriate word(s) by underlining, numbering or filling a blank on an answer sheet as in "The girl/girls are from a small town"; "They _____ (like/likes) to go the movies."
B. Answer questions such as "What time do you get up? _____."
C. Combine sentences.
D. Complete sentences.
E. Match the stimuli with possible responses.
F. Detect ungrammatical sentences within a passage.
G. Perform transformations such as active to passive, present to future, statements to questions.

The four steps that Ur recommends for presenting explicit grammatical instruction are useful in terms of a pedagogical framework. However, grammatical drills at the sentence level may not be particularly relevant to learners when they have to comprehend and produce oral or written discourse. Grammar should be seen as a tool or resource for creating meaning and texts (Celce-Murcia, 1991).

From an interactive perspective, oral grammar exercises can be created to stress the practice of language forms through group activities. Students working in pairs, for instance, can fill in blanks in dialogues, write their own dialogues based on visual cues, create dialogues based on defined situations, and conduct interviews to elicit answers to specific types of questions. They can also relate grammar points (adjectives, imperatives, prepositions) to personality types and prepare questions or statements for guessing games. Teachers, in turn, can direct their students to respond to commands using different forms (imperatives, questions as indirect commands, statements as indirect commands). Students can also complete sentences with their own personal responses (If I were the teacher, I would. . . .). Comeau (1987) recommends that interactive grammar exercises should complement rather than replace traditional exercises like the one outlined above by Ur. Exercises requiring fill-in answers, completions, transformations, or a combination of items are effective tools for language learning, particularly at the manipulative or mechanical phase. These activities can also be used in conjunction with interactive exercises that place instruction in a more meaningful, communicative mode.

DEVELOPING PRONUNCIATION ACCURACY

Pronunciation is another aspect of language associated with the accuracy issue. In the Audio-Lingual Method, techniques for teaching the pronunciation of specific sounds tended to be organized according to aural discrimination (usually of sound in the context of words as in "b*i*t," "bet," "b*a*t") and the production of individual sounds within words, phrases, and sentences. Remedial training exercises were recommended at later stages of learning. In the Communicative Approach, relatively little attention has been given to pronunciation. The question of pronunciation seems to be an important consideration in ESL instruction around the world (Hubbard et al., 1983), but many of these concerns have more to do with the choice of a standard variety or dialect of English and the limited proficiency of many nonnative teachers (Von Schon, 1987). Music and jazz chants, in particular, have been found by ESL teachers to be highly effective for dealing with word stress, intonation, and acceptable pronunciation. Unlike the Audio-Lingual Method, which usually stressed pronunciation practice out of context, songs have a topic and present sounds in context. Poetry has also been recommended as a natural language activity since the patterns of sound and word stress are often repeated in a regular sequence, making it possible for everyone to practice without appearing to be doing a mechanical drill (Maley, 1987).

Since the sound system is an integral part of language, the teaching of pronunciation should be an important consideration for the development of oral communication. Teaching pronunciation requires more than simply having students imitate the teacher. Robinett (1984) points out that students often need more direct help to achieve greater levels of accuracy. Such help might involve the use of visual aids to indicate how individual sounds are produced, specific pronunciation exercises, and practice opportunities.

The sound system of a language can be described in terms of the following categories:

1. *Phonemes*: the individual sounds of the language (consonants and vowels) that are systematically distinguished from each other (e.g., *t*in vs. *s*in)
2. *Syllabus structure*: the way in which consonants and vowels may be combined into syllables in a particular language
3. *Syllable stress*: the relative prominence given to one syllable (présent/presént)
4. *Juncture*: the manner in which sounds are connected to each other (e.g., nitrate vs. night rate)
5. *Intonation*: the rise and fall in pitch of the voice during speech production, as in these sentences:

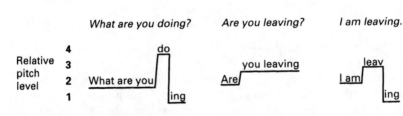

Murphy (1991) argues that pronunciation needs should be approached from the level of macro and micro subskills. At the macro level, suprasegmental features of the sound system such as stress, intonation, juncture, and rhythm should be given a primary role. Segmental features—the individual consonant and vowel sounds of the language—should be assigned a secondary or micro-level role in oral communication. Both the segmental and suprasegmental levels of the sound system, along with phenomena such as voice quality and body language, form an integrated system of various oral communication subskills.

Attainment of better pronunciation seems to be closely linked with students' affective states. Some students might actually be embarrassed if they are corrected before their peers; thus, calling attention to nonstandard speech patterns could be a counterproductive strategy (Stevick, 1978). The attainment of pronunciation accuracy might also be seen in light of the students' motivation or desire to identify (acculturate) with members of the target culture. Since pronunciation improvement seems to depend significantly on the learner, a student may have to agree to specified amounts of weekly practice in order to overcome "fossilized" nonstandard speech forms (Acton, 1984).

The teaching procedures required to develop pronunciation accuracy need both teacher and learner involvement. The teacher can plan instructional activities that call attention to segmental as well as suprasegmental levels of language. At the same time, the practice of pronunciation subskills can be linked to speaking and listening tasks. Morley (1991) outlines the following contexts for speech/pronunciation practice:

1. *Pronunciation/speech practice*, consisting of a mix of activities ranging from imitative practice (e.g., repetition exercises), rehearsed practice (guided self-practice using a script, poem, role play), and extemporaneous speaking practice (unplanned talks, question-and-answer sessions)
2. *Pronunciation-oriented listening practice*, focusing on auditory perception and identification of segmental features (vowel and consonant sounds and their combinations) and suprasegmental features (intonation, juncture, stress, tone of voice)
3. *Spelling-oriented pronunciation practice*, using cues from spelling patterns, with consistent reference to phonological information as cues to syllable stress, word blending patterns, and the use of contracted forms typical in casual speech; and from intonational patterns at the sentence level.

Learners, particularly those in adult ESL situations, can be guided toward an awareness of how speech functions and how to monitor one's own speech habits. Morley (1991) suggests that it is possible for ESL/EFL teachers who work with highly motivated students to offer strategies for self-involvement in pronunciation and speech development. Teachers can assist students in formulating pronunciation goals, establishing learning and practice tasks, developing self-monitoring skills, and defining speech modification objectives. It is important to note that the development of pronunciation accuracy is a gradual process with considerable variability among learners. Audio and/or video recordings are useful in making students aware of their speech problems and degree of change as a result of instruction and self-involvement.

According to Carruthers (1987), teachers can plan pronunciation study by anticipating the problems that students encounter in the linguistic content presented in a specific lesson or unit. These may occur at the suprasegmental and segmental levels of phonology. At the segmental level, for example, some of the problems associated with producing consonant sounds in a target language could be identified by comparing phonemic charts contrasting the differences and similarities in consonant systems of, say, English, French, German, and Spanish (see Figure 5.2).

Individual consonant sounds can be classified according to their place of articulation (bilabial, labiodental, retroflex, velar) and the manner of articulation (stop, fricatives, nasals, flap) as the airstream moves through the speech organs. German speakers do not have the /w/ phoneme, as in "*w*ater," and will likely substitute /v/ to result in "*v*ater." English speakers do not use the French uvular /r/, as in "*r*ue," and will tend to use the retroflex /r/ as in "*r*ather." English speakers do not have the trilled /R/ and will substitute the retroflex /r/ by pronouncing Spanish "pe*rr*o" (dog) as "pe*r*o" (but). Certain sound sequences may be absent in

FIGURE 5.2   Phonemic charts contrasting the consonant systems for English, French, German, and Spanish

SOURCE: Adapted from Politzer and Politzer (1972), pp. 56–57.

	Bilabial	Labio-Dental	Dental	Alveolar	Retroflex	Alveo-Palatal	Velar	Uvular	Glottal
ENGLISH stop	p, b			t, d			k, g		
affricate						č, ǰ			
fricative slit		f, v	θ, ð						h
fricative groove				s, z		ʃ, ʒ			
lateral				l					
nasal	m			n			ŋ		
semivowel	w				r	y (palatal)			

FRENCH stop	p, b		t, d				k, g		
fricative slit		f, v							
fricative groove			s, z			ʃ, ʒ			
lateral			l						
vibrant								r	
nasal	m		n			ɲ			
semivowel	w					y, ɥ			
GERMAN stop	p, b		t, d				k, g		
affricate	(pf)		(ts)			(tʃ)			
fricative slit		f, v				ç	χ		h
fricative groove			s, z			ʃ, ʒ			
lateral			l						
vibrant								R	
nasal	m		n			ŋ			
semivowel						y			
SPANISH stop	p, b		t, d				k, g		
affricate						č			
fricative slit		f	θ				χ		
fricative groove			s						
lateral			l			λ (palatal)			
nasal	m		n			ɲ			
trill		R							
flap		r							
semivowel	w					y			

FIGURE 5.2 (continued)

the learner's native language, as in the case of three-consonant sequences (C-C-C in "*street*" and "*asked*"). The Spanish speakers will have trouble producing such words as "*scroll*," "*script*," and "*spring*," in which /s/ is the first element. They will most likely add a vowel before the initial /s/, resulting in "*escroll*," "*escript*," and "*espring*.*" French admits a number of consonant sequence patterns (C-C-C as in "*spl*endide," "*scr*upule," and C-C as in "*pr*endre" and "*dr*ogue"), but the occurrence is governed by the "law of three consonants," which states that a combination of three consonants is possible only if a group of consonants remaining after omitting the first can occur in word-initial position (e.g., pe*rdre*, d*rogue*).

A second way to address pronunciation problems is to develop lessons that focus on student speech errors. Teachers can isolate problems at the level of accent, intonation, and syllable stress. Carruthers (1987) points out that pronunciation drills can be built using vocabulary and sentences from the day's lesson or the student's own speech samples. A few minutes could be devoted at the end of a class period for correcting pronunciation errors. Traditional teaching strategies such as the use of minimal pairs, articulatory charts, tongue twisters, poems, songs, and drawings or illustrations could all play a role in developing pronunciation accuracy. Minimal-pair exercises are useful for teaching individual vowel and consonant contrasts and can provide students with opportunities for recognizing and producing specific sounds. Figure 5.3 contrasts the vowel systems for English, French, German, and Spanish. The vowels are classified according to the shape of the oral cavity and the movement of the tongue from front to back and from high to low during the production of specific sounds. A discrimination drill of minimal vowel contrasts asks students to listen and indicate which of the words are the same or different:

	A	*B*	*C*	*A*	*B*	*C*
English:	*ship* / sheep / *ship*			*leave* / *leave* / live		
French:	doux / *du* / *du*			*roue* / rue / *roue*		
German:	*bitte* / *bitte* / bitter			Wette / *Wette* / *Wette*		
Spanish:	*coma* / come / *coma*			*van* / ven / *van*		

In a production exercise, students write a list of words with the same sound (vowel or consonant) in initial, medial, or final positions:

English:	/ θ /	*th*ing, pa*th*, *th*eme wi*th*, leng*th*
French:	/ e /	les, parlé, parl*ai*, n*ei*ger
German:	/ ts /	*z*um, ka*tz*e, na*t*ion, *z*u
Spanish:	/ y /	*y*o, *h*ierro, el*l*a, *ll*anto

A simple diagram or wall chart representing the speech organs might prove to be a useful teaching tool for indicating the production of individual sounds. Figure 5.4 illustrates the place of articulation for consonant sounds in English. It can be used to point out how consonant sounds are produced in French, German, and Spanish, using the sounds presented in Figure 5.2.

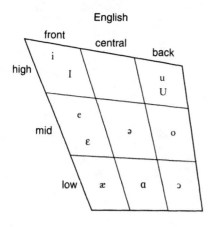

English

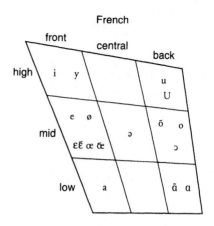

French

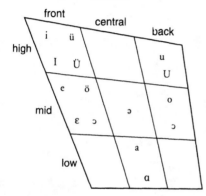

German

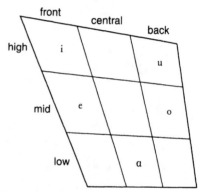

Spanish

Phonemes with Examples in Specific Languages

English		French		German		Spanish	
/i/	see	/i/	lit	/i/	Lied	/i/	dormir
/I/	hit	/y/	du	/ü/	Güte	/e/	pero
/e/	laid	/e/	les	/I/	bitte	/a/	padre
/ɛ/	bed	/ø/	peu	/Ü/	Mütter	/u/	una
/æ/	bat	/ɛ/	dette	/e/	beten	/o/	total
/ɑ/	cod	/ɛ̃/	vin	/ö/	Goethe		
/ə/	mud	/œ/	peur	/ɛ/	Bett		
/u/	move	/œ̃/	un	/ɔ̈/	Götter		
/U/	put	/a/	patte	/ə/	Rosen		
/o/	know	/ə/	le	/a/	Stadt		
/ɔ/	raw	/u/	doux	/ɑ/	Staat		
		/õ/	mon	/u/	gut		
		/o/	beau	/U/	mutter		
		/ɔ/	botte	/o/	Sohn		
		/ã/	tante	/ɔ/	Gott		
		/ɑ/	bas				

FIGURE 5.3 Phonemic charts contrasting the vowel systems for English, French, German, and Spanish

SOURCE: Based on Politzer and Politzer (1972), pp.61–62; 79–80.

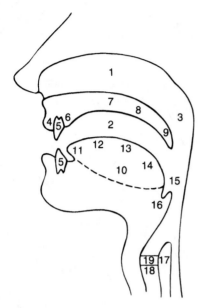

1. Nasal cavity
2. Oral cavity
3. Nasal passage
4. Lips
5. Teeth
6. Alveolae (ridge behind upper teeth)
7. Hard palate
8. Soft palate (velum)
9. Uvula
10. Tongue
11. Tip of tongue
12. Front of tongue
13. Middle of tongue
14. Back of tongue
15. Pharynx
16. Epiglottis
17. Glottis
18. Larynx
19. Vocal cords

Type of sound	Place of articulation	Examples
bilabial	lower (4) and upper lip (4)	pin, rubber, ham
labio-dental	lower lip (4) and upper teeth (5)	vat, coffee, leaf
dental	tip of tongue (11) and upper teeth (5)	thin, either, breath
alveolar	tip of tongue (11) and alveolae (6)	team, basic, mail
retroflex	tip of tongue curled back (11) and palate (7)	rather, very, far
alveo-palatal	front of tongue (12) and alveolae (6)	chin, ridge, rush
palatal	back of tongue (13/14) and back of palate (7)	yes, vignette
velar	back of tongue (14) and velum (8)	good, bigger, back
uvular	back of tongue (14) and uvula (9)	French rue
glottal	vocal cords (19)	hat, cohort

FIGURE 5.4   Place of articulation for consonant sounds

SOURCE: Adapted from Politzer and Politzer (1972), pp. 56–57.

Intonational patterns can be represented through line drawings superimposed over sentences. In English, for example, sentence patterns are often described according to four pitch levels: (1) low, (2) normal or mid, (3) high, and (4) extra-high for emphasis or contrast. The 2, 3, 1 pattern is used for most declarative sentences, requests, or commands, and *wh-* (who, what, when, where) questions (Paulston & Bruder, 1976, pp. 93-94):

1. I'm going downtown.

2. Please get me some ice cream.

3. Stop talking.

4. Where are you going?

The pattern for yes/no questions or questions with declarative word order is 2, 3, 3 (Paulston & Bruder, 1976, pp. 93-94):

1. Are you leaving?

2. Will you be here later?

3. It's time to go to bed?

Contour lines may be useful for illustrating intonational patterns and phonic groupings, as in the Spanish examples below (Azevedo, 1992, pp. 90-91):

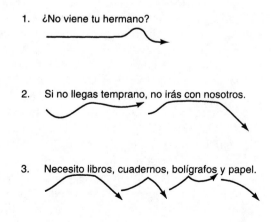

1. ¿No viene tu hermano?

2. Si no llegas temprano, no irás con nosotros.

3. Necesito libros, cuadernos, bolígrafos y papel.

Major sentence stress and word-series emphasis can be indicated through the use of boxes and bold print. The German examples below combine the use of boxes for sentence stress, bold print for words in series stress, and underlining for syllable stress (Lederer, 1969, pp. 637–638):

1.   Auf den **Straßen und Plätzen** fanden sich ⃞ viele junge Leute ⃞ ein.

2.   **Mittel und Wege** müssen zur Lösung ⃞ der Schwierigkeit ⃞ gefunden werden.

3.   Wir schenkten **dem Mädchen und dem Jungen** ein Stück ⃞ Schokolade. ⃞

Tongue twisters, songs, and poems create additional opportunities for pronunciation practice. Most tongue twisters contrast similar sounds, and some can be used to practice sentence intonational patterns (Allen & Valette, 1977, p. 68):

Spanish /rr/:   Erre con erre cigarro,
                Erre con erre barril.
                Rápido corren los carros
                Por la línea del ferrocarril.
French /ʃ/ and /s/: Un chasseur sachant chasser chasse sans chiens.
German /ʃ/ and /s/, /fr/ and /f/: Fischer frißt frische Fische.
French vowels: Didon dîna, dit-on, du dos d'un dodu dindon.
ESL /s/ and /ʃ/: She sells sea shells by the seashore.
ESL /θ/ and /ð/: What's this thing he works with? It's a lathe.

ERROR CORRECTION PROCEDURES

Teachers' corrective feedback on learner errors is seen as a way to provide students with useful information necessary to modify their transitional, developing grammatical systems. The question of which errors to correct, when to treat them, and how to correct them is an exceedingly complex matter. As Chaudron (1988) points out, the nature of teacher-pupil interaction in the L2 classroom "is perhaps the most critical issue concerning formal second language learning" (p. 152). Such instructional practices as correcting errors or providing feedback to learners may be both effective and detrimental to the development of second language proficiency. According to Vigil and Oller (1976), error correction must be optimal in order to be effective. Too much negative feedback ("No, you don't say it that way." "Will you repeat that?" and "Listen to me say it.") may lead learners to stop their attempts at communicating. Error correction may be positive, neutral, or negative depending on the particular circumstances. Students need to be assured that feedback on errors is not an indication of failure.

Hendrickson (1978), for instance, suggests correcting errors on the basis of reactions among native speakers of the target language. This would include:

1. Errors that impair communication significantly
2. Errors that have highly stigmatized effects on the listener or reader
3. Errors that recur frequently in the students' speech or writing

Walz (1982) proposed four basic considerations to keep in mind when correcting learner errors:

1. *Comprehensibility*. Correct first those errors that interfere with understanding (meaning).
2. *Frequency*. Correct the most frequently occurring errors in a consistent manner.
3. *Pedagogical forms*. Correct those errors that reflect misunderstanding or inadequate learning of current classroom instruction.
4. *Individual student concerns*. Treat errors according to the learner's abilities and reactions to feedback. Some students profit more than others with correction of errors in language forms. Others should only be corrected on errors related to meaning.

Chaudron's (1988) review of research reveals that error correction is not a major instructional activity in communicative-oriented classrooms. Actual error correction rates seem to reflect a concern for accuracy matters (grammatical errors 56%, phonological deviations 29%) rather than communicative concerns (lexical errors 11%, discourse features 8%, inappropriate context 6%). Moreover, teachers are not likely to correct the most frequent error types.

In classroom situations, teachers engage in a number of corrective feedback behaviors, ranging from ignoring the problem to correcting specific errors or calling on a student who knows the answer. Table 5.2 includes a list of typical corrective behaviors that occur during teacher-centered lessons. These forms of correction usually involve different types of modification of original student utterances (reduction, expansion, repetition). These are intended to signal an error that should be corrected. However, the alternatives might be perceived as other ways of expressing the same meaning since teacher "acceptances," "approvals," and "repeats without corrections" are frequent in classroom teacher talk.

It is important to remember that error correction does not necessarily lead to student improvement in accuracy levels. Teaching behaviors such as correction, questioning, and formal explanation may have a positive influence with some learners in certain situations. Ellis (1990) believes that there are grounds for concluding that form-focused instruction helps the acquisition of linguistic competence (grammatical and phonological accuracy). Instruction can promote conscious knowledge of linguistic features that, in turn, may reduce the fossilization of nonstandard language forms. Van Patten (1992) also concludes that classroom learners tend to acquire higher proficiency levels and have greater accuracy in

TABLE 5.2 Examples of features and types of teachers' corrective reactions

Features or Type of "Act" (F and/or T)	Description	Example of Exponent of Expression
Ignore (F)	Teacher ignores Student's ERROR, goes on to other topic, or shows ACCEPTANCE of content.	
Interrupt (F)	T interrupts S utterance (ut.) following ERROR, or before S has completed.	
Delay (F)	T waits for S to complete ut. before correcting. (Usually not coded, because INTERRUPT is "marked")	
Acceptance (T)	Simple approving or accepting word (usually as sign of reception of ut.), but T may immediately correct a linguistic ERROR.	Bon, oui, bien, d'accord
Attention (T, F)	Attention-getter; probably quickly learned by Ss.	Euhh, regarde, attention, allez, mais.
Negation (T, F)	T shows rejection of part or all of S ut.	Non, ne . . . pas
Provide (T)	T provides the correct answer when S has been unable or when no response is offered.	S: Cinquante, uh . . . T: Pour cent.
Reduction (F)	T ut. employs only a segment of S ut.	S: Vee, eee . . . (spelling) T: Vé . . . c.
Expansion (F)	T adds more linguistic material to S ut., possibly making more complete.	S: Et c'est bien. T: Ils ont pensé que c'etait bien?
Repeat (T)	T requests S to repeat ut., with intent to have S self-correct.	
Repeat (implicit)	Procedures are understood that by pointing or otherwise signaling, T can have S repeat.	
Transfer (T)	T asks another S, or several, or class, to provide correction.	

SOURCE: "A Descriptive Model of Discourse in the Corrective Treatment of Learners' Errors" by Craig Chaudron, 1977, *Language Learning, 27*, pp. 38–39. Reprinted with permission.

performance than their nonclassroom peers. Nevertheless, correcting errors in learner output has a negligible effect on the developing language system of most learners. Explicit grammar instruction does not seem to alter the natural route of acquisition. Explicit grammar instruction generally results in temporary gains unless the learner is psycholinguistically ready for such instruction.

From a learner perspective, students can be made aware of their role in the acquisition process. Students can learn to use a broad range of strategies involving such behaviors as planning, self-monitoring, problem identification, repetition, questioning, and collaboration. These strategies are discussed more fully in Chapter 6.

Omaggio (1986) offers a number of self-correction strategies that learners can engage in with the teacher's help. These range from pinpointing an error to renegotiating for an acceptable response (Figure 5.5). These strategies represent a col-

1. *Pinpointing.* The teacher localizes the error without providing the correct form by repeating the student's response up to the point at which the error is made, hesitating, and exaggerating the last word a little with a rising intonation:

   S: Demain, je vais aller à le supermarché.
   T: Je vais aller . . .
   S: Je vais aller au supermarché.

   S: Yo veo mi amigo.
   T: Yo veo . . .
   S: Yo veo mi amigo.

2. *Rephrasing the question.* The teacher rephrases the question to a fewer number of words or simpler format if the student fails to understand:

   T: Warum ist er denn so spät nach Hause gekommen: (*Why did he come home so late?*)
   S: Uh . . . (*hesitates*)
   T: Warum kommt er spät? (*Why is he late?*)

3. *Cuing.* Instead of supplying the correct answer, the teacher provides some options for the incorrect or missing element, as in an oral multiple choice:

   T: When did you come to this part of the United States?
   S: I . . . I . . . (hesitates over the verb form)
   T: Come, came, have come . . .
   S: I came last year.

4. *Explaining a key word.* The teacher may write a difficult word on the board or act it out if it seems to be the source of confusion or hesitation on the part of the student:

   T: D'où viens tu?
   S: (*No response*)
   T: (*Writes d'où in the board*)
   S: Oh! Je viens du Kentucky.

   T: ¿Sabe Ud. conducir un coche?
   S: (*No response*)
   T: (*Gestures with hands on an imaginary steering wheel*)
   S: Oh, sí! Yo sé conducir un coche.

5. *Questioning.* If the student uses a word that the teacher does not understand, the teacher may want to ask futher questions to elicit the meaning more clearly from further contextual support:

   S: I would like to study (*incomprehensible word*).
   T: Oh, why would you like to study that?
   S: I like to help people.
   T: How do you think that will help them?
   S: If I help them, they can see better.
   T: Yes, being an optometrist is a good chioce.

6. *Providing your own answer.* In this technique, the teacher cues the student by providing his or her own answer to the question, supplying a model:

   T: Qu'est-ce que tu vas faire ce week-end?
   S: Uh, j'aller . . . (*hesitates*)
   T: Moi, je vais voir un film avec un ami.
   S: Je vais au resaturant avec mes amis.

(continued)

FIGURE 5.5 Student self-correction strategies with teacher's help

SOURCE: From *Teaching Language in Context* (pp. 295–297) by Alice C. Omaggio, 1986. Boston: Heinle & Heinle. Reprinted with permission.

7. *Repetition of answer, with correction.* Without making an overt correction, the teacher repeats the student's response, subtly correcting the mistake. Some students will pick this up, while others may not notice:

T: Avez-vous des disques de rock?
S: Non, je n'ai pas des disques.
T: Oh, tu n'as pas de disques. As-tu des cassettes?
S: Non, je n'ai pas de cassettes.

8. *Rephrasing a question, after a formally correct, but inappropriate response to the original formulation:*

T: When are you leaving for vacation?
S: I am going to Florida.
T: Oh, that's nice! But when are you leaving? Monday, Tuesday . . .?
S: I am leaving on Sunday.

FIGURE 5.5 (continued)

laborative effort between teacher and student and tend to be more communicative in nature. Language forms are negotiated through the use of such conversational strategies as hesitation, questioning, cuing, and rephrasing.

SUMMARY

Teaching methods differ in their views of language, the learning process, the roles assigned to students and teachers, and the selection of specific instructional techniques. Some confusion exists in the use of terms such as method, approach, procedure, and curriculum models. Methods described as Grammar Translation, Direct, Reading, Structural, Audio-Lingual, Situational, and Functional-Notional have different language learning goals and ways of structuring classroom activities. More recent approaches with a communicative orientation include the Dartmouth Intensive Model, Comprehension Approach, Total Physical Response, Natural Approach, Silent Way, Community Language Learning, and Suggestopedia. Some of these approaches incorporate insights from second language acquisition research and address both cognitive and affective issues. In general, the term *approach* is used to refer to the theoretical basis or set of principles that determine the method for presenting and teaching the language. Teaching techniques are the individual instructional strategies used to implement a methodology. How different sets of teaching activities are used in the learning sequence distinguishes more accurately the implementation of one method from another.

The selection of particular teaching techniques is conditioned by such issues as program goals, learner characteristics, teaching methodology, and local resources. A task-oriented perspective offers a framework for relating teaching techniques or procedures to both learning objectives and language content. Specific examples are presented in later chapters for listening situations (Chapter 7), reading contexts (Chapter 8), speaking activities (Chapter 9), and writing tasks (Chapter 10).

Grammar instruction needs to be addressed in terms of the uses of language forms in listening, speaking, reading, and writing situations. The teaching of grammatical forms should be guided by concerns about the type of learner, the means for rule explication or presentation, the range of contexts for practice, and the relationship to meaning-focused activities. The development of pronunciation accuracy should be approached from both macro-level features (intonation, stress, juncture, and rhythm) and micro-level, segmental elements (individual consonant and vowel sounds). Pronunciation practice can occur as speech rehearsal (repetition, guided practice, unplanned talk), listening-oriented training (auditory perception and identification of segmental and suprasegmental features), and spelling-oriented experience (orthographic information as cues to syllable stress, word blending patterns, and intonational sequences). Learners play an important role in the development of both grammatical and phonological accuracy since both aspects of linguistic competence require a significant level of personal involvement and commitment.

Error correction is a critical issue that affects instructional practices. Some teaching behaviors, such as overt corrections, questions, repetitions, and expansions, may not be effective unless most students are psycholinguistically ready for such feedback. Instruction can promote conscious awareness of specific linguistic features, and learners can profit from such strategies as self-monitoring, problem identification, and collaboration.

ACTIVITIES

1. Observe a language classroom and characterize it in terms of (1) the assumptions about second language learning, (2) teacher and learner roles, and (3) the kinds of instructional activities utilized.
2. What do you think of Richards's definition of methodology in language teaching? Compare your opinions with those of other students.
3. Read more about various teaching methods as described by one of the authors mentioned (e.g., Kelly, Oller & Richard-Amato, Richards & Rodgers, Larsen-Freeman, or Finocchiaro & Brumfit), and compare two teaching approaches with respect to design and procedure.
4. Consider the usefulness of such approaches as Suggestopedia, Counseling-Learning, and Total Physical Response. When can they be used most appropriately to teach various aspects of language?
5. Review one of the many books recommended in this chapter that offer numerous examples of different kinds of instructional techniques. Which techniques do you find easiest to implement in regular classroom situations? Which techniques would require special preparation of materials?
6. How useful do you find Nuessel's framework for supplementing the use of teaching techniques in a meaningful, organized manner?
7. Interview a teacher to determine on what basis he or she selects different teaching techniques for various lessons.

8. Using Ur's four-stage framework for teaching grammar, outline the presentation of one grammatical aspect to a specific group of learners.
9. Collect an oral language sample from a student. Identify some of the major phonological problems in the vowels, consonants, stress, and juncture. Outline some pronunciation exercises to correct the major speech errors using techniques recommended by Carruthers.
10. What are your notions about error correction? Compare your opinion with those of other students.
11. Interview several teachers to ascertain their philosophy about grammar and the role it should play in relation to listening, speaking, reading, and writing abilities. Do they all share the same ideas?
12. Observe a language classroom to determine the teacher's error correction policy. What and how are errors corrected? Does the teacher's plan correspond to the considerations proposed by Hendrickson or Walz?

REFERENCES

Acton, W. (1984). Changing fossilized pronunciation. *TESOL Quarterly*, *18*(1), 71–86.

Allen, E. D., & Valette, R. (1977). *Classroom techniques: Foreign languages and English as a second language*. New York: Harcourt Brace Jovanovich.

Asher, J. (1982). *Learning another language through actions: The complete teacher's guidebook* (2nd ed.). Los Gatos, CA: Sky Oaks Productions.

Azevedo, M. M. (1992). *Introducción a la lingüística española*. Englewood Cliffs, NJ: Prentice-Hall.

Birckbichler, D. W. (1982). *Creative activities for the second language classroom*. Washington, DC: Center for Applied Linguistics.

Bowen, J. D., Madsen, H., & Hilferty, A. (1985). *TESOL techniques and procedures*. New York: Newbury House.

Carruthers, R. (1987). Teaching pronunciation. In M. H. Long & J. C. Richards (Eds.), *Methodology in TESOL* (pp. 191–200). New York: Harper & Row (Newbury House).

Celce-Murcia, M. (1991). Grammar pedagogy in second and foreign language teaching, *TESOL Quarterly*, *25*(3), 459–480.

Chastain, K. (1987). Examining the role of grammar explanation, drill, and exercises in the development of communication skills. *Hispania*, *70*(1), 160–166.

Chastain, K. (1988). *Developing second-language skills: Theory and practice* (3rd ed.). New York: Harcourt Brace Jovanovich.

Chaudron, C. (1977). A description model of discourse in the corrective treatment of learners' errors. *Language Learning*, *27*, 29–46.

Chaudron, C. (1985). Comprehension, comprehensibility, and learning in the second language classroom. *Studies in second language acquisition*, *7*(2), 216–232.

Chaudron, C. (1988). *Second language classrooms*. Cambridge, England: Cambridge University Press.

Comeau, R. (1987). Interactive oral grammar exercises. In W. M. Rivers (Ed.), *Interactive language teaching* (pp. 57–69). Cambridge, England: Cambridge University Press.

Curran, C. (1976). *Counseling-learning in second languages*. Apple River, IL: Apple River Press.

Eisenstein, M. R. (1987). Grammatical explanations in ESL: Teach the student, not the method. In M. H. Long & J. C. Richards (Eds.), *Methodology in TESOL* (pp. 282-292). New York: Harper & Row (Newbury House).

Ellis, R. (1990). *Instructed second language acquisition*. Oxford: Basil Blackwell.

Finocchiaro, M., & Brumfit, C. (1983). *The functional-notional approach: From theory to practice*. Oxford: Oxford University Press.

Frisby, A. W. (1957). *Teaching English: Notes and comments on teaching English overseas*. London: Longman.

Garrett, N. (1986). The problem with grammar: What kind can the language learner use? *Modern Language Journal, 70*(2), 133-148.

Gattegno, C. (1976). *The common sense of foreign language teaching*. New York: Educational Solutions.

Guntermann, G., & Phillips, J. K. (1982). *Functional-notional concepts: Adapting the FL text-book* (Language in Education: Theory and Practice, Vol. 44). Washington, DC: Center for Applied Linguistics.

Hammond, R. M. (1988). Accuracy versus communicative competence: The acquisition of grammar in the second language classroom. *Hispania, 71*(2), 408-417.

Hendrickson, J. M. (1978). Error correction in foreign language teaching: Recent theory, research, and practice. *Modern Language Journal, 62*, 387-398.

Higgs, T. V. (1985). Teaching grammar for proficiency. *Foreign Language Annals, 18*, 289-296.

Higgs, T. V., & Clifford, R. (1982). The push towards communication. In C. James (Ed.), *Curriculum, competence, and the foreign language teacher* (pp. 57-78). Lincolnwood, IL: National Textbook.

Hubbard, P., Jones, H., Thornton, B., & Wheeler, R. (1983). *A training course for TEFL*. Oxford: Oxford University Press.

Kelly, L. G. (1969). *Twenty-five centuries of language teaching*. New York: Newbury House.

Krashen, S. D., & Terrell, T. D. (1983). *The natural approach: Language acquisition in the classroom*. Oxford: Pergamon Press.

Larsen-Freeman, D. (1986). *Techniques and principles in language teaching*. Oxford: Oxford University Press.

Larsen-Freeman, D. (1987). From unity to diversity: Twenty-five years of language teaching methodology. *English Language Teaching Forum, 25*(4), 2-10.

Lederer, H. (1969). *Reference grammar of the German language*. New York: Charles Scribner's Sons.

Lozanov, G. (1982). Suggestology and suggestopedia. In R. W. Blair (Ed.), *Innovative approaches to language teaching* (pp. 146-159). New York: Newbury House.

Macdonald, M., & Rogers-Gordon, S. (1984). *Action plans*. Rowley, MA: Newbury House.

Magnan, S. S. (1988). Grammar and the ACTFL oral proficiency interview: Discussion and data. *Modern Language Journal, 72*(3), 266-276.

Maley, A. (1987). Poetry and song as effective language-learning activities. In W. M. Rivers (Ed.), *Interactive language teaching* (pp. 93-109). Cambridge, England: Cambridge University Press.

Morley, J. (1991). The pronunciation component in teaching to speakers of other languages. *TESOL Quarterly, 25*(3), 481-520.

Moskowitz, G. (1978). *Caring and sharing in the foreign language class*. New York: Newbury House.

Murphy, J. M. (1991). Oral communication in TESOL: Integrating speaking, listening, and pronunciation. *TESOL Quarterly, 25*(1), 51-75.

Nelson, G., & Winters, T. (1980). *ESL operations: Techniques for learning while doing*. New York: Newbury House.

Nuessel, F. (1989). Selected enrichment techniques for the second language classroom. *Canadian Modern Language Review, 45*(2), 294-317.

Nunan, D. (1989). *Designing tasks for the communicative classroom*. Cambridge, England: Cambridge University Press.

Oller, J. W., Jr., & Richard-Amato, P. A. (Eds.). (1983). *Methods that work: A smorgasbord of ideas for language teachers*. New York: Newbury House.

Omaggio, A. C. (1986). *Teaching language in context*. Boston, MA: Heinle & Heinle.

Pattison, P. (1987). *Developing communication skills*. Cambridge, England: Cambridge University Press.

Paulston, C. B., & Bruder, M. N. (1976). *Teaching English as a second language: Techniques and procedures*. Cambridge, MA: Winthrop.

Penfield, J. (1987). *The media: Catalysts for communicative language learning*. Reading, MA: Addison-Wesley.

Politzer, R. L., & Politzer, F. N. (1972). *Teaching English as a second language*. Lexington: MA: Xerox College Publishing.

Postovsky, V. A. (1982). Delayed oral practice. In R. W. Blair (Ed.), *Innovative approaches to language teaching* (pp. 67-76). New York: Newbury House.

Rassias, J. A. (1983). New dimensions in language training: The Dartmouth College experiment. In J. W. Oller, Jr., & P. A. Richard-Amato (Eds.), *Methods that work: A smorgasbord of ideas for language teachers* (pp. 363-374). New York: Newbury House.

Richards, J. C. (1990). *The language teaching matrix*. Cambridge, England: Cambridge University Press.

Richards, J. C., & Rodgers, T. S. (1986). *Approaches and methods in language teaching*. Cambridge, England: Cambridge University Press.

Rivers, W. M. (1986): Comprehension and production in interactive language teaching. *Modern Language Journal, 70*(1), 1-7.

Robinett, B. W. (1984). Simple classroom techniques for teaching pronunciation. In *Teaching English as a second language: Perspectives and practices* (pp. 111-119). Albany, NY: State Education Department.

Sadow, S. A. (1982). *Idea bank: creative activities for the language class*. Rowley, MA: Newbury House.

Scarcella, R. C., & Oxford, R. L. (1992). *The tapestry of language learning*. Boston, MA: Heinle & Heinle.

Stevick, E. W. (1978). Toward a practical philosophy of pronunciation: Another view. *TESOL Quarterly, 12*(2), 145-150.

Terrell, T. D. (1982). The natural approach to language teaching: An update. *Modern Language Journal, 70*, 121-132.

Ur, P. (1988). *Grammar practice activities: A practice guide for teachers*. Cambridge, England: Cambridge University Press.

Van Patten, B. (1992). Second language acquisition research and foreign language teaching, Part 2. *ADFL Bulletin, 23*(3), 23-27.

Vigil, N., & Oller, J. (1976). Rule fossilization: A tentative model. *Language Learning, 26*, 281-295.

Von Schon, C. V. (1987). The question of pronunciation. *English Language Teaching Forum, 25*(4), 22-27.

Walz, J. C. (1982). *Error correction techniques for the foreign language classroom*. Washington, DC: Center for Applied Linguistics.

Winitz, H. (Ed.). (1981). *The comprehensive approach to foreign language instruction.* New York: Newbury House.

Wright, A. (1989). *Pictures for language learning.* Cambridge, England: Cambridge University Press.

Wright, A., Betteridge, D., & Buckby, M. (1984). *Games for language learning* (rev. ed.). Cambridge, England: Cambridge University Press.

chapter 6

Differences among Language Learners

Within the microsociety of the classroom, learners will vary in the ways they react to and interact with teachers and other students, as well as with learning tasks. These social preferences reflect various manifestations of inward (self) or outward (other) direction and derive from the interaction of cognitive, personality, and affective learner variables. Students will thus display distinctly different constellations and degrees of such traits as independence, responsibility, competitiveness, risk-taking tendency, and initiative as demonstrated by varying needs for attention, direction, structure, freedom, and praise. Some of these behaviors and needs may vary from one situation to another.

V. Galloway and A. Labarca, 1990

The role that learner characteristics play in the process of second language acquisition is not fully understood nor comprehensive at this time. Personality traits, learning styles, learning strategies, attitudes, and motivation appear to be important variables that have a direct bearing on how learners respond to different instructional activities, and that can influence the ultimate learning outcomes. Learners utilize a number of strategies—analogy, generalization, transfer, simplification—in the process of acquisition. Similarly, they make use of various communication strategies to convey meaning even with a limited command of the second language. Determining the learner's attitudes toward learning activities, preferred learning styles and strategies, and how they characterize effective teaching are important questions that need to be asked when analyzing language programs.

This chapter examines the role of learner differences in second language acquisition. Some of the issues raised have to do with the following questions:

1. How can one characterize second language learning?
2. What are some of the major processes involved in second language learning?
3. What role do learning styles play in the acquisition process?
4. What types of learning strategies are used by learners?
5. What types of communication strategies do learners use to compensate for an imperfect knowledge of the target language?
6. What role do attitudes, motivation, and anxiety play in second language learning?

LANGUAGE LEARNING

The learning of a second language can be affected by a multitude of factors. According to Izzo (1981), they can be grouped into three broad categories: personal (age, psychological traits, attitudes, motivation, learning strategies), situational (setting, instructional approaches, teacher characteristics), and linguistic aspects (differences between the first and second languages with respect to such features as pronunciation, grammar, discourse patterns).

These factors, in turn, have been described by various theoretical models attempting to explain what aspects of the second language are acquired, how they are acquired, and why are they acquired. Schumann's (1978) acculturation model includes such cognitive processes as imitation, generalization, inference, and memory, which all influence *how* the second language is acquired, and initiating factors that focus on *why* the process takes place. This also involves the degree of social and psychological distance between the learner and the target language culture, along with the learner's language attitudes, motivation, and degree of anxiety.

Gardner's (1979) social psychological model emphasizes the social conditions under which the second language is learned. Individual differences (the role of intelligence, language, aptitude, motivation, learning anxiety) can interact with social conditions and instructional factors, resulting in differential learning outcomes. The framework proposed by Dulay, Burt, and Krashen (1982) attempts to account for variation in the learner's verbal performance by postulating an "internal processing" mechanism that affects the type of "input" the learner processes from the language environment. Based on certain learner characteristics (age, personality traits, past language experience, and proficiency level in the first language) and involvement of the socioaffective "filter" (self-confidence, motivation, language learning anxiety), the student subconsciously processes and "organizes" linguistic data, which can then be "edited" by monitorlike conscious knowledge that acts on the verbal output. McLaughlin (1987) describes the acquisition process from a cognitive perspective. Language learning is the acquisition of a complex cognitive skill involving various tasks that must be practiced until they are automatized. Internal representations based on the language system are constantly restructured as learners gain control over the procedures for selecting appropriate vocabulary, grammatical rules, and pragmatic conventions regulating language use in different situations.

ACQUISITION PROCESSES

Learners are actively involved in the language learning process. Instead of merely repeating and imitating what they hear, they are engaged in developing an internal rule system, an interim grammar that approximates the target language in successive stages. This language has been referred to as *interlanguage* (Selinker, 1974), which can be located on a continuum between the mother tongue and the target language. Many of the "errors" (deviations from the target language norms) committed by learners are systematic in nature. These errors can be classified according to global categories (Corder, 1971): addition ("Does can she swim?" for "Can she swim?"), omission ("He not home" for "he is not at home"), substitution ("Did you cook the cake?" for "Did you bake the cake?"), and word order ("He to the movies went" for "He went to the movies").

Each error type can be considered within the different levels of language: phonology/orthography, lexicon, grammar, and discourse. Thus, the substitution of "cook" for "bake" represents a problem at the level of lexicon, while the word-order confusion of "He to the movies went" affects the grammaticality of the sentence. The source of an error can be described in terms of native-language transfer ("interlingual" errors) or errors made in the process of second language learning ("intralingual" errors), often similar to what children produce while learning their mother tongue, involving overgeneralization and simplification strategies.

Overgeneralization errors result from application of a previously available rule to a new situation where the rule does not apply, as in "John/Mary/He/She eats" becoming "I eats," or "I climbed/jumped/traveled" to "I goed/swimmed/singed."

Simplification strategies can involve the omission of certain semantic or propositional elements of a sentence, as in "She walking" (agent + action process) or "She class" (agent + destination) for "She is walking to class" (agent + action process + destination). The learner's omission of "walking," the verb form used to express ongoing action, or "to class," the adverbial phrase needed to denote destination, may reflect the limited linguistic resources available in the early stages of second language acquisition (Ellis, 1982; 1984). Simplification can also involve the omission of form words ("Is teacher" for "He is a teacher") and affixes ("She play chess" for "she plays chess").

Figure 6.1 provides a number of examples involving overgeneralization and transfer errors in English, French, and German. It should be noted that the source of some errors may not always be clear. The use of the expression *J'ai parti* instead of *Je suis parti*, as produced by an English speaker, could be seen as a transfer error (the English *have*-plus-past-participle rule, as in "I have gone") or an overgeneralized use of the French rule for forming the perfect tense with *avoir*, as in *J'ai fini*. At the same time, both types of errors could be seen as different forms of simplification. The utterance "No want go" for "I don't want to go" could be seen as a transfer error from Spanish *no quiero ir* as well as an example of redundancy reduction by omitting certain linguistic elements. Trying to identify the exact source of errors is not easy, since some of them may be "mistakes" (nonsystematic errors due to lapses in memory or slips of the tongue) while others may be the

Overgeneralization Errors in English

1 We are not knowing the rules. (Overgeneralized use of the rule for forming progressives.)
2 This shows that how sensitive he is. (Overgeneralized use of *that* for introducing a noun clause.)
3 Who can Angela sees? (Overgeneralized third-person ending.)
4 Who did write this book? (Overgeneralization of the rule for inserting *do* into interrogatives.)
5 You are not expected to make noise here. (*Noise* is classed as 'unaccountable' so a is omitted.)

Overgeneralization Errors in French

1 J'entends quelqu'un frappe à la porte. (Third-person verb form used after *quelqu'un*, but the infinitive is needed here)
2 Il fait du beau jour. (Compare *Il fait du soleil*, etc.)
3 Vous avez gagné une voiture nouvelle rouge. (The rule that places most adjectives after their noun is overgeneralized to *nouvelle*)
4 Peux-je il téléphoner? (Overgeneralized use of *peux* and *il*)
5 Vous disez votre père n'est pas ici. (*Disez* would be the expected form by analogy: cf. *lisons/lisez* and others. This sentence also contains an example of transfer—see next section.)

Overgeneralization Errors in German

1 Julia habe gern das Land. (Overgeneralized use of first person singular verb ending)
2 Wir haben Tischtennis gespielen. (Past participle formed on the pattern of many irregular verbs)
3 Da war eine Party und war ich spät nach Hause. (Inversion of subject and verb is inappropriate after *und*.)
4 Ich habe nach Hause um halb eins gekommen. (Past tense formation with *haben* overgeneralized to *kommen*, which requires *sein*)
5 Dann ein Polizeiauto entlang die Strasse komme. (Several errors, including overgeneralized first person singular verb and overgeneralized use of a rule placing the main verb at the end of a subordinate, not main, clause.)

Transfer Errors among Italian- and German-Speaking Learners of English
1 We think to come by car. (Italian construction after *pensare* transferred to English)
2 It's a long time she helps me with the home. (Use of Italian comstruction for expressing duration from the past into the present)
3 I promised it to you at the telephone. (German: *am Telefon*)
4 David always fools so much about. (*About* placed at the end of the clause like German 'separable prefix')
5 Jan sleeps long. (Tense and adverb as in German: Jan schläft lange.)

Transfer Errors among English-Speaking Learners of French

1 Puis-je aider vous? (English position for object pronoun)
2 Je suis fait mon devoir. (Attempt to form a 'present continuous' tense on the pattern of English)
3 Je vais et ouvre la porte. (Compare *I go and open* . . .)
4 Elle montre Madame Rouchon les exemples. (Two unmarked objects can follow English *show* but not French *montre*)
5 Je suis pardon. (Compare English *I am sorry*)

Transfer Errors among English-Speaking Learners of German

1 Heute er findet eine Spinne. (English word order)
2 Ich war gerade gehen in der Café. (Compare English: *I was just going* . . .)
3 Unsere Familie fahren auf dem Lande. (English, but not German, allows a plural verb after *family*)
4 Warst du da alles Abend? (Compare English: *all evening*)
5 Er bekam sehr zornig. (Compare English: *He became* . . .)

FIGURE 6.1 Examples of overgeneralization and transfer errors in English, French, and German

SOURCE: From *Foreign and Second Language Learning: Language Acquisition Research and Its Implications for the Classroom* (pp. 24–27) by William T. Littlewood, 1984, Cambridge, England: Cambridge University Press. Reprinted with permission.

result of formal instruction or the learner's personality, motivation for learning, and learning styles.

Some learner errors might be explained on the basis of a "natural" route of language development. Ellis (1985), for example, notes that there is sufficient evidence to show that L2 learners follow a particular order of acquisition for specific linguistic features, such as negatives, interrogatives, and syntactic structures. In the area of *wh-* questions (who, what, when, where, how constructions in English), Hatch (1983) notes the following sequence among ESL learners: (1) the *wh-* word is placed at the beginning of the question and is followed by declarative word order (Where he is?); (2) the *be* verb form is placed before the subject (Where is he?); (3) the *be* verb form is placed correctly in *wh-* questions, and the *do* support form appears in yes-or-no questions (Do you know him?), followed by its incorporation in *wh-* questions (Where does she live?).

Developmental stages have also been observed for such features as negation, word order, pluralization, tense and aspect, determiners, and possessives (Ellis, 1985). To characterize the so-called natural route of second language acquisition (SLA), Ellis (1984) has proposed four broad stages of development based on a number of longitudinal studies. The first stage consists of standard word order along with the omission of sentence constituents (No want go; Me house; Where you go?). In the next stage of development, the learner begins to vary the word order in accordance with L2 language norms (I not want to go; This my house; Where you are going?). The third stage of development is characterized by systematic and meaningful use of grammatical morphemes (*do* support form: I don't want to go; *be* form in declaratives: This is my house; *be* form in *wh-* questions: Where are you going?). The fourth stage reflects the use of complex sentence structures such as embedded *wh-* questions (I don't know where they live; Tell me why I need to do this now) and relative clauses modifying the main subject of the sentence (The man who is wearing a gray raincoat is from France). Ellis emphasizes the fact that the stages of development are not clearly delineated and, at times, appear to fuse various features during the same period. Furthermore, there are individual differences due to learner characteristics (age, learning styles, personality traits, motivation, attitudes) and the social context of learning. Wong-Fillmore's research (1976), for example, stresses the importance of social factors in SLA. The learner has to establish a social relationship with an interlocutor in order to have access to L2 input and develop language proficiency. Hatch (1978) argues in her discourse theory of SLA that syntactic development grows out of conversations between interlocutors. The conversational strategies used to negotiate meaning and the resulting adjusted speech influence both the rate and route that SLA will follow. Social interactions do provide the learner with excellent linguistic data to work with, but there are a number of psychological processes involved, including memory, cognitive styles, and information processing strategies.

At any given time a learner's interlanguage is the manifestation of a complex system of linguistic rules. The interlanguage of some L2 learners evolves and eventually approximates the system used by native speakers. However, there are cases in which L2 speakers reach a plateau or a fossilization of interlanguage structures, thus failing to reach target language norms. It is not uncommon to hear some members of immigrant groups speak with marked accents and produce ungrammatical sentences. Affective factors such as attitudes toward the L1 and L2, personality characteristics (shyness, high level of anxiety, low self-esteem), ethnocentrism, and motivational orientations appear to be crucial in determining the proficiency level reached in L2 (Brown, 1981). Learner differences go beyond individual characteristics such as age, personality, sex, cognitive style, and motivation. There could be significant group differences in terms of cultural needs and expectations (Ashworth, 1985). Members of ethnolinguistic minority groups might have specific linguistic, social, and economic reasons for learning a second language (e.g., Mexican Americans learning English in the United States, Turkish guest workers in Germany, Moroccans learning French). Members from language majority groups might learn a second language to fulfill an educational requirement, increase career options, or obtain a better understanding of an interdependent world.

Learners from language minority groups may experience identity problems and suffer the loss of first language skills as they add a second language to their linguistic repertoire. The cultural beliefs of a community regarding the relative use of L2 learning could greatly influence linguistic outcomes. In addition, the nature of interethnic contact can also affect L2 development, particularly among immigrant and language minority groups. Meisel (1980) has proposed that guest workers in Germany who have a segregative social orientation are more likely to fossilize than integrative learners who seek leisure contact and maintain positive interethnic contacts with German speakers. Along the same lines, Richards (1972) has argued that it might be difficult for persons of certain ethnolinguistic groups to learn the language of the dominant social class if membership in the host group is restricted. He points out that German Americans, who, unlike Puerto Ricans, do not live in linguistic ghettoes, tend to learn English with relative ease and attain high levels of L2 proficiency. Moreover, the German interference present in their English does not appear to result in obvious social discrimination. The case of the Puerto Ricans illustrates, to a certain extent, the linguistic impact that economic and social structures have on the acquisition process and level of L2 proficiency. Ma and Herasimchuk (1968) have observed that many members of the Puerto Rican community in New York City interact with each other using both English and Spanish far more frequently than they communicate with members of the surrounding English-speaking, monolingual community. Given this situation, speakers generate their own bilingual norms of correctness for both L1 and L2.

LEARNING STYLES

Individuals differ in the way they learn the same content. Every person has a learning style, that is, a composite of personal characteristics, environmental and perceptual preferences, cognitive orientation, and social needs (Galloway & Labarca, 1990). Learning style encompasses cognitive, affective, and physiological traits that are relatively stable indicators of how learners perceive, interact with, and respond to the learning environment (Keefe, 1979, p. 4). Many different learning styles can exist within one classroom, and teaching styles match some learning styles better than others.

Papalia (1986) developed an individual-differences inventory to determine how students in high schools process information and approach language tasks. The questionnaire presented in Figure 6.2 assesses seven aspects: (1) cognitive styles, (2) sensory modes, (3) interactive learning modes, (4) work habits, (5) personal traits, (6) intellectual dependence, and (7) intellectual independence and originality. The instrument, developed in collaboration with foreign language practitioners, enables the teacher to diagnose students' learning styles and plan instructional changes accordingly.

FIGURE 6.2   Individual differences inventory

SOURCE: From "Avoid Malpractice: An Individual-Differences Inventory" by Anthony Papalia, 1986, *Language Association Bulletin*, pp. 21–22. Reprinted with permission.

Use the following scale to assess students' behaviors:
1   Never
2   Rarely
3   Occasionally
4   Often
5   Very frequently

Cognitive styles

Proceeds from specific to general (inductive)   _____
Proceeds from general to specifics (deductive)   _____
Uses examples of nonpersonal and abstract thinking   _____
Uses examples of personal and concrete experiences   _____
Learns step by step   _____

Sensory modes

Learns best by acting out dialogue (role-playing)   _____
Learns best by seeing   _____
Learns best by listening   _____
Learns best by touching   _____
Learns best by using a combination of senses   _____

Interactive learning modes

Learns best in one-to-one situations   _____
Learns best in small-group work   _____
Learns best by working alone at own rate   _____
Learns best in large-group structured lecture   _____
Adapts well to any grouping situation   _____

Work habits

Has work well organized   _____
Turns in assignments on time   _____
Has tolerance for disliked tasks   _____

The learning-style questionnaire in Figure 6.3 developed by Reid (1987) identifies students' preferred learning styles with respect to four basic perceptual learning modalities: (1) visual (reading, studying charts), (2) auditory (listening to lectures, audiotapes), (3) kinesthetic learning (physical involvement with the learning situation), and (4) tactile (constructing models, doing laboratory experiments). Identification of learning styles should be approached with caution. There are dangers associated with misuse of learning-style information and the resulting instructional prescriptions. Students might be stereotyped on the basis of responses on a questionnaire that may not be a reliable assessment instrument. Students might not self-report accurately what they actually do during specific learning tasks, or they might report their "adapted" preferences as a result of instructional practices rather than preferred learning styles. The instruments themselves are exclusive since they focus on some aspects and leave out others. It appears that no single instrument can satisfy all learning situations because classroom learning involves cognitive, affective, perceptual, and environmental considerations (Reid, 1987). To be sure, though, an understanding of the student as learner is an important factor in designing curricula and planning instructional activities.

FIGURE 6.2 (continued)

Completes assignments to "get it over with"   _____
Works cautiously (reflective)   _____
Works at variable pace depending on the task   _____
Works without teacher's prodding   _____
Participates actively in small group discussions   _____

Personal characteristics

Is competitive and tries to outdo classmates   _____
Enjoys helping others learn   _____
Blames the teacher or external circumstances when things don't go well   _____
Is flexible; adapts easily to change   _____
Restless activity, unable to sit still   _____
Annoys or interferes with work of peers   _____
Has to be reprimanded or controlled by the teacher because of behavior   _____
Nervous about taking tests   _____

Intellectual dependence

Reliant upon the teacher to be told how to do things   _____
Wants the teacher to make things easy   _____
Becomes confused easily   _____
Prone to want quick black-or-white answers to questions   _____

Intellectual independence and originality

Shows persistence in a task and does not quit when something is difficult   _____
Brings up topics to be explored   _____
Brings things to class that relate to the current topic   _____
Comes up with original and unique ideas for projects   _____
Proposes alternative ways to solve a problem   _____
Shows initiative   _____

Directions:

People learn in many different ways. For example, some people learn primarily with their ears (auditory learners); some people prefer to learn by experience and/or by hands-on tasks (kinesthetic or tactile learners); some people learn better when they work alone, while others prefer to learn in groups.

This questionnaire has been designed to help you identify the way(s) you learn best—the way(s) you *prefer* to learn.

Read each statement on the following pages. Please respond to the statements AS THEY APPLY TO YOUR STUDY OF ENGLISH. Decide whether you agree or disagree with each statement. Mark one of the following applicable to your answer:

Strongly agree = SA   Disagree   = D
Agree   = A   Strongly disagree = SD
Undecided   = U

Please respond to each statement quickly, without too much thought. Try not to change your responses after you choose them. Please use a pen to mark your choices.

Questionnaire statements

		SA	A	U	D	SD
1.	When the teacher tells me the instructions, I understand better.					
2.	I prefer to learn by doing something in class					
3.	I get more work done when I work with others.					
4.	I learn more when I study with a group.					
5.	In class, I learn best when I work with others.					
6.	I learn better by reading what the teacher writes on the chalkboard.					
7.	When someone tells me how to do something in class, I learn it better.					
8.	When I do things in class, I learn better.					
9.	I remember things I have heard in class better than things I have read.					
10.	When I read instructions, I remember them better.					
11.	I learn more when I can make a model of something.					
12.	I understand better when I read instructions.					
13.	When I study alone, I remember things better.					
14.	I learn more when I make something for a class project.					
15.	I enjoy learning in class by doing experiments.					
16.	I learn better when I make drawings as I study.					
17.	I learn better in class when the teacher gives a lecture.					
18.	When I work alone, I learn better.					
19.	I understand things better in class when I participate in role playing.					
20.	I learn better in class when I listen to someone.					
21.	I enjoy working on an assignment with two or three classmates.					
22.	When I build something, I remember what I have learned better.					
23.	I prefer to study with others.					
24.	I learn better by reading than by listening to someone.					
25.	I enjoy making something for a class project.					
26.	I learn best in class when I can participate in related activities.					
27.	In class, I work better when I work alone.					
28.	I prefer working on projects by myself.					
29.	I learn more by reading textbooks than by listening to lectures.					
30.	I prefer to work by myself.					

FIGURE 6.3 Perceptual learning style preference questionaire

SOURCE: Adapted from "The Learning Style Preferences of ESL Students" by J. M. Reid, 1987, *TESOL Quarterly, 21,* pp. 110–111. Copyright 1987 by Teachers of English to Speakers of Other Languages. Used with permission.

LEARNING STRATEGIES

Students can learn a second language in many different ways. For example, some may create mental pictures of words, write sentences to practice new grammar rules, and guess the meaning of a conversation from the gestures of the speakers. Other students may seek help from other persons by asking questions, or decide in advance what to pay attention to and how to relate new material to what they have already learned. The techniques, approaches, or tactics that learners use are classified as learning strategies. These strategies enable students to develop competence in the target language through the use of various techniques to help them comprehend, store, and remember new information and skills (Chamot & Kupper, 1989). Since the 1970s, there have been numerous studies of the use of learning strategies among successful second language learners. These studies have utilized different methodological approaches: anthropological techniques (Rubin, 1975), classroom observation and intensive introspective interview (Naiman, Fröhlich, Stern, & Todesco, 1978), longitudinal case studies (Wong-Fillmore, 1976), "think-aloud" introspections while performing a language task (Hosenfeld, 1979), and use of a self-report learning modalities inventory (Papalia & Zampogna, 1977).

A number of manuals offer advice to students on how to use second language learning strategies (Rubin & Thompson, 1993; Brown-Azarowics, Stannard, & Goldin, 1986), as well as suggestions to teachers on the use of classroom activities to enhance learning among unsuccessful pupils (Omaggio, 1981). In the study of *The Good Language Learner* (Naiman et al., 1978), the researchers found, for example, that "tolerance for ambiguity" was a significant predictor of success in French in grade 8 but not in grades 10 or 12. Along the same line, the traits of "conformity" and "control" were found to be associated with high French achievement among high school students in a traditional, formal grammar-oriented language program and with low achievement in French among a comparable group of students enrolled in a French immersion program (Hamayan, Genesee, & Tucker, 1977). It appears that "conformity" or "control"—unwillingness to take risks or to communicate when grammatical features are unresolved—proved to be unsuccessful strategies in the immersion language program, which emphasized experimentation and functional language use. These findings suggest that some strategies are more useful than others at different levels of language study and in different types of language programs.

Investigations among university-level students point to the relative success of certain learning strategies through the acquisition process. Students learning French in a Canadian university were found to place different emphasis on given cognitive strategies as they became more proficient in the language (Prokop, Fearon, & Rochet, 1982). Beginning students were more likely to use reading, translation, and writing behaviors (psychomotor support strategies) while participating in language learning activities. More advanced students, on the other hand, indicated that they paid more attention to the systematic features of the target language and made greater use of contextual clues. American college students learning French, German, and Spanish (Politzer, 1983) were found to differ in the use of some language learning behaviors according to the target language and proficiency level. At the same time, the learning behaviors that related to achievement varied with the type of language test used for evaluation. In a second study using the same questionnaire among international graduate students learning English as a second language (Politzer & McGroarty, 1985), use of specific language learning behaviors was found to vary depending on such factors as the student's proficiency level, cultural background (Asian or Hispanic), and type of language test (aural comprehension, grammatical competence, and communicative proficiency). These studies of college-age students indicate that significant differences exist in the use of second language learning strategies.

Learner strategy use among high school students has been examined by Ramírez (1986) and Chamot and Kupper (1989). Ramírez, for example, found that among adolescents studying French in secondary schools, years of language study influenced the use of and need for different sets of strategies for different language skills. Overall, eight strategies contributed differentially to the general success of these learners: (1) asking for clarification or verification, (2) using inferencing skills or deductive reasoning, (3) creating opportunities for practice, (4) memorizing, (5) using vocabulary learning techniques, (6) employing available linguistic and contextual cues, (7) being able to self-monitor performance, and (8) practicing. Chamot and Kupper (1989) conducted a study among high school students to demonstrate the use of three general learning categories: (1) metacognitive strategies, which involve thinking about the learning process, planning for learning, monitoring the learning task, and evaluating how well one has learned; (2) cognitive strategies, which include interacting with the material to be learned, manipulating the material, and applying specific techniques to complete a learning task; and (3) social and affective strategies, which involve interacting with another person, or using effective control, to assist learning a task. The findings of the longitudinal study resulted in the refinement of various strategies with respect to specific kinds of language tasks, as can be seen in Figure 6.4.

The researchers noted that a number of factors influenced the learners' choice of strategies in the longitudinal study. Among these were the type of language classroom (classrooms stressing grammar vs. those focusing on proficiency), prior language study, type of language task (reading comprehension, vocabulary learning, or oral production) and the degree of task difficulty (summarizing a text, completing a cloze exercise, or written communication), and the student's motivation to learn. Successful students tended to use a greater variety of strategies, more frequently, and more appropriately for task completion. Unsuccessful students tended to use fewer strategies that were often inappropriate for successful task completion.

Some of the successful learning behaviors noted above correspond to the four basic strategies identified by Stern (1983). These include (1) an active planning strategy (select goals or subgoals, recognize stages, and participate actively in the learning process), (2) an explicit learning strategy (paying attention to linguistic features of the target language, conscious learning, practice, memorization, and

Metacognitive strategies involve thinking about the learning process, planning for learning, monitoring the learning task, and evaluating how well one has learned.

1. *Planning:* Previewing the organizing concept or principle or an anticipated learning task ("advance organizer"); proposing strategies for handling an upcoming task; generating a plan for the parts, sequencing main ideas, or language functions to be used in handling a task.
2. *Directed attention:* Deciding in advance to attend in gereral to a learning task and to ignore irrelevant distractors; maintaining attention during task execution.
3. *Selective attention:* Deciding in advance to attend to specific aspects of language input or situational details that assist in performance of a task; attending to specific aspects of language input during task execution.
4. *Self-management:* Understanding the conditions that help one successfully accomplish language tasks and arranging for the presence of those conditions; controlling one's language performance to maximize use of what is already known.
5. *Self-monitoring:* Checking, verifying, or correcting one's comprehension or performance in the course of a language task. This has been coded in think alouds the following ways:
   - Comprehension monitoring: checking, verifying or correcting one's understanding
   - Production monitoring: checking, verifying, or correcting one's language production
   - Auditory monitoring: using one's "ear" for the language (how something sounds) to make decisions
   - Visual monitoring: using one's "eye" for the language (how something looks) to make decisions
   - Style monitoring: checking, verifying, or correcting based upon an internal stylistic register
   - Strategy monitoring: tracking use of how well a strategy is working
   - Plan monitoring: tracking how well a plan is working
   - Double check monitoring: tracking across the task previously undertaken acts or possibilities considered
6. *Problem identification:* Explicitly identifying the central point needing resolution in a task, or identifying an aspect of the task that hinders its successful completion.
7. *Self-evaluation:* Checking the outcomes of one's own language performance against an internal measure of completeness and accuracy; checking one's language repertoire, strategy use or ability to perform the task at hand. This has been coded in the think alouds as:
   - Production evaluation: checking one's work when the task is finished
   - Performance evaluation: judging one's overall execution of the task
   - Ability evaluation: judging one's ability to perform the task
   - Strategy evaluation: judging one's strategy use when the task is completed
   - Language repertiore evaluation: judging how much one knows of the L2, at the word, phrase, sentence, or concept level

Cognitive strategies involve interacting with the material to be learned, manipulating the material mentally or physically, or applying a specific technique to a learning task.

1. *Repetition:* Repeating a chunk of language (a word or phrase) in the course of performing a language task.
2. *Resourcing:* Using available reference sources of information about the target language, including dictionaries, textbooks, and prior work.
3. *Grouping:* Ordering, classifying, or labeling material used in a language task based on common attributes; recalling information based on grouping previously done.

(continued)

FIGURE 6.4 Learning strategies and their definitions

SOURCE: From "Learning Strategies in Foreign Language Instruction" by Anna Uhl Chamot and Lisa Kupper,1989, *Foreign Language Annals, 22,* pp.15–17. Reprinted with permission.

159

4. *Note-taking:* Writing down key words and concepts in abbreviated verbal, graphic, or numerical form to assist performance of a language task.
5. *Deduction/induction:* Consciously applying learned or self-developed rules to produce or understand the target language.
6. *Substitution:* Selecting alternative approaches, revised plans, or different words or phrases to accomplish a language task.
7. *Elaboration:* Relating new information to prior knowledge; relating different parts of new information to each other; making meaningful personal associations to information presented. This has been coded in the think aloud data in the following ways:
   - Personal elaboration: making judgments about or reacting personally to the material presented
   - World elaboration: using knowledge gained from experience in the world
   - Academic elaboration: using knowledge gained in academic situations
   - Between parts elaboration: relating parts of the task to each other
   - Questioning elaboration: using a combination of questions and world knowledge to brainstorm logical solutions to a task
   - Self-evaluative elaboration: judging self in relation to materials
   - Creative elaboration: making up a story line, or adopting a clever perspective
   - Imagery: using mental or actual pictures or visuals to represent information; coded as a separate category, but viewed as a form of elaboration
8. *Summarization:* Making a mental or written summary of language and information presented in a task.
9. *Translation:* Rendering ideas from one language to another in a relatively verbatim manner.
10. *Transfer:* Using previously acquired linguistic knowledge to facilitate a language task.
11. *Inferencing:* Using available information: to guess the meanings or usage of unfamiliar language items associated with a language task; to predict outcomes; or to fill in missing information.

Social and affective strategies involve interacting with another person to assist learning, or using effective control to assist a learning task.

1. *Questioning:* Asking for explanation, verification, rephrasing, or examples about the material; asking for clarification or verification about the task; posing questions to the self.
2. *Cooperation:* Working together with peers to solve a problem, pool information, check a learning task, model a language activity, or get feedback on oral or written performance
3. *Self-talk:* Reducing anxiety by using mental techniques that make one feel competent to do the learning task
4. *Self-reinforcement:* Providing personal motivation by arranging rewards for oneself when a language learning activity has been successfully completed

FIGURE 6.4   (continued)

progress monitoring), (3) a social learning strategy (seek communication with target language users and language community, develop communication strategies, become involved as participants in authentic language use), and (4) an affective strategy (approach task with positive frame of mind, develop necessary energy to overcome frustrations, and cope with emotional and motivational problems). Other strategies can be seen in light of the profile of the "good language learner" offered by Rubin (1975). Good language learners:

1. Are willing and accurate guessers
2. Have a strong, persevering drive to communicate

3. Are often uninhibited and willing to make mistakes in order to learn or communicate
4. Focus on form by looking for patterns, classifying, and analyzing
5. Take advantage of all opportunities to practice
6. Monitor their own speech and the speech of others
7. Pay attention to meaning

A number of the strategies used by the "good learner" are related to cognitive factors (1, 4, 6, and 7), while others are associated with affective variables (2, 5) and personality characteristics (3).

Guiding students to develop more-effective strategies for language learning means that teachers have to make changes in their instructional plans. Students require more time for self-monitoring, rehearsing different strategies, and processing problem-solving tasks. Teachers have to reflect on the complexity of learning tasks rather than focusing on classroom techniques (Galloway & Labarca, 1990). Chamot (1988) advocates the use of direct strategy training as part of the instructional process in second language classrooms. Teachers can assist learners by:

1. Identifying students' current learning strategies
2. Assessing students' strategy needs in relation to course objectives and demands of the learning tasks
3. Modeling more-effective strategies through think-aloud procedures, thus demonstrating the steps involved in approaching and completing the language task
4. Labeling the strategies used so students can readily identify them
5. Providing guided practice in the use of strategies on similar language tasks
6. Gradually reducing reminders on the use of strategies on similar language tasks
7. Providing varied practice on appropriate use of specific strategies with different tasks

COMMUNICATION STRATEGIES

Learners are often faced with the need to communicate with an imperfect knowledge of the target language. To get the message across, second language learners often use a number of "production tricks" to compensate for gaps in their linguistic repertoire. They resort to a number of communication strategies, such as use of mime, appeals for assistance, word coinage, circumlocution, translation, message abandonment, and topic avoidance. These communication strategies, according to Faerch and Kasper (1983, p. 36), represent "potentially conscious plans for solving what to an individual presents itself as a problem in reaching a particular communicative goal."

Various typologies of communication strategies have been proposed. Tarone's (1980) typology takes an interactional perspective in that communication strategies serve to bridge the gap between the linguistic knowledge of the L2 learner and that of the interlocutor in real communication situations. To overcome communication problems, the learner can utilize *transfer strategies* from L1 (literal translation, language switch, mime), second language strategies (paraphrase: approximation, word coinage, and circumlocution), or *reduction strategies* (topic avoidance and message abandonment). Drawing largely from the work of Faerch and Kasper (1983), Willems (1987) developed a typology of communication strategies that includes both "positive" (achievement-oriented) strategies and "negative" (reduction) strategies. It also includes interlingual strategies and foreign-language-based intralingual strategies, or psycholinguistic plans, along with the use of non-verbal, paralinguistic strategies. Figure 6.5 presents a typology for coding observable communication strategies. Willems believes that learners need to be able to use communication strategies appropriately in order to bridge the gap successfully between the traditional classroom setting and real communicative situations. With the aid of this typology, teachers can develop a series of exercises and procedures to enable students to communicate with the use of these compensatory strategies.

Ellis (1985) points out, in summarizing the empirical research on communication strategies, that it is not clear what effect communication strategies ultimately have on linguistic development. The use of different strategies seems to be influenced by such factors as the learner's proficiency level, learning situation, learner's personality, and type of linguistic problem. In an interactive, proficiency-oriented classroom, development of communication strategies among learners should be an important instructional goal directed toward the acquisition of strategic competence.

FIGURE 6.5 A typology of communication strategies

SOURCE: Reprinted from "Communication Strategies and Their Significance in Foreign Language Teaching," by G. M. Willems, 1987, *System, 15,* p. 355. Copyright 1987, with permission from Pergamon Press Ltd, Headington Hill Hall, Oxford OX 30BW, UK.

Reduction strategies
(Often difficult to identify. Introspection may be guide here.)

Formal

Phonological: Avoidance of words containing "difficult" segments
Morphological: Avoidance of talking about yesterday to avoid past tense form.
Syntactic: Avoidance of speaking about what might happen for fear of using conditionals
Lexical: Avoidance of certain topics because the necessary vocabulary is lacking

Functional

Message abandonment: "Oh, I can't say this, let's talk about something else."
Meaning replacement: Saying almost what you want to say; saying something less politely than you would in your L1 ("modality reduction").

Topic avoidance: Saying nothing at all.

"Meaning replacement" and "topic avoidance" form extremes of a continuum.

N.B. "Meaning replacement" resembles closely what is called "approximation" or "generalization" under "Achievement strategies."

Achievement strategies
(Classification depends on resources used.)

Paralinguistic strategies

      I. The use of mimetic gestures, facial expressions etc. to replace speech.

Interlingual strategies involving the interpolation of a L different from the one in which the conversation is taking place.

      II. *Borrowing or "code switching;"* a native language word or phrase is used with a native language pronunciation, e.g. "Please Sir, have you a 'krijtje' " (Du. for "piece of chalk").

     III. *Literal translation:* a literal translation from L1 to L2 of lexical items, idioms, or compound words, e.g. "make it a little" (Du. for "Come off it"); "nighttable" (for Ger. "Nachttisch"="bedside table"); "greens" for "vegetables" (from Du. "groente"); "Je suis pardon" for "I am sorry"; "cool-box" for "refrigerator" (from Du. "koelkast").

     IV. *"Foreignizing":* Using a word or phrase from the L1 with L2 pronunciation, e.g. "/'Knælə/" from Da. "knallert" for "moped;" "/,sɔːkjə'leiʃn/" from Fr. "/'siʁkylasiõ/" for "traffic" in: "There was a lot of circulation."

Intralingual strategies exploit generally only the L in which the conversation is taking place. (Interlingual strategy may be embedded.)

     V. *Approximation* (generalization): The use of an L2 word that shares essential semantic features with the target word: "birds" for "ducks," "animals" for "rabbits," "rose" for "flower," or "lorry" for "van".

    VI. *"Word coinage":* An L2 word is made up on basis of supposed rule: "intonate" from "intonation", "inunded" for "flooded".

   VII. *Paraphrase:*
        a. description:
           1. *physical properties:* Colour, size, spatial dimensions
        b. circumlocution:
           2. *specific features:* "It has a motor. . . ."
           3. *functional features:* "It is used in. . . ."
           4. *locational features:* "You find it in a factory"
           5. *temporal features:* "It's between summer and autumn"
        c. exemplification: subordinate terms used instead of unavailable subordinate terms like: trade names: "Puch" for "moped".

   VIII. *"Smurfing":* The use of empty or meaningless words to fill gaps in vocabulary command like: "thing," "whatsit," "what-do-you-call-it."

    IX. *Self-repair* (restructuring): Setting up a new speech-plan when the original one fails.

     X. *Appeals for assistance:*
        a. *Explicit:* "what d'you call"; "Speak more slow," "I am foreign;" "Do you understand?"

        b. *Implicit:* pauses, intonation, drawls, repetition, or "I don't know what to call this" and the like

        c. *Checking questions:* To make sure something is correctly understood: "Do I hear you say . . ."; "Are you saying that . . ."

    XI. Initiating repair: "I am sorry, there must be some misunderstanding. Does . . . mean . . .? I took it to mean . . . I hope you don't mind my asking . . ."

FIGURE 6.5 (continued)

ATTITUDES, MOTIVATION, AND ANXIETY

Second language learning requires, among other things, the use of conscious learning strategies, a willingness to practice, a strong desire to communicate, and a positive attitude about the target language. Gardner and Lambert (1972) introduced the constructs of *integrative* and *instrumental* motivation to characterize the learning of a nonnative language. A learner with integrative motivation wants to learn the second language because of "a sincere and personal interest in the people and culture" (Gardner & Lambert, 1972, p. 132), while the instrumentally motivated student is interested in the language as a means for furthering other personal goals such as passing an examination or improving employment opportunities. The difference between the two main types of motivation can be expressed with the following formats:

I. I am studying French because
   A. I feel it may be helpful in getting a job.
   B. I want to be able to use it with French-speaking friends.
II. I need to pass two years of a foreign language in order to fulfill my college requirement.

Strongly agree	Agree	No opinion	Disagree	Strongly disagree
_____	_____	_____	_____	_____

III. Knowing another language will enable me to meet and converse with a wider group of people.

Strongly agree	Agree	No opinion	Disagree	Strongly disagree
_____	_____	_____	_____	_____

(Adapted from Hahn, Stassen, & Reschke, 1989, p. 249)

The instrumental-integrative dichotomy has been called into question by research findings suggesting that the two types of motivation are not mutually exclusive. A learner may study a second language initially for instrumental purposes (an interest in occupational uses of the language) and later manifest an integrative motive (a desire to associate with members of target community). Brown (1981) identifies three types of motivation: (1) global motivation, associated with a general orientation to the goal of learning, (2) situational motivation, which can vary according to the context where the learning takes place (classroom or naturalistic setting), and (3) task motivation, which corresponds to the motivational drive for performing different learning tasks. Ely (1986) suggests that some learners may have a desire to learn a second language that is not related to either instrumental or integrative motives. Some may learn a language as a means of promoting social respect, developing a better understanding of the world, or gaining a well-rounded education.

Figure 6.6 presents the survey questionnaire that he developed to establish the motivational patterns among first-year university students learning Spanish. Ely recommends that instructional materials be prepared to appeal to the cluster of items that relate to at least the two basic motivational patterns. In addition, both types of motivational drives should be encouraged in the classroom.

Language attitudes is another term closely associated with motivation. Attitudes can be used to refer to the set of beliefs that a learner holds about the community and people who speak the target language. For example:

Spanish-speaking people may be rated as:

interesting	____	____	X	____	____	____	____	boring
honest	____	____	____	____	X	____	____	dishonest
friendly	____	____	____	X	____	____	____	unfriendly
kind	____	X	____	____	____	____	____	unkind

Attitudes can also refer to the language itself:

I find studying German:

_____ (a) very interesting

_____ (b) interesting

__X__ (c) no more interesting than most subjects

_____ (d) not interesting at all

(Based on Burstall, Jamieson, Cohen, & Hargreaves, 1974, p. 154)

Attitudes may also be related to the learning task itself:

The study of French this semester is:

dull	____	____	____	____	X	____	____	exciting
hard	____	X	____	____	____	____	____	easy
disorganized	____	____	____	____	X	____	____	organized
discouraging	____	____	____	____	____	X	____	rewarding

(Adapted from Lafayette & Buscaglia, 1985, p. 342)

What I like about learning French is _____.

What I don't like about learning French is _____.

(Adapted from Burstall et al., 1974, p. 255)

The relationship between attitudes and motivation is not always clear. Some investigators use the term *attitudes* to refer to motivational tendencies. Others use the concept of motivation for describing course-related attitudes and opinions about specific learning tasks. Given the abstractness of the two concepts and the types of relationships that can exist between the two constructs, it is difficult to establish precisely how attitudes and motivation affect second language learning.

Please rate the following reasons for studying Spanish by circling the appropriate choice:

Not important   (NI)
Slightly important   (SI)
Moderately important   (MI)
Highly important   (HI)

I am taking Spanish:

1. Because I want to use Spanish when I travel to a Spanish-speaking country.
   NI   SI   MI   HI

2. Because I need to study a foreign language as a requirement for my major.
   NI   SI   MI   HI

3. Because I want to be able to converse with Spanish speakers in the U.S.
   NI   SI   MI   HI

4. Because I am interested in Hispanic culture, history, or literature.
   NI   SI   MI   HI

5. Because I feel it may be helpful in my future career.
   NI   SI   MI   HI

6. Because I need it for study abroad.
   NI   SI   MI   HI

7. Because I feel it is mentally challenging and provides mental exercise.
   NI   SI   MI   HI

8. Because I want to be able to use it with Spanish-speaking friends.
   NI   SI   MI   HI

9. Because I need it to fulfill the university foreign language requirement.
   NI   SI   MI   HI

10. Because of interest in my own Hispanic heritage.
    NI   SI   MI   HI

11. Because I think it will help me to understand English grammar better.
    NI   SI   MI   HI

12. Because I feel the classes are less demanding than other five-unit courses.
    NI   SI   MI   HI

13. Because I want to be able to speak more languages than just English.
    NI   SI   MI   HI

14. Because I want to learn about another culture to understand the world better.
    NI   SI   MI   HI

15. Because it may make me a more qualified job candidate.
    NI   SI   MI   HI

16. Because I want to communicate with relatives in Spanish.
    NI   SI   MI   HI

17. Because I think foreign language study is part of well-rounded education.
    NI   SI   MI   HI

18. Because I feel Spanish is an important language in the world.
    NI   SI   MI   HI

FIGURE 6.6 Language learning motivation

SOURCE: From "Language Learning Motivation: A Descriptive and Causal Analysis" by Christopher M. Ely, 1986, *Modern Language Journal*, 70, pp. 34–35. Reprinted with permission.

There can be no doubt, however, that both motivation and attitudes are powerful factors helping to determine the level of proficiency attained by different learners (Gardner & Lambert, 1972; Gardner, 1980). Savignon (1976) believes that attitude is the single most important variable in second language learning.

It is not clear at this point if motivation contributes to successful learning or if successful classroom experiences enhance motivation. MacNamara (1973) argues that the most important part of motivation may lie in the act of communication itself, instead of any general motivation orientation as reflected by an instrumental-integrative difference. It may be possible to foster a more favorable language attitude and motivational orientation by selecting appropriate learning tasks based on the learner's motives, interests, and needs. The "German Attitude Survey" (Figure 6.7) prepared by Hahn et al. (1989) represents an attempt to determine the learner's attitudes toward foreign language study, reasons for studying German, and opinions about oral language activities. The authors recommend that some form of student evaluation or informal assessment be used to determine the appropriateness of learning activities and testing procedures. Grading policies and certain types of language activities can affect the stress factor as well as motivation attitudes. Teachers may decide to use a case-study approach as a means of comparing attitudes (motivation of selected students, such as successful vs. unsuccessful language learners).

Language anxiety is another important issue in second language learning. Anxiety, defined as "a state of apprehension, a vague fear" (Scovel 1978, p. 134), can have a negative effect on motivation and can result in poor performance, which in turn produces even more anxiety. Some level of anxiety might facilitate language learning, while the bad or debilitating form of anxiety may result in avoidance behaviors (not participating in class activities, not completing homework assignments) and physical actions (squirming, nervousness, stammering).

Language anxiety can be diagnosed with the use of surveys, diaries and dialogue journals, and interviews (Scarcella & Oxford, 1992). Questions such as the ones below illustrate some of the classroom dimensions of the problem:

SA = strongly agree; A = agree; N = neither agree nor disagree; D = disagree; SD = strongly disagree

1. I tremble when I know that I'm going to be
   called on in language class.   SA   A   N   D   SD
2. I am usually at ease during tests in my
   language class.   SA   A   N   D   SD
3. Even if I am well prepared for language class, I
   feel anxious about it.   SA   A   N   D   SD
4. It embarrasses me to volunteer answers in my
   language class.   SA   A   N   D   SD

(Horwitz, Horwitz, & Cope, 1991, pp. 32-33).

For each of the following decide whether you strongly agree (SA), agree (A), have no opinion (NO), disagree (D), or strongly disagree (SD) and circle the appropriate choice:

1. It is important to me to speak the language like a native speaker.   SA   A   NO   D   SD
2. I would like to be able to read the target language without the aid of a dictionary.   SA   A   NO   D   SD
3. Learning to speak a language well is more important than learning to read or write it well.   SA   A   NO   D   SD
4. The study of a foreign language is a waste of time.   SA   A   NO   D   SD
5. A lack of knowledge of a foreign language can account for some of our political difficulties.   SA   A   NO   D   SD
6. It is not necessary to know a foreign language in order to travel or conduct business abroad, since everyone speaks English.   SA   A   NO   D   SD
7. I think that a stay abroad for a year or more would be one of the most valuable experiences of my life.   SA   A   NO   D   SD
8. I believe a foreign language should be required.   SA   A   NO   D   SD

Read and rate the following attitudes toward studying a foreign language according to how you feel it describes your own case:

9. Knowing how to speak and read a foreign language will help me get a good job.   SA   A   NO   D   SD
10. Another language will help me understand other people and their way of life.   SA   A   NO   D   SD
11. Knowing another language will enable me to meet and converse with a wider group of people.   SA   A   NO   D   SD
12. I need to pass two years of a foreign language in order to fulfill college requirements.   SA   A   NO   D   SD
13. I would like to study a language other than German.   SA   A   NO   D   SD
14. I would like to be able to belong to another culture.   SA   A   NO   D   SD
15. I like learning German.   SA   A   NO   D   SD
16. I plan to continue my German study.   SA   A   NO   D   SD
17. I feel there is too much homework.   SA   A   NO   D   SD
18. I work harder on activities that are graded.   SA   A   NO   D   SD

Read and rate the following statements concerning the oral activities done in class:

19. The situations in the activities are realistic.   SA   A   NO   D   SD
20. I think the content of the activities is up-to-date.   SA   A   NO   D   SD
21. I think the content of the activities is appropriate for my level.   SA   A   NO   D   SD
22. I think the content of the activities is useful.
23. I think the oral activity situations are clearly explained.   SA   A   NO   D   SD
24. I feel prepared for the oral activities.   SA   A   NO   D   SD
25. I feel the oral activities are not stressful.   SA   A   NO   D   SD
26. I think the oral activities should be graded.   SA   A   NO   D   SD
27. I like being interviewed by a native speaker.   SA   A   NO   D   SD

Read and answer the following questions:

28. German class would be better if _____
29. I like German class, because _____
30. I liked/disliked the oral activities. Why or why not? _____

FIGURE 6.7 German attitude survey

source: From "Grading Classroom Oral Activities: Effects on Motivation and Proficiency" by Sidney L. Hahn, Tamara Stassen, and Claus Reschke, 1989, *Foreign Language Annals, 22,* pp. 248–251. Reprinted with permission.

SUMMARY

Learning a second language can be influenced by any number of factors. Some of the factors have to do with the social context where the learning takes place: the classroom, interaction in the community with native or bilingual persons, and cultural beliefs about learning and the status of the target language. Other factors are associated with the learning process itself—universal learning tendencies, such as use of overgeneralization, transfer, and simplification strategies.

Learners are actively involved in the acquisition process and utilize various strategies that can be classified as metacognitive, cognitive, and socioaffective. In addition, students have preferred learning styles, reflected by the way they perceive, interact, and respond to the teaching environment. It is important for teachers to determine the ways their students learn in order to help them acquire the language more efficiently.

Learners create their own interlanguage and use numerous communication strategies to get their message across. Language attitudes and motivation play a major role in the learning process and can affect in significant ways the proficiency levels ultimately attained. Language anxiety is another factor influencing student participation in classroom activities and test performance. Paying special attention to the characteristics of learners should be a key concern when designing learning tasks.

ACTIVITIES

1. Why are some languages taught more widely than others in schools and colleges? Consider issues such as cultural attitudes, language status and use, learning difficulty, and career opportunities.
2. Make a list of the reasons why you learned a second language. Compare your list with those of students, and determine which reasons are based on personal concerns, social factors, or school-related issues.
3. Collect oral or written language samples from L2 learners and determine the different types of "errors" due to overgeneralization, transfer, and simplification strategies. Which "error" types (grammar, pronunciation, vocabulary) may have more than one cause or explanation? Which errors appear to be "mistakes"?
4. Administer Papalia's individual-differences inventory to a few learners, and compare the response patterns for the seven categories. What information would you offer to a classroom teacher, based on the responses of these students?
5. Administer Reid's preferred learning styles to a group of students who appear to be successful learners in a class. What are their basic perceptual learning modalities?
6. Interview a group of L2 learners to determine how they learn vocabulary items, read a text, and study for a language test. How do these strategies compare to the ones identified and described by Chamot and Kupper?
7. Analyze your own experiences as a teacher-learner of a second language. Do you have many of the characteristics listed by Rubin in her profile of the "good language learner"? What would be the profile of a "poor language learner"?

8. Record a conversation with an L2 learner and try to determine the conversation strategies used to get the message across. Transcribe a few minutes of the conversation and use the typology proposed by Willems. Contrast the number and type of reduction and achievement strategies.

9. Administer Ely's language learning motivation questionnaire (adapt according to target language group—English, French, German) to a few students. Is there any pattern of association between motivational orientation (integrative vs. instrumental) and classroom behavior, course grade, or proficiency level?

10. Consider items 19-30 in the German Attitude Survey by Hahn et al. In what way could these items be rewritten to get information about reading activities, writing tasks, and listening situations?

11. Develop a list enumerating the ways in which language anxiety could facilitate learning different aspects of language.

12. Discuss with others the types of language anxiety they encountered while learning language. What recommendations would you offer to teachers?

REFERENCES

Ashworth, M. (1985). *Beyond methodology.* Cambridge, England: Cambridge University Press.

Brown, H. (1981). Affective factors in second language learning. In J. Alatis, H. Altman, & P. Alatis (Eds.), *The second language classroom: Directions for the 1980s* (pp. 113-129). New York: Oxford University Press.

Brown-Azarowics, M., Stannard, C., & Goldin, M. (1986). *Yes! You can learn a foreign language.* Lincolnwood, IL: Passport Books.

Burstall, C., Jamieson, M., Cohen, S., & Hargreaves, M. (1974). *Primary French in the balance.* Windsor: NFER Publishing.

Chamot, A. U. (1988). *Learning strategy instruction for writing in French: A possible script.* McLean, VA: Interstate Research Associates.

Chamot, A. U., & Kupper, L. (1989). Learning strategies in foreign language instruction. *Foreign Language Annals, 22,* 13-24.

Corder, S. P. (1971). Idiosyncratic dialects and error analysis. *International Review of Applied Linguistics, 9,* 147-159.

Dulay, H., Burt, M., & Krashen, S. (1982). *Language two.* New York: Oxford University Press.

Ellis, R. (1982). *Discourse processes in classroom second language development.* Unpublished doctoral dissertation, University of London.

Ellis, R. (1984). *Classroom second language development.* Oxford: Pergamon.

Ellis, R. (1985). *Understanding second language acquisition.* Oxford: Oxford University Press.

Ely, C. M. (1986). Language learning motivation: A descriptive and causal analysis. *The Modern Language Journal, 70*(1), 28-35.

Faerch, C., & Kasper, G. (1983). On identifying communication strategies. In C. Faerch and G. Kasper (Eds.), *Strategies in interlanguage communication.* London: Longman.

Galloway, V., & Labarca, A. (1990). From student to learner: Style, process, and strategy. In D. W. Birckbichler (Ed.), *New perspectives and new directions in foreign language education* (pp. 111-158). Lincolnwood, IL: National Textbook.

Gardner, R. C. (1979). Social psychological aspects of second language acquisition. In H. Giles & R. N. St. Clair (Eds.), *Language and social psychology*. Oxford: Basil Blackwell.

Gardner, R. (1980). On the validity of affective variables in second language acquisition: Conceptual, contextual, and statistical considerations. *Language Learning, 30*, 255-270.

Gardner, R. C., & Lambert, W. E. (1972). *Attitudes and motivation in second language learning*. Rowley, MA: Newbury House.

Hahn, S. L., Stassen, T., & Reschke, C. (1989). Grading classroom oral activities: Effects on motivation and proficiency. *Foreign Language Annals, 22*(3), 241-252.

Hamayan, E., Genesee, F., & Tucker, G. R. (1977). Affective factors and language exposure in second language learning. *Language Learning, 27*, 224-241.

Hatch, E. (1978). Discourse analysis and second language acquisition. In E. Hatch (Ed.), *Second language acquisition: A book of readings* (pp. 401-435). New York: Newbury House.

Hatch, E. (1983). *Psycholinguistics: A second language perspective*. New York: Newbury House.

Horwitz, E. K., Horwitz, M. B., & Cope, J. A. (1991). Foreign language classroom anxiety. In E. K. Horwitz & D. J. Young (Eds.), *Language anxiety: From theory and research to classroom implications* (pp. 27-36). Englewood Cliffs, NJ: Prentice-Hall.

Hosenfeld, C. (1979). Cindy: A learner in today's foreign language classroom. In W. Bonn (Ed.), *The foreign language learner in today's classroom environment. Northeast Conference Reports* (pp. 53-75). Middlebury, VT: Northeast Conference on the Teaching of Foreign Languages.

Izzo, S. (1981). *Second language learning: A review of related studies*. Rosslyn, VA: National Clearinghouse for Bilingual Education.

Keefe, J. W. (1979). Learning style: An overview. In J. W. Keefe (Ed.), *Student learning styles: Diagnosing and prescribing programs* (pp. 1-17). Reston, VA: National Association of Secondary School Principals.

Lafayette, R., & Buscaglia, M. (1985). Students learn language via a civilization course: A comparison of second language classroom environments. *Studies in Second Language Acquisition, 7*, 323-342.

Littlewood, W. T. (1984). *Foreign and second language learning: Language acquisition research and its implications for the classroom*. Cambridge, England: Cambridge University Press.

Lund, R. J. (1991). A comparison of second language listening and reading comprehension. *Modern Language Journal, 75*(2), 196-204.

Ma, R., & Herasimchuk, E. (1968). Linguistic dimensions of a bilingual neighborhood. In J. A. Fishman, R. L. Cooper, & R. Ma (Eds.), *Bilingualism in the barrio (Final report)*. Washington, DC: U. S. Office of Education.

MacNamara, J. (1973). Nurseries, streets, and classrooms: Some comparisons and deductions. *Modern Language Journal, 57*, 250-254.

McLaughlin, B. (1987). *Theories of second language learning*. London: Edward Arnold.

Meisel, J. (1980). Linguistic simplification. In S. Felix (Ed.), *Second language development: Trends and issues* (pp. 13-40). Tübingen: Narr.

Naiman, N., Fröhlich, M., Stern, H. H., & Todesco, A. (1978). *The good language learner. Research in education, Series 7*. Toronto: Ontario Institute for Studies in Education.

Omaggio, A. (1981). *Helping learners succeed: Activities for the foreign language classroom*. Washington, DC: Center for Applied Linguistics.

Papalia, A. (1986). Avoid malpractice: An individual-differences inventory. *Language Association Bulletin, 38*(2), 21-22.

Papalia, A., & Zampogna, J. (1977). Strategies used by foreign language students in deriving meaning from a written text and in learning vocabulary. *Language Association Bulletin*, *23*, 7-8.

Politzer, R. L. (1983). An explatory study of self-reported language learning behaviors and their relation to achievement. *Studies in Second Language Acquisition*, *6*, 54-65.

Politzer, R. L., & McGroarty, M. (1985). *An exploratory study of learning behaviors and their relation to gains in linguistics and communicative competence*. Unpublished manuscript, Stanford University.

Prokop, M., Fearon, D., & Rochet, B. (1982). *Second language learning strategies in formal instructional context*. Edmonton, Alberta: University of Alberta.

Ramírez, A. G. (1986). Language learning strategies used by adolescents studying French in New York schools. *Foreign Language Annals*, *19*(2), 131-141.

Reid, J. M. (1987). The learning-style preferences of ESL students. *TESOL Quarterly*, *21*(1), 87-111.

Richards, J. (1972). Social factors, interlanguage, and language learning. *Language Learning*, *22*(2), 158-188.

Rubin, J. (1975). What the good language learner can teach us. *TESOL Quarterly*, *10*, 77-98.

Rubin, J., & Thompson, I. (1993). *How to be a more successful language learner*. Boston: Heinle & Heinle.

Savignon, S. J. (1976). On the other side of the desk: Teacher attitudes and motivation in second language learning. *Canadian Modern Language Review*, *32*, 295-304.

Scarcella, R. C., & Oxford, R. L. (1992). *The tapestry of language learning*. Boston, MA: Heinle & Heinle.

Schumann, J. (1978). The acculturation model for second language acquisition. In R. Gingras (Ed.), *Second language acquisition and foreign language teaching* (pp. 27-50). Arlington, VA: Center for Applied Linguistics.

Scovel, T. (1978). The effect of affect on foreign language learning: A review of the anxiety research. *Language Learning*, *28*, 129-142.

Selinker, L. (1974). Interlanguage. In J. Schumann & N. Stenson (Eds.), *New frontiers in second language learning*. Rowley, MA: Newbury House.

Stern, H. H. (1983). *Fundamental concepts of language teaching*. New York: Oxford University Press.

Tarone, E. (1980). Communication strategies, foreigner talk, and repair in interlanguage. *Language Learning*, *30*, 417-31.

Willems, G. M. (1987). Communication strategies and their significance in foreign language teaching. *System*, *15*(3), 351-364.

Wong-Fillmore, L. (1976). *The second time around: Cognitive and social strategies in second language acquisition*. Unpublished doctoral dissertation. Stanford University.

chapter 7

Listening to Language in Context

> *When planning listening exercises it is essential to bear in mind the kind of real-life situations for which we are preparing students, and also the specific difficulties they are likely to encounter and need practice to overcome. But we also need to take into account a further complex factor: the nature of the classroom teaching-learning process itself. There are physical considerations such as the size and arrangement of the classroom, or the number of students; technical ones such as may be involved in the use of tape recorders or other equipment; and a mass of pedagogical ones: how to improve student motivation, concentration and participation; how to correct, or give feedback; how to administer exercises efficiently, and so on.*
>
> *P. Ur, 1984*

Listening in L2 classrooms involves a number of considerations about the nature of language learning, listening situations, and classroom activities. Listening to language in context entails a close examination of the uses of spoken discourse in a variety of circumstances. Spoken language has a number of characteristics that differentiate it from written texts. Comprehension of spoken discourse is influenced by a multitude of factors, including linguistic elements, knowledge systems, and cognitive demands. Research studies provide some insight about the dynamics of oral language comprehension and the nature of learning strategies. Instructional activities can be planned and sequenced in ways that relate listening tasks to specific situations and guide students toward global listening proficiency. The use of authentic texts and real-life situations enhances the students' abilities to understand natural discourse.

This chapter considers a number of issues related to the teaching of listening skills in different contexts. The following questions are addressed:

1. What is the role of listening in L2 classrooms?
2. How can one characterize the types of listening situations?
3. What is involved in comprehension of spoken language?
4. What are some of the research findings in listening comprehension?
5. What considerations need to be taken into account when designing listening activities?
6. What are some examples of listening tasks?

LISTENING IN L2 CLASSROOMS

The role that listening should play in L2 classrooms is more a matter of opinion than certainty (Anderson & Lynch, 1988). There is still the view among some practitioners that language learning is a linear process, starting with the spoken language medium (listening and speaking) and then moving to the written medium (reading and writing). Listening is the means to initiate oral production, which tends to be an imitation of spoken texts. A second view places listening along with the other three language modalities (speaking, reading, and writing) in an interactive mode. All four modalities should be taught simultaneously, so that practice in one area can reinforce and develop the other forms of communication (Rivers, 1987). This holistic view of language is especially reflected in the "whole language" movement in ESL, which sees language as the principal means by which one creates and communicates meaning. Language is both an individual and a social activity. Rather than being a transmitter of linguistic content, the teacher collaborates with the students in creating meaning and transmitting information (Rigg, 1991).

A third view emphasizes listening as the primary source of linguistic input, which activates the language learning process. Espoused by the Comprehension Approach and the Natural Approach (see Chapter 5), this view is based on the premise that students must first develop the ability to comprehend and process oral language before being asked to speak. Oral language input activates the individual's internal mental processes, which, in turn, lead to creation of a learner's system reflected in spontaneous utterances. This comprehension-focused model emphasizes the parallels with first language acquisition and informal (out-of-class) L2 learning. Littlewood (1984) characterizes this as a creative construction process, in contrast to teaching approaches that promote L2 acquisition as a form of skill learning. The two models, as conceived by Littlewood, are presented in Figure 7.1.

In the skill-learning model, instructional input consists of controlled language samples together with classroom activities intended to guide the system created by the learner. However, learners still engage in their own process of creative construction, determined by their own internal language processing mechanisms rather than external curriculum designs. Still, for successful language acquisition in classroom settings, learners require access to comprehensible and meaningful input (Van Patten, 1992). Some features of comprehensible input are the use of pictures, visual aids, and authentic materials. Key words related to the topic or sit-

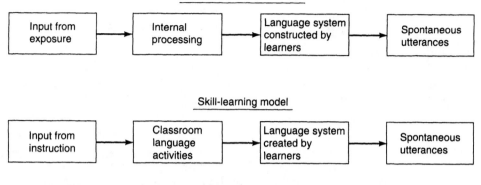

FIGURE 7.1 Models of second language learning

SOURCE: Adapted from *Foreign and Second Language Learning: Language Acquisition Research and Its Implications for the Classroom* (p. 73) by William T. Littlewood, 1984, Cambridge, England: Cambridge University Press. Used with permission.

uation are highlighted. Comprehension of meaning is facilitated with the use of nonverbal devices (gestures, mime, facial expressions), communication strategies (repetition, paraphrase, circumlocution), and contextual cues. Listening is a crucial skill since it interacts with other language modalities. For many foreign language students, the classroom is the only source of oral linguistic input, making listening an important teaching area.

TYPES OF LISTENING SITUATIONS

Second language learners may find themselves listening to the target language in a variety of situations. These situations can vary significantly: messages transmitted over loudspeakers at train or bus stations; short presentations on radio or television; information provided by hotel personnel, police, salespersons, and bank tellers; songs, live or recorded; feature programs on television, at the movies, and on the radio. Some of the situations involve listening to planned discourse that approximates written discourse, such as readings of the news on radio or television, academic lectures, political speeches, and religious sermons. Other contexts may consist of informal everyday conversational language with strangers, familiar adults, children, and family members. This unedited language contains pauses, repetition of words and phrases, and incomplete sentences. The participants may shift from one topic to another and use restatements and paraphrases to clarify misunderstandings.

While no taxonomy exists to classify all the different kinds of listening situations (Ur, 1984), it may be possible to classify listening activities along various continua:

planned. . . . . . unplanned discourse

interactive. . . . . . noninteractive situations

familiar. . . . . . unfamiliar topic

recognize/understand. . . . . . comprehend/react mode

Listening to a French lecture about contemporary art trends would entail, for the most part, hearing the reading of a prepared talk with explicit text organizers that enable the audience to follow the script. The audience would not interact with the speaker, ask clarifying questions, or expect to be tested orally on the subject. Some members of the audience might comprehend the lecture better than others because of their familiarity with and interest in the topic, above and beyond simple recognition of sounds and knowledge of vocabulary, grammar, or discourse connectors. Chatting at a party or social gathering means having to participate in unplanned discourse, which could cover a variety of topics: self-identification, family members, personal interests, and opinions. The conversation follows a series of question-and-answer sequences, with each participant playing the role of both listener and speaker. Cultural differences might affect the directness or indirectness of expression (Are you enjoying yourself? Isn't this a nice party?), ways of shifting topics to avoid cultural taboos, and rules for taking turns at speaking (when and how to interrupt). A weather report on the radio evokes a particular type of reaction from the listener: deciding whether or not to take an umbrella and raincoat as one leaves the hotel room. Listening to a song, on the other hand, might require attending to the poetic uses of language—repetition of certain words and the use of metaphors—without having to worry about the author's intent. The use of authentic, realistic listening situations should be a major consideration in preparing listening tasks.

COMPREHENDING SPOKEN LANGUAGE

Spoken language tends to occur in four basic modes, according to Byrnes (1984, p. 319):

1. *Spontaneous free speech*, characterized by the interactiveness of the situation and by "flaws" in the speaker's manner of speech production
2. *Deliberate free speech*, as it occurs in interviews and discussions, which has higher information value but maintains interactive and spontaneous qualities
3. *Oral presentation of a written text*, as in newscasts and lectures, where transmission of information is the objective and intentional considerations are much more covert
4. *Oral presentation of a fixed, rehearsed script*, such as on stage or in film, with its highly stylized ordering of linguistic elements and manner of delivery

Spontaneous free speech, while characterized by the use of reduced forms (e.g., "gonna" for "going to"; "sposta" for "supposed to"), ungrammatical utterances, false starts, and pauses and hesitations, occurs within a real time frame and is produced cooperatively by a speaker and a hearer who utilize a variety of verbal and nonverbal signals during the course of the conversation. Comprehension of this type of oral text, Joiner (1986) notes, is aided by both the characteristics of spoken language (hesitations, repetitions, paraphrases, speaking in clause units rather than sentence forms) and extralinguistic cues (gestures, facial expressions, situational clues). Listeners can also ask for further clarification, elaboration, and repetition of information to facilitate comprehension. Coakley and Wolvin (1986) point out in their review of research on listening in the native language that as much as 93% of the total meaning of a message can be based on such visual cues as the speaker's facial expressions, posture, gestures, and appearance.

Comprehension of the second mode, deliberate free speech, such as interviews and discussions, is also characterized by many of the features of spontaneous free speech, but greater emphasis is given to imparting information on various topics (health, education, economic and social conditions), developed collaboratively through the use of various language functions (requests for information, expressions of personal opinion, assertions, evaluations). The listener's lack of knowledge about the topics under discussion could greatly influence the comprehensibility of the message (Long, 1989). In addition, the listener's unfamiliarity with the cultural conventions the participants follow, as they initiate and switch topics, take and relinquish the floor, and make use of such genres as jokes, anecdotes, and debates, might contribute to misunderstandings (Richards, 1985).

When listening to oral language in noninteractional settings as in radio newscasts, lectures, loudspeaker announcements, and TV programs, the contextual or visual clues may be limited or totally absent. For example, the listener does not have the option of asking questions for clarification. These oral situations have more in common with written texts than with spoken language, since the presentations often involve the reading of fixed, rehearsed scripts. At the same time, usually the listener neither controls the delivery speed nor has the opportunity to ask for the text to be repeated.

The process of comprehending spoken language in different situations consists of a number of elements. The activity involves such aspects as anticipation and listening with a purpose in mind (Ur, 1984), actively attending to and assigning meaning to aural stimuli (Coakley & Wolvin, 1986), and skillfully bringing together "an interplay between all types of knowledge—phonological, lexical, and semantic" (Byrnes, 1984, p. 322). Richards (1983) points out that much of our knowledge of the world is organized around *scripts*, also called frames or schemata. These scripts enable individuals to make inferences and interpretations of typical episodes that occur in well-known situations. Because scripts consist of "predetermined, stereotyped sequences of actions" (Schank & Abelson, 1977, p. 41), they are helpful in understanding commonplace situations even when incoming information is incomplete. Listeners and readers make use of their scripts for "eating at fast food restaurants," "a visit to the dentist," and "renting an apartment."

In some second language situations, scripts may facilitate comprehension, particularly when the native-culture scenario is compatible with that of the target culture. On the other hand, this may prove deceptive. A typical American "eating dinner at home" script, for example, would be different from the script of having dinner with foreign friends in their homes in France or Spain.

Textual and content schemata are also essential to comprehension (Anderson, Pichert, & Shirey, 1979). The term *textual schemata* is used to refer to knowledge about discourse-level conventions of a text: general organization, information structure or sequence followed by a particular text type (e.g., sequence for reporting the news, structure followed by a short story, conventions for making an appointment with a doctor). The term *content schemata* refers to the knowledge an individual acquires through life experiences: attending weddings, parties, funerals, school; shopping for groceries, furniture, clothing; traveling by car, train, bus; going to museums, festivals, concerns, movies. The relative importance of one type of schemata over another in the comprehension process might be difficult to establish, since it is probably the situation that "determines which schemata are most pertinent at a given time" (Long, 1989, p. 33).

Research efforts in the area of receptive skills suggest that reading and listening comprehension require different types of cognitive processes associated with particular text types. Lee and Musumeci (1988), for example, offer a framework for considering the interrelationship among performance levels (a 0–5 proficiency scale), text types, reading and listening functions, and reading and listening strategies. Reading names and street signs has to do with discerning discrete elements of memorized information. Following directions implies an understanding of the facts and the sequence of events. Cognitive strategies such as inferring, hypothesizing, and analyzing are associated with listening or reading texts that are evaluative (editorial, movie review) or projective (research reports, monographs). Table 2.4 in Chapter 2 presents the parallel hierarchies of text types and the reading skills or cognitive processes. It appears that the efficient listener engages constantly in reconstructing the language of the speaker (Lundsteen, 1979), based on textual and extratextual considerations. The listening act incorporates a broad range of linguistic competencies, knowledge systems, and cognitive strategies. The nature of speech (spontaneous, as opposed to reading of prepared texts), topic familiarity, cultural scripts, and listening purpose contribute in different ways to comprehension problems.

SECOND LANGUAGE LISTENING RESEARCH

The research on second language listening is not extensive and tends to follow developments in first language listening. Conrad (1985) found that more-advanced nonnative listeners of English relied more on semantic-level (meaning) cues than on the grammatical or phonological features of the spoken text. Advanced students were able to complete more of the blank items from a listening passage by relying on meaning cues from the text content rather than by focusing on the grammatical cues of specific sentences. Students at lower levels of proficiency, on the other hand, paid more attention to maintaining sentence grammaticality at the expense of meaning.

Wolff (1987) noted that German students learning English as a second language utilized comprehension strategies similar to those employed by native speakers, particularly at the level of script activation. Students listened to English stories and recalled the texts in German. This procedure enabled the students to make use of their world knowledge when they encountered problems with their linguistic knowledge (e.g., lexical, syntactic, discourse deficiencies in English). Thus, top-down strategies (involving the use of context, knowledge structures, and schemata) play a significant role in L2 processing. Voss's (1984) experiments among German students studying to become English teachers reveal that learners engaged in both top-down along with bottom-up strategies. Bottom-up strategies start with lower-order acoustic elements (sounds $\longrightarrow$ syllables $\longrightarrow$ words) and then continue to larger language units (sentences $\longrightarrow$ paragraphs $\longrightarrow$ texts). Unsuccessful listeners tend to rely more on bottom-up processing than on top-down strategies. The overreliance on bottom-up strategies results in microcomprehension, which is the ability to repeat or recall the linguistic forms that occur in the spoken text. Successful speech perception entails the ability to focus on the content of the message rather than simply recalling specific details or linguistic elements. This type of macrocomprehension involves the ability to paraphrase and answer general comprehension questions (Long, 1989). Top-down and bottom-up processing listening activities are discussed in the next section of this chapter.

Long's (1990) study of American college students learning Spanish revealed that bottom-up strategies were utilized more extensively when appropriate schemata were not available to the listener. When listeners do possess the relevant schemata, they seem to make less use of their linguistic knowledge in favor of knowledge structures (top-down strategies). Knowledge of textual schemata along with information about specific topics was found to increase aural comprehension significantly, especially when the listeners were trained to use strategies such as identifying key semantic elements, making associations, and anticipating the content of specific texts in radio newscasts (Weissenreider, 1987). Visual contextual cues were also found to facilitate listening comprehension among beginning students of German. Visual presentations depicting the participants in the text, their relationship, and the cultural setting served as script activators and enhanced the recall in English of a German passage. The visual cues were effective when used as a prelistening or a postlistening activity. The use of visual cues, however, was less important for the more proficient students, who could make use of their linguistic knowledge without the support of visual organizers (Mueller, 1980). In a recent study, Lund (1991) has noted that as listeners, college students learning German tended to rely on more top-down processing strategies, resulting in a higher number of text misinterpretations. He suggests that listeners may need extra training in order to use abilities to infer more successfully and consider textual cues in the process of confirming or modifying assumptions about meaning.

Research conducted by Chamot and Kupper (1989) among students learning Spanish indicated that successful pupils used prelistening tasks (e.g., written comprehension questions) to activate what they knew about the topic and predict possible text context. The students also focused selectively on the context during the listening phase, relating the new information to what they knew about the topic and confirming or correcting their predictions. Successful listening comprehension required the use of both metacognitive strategies (self-monitoring by checking, verifying, or correcting one's comprehension in the course of a language task) and cognitive strategies (inferencing by guessing meanings or predicting outcomes on the basis of available information; elaboration by relating new information to prior knowledge). To determine some of the strategies utilized by students during listening situations, Chamot and Kupper (1989) suggest the use of oral interview procedures. Specific tasks can be delineated to make students aware, individually or in groups, of what learning strategies come into play during the listening process. For instance, students could be asked:

> Your teacher speaks to you in Spanish, explaining grammar rules, making conversation, giving you directions and assignments. There are several words you do not know in what your teacher says. You have to guess at the meanings of these words. How do you figure out the meanings of the new words? Do you have special tricks or ways that help you understand what the teacher says in Spanish? What is your general approach to listening in Spanish? What do you do if you don't understand the Spanish you hear? (Chamot & Kupper, 1989, pp. 22–23)

In summary, listeners are actively involved in the comprehension of oral texts. The major findings of the studies reviewed suggest the following:

1. Advanced learners rely more on semantic-level cues than on the syntactic or phonological features of the spoken text.
2. Some learners are able to rely on both top-down and bottom-up strategies.
3. Unsuccessful listeners tend to rely more on bottom-up strategies, resulting in the recall of some linguistic forms rather than the comprehension of meaning.
4. Listeners will make more extensive use of bottom-up strategies if they do not possess the relevant schemata.
5. Visual contextual cues facilitate listening comprehension, especially among beginning students.
6. Prelistening tasks can activate listeners' top-down processing strategies.
7. Successful comprehension skills require the use of both metacognitive and cognitive strategies.
8. Teachers can help students to become aware of the strategies they use during listening situations.

TEACHING CONSIDERATIONS

Various frameworks have been proposed for organizing listening activities. Joiner (1986) suggests considering some of the perspectives from first language listening processes (receiving, attending, assigning meaning, remembering, and verbal response) or listening purposes (auditory discrimination, visual discrimination, comprehensive, therapeutic, critical, and appreciative). Omaggio (1986) organizes listening activities on the basis of ACTFL proficiency levels (novice, intermediate, advanced, and superior) and performance descriptions with respect to language functions (identification of text types, understanding main ideas, and detecting the speaker's attitudes), context (personal information, food, travel, lodging), and degree of accuracy in comprehension (understanding of simple memorized words, expressions, need for repetition of speech delivered at normal rate, inability to detect irony or satire). Listening units can also be sequenced on the basis of situations (going on a trip, at the airport, eating at a restaurant, finding accommodations) and the tasks the learners have to perform (making inquiries, using the telephone, listening for main ideas), given the particular needs of learners (Yalden, 1987).

Specific listening activities can be approached in terms of two distinct processes involved in listening comprehension: bottom-up and top-down processing (Chaudron & Richards, 1986). *Bottom-up processing* focuses on the specific elements of the text—sounds, words, clauses, and utterances—that can be analyzed at successive levels of organization until the meaning of the message is comprehended. Richards (1990) offers a number of exercises that involve bottom-up listening and require the learner to engage in different kinds of processes:

Exercises that require bottom-up processes develop the learner's ability to do the following:

- Retain input while it is being processed
- Recognize word divisions
- Recognize key words in utterances
- Recognize key transitions in a discourse
- Use knowledge of word-order patterns to identify constituents in utterance
- Recognize grammatical relations between key elements in sentences
- Recognize the function of word stress in sentences
- Recognize the function of intonation in sentences (p. 51)

Some exercises might require the learner to do the following tasks:

- Identify the references of pronouns used in a conversation
- Recognize if a sentence is active or passive

- Distinguish between sentences containing causative and noncausative verbs
- Identify major constituents in a sentence, such as subject and object, verb and adverb
- Distinguish between sentences with and without auxiliary verbs
- Recognize the use of word stress to mark the information focus of a sentence
- Distinguish between sentences containing similar-sounding tenses
- Identify prepositions in rapid speech
- Recognize sequence markers
- Distinguish between yes/no and *wh-* questions (p. 51)

Top-down processing requires the use of background knowledge in order to understand the meaning of the text. This knowledge can be in the form of scripts or schemata, awareness of textual features, information about different topics, or personal experiences. To approach reading as a top-down process, Richards (1990) suggests a number of activities and tasks that lead the listener to concerns that are stated implicitly or exist beyond the spoken text. Exercises that require top-down processes develop the learner's ability to do the following:

- Use key words to construct the schema of a discourse
- Construct plans and schema from elements of a discourse
- Infer the topic of a discourse
- Infer the outcome of an event
- Infer the cause or effect of an event
- Infer unstated details of a situation
- Infer the sequence of a series of events
- Infer comparisons
- Distinguish between literal and figurative meanings
- Distinguish between facts and opinions (p. 51)

Exercises that address these goals might require the learner to do tasks such as:

- Listen to part of the conversation and infer the topic of the conversation
- Look at pictures and then listen to conversations about the pictures and match them with the pictures
- Listen to conversation and identify the setting
- Read a list of key points to be covered in talk and then number them in sequence while listening to the talk

- Read information about a topic, then listen to a talk on the topic and check whether the information was mentioned or not
- Read one side of a telephone conversation and guess the other speaker's responses; then listen to the telephone conversation
- Look at pictures of people speaking and guess what they might be saying or doing, then listen to their actual conversations
- Complete a story, then listen to how the story really ended
- Guess what news headlines might refer to, then listen to news broadcasts about the events referred to (Richards, 1990, pp. 60-61)

Richards (1990) also points out the need to consider the interactional and transactional functions of language. Interactional uses of language involve the social functions of language, such as greetings, compliments, joking, praising, using markers of social distance among speakers, and engaging in a real conversation versus chatting with friends to pass the time. Transactional uses of language consist of occasions when language is used to transmit information, as in providing instructions, giving advice, making requests, lecturing about specific topics, and informing on news broadcasts.

A taxonomy for structuring listening activities has been proposed by Lund (1990), who states that at least five elements should be considered in the design of listening tasks:

1. Function or aspects of the message that listener may attempt to process: (1) identification, (2) orientation, (3) main-idea comprehension, (4) detail comprehension, (5) full comprehension, and (6) replication
2. Listener response involving one of these nine reactions: (1) doing (physical response), (2) choosing (selecting from alternatives such as pictures, objects, actions, and graphics), (3) transferring (receiving information in one form and drawing a picture based on a text or making a map), (4) answering questions about the text, (5) condensing the message as in an oral summary outline, or written abstract, (6) extending the text such as providing an ending to a story or solving a problem, (7) duplicating the message in another modality, for example, dictation, oral repetition, or translation, (8) modeling a feature of the text such as intonation or trying to create a similar example of the whole text such as preparing a weather report based on a radio newscast, and (9) conversing by responding interactively with another participant regarding the content of a particular oral text
3. Text type, such as an advertisement, a newscast, a conversation between buyer and seller, ordering a meal at a restaurant, making a reservation for a hotel room by telephone
4. Topic of the text, for example, food, clothing, train travel, shopping in a department store, checking in at a hotel, going to the movies

5. Method of presentation, through the use of such means as a prelistening activity, video, audio recording, or written script

Each listening activity should have a specific objective or set of objectives. The objective may approach listening from a top-down or a bottom-up perspective and include interactional or transactional uses of language (Richards, 1990). The syllabus should offer learners the opportunity to comprehend language according to these six different functions and nine ways of responding to an oral text, as well as offer a range of text types and topics appropriate to the students' proficiency level (Lund, 1990).

A four-stage sequence for guiding students toward global listening proficiency has been outlined by Glisan (1988). The plan, based on a reading model (Phillips, 1984), integrates both listening and cognitive skills. Other language areas such as speaking and writing are also included in the sequence:

1. *Preteaching or preparation stage:* Students listen to a brief introduction about the text, which can include the title, first sentence, or several phrases. Students then discuss possible content, vocabulary, structures, and organization of the text, thereby calling to mind background knowledge, schemata, or scripts.
2. *Skimming and scanning stages:* Students listen to the text for the gist of the message in order to determine the main idea without attending to all the details, as in a newscast, announcement, interview, or commercial. Students can also "scan" or focus on specific items of information included in the text, such as the possibility for rain as noted in the weather report, the location of a clothing sale as reported in a radio commercial, or the names of the persons involved in a traffic accident mentioned in a newscast.
3. *Comprehension stage:* Students receive feedback on a comprehension check of the entire text. Comprehension exercises can involve different types of responses (writing a summary in the native language; choosing an appropriate title or main idea; completing a diagram, chart, or picture with information from the spoken text) and can combine both oral and written modalities.
4. *Transferable/integrating skills stage:* Students link the listening text to oral and written language as they express their feelings and attitudes about the topic through such activities as role-playing situations, pair or group interviews, writing character sketches, or written essays.

The four-stage sequence for extracting meaning from spoken discourse also enables students to apply a number of "cognitive strategies aimed at uncovering a speaker's message" (Dunkel, 1986, p. 100). Listeners will be able to (1) predict or anticipate the content of the message during prelistening or preparation stage; (2) monitor for discrepancies in the message received, with the meaning predicted or anticipated during the skimming and comprehension phases; (3) select relevant and ignore irrelevant aspects of the message during the comprehension stage; and (4) check the accuracy of comprehension, especially during the comprehension and transferable phases (Rixon, 1981).

Dunkel (1986) states that teachers also need to provide students with extensive listening and a broad range of authentic spoken discourse through audio and video tapes. Authentic texts, whether planned or unplanned, can be successfully incorporated into the syllabus, particularly if one considers the nature of the task (the function for listening, type of listener's response, and special features of the spoken text) instead of solely the linguistic complexity of the discourse (Lund, 1990).

Borges (1987) urges teachers to pose the following questions when considering use of commercial recordings with particular types of students:

1. Does the recording presuppose knowledge of vocabulary not previously introduced, or words that students may not recognize at a normal rate of speed?
2. Does the listening task require that students respond to many levels of comprehension?
3. Is the rate of speed of the recording too fast for the particular class level?
4. Does the topic of the recording presuppose types of knowledge (textual, content, cultural script) that students do not possess?
5. Does the content of the selection involve grammatical features not yet examined or mastered in class?

The answers to some of these questions can be formulated by following procedures offered by Glisan (1988) in her four-stage sequence toward global listening comprehension. Lund's (1990) taxonomy for structuring listening activities can also offer a specific set of strategies, making it possible to use a wide range of text types and topics with students at different proficiency levels.

It is important to note that listening activities may require students to respond in a variety of ways. Byrnes (1984) lists a number of tasks that do not entail considerable language-production demands: multiple-choice, fill-ins, true-false answers, matching, and arranging sentences according to a proper sequence. Tasks such as open-ended questions; oral and written summaries; story endings; and predicting outcomes, causes, and relationships involve considerable production requirements. Richards (1983) stresses the need to establish a set of criteria for evaluating the appropriateness of listening activities. Questions such as the following should be asked to ensure that listening tasks place language in realistic contexts:

1. Does the listening activity involve language skills and behaviors that are associated with listening in the real world rather than relying on other abilities (e.g., visual discrimination or general intelligence)?
2. Does the listening activity focus on the listening process rather than on the recall of facts, details, or events that entail memorizing abilities?

3. Are the listening tasks (cloze technique, multiple-choice items, oral or written summaries), typical of real-life situations?
4. Is the listening task a teaching strategy (e.g., prelistening comprehension check) or a testing situation (e.g., comprehension questions after listening to text)?
5. To what extent does the listening text resemble the natural language of native speakers?

DESIGNING LISTENING TASKS

Listening tasks may require learners to speak, read, write, and act in response to a particular oral situation. At the same time, listening tasks might entail top-down or bottom-up strategies involving different (1) genres (announcement on the radio, song, taped dialogue, oral description with visuals), (2) topics (food, weather, family, sports), (3) language functions (inform, warn, convince, praise, direct), (4) discourse structures, and (5) linguistic elements. Many types of reactions to the spoken texts are possible. Students might be asked to:

1. Write a summary
2. Answer comprehension questions
3. Listen selectively for specific information
4. Draw a picture based on the description
5. Dramatize the oral text using pictures and real objects
6. Report orally the main points of the spoken text
7. Prepare an outline
8. Complete a chart
9. Repeat the language of the spoken text
10. Ask questions about the content
11. Prepare a dialogue based on the content
12. Create a similar oral text

The 10 listening tasks that follow represent a broad range of oral text types or genres and involve a number of learner behaviors and cognitive strategies. Table 7.1 classifies each activity according to genre, learning objective, and task demands. Each task can be adapted to other proficiency levels and languages.

Listening tasks A, B, F, and J from Table 7.1 do not require interaction with written texts. Comprehension checks for tasks G and H are assessed through writing, and tasks C and I include reading. Analysis of the television commercial (task J) is accomplished through group discussions. It is important to note that the sequence of behaviors can be varied for each task:

1. listen; nonverbal response
2. listen; read; oral response
3. listen; write; oral response

TABLE 7.1 Components of listening tasks

Text/Genre	Learning Objective	Listening Skill
A Commands	Perform directions	Recognize oral commands and perform the acts
B Directions	Draw picture	Translate oral to visual
C Description with visuals	Complete sentences	Relate information
D Conversation	Check off items	Selective recalls
E Radio announcement	Label map	Solve/demonstrate
		Translate oral to visual information
F Narrative	Arrange pictures	Translate oral to visual information
G Narrative	Fill in chart	Classify information
H Telephone calls	Take notes	Rephrase/reduce information
I Conversation	Answer comprehension questions	Recall details
J Television commercial	Analyze message	Evaluate information

4. listen; role play
5. listen; interact; solve problem

Some tasks are easier than others, based on textual factors (language familiarity, organization of information, density of facts), learner considerations (prior learning experiences, language skills, motivation to compete task), and task complexity (number of steps to solve, type of context provided, availability of help, and time to complete). Nunan (1989) points out that task difficulty needs to be taken into account in the planning of classroom activities. The listening tasks on the following pages also specify the topic, language function, and linguistic elements. The procedures identify the situation and the conditions under which each task is being undertaken. Some listening tasks require a prelistening phase to introduce students to culturally relevant information, vocabulary, or genre structure. Postlistening activities can extend the oral text to related reading or speaking situations. Students may also respond to the text in a personal way by relating it to their own experiences, interests, or concerns. For example, listeners may hear a song and write a few sentences about their feelings or associations with the lyrics.

In grading listening exercises, one should keep in mind three major aspects of listening: (1) the type of input, (2) the support provided by the context, and (3) the kind of task involved (Anderson & Lynch, 1988). The type of input can be static, dynamic, or abstract (Brown & Yule, 1983). A static text, such as describing an object or giving someone directions to get to a destination, establishes relationships in a fixed manner. Describing an incident or telling a story, on the other hand, makes dynamic use of language. These situations usually involve shifts of time and scenes. The relationships among persons or characters may change, as in the case of family members growing older or moving to another home. There are also abstract listening texts where the focus is on opinions and beliefs rather than concrete objects or specific actions and persons. Texts of this type might involve political speeches, movie reviews, and talk shows.

Text difficulty increases as one moves across different types of input: static ⟶ dynamic ⟶ abstract. This is further compounded by the number of potentially confusable elements found in each type of text. Within the dynamic category, for example, listening to a story with four characters from different backgrounds is more difficult than following a narrative involving a brother and sister. Visual supports (using pictures, illustrations, simple line drawings) enhance aural comprehension abilities among listeners. Some helpful prelistening activities to consider are (1) a brief preview of the text, (2) discussions about the cultural content, key words, expressions, or text organization, (3) formulation of a list of prelistening questions, and (4) directions on how to listen—in other words, the listening purpose.

TASK A

Task:	Recognize and perform oral commands
Genre:	Oral instructions
Topic:	Parts of the body
Function:	Follow and direct others to follow a course of action
Linguistic elements:	Prepositions of location; action verbs; vocabulary related to parts of the body
Objective:	Students will act out the teacher's oral commands about location of parts of the body and then give each other instructions to follow.
Procedure:	Teacher models the behaviors in front of the class.

1. Stand up
2. Place your left hand on your head
3. Close your eyes
4. Open your mouth
5. Touch your left knee with your right hand
6. Smile
7. Jump up and down
8. Sit down at your desk

Teacher then gives instructions to the whole class and to specific students. Students reverse roles and direct each other to follow commands.

TASK B

Task:	Draw a picture based on oral description
Genre:	Oral description
Topic:	Physical environment

Function: Follow directions and provide information to others

Linguistic elements: Locative phrases; nouns (lake, tree, bird, fish, rock, sun); articles

Objective: Students will draw a picture based on the teacher's description of a country setting.

Procedures: Teacher reads the directions to the students:

1. Draw a lake in the center of your paper.
2. Draw two trees next to the lake. Draw the trees on the right side of the lake.
3. Draw a fish in the lake.
4. Draw a sun over the lake.
5. Draw a cloud near the trees.
6. Draw three birds near the cloud.
7. Draw some grass around the lake.

Students show their pictures to the class and describe the contents.

Task B is adapted from Nelson & Winters, 1980, p. 12.

TASK C

Task: Note specific information

Genre: Oral presentation with visuals

Topic: Furniture in a house

Function: Identify the location of furniture in a room

Linguistic elements: Prepositional phrases, verb *poner*, room furniture

Objective: Students will identify the location of room furniture upon hearing a description.

Procedures: Students are provided a floor plan of a bedroom that contains the location of furniture. In order to achieve the aforementioned objective, a prelistening warm-up activity is necessary to ensure that students understand the prepositional phrases. The prepositional phrases are written on the board. The teacher makes various true/false statements concerning the furniture in the target language. Students respond orally and corrections are made by other students in the target language. Students listen to a cassette recording and indicate on a worksheet the location of specific furniture items. The tape contains sentences such as:

1. Debajo de la ventana Daniel pone su _____
2. Los chicos cubren el piso con una _____

3. El escritorio está al lado de _____
4. Frente al escritorio hay una _____
5. A la izquierda de la puerta hay una _____
6. Sobre la mesita de noche Daniel pone su _____
7. Contra la otra pared, al lado del librero, hay una _____
8. Debajo de la cama Daniel deja sus _____

Task C is adapted from Shiland, 1988.

TASK D

Task:	Note specific information
Genre:	Recorded conversation
Topic:	Food items in a French restaurant
Function:	Aurally identify food and drink items
Linguistic elements:	Food and drink items on listening-unit card
Objective:	Students will identify from a cassette recording the orders placed by other customers in a restaurant.
Procedure:	Teacher establishes the listening situation by informing students that a group of American students, seated in a French restaurant, overhear various customers placing their orders.

Each student is given a listening grid as shown below, listing in English various food and drink items available in a French restaurant and designating customers 1, 2, and 3. The teacher plays a cassette recording on which French natives (a monsieur, a madame, a young person) are heard placing their orders. After each customer has placed his or her order, students check those items ordered.

Listening Grid

Food/Drink	Customer 1	Customer 2	Customer 3
soup			
beef	X		
ham			
chicken			
fish			
potatoes	X		
peas			
carrots			
green beans	X		

Food/Drink	Customer 1	Customer 2	Customer 3
salad	X		
cheese			
fruit			
coffee			
tea			
wine	X		

Task D is adapted from Porter, 1987, p. 326.

TASK E

Task:	Note specific information from oral report
Genre:	Radio announcement
Topic:	Weather
Function:	Aurally identify weather conditions and give to others a course of action appropriate to the weather conditions
Linguistic elements:	Commands; personal pronouns and vocabulary about directions; temperature, weather conditions
Objective:	Students will identify from a radio announcement the weather conditions on a German map and will give advice to others on the course of action to follow.
Procedure:	Students listen to a recorded weather report in German. On a map they draw the symbols for rain, snow, sunshine, and cloudy for the corresponding regions. The day's temperatures are also indicated for selected cities.

Task E is adapted from Buhr, 1988.

TASK F

Task:	Match pictures with oral description
Genre:	Oral narrative with visuals
Topic:	Marriage problems
Function:	Obtain information to arrange visuals
Linguistic elements:	Adverbs of time; expressions of anger; apologies
Objective:	Students will arrange visuals in a sequence that matches the oral description.

Procedure: Teacher introduces the topic to the class. The linguistic elements are reviewed, and students receive a series of pictures in a set order. Students listen to the teacher's description of the situation and number each picture according to the sequence of events in the oral narrative. Excerpts from the oral text:

Couple started quarreling . . .
Got really fierce . . .
Wife walked out . . .
Husband begged her to come back . . .
Made it up.

Task F is adapted from Ur, 1984, pp. 98–99.

TASK G

Task: Listen for specific information

Genre: Recorded passage

Topic: Mother's birthday celebration

Function: Obtain information to complete a chart

Linguistic elements: Use of *quel* in exclamations; possessive pronouns; vocabulary related to gifts; birthdays; expressions for socializing

Objective: Students will complete chart with information about persons and gifts mentioned in oral text.

Procedure: Students listen to recorded passage and complete a chart based on information provided in the oral narrative.

Then students compare their charts, discuss the text, and review ways of "thanking," "complimenting," and expressing affection.

Transcript of the oral narrative.

"Bon anniversaire, Maman!"
Toute la famille est réunie. C'est l'anniversaire de Mme. Dupont. "Bon anniversaire, Maman chérie!" Un à un, les enfants lui donnent leurs cadeaux et l'embrassent sur les deux joues.
"Oh, les jolies fleurs! Merci, Xavier, elles sont ravissantes!"
"Quel joli foulard! Il ira parfaitement avec ma nouvelle robe! Les couleurs sont comme le tien, n'est-ce pas? Merci, Françoise. C'est un très bon choix!"

"Et Vincent! Quels jolies bracelets! C'est un très bon choix!"

"Une montre! Quelle surprise! Merci, Claude. Tu n'aurais pas dû, mon chéri!"

"Merci à tous encore une fois."

"Et maintenant, je vous emmène tous au restaurant," dit M. Dupont. "J'ai réservé une table pour sept heures et demie. Alors, en route!"

Persons mentioned	Gifts mentioned

Task G is adapted from Rayder, 1988.

TASK H

Task:	Take notes while listening to telephone calls
Genre:	Recorded telephone messages
Topics:	Renting or buying a home or apartment, rooms in a house
Function:	Obtain information about a person's housing needs and report details to others
Linguistic elements:	Expressions of housing needs
Objective:	Students will record basic information from telephone calls made by prospective home buyers or renters.
Procedure:	Teacher tells students that they will receive five telephone calls from prospective home buyers or renters. As a warm-up activity, the parts of the house are reviewed.

Students hear recorded telephone calls and jot down basic information. Then, working in pairs, the students refer to newspaper housing ads previously distributed and decide which advertisement best matches each caller's wishes. Each pair of students reports the results to the class.

Sample scripts:

Buenos días. Me llamo Miguel González. Mi esposa y yo deseamos comprar una casa. Tenemos dos hijos y por eso nos gustaría una casa con tres cuartos de dormir y dos baños. También es importante que tenga un garaje para dos coches.

Buenas tardes. Me llamo María Ramos. He venido a Miami a pasar mis vacaciones. Desearía ver un apartamento donde pueda quedarme y a la vez jugar mis deportes favoritos.

Buenos días. Me llamo Juan Ayala. Yo busco una casa más bien grande porque tengo una familia numerosa. Necesitamos una sala de estar amplia y nos gustaría tener un comedor grande donde podamos estar los siete.

Buenos días. Me llamo Héctor Santos y llegué de España ayer. Necesito encontrar una casa amueblada con cuatro dormitorios. Mi familia va a llegar en fecha próxima. ¿Tiene usted una casa con estas condiciones?

Hola. Le habla Julio Olivares. Yo busco una casa moderna, lista para habitar y con buen sistema de seguridad. También desearía que tuviera una piscina porque me gusta nadar.

Task H is adapted from Shiland, 1988.

TASK I

Task:	Note specific information and recreate a similar situation
Genre:	Recorded conversation
Topic:	Hotel, lost luggage
Function:	Obtain and provide information about a situation between a hotel receptionist and an angry customer
Linguistic elements:	Complaints; expressions of time, location, and luggage
Objectives:	Students will answer comprehension questions to indicate understanding of hotel situation.
Procedure:	Teacher informs students about the conversation they will hear on tape. Students are asked to listen once for the gist of the situation, and then they are told to listen again for specific details:

1. Why is the customer so upset?
2. Who saw the customer's suitcase?
3. What does the hotel receptionist tell the angry customer?

4. How does the customer respond to the hotel receptionist?

Later, students work in pairs to create similar role-playing situations in which there are reports of lost articles, and they use assertive expressions and complaints.

Task I is adapted from Herman, 1988

TASK J

Task:	Evaluate the contents of an advertisement
Genre:	Television commercial
Topic:	Transportation—automobile
Function:	Obtain information about a product aurally/visually and provide personal evaluation.
Linguistic elements:	Parts of an automobile; adjectives and adverbs related to expressions of elegance, safety, and durability
Objective:	Students will watch a television commercial about a European car and then evaluate the commercial.
Procedure:	Students watch a two-minute television commercial in the target language twice.

Students meet in small groups and discuss (1) the effect the commercial tries to achieve and the means used, (2) the image the product tries to project, (3) the population targeted to buy the product, and (4) the artistic or aesthetic merits of the advertisement.

Student groups report to the class and compare their evaluations.

SUMMARY

Listening situations can vary significantly in terms of situations (airport, hotel, theater, department store), topics (weather, shopping, food, politics), participants (friend, stranger, common service providers, children), and genres (public announcement, news, lecture, conversation, song). Spoken language has many features absent from written texts, including the use of reduced forms, false starts, hesitations, and repetitions. Comprehending spoken language involves both linguistic and nonlinguistic elements, including textual and content schemata. Contextual or visual clues may be limited or totally absent, as in the case of noninteractional situations such as radio programs and announcements at train stations. Research findings indicate that important differences in listening comprehension are due to how listeners process aural input, how they make use of schemata and contextual cues, and how teachers present listening tasks. Unsuccessful listeners tend to rely on more bottom-up strategies when they lack the relevant schemata. Teachers can assist learners by developing listening tasks that have a specific set of objectives and by relating listening to other language modalities.

Listening activities can be organized according to proficiency notions, sociocultural situations, and bottom-up or top-down processes. Listening activities can also be structured in terms of such aspects as function, topic, text type, listener response, and method of presentation. Some listening tasks might be based on insights from reading as a process. This might consist of the following stages: (1) prelistening or preparation stage, (2) skimming and scanning stages, (3) comprehension stage, (4) transferable/integrating skills stage. Students should be exposed to a broad range of authentic spoken discourse by making use of audio and video-tapes. Listening tasks can range from oral commands to mass media and might require oral, written, or psychomotor responses. The nature of oral texts, as well as learner and task complexity need to be considered when designing listening activities.

ACTIVITIES

1. Prepare a list of typical listening tasks a learner would encounter in the following situations: airport, hotel, restaurant, and theater.
2. Write a one-page dialogue in the target language with a fellow student, and then consider the issues related to (1) the topics covered, (2) the question-and-answer sequence along with the opening and closing segments, and (3) the use of different language functions.
3. Compare typical scripts for the following situations: (1) eating at a U.S. restaurant versus a comparable one in the target culture, (2) visiting the home of a friend here and abroad, and (3) shopping for clothing in one's home town and in the target country.
4. Select a dialogue from an intermediate or advanced language textbook, and describe the possible role textual and content schemata play in the comprehension of such oral discourse.
5. Observe a language class and make an inventory of the types of listening activities included, using the framework proposed by Byrnes.
6. Examine a few lessons from a language text and determine (1) the importance given to the development of listening skills, (2) the types of listening activities (bottom-up and top-down), and (3) the use of authentic listening situations.
7. Based on the research findings in this chapter with respect to successful listening comprehension strategies in teaching and learning, prepare a list of suggestions for a beginning teacher.
8. Develop a listening activity that requires both bottom-up and top-down processes based on Richards's list of tasks. Compare your approach with those of other students, and discuss the implications for the learner.

9. Review Lund's taxonomy for structuring listening activities and plan two listening tasks for a specific group of learners. Discuss the implications for the development of listening comprehension from this perspective.

10. Choose an authentic listening task and prepare a lesson that incorporates Glisan's four-stage sequence.

11. Prepare a listening task based on a radio announcement or a telephone call.

12. Analyze a listening activity in terms of the task requirements, topic, functions, linguistic elements, and learner behaviors.

REFERENCES

Anderson, A., & Lynch, T. (1988). *Listening*. Oxford: Oxford University Press.

Anderson, R. C., Pichert, J., & Shirey, L. I. (1979). *Effects of the reader's schemata at different points in time* (Tech. Rep. No. 119). Urbana, IL: University of Illinois, Center for the Study of Reading.

Borges, D. (1987). A few practical suggestions toward solving the listening dilemma. *Hispania, 70*(1), 171-173.

Brown, G., & Yule, G. (1983). *Teaching the spoken language*. Cambridge, England: Cambridge University Press.

Buhr, M. (1988). Materials prepared for a course. Albany: State University of New York, School of Education.

Byrnes, H. (1984). The role of listening comprehension: A theoretical base. *Foreign Language Annals, 17*(4), 317-329.

Canale, M. (1984). Considerations in the testing of reading and listening proficiency. *Foreign Language Annals, 17*(4), 349-391.

Chamot, A. U., & Kupper, L. (1989). Learning strategies in foreign language instruction. *Foreign Language Annals, 22*(1), 13-24.

Chaudron, C., & Richard, J. C. (1986). The effect of discourse markers on the comprehension of lectures. *Applied Linguistics, 7*(2), 113-127.

Coakley, C. G., & Wolvin, A. D. (1986). Listening to the native language. In B. H. Wing (Ed.), *Listening, reading, writing: Analysis and application* (pp. 11-42). Middlebury, VT: Northeast Conference on the Teaching of Foreign Languages.

Conrad, L. (1985). Semantic versus syntactic cues in listening comprehension. *Studies in Second Language Acquisition, 7*(1), 59-68.

Dunkel, P. A. (1986). Developing listening fluency in L2: Theoretical principles and pedagogical considerations. *Modern Language Journal, 70*(2), 99-106.

Glisan, E. W. (1988). A plan for teaching listening comprehension: Adaptation of an instructional reading model. *Foreign Language Annals, 21*(1), 9-16.

Herman, N. (1988). Materials prepared for a course. Albany: State University of New York, School of Education.

Joiner, E. G. (1986). Listening in the foreign language. In B. H. Wing (Ed.), *Listening, reading, writing: Analysis and application* (pp. 43-69). Middlebury, VT: Northeast Conference.

Lee, J. F., & Musumeci, D. (1988). On hierarchies of reading skills. *Modern Language Journal, 72*(2), 173-187.

Littlewood, W. (1984). *Foreign and second language learning*. Cambridge, England: Cambridge University Press.

Long, D. R. (1989). Second language listening comprehension: A schema-theoretic perspective. *Modern Language Journal*, 73(1), 32–40.

Long, D. R. (1990). An exploratory study of background knowledge and second language listening comprehension. *Studies in Second Language Acquisition*, 12(1), 65–75.

Lund, R. J. (1990). A taxonomy for teaching second language listening. *Foreign Language Annals*, 23(2), 105–115.

Lund, R. J. (1991). A comparison of second language listening and reading comprehension. *Modern Language Journal*, 75(2), 196–204.

Lundsteen, S. W. (1979). *Listening: Its impact on reading and the other language arts*. Urbana, IL: NCTE, ERIC. National Council of Teachers of English (NCTE), Education Resources Information Center (ERIC).

Mueller, G. (1980). Visual contextual cues and listening comprehension: An experiment. *Modern Language Journal*, 64, 335–340.

Nelson, G., & Winters, T. (1980). *ESL operations: Techniques for learning while doing*. Rowley, MA: Newbury House.

Nunan, D. (1989). *Designing tasks for the communicative classroom*. Cambridge, England: Cambridge University Press.

Omaggio, A. C. (1986). *Teaching language in context*. Boston: Heinle & Heinle.

Phillips, J. K. (1984). Practical implications of recent research in reading. *Foreign Language Annals*, 17, 285–296.

Porter, L. P. (1987). Using the ACTFL proficiency guidelines to achieve goals of exploratory language courses. *Foreign Language Annals*, 20(4), 323–330.

Rayder, C. (1988). Materials prepared for a course. Albany: State University of New York, School of Education.

Richards, J. C. (1983). Listening comprehension: Approach, design, procedure. *TESOL Quarterly*, 17, 219–240.

Richards, J. C. (1985). *The context of language teaching*. Cambridge, England: Cambridge University Press.

Richards, J. C. (1990). *The language teaching matrix*. Cambridge, England: Cambridge University Press.

Rigg, P. (1991). Whole language in TESOL. *TESOL Quarterly*, 25(3), 521–542.

Rivers, W. M. (1987). *Interactive language teaching*. Cambridge, England: Cambridge University Press.

Rixon, S. (1981). The design of materials to foster particular listening skills. *The teaching of listening comprehension. ELT Documents*, 121, 68–106.

Schank, R., & Abelson, R. P. (1977). *Scripts, plans, goals, and understanding*. Hillsdale, NJ: Erlbaum.

Shiland, M. (1988). Materials prepared for a course. Albany: State University of New York, School of Education.

Ur, P. (1984). *Teaching listening comprehension*. Cambridge, England: Cambridge University Press.

Ur, P. (1988). *Grammar practice activities: A practice guide for teachers*. Cambridge, England: Cambridge University Press.

Van Patten, B. (1992). Second language acquisition research and foreign language teaching. Part 2. *ADFL Bulletin*, 23, 23–27.

Voss, B. (1984). *Slips of the ear: Investigations into the speech perception behavior of German speakers of English*. Tübingen: Narr.

Weissenreider, M. (1987). Listening to the news in Spanish. *Modern Language Journal,* 71(1), 18-27.

Wolff, D. (1987). Some assumptions about second language text comprehension. *Studies in Second language Acquisition, 9*(3), 307-326.

Yalden, J. (1987). *Principles of course design for language teaching.* Cambridge, England: Cambridge University Press.

chapter 8

Reading for Different Purposes

Interactive reading is an integral part of communicative language learning. Consider the processes that must be practiced and assessed. Prereading reviews language. In asking students to decide what the text is about (text schema) and what they know about this subject (reader schema), the teacher has students practice language in context. Strategies reinforce discourse gambits. To learn strategies, students need to articulate their processing an L2 metalanguage, thinking aloud about how understanding is achieved. Instead of labeling answers "right" and "wrong," the interactive class emphasizes expanding what the reader knows. Reading becomes a reasoning task connected to a language task.

J. K. Swaffar, 1988

Reading in L2 classrooms encompasses a number of issues related to such matters as the type of text, reader characteristics, instructional approaches, and reading as an interactive process. Reading second language texts involves a wide range of genres, from literary forms to orientational materials such as schedules, maps, and pictures with captions. Written texts can be read with different purposes in mind, requiring a number of cognitive processes to reconstruct the meaning. Research on the comprehension of written discourse suggests that learners' characteristics, proficiency levels, background knowledge, and use of reading strategies can influence reading performance. Determining reading comprehension strategies among students should be an important instructional consideration. Classroom reading tasks can be planned and sequenced in ways that promote the development of reading proficiency in relation to other language abilities.

This chapter considers a number of issues related to the teaching of reading skills as an interaction with written texts. The following questions are addressed:

1. What is the nature of reading in L2 classrooms?
2. What are the different types of reading texts?
3. What is involved in the comprehension of written language?
4. What are some of the research findings in reading comprehension?
5. What considerations need to be taken into account when designing reading activities?
6. What are some examples of reading tasks?

READING IN L2 CLASSROOMS

As in L1, reading in L2 has to do with the interpretation of texts. The comprehension of written texts is a complex process involving many linguistic subskills and systems of knowledge, including the social uses of written language and structures for organizing information. The reading process can be conceived of as an interaction between the writer (author of the text) and the reader. The reader constructs the meaning of the text through use of comprehension strategies, awareness of textual features (rhetorical structure, vocabulary, grammar) and knowledge of extratextual elements (topic familiarity, cultural situations, and text types).

Reading might be seen as a source of language input, influencing the development of writing abilities. The reading-writing connection appears to be a reciprocal process affected by such factors as proficiency levels, learner characteristics, and instructional approaches. Written texts can serve multiple functions in L2 classrooms. Wallace (1992) points out that a text can be used as:

1. A vehicle for teaching specific language structures and vocabulary
2. An opportunity to promote key reading strategies
3. An occasion to present content that is familiar and of interest to the learners
4. A cultural context to present authentic, naturally occurring social messages
5. A situation to exploit other modalities of communication (listening, speaking, and writing) and language subskills

TYPES OF READING SITUATIONS

Reading in a second language can include a broad range of *text types*. These texts may come from literary genres such as plays, short stories, essays, poems, and novels. They may also involve informative materials (labels, warnings, recipes, handbooks, instructions, notices, rules and regulations), orientational texts (travel brochures, menus, plane and train schedules, catalogs, posters, signs, TV and radio guides, advertisements), evaluative reports (editorials, magazine articles, travel essays, reviews, biographies), and visuals with texts (comic strips, cartoons, maps, pictures with captions, charts, diagrams). The reader may only need to understand explicitly stated information (e.g., recognize the names and numbers on a street sign), or the reader may be required to go beyond the text as in the case of having to judge fairness in reporting an incident (e.g., a newspaper editorial).

At present there is no comprehensive taxonomy able to classify the extensive variety of text types. Child (1987), for example, has proposed a classification scheme based on the degree to which the reader and writer share background information. These text types are organized hierarchically to correspond with the ACTFL's proficiency levels (1986) and include four basic purposes: orientation, instructive, evaluative, and projective. Lee and Musumeci (1988) have extended Child's (1987) system to include the reading skills that parallel the hierarchies of text types. Table 2.4, presented in Chapter 2, provides specific examples of the genres that correspond to each level and text type. For example, orientational texts (travel and registration forms, schedules, menus) require reading skills such as skimming and scanning. Instructive texts (ads, labels, directions, newspaper accounts) are linked to skills in decoding and classifying. Evaluative texts (editorials, analyses, library texts) call for interpretation and inferring skills.

Nevertheless, Lee (1988) notes that many factors can affect text difficulty, making Child's (1987) hierarchy questionable. Some difficulties found with text types might be attributed to such factors as the topic, passage density associated with the proportion of concepts or information units in the passage, or the cognitive strategies the reader needs to employ to accomplish particular comprehension tasks. How learners actually interact with written texts is discussed in the section on reading research.

There appear to be at least two main reasons for reading texts: for pleasure and for obtaining information (Byrnes, 1985). When we read, we tend to approach written texts in four basic ways (Grellet, 1981, p. 4):

1. *Skimming*: to read a text superficially and rapidly in order to obtain the gist or main idea
2. *Scanning*: to read a text quickly in order to locate a specific item of information
3. *Extensive reading*: reading longer text, usually for one's own pleasure and for the purpose of global understanding and fluency development
4. *Intensive reading*: reading shorter texts to extract information and to develop accuracy in comprehension at the level of detail

Reading often involves the act of reconstructing meanings sent by a writer at a remote time and place. Much of the language of written texts is carefully "edited" (i.e., complete sentences, fewer redundancies) and contains a number of conventional features: paragraphing, spelling rules, and punctuation marks. Since the meaning cannot be negotiated between the participants as with speaking situations, a considerable amount of information has to be made explicit to the reader in order to facilitate comprehension (Stubbs, 1980).

COMPREHENDING WRITTEN TEXTS

Reading has been viewed as a *bottom-up process* of decoding written symbols, starting from the smaller segments (individual letters, syllables, words) and working to the larger units (clauses, sentences, paragraphs). Reading comprehension involves the use of various strategies that the reader uses to build progressively larger units of the language until meaning can be extracted. Reading has also been described as a *top-down process* in which the reader brings to the task an array of information, ideas, and beliefs about the text. The reader initiates the process by making predictions about the meaning of the text as he or she employs knowledge of vocabulary, syntax, discourse, and the world. Reading competence depends on efficient interaction between linguistic knowledge and background knowledge associated with the topic.

A third perspective assumes that readers use both text-based (bottom-up) and reader-based (top-down) strategies. Readers make guesses, and those predictions in turn facilitate the decoding. As readers decode, they are able to relate the text to their own background knowledge. Thus, meaning is created through the interaction of text and reader. Stanovich (1980) has noted that efficient L2 reading may require the integration of both strategies.

Background knowledge is particularly significant for L2 readers. According to schema theory, readers can adequately comprehend a text if they have the preexisting structures to organize knowledge of language and the world. Carrell and Eisterhold (1983) have observed that efficient readers rely on information processing based on linguistic data from the text, which is then mapped against the readers' schemata. Nunan (1984), for example, found that among high school ESL readers, background knowledge about the topic was a more important factor in reading comprehension that the syntactic complexity of the text. Similarly, Hudson (1982) demonstrated that the importance of schemata in the interpretation of texts by showing that relevant background knowledge can compensate for a student's level of language proficiency as a factor in reading comprehension.

Readers employ many different types of strategies, more or less successfully, when reading a text. Van Parreren and Schouten-Van Parreren (1981) point out that students may need to acquire at least six crucial subskills and learn when to apply each subskill based on the requirements of the task:

1. Recognize the type of text (fictional, informative, persuasive)
2. Recognize different types of text structure (story schema, expository prose)
3. Predict and summarize the content of a text or passage
4. Make references with respect to information that is textually implicit
5. Determine the meaning of unknown words from the context
6. Analyze the word morphology of unknown words

Studies of actual reading strategies have shown that students are actively engaged in the process of constructing meaning. Hosenfeld, Arnold, Kirchoffer,

Laciura, and Wilson (1981) found that successful readers used a variety of strategies that involved both bottom-up and top-down processes. For example, readers skipped unnecessary words and guessed contextually, relied on illustrations and titles to make inferences, kept meaning in mind, made use of their knowledge of the world, identified words according to grammatical category, looked up words, used side glosses, evaluated their guesses, and used context from preceding and succeeding sentences and paragraphs as they tried to make sense of the text. Block (1986) also observed that college ESL readers brought their knowledge of the reading process and strategies to the second language task. However, the use of various comprehension strategies did not correspond to language-specific features. Readers who were aware of text structure and who monitored their reading skills tended to learn course content more efficiently. The reading act incorporates a broad range of language competencies, knowledge systems, and cognitive strategies. Topic familiarity, reading purpose, and the use of specific reading strategies contribute in different ways to text comprehension.

RESEARCH FINDINGS IN L2 READING

Considerable research in L2 reading has been conducted in the past decade. Major research themes include such concerns as the reading behavior of L2 learners, the role of background knowledge in text comprehension, ACTFL reading proficiency guidelines, readers' interactions with texts, and readers' strategy instruction.

Among those studies attempting to describe the reading behavior of L2 learners, there has been considerable interest in characterizing the differences between first and second language reading abilities. Cziko (1978), for example, compared differences among native and nonnative speakers of French, focusing on the use of syntactic, semantic, and discourse constraints (using passages with words systematically deleted). Three groups of seventh grade students were involved: two English-speaking groups (one "intermediate" group of students that had participated in a year-long French immersion program and an "advanced" group of pupils that had received six years of immersion education) and a French control group. The results suggest a developmental order in the ability of L2 learners to use contextual constraints. Sensitivity to syntactic constraints develops before sensitivity to both semantic and discourse aspects. In another study, Cziko (1980) also examined differences in L2 reading strategies that were due to L2 competence. He found that the intermediate group of French learners made a significantly lower proportion of deletion-and-insertion errors than did the advanced group—or the native speakers. The intermediate group made a significantly higher proportion of substitution errors that graphically resembled the text than did the French group. The errors made by the intermediate group suggest greater reliance on graphic information, while the advanced learners and native speakers used both graphic and contextual information to derive meaning from the text. Sensitivity to contextual information is reflected by fewer errors that violate the syntactic, semantic, or discourse constraints of the text.

Block (1986) compared the comprehension strategies used by native English speakers and nonnative students at the college level. No pattern of strategy use seemed to distinguish ESL readers (Spanish and Chinese speakers) from native English speakers. Instead, in each language group, one reader tended to integrate information more consistently, recognized text structure, and referred less frequently to personal experiences than the other readers. Other readers tended to make more personal associations, paid less attention to text structure, and neglected to integrate textual information. Langage background did not seem to account for the use of particular strategies or patterns of behavior, suggesting processing phenomena not linked to specific language features.

The question, "Do reading strategies transfer from L1 to L2?" has been addressed in a number of studies. Clarke (1980) noted that "good" readers in both L1 and L2 tend to perform better than "poor" readers in both languages, as in this case of Spanish speakers learning English as adults. Nevertheless, text complexity can cause L2 readers to revert to poor reading strategies that are due to limited L2 proficiency. In the case of French, Hauptman (1979) found that poor readers in English (L1) were inclined to use similar strategies when reading French texts. They experienced difficulty in both languages, especially in using content information, relying on contextual cues, and making guesses. Hosenfeld (1979) found in case studies of ninth grade students who were learning French that successful readers tended to keep the meaning of the passage in mind, skipped nonessential words, read in broad phrases, and used context as a way to determine word meaning. Poor readers, by contrast, lost sentence meaning as soon as they decoded it, rarely skipped words, read word-by-word or in short phrases, and turned to the glossary frequently for the meaning of unknown words.

The roles of background knowledge and cultural schemata in L2 reading comprehension have been addressed in a number of studies. Investigations into the role of schemata have noted that native English-speaking readers read faster, recall more accurately, and make more appropriate inferences from texts that have familiar content that from text for which they lack the appropriate background knowledge (Anderson, Spiro, & Anderson, 1978). The term *schema* is generally used to mean that "based on one's experience of the world in a given culture, one organizes knowledge about the world and uses this knowledge to predict interpretations and relationships regarding new information, events, and experiences" (Tannen, 1979, p. 139). Schemata function as knowledge structures that allow for the organization of information in long-term memory.

Lalas (1982), for instance, noticed the influence of prior cultural experience on ESL reading among secondary and elementary school bilingual Filipino students living in the United States in the Pacific Northwest. The students were asked to read aloud a story about an old man, his son, and a donkey. The high school students' concept of the farmer, his home, his use of animals, and the type of crops harvested differed from the notions held by the elementary pupils. The high school students maintained the Filipino farming schema (rice fields, nipa huts, the carabao as the beast of burden, and the barefooted farmers). The elementary pupils, on the other hand, added or acquired a new set of schemata for farming (corn fields, wheat, a cabin or barn, horses and cows, and a moustached farmer wearing a checkered shirt and blue jeans) based on their cultural experiences in the United States.

Both Carrell (1981) and Johnson (1981) found in their studies that the cultural origin of the text had more effect on the comprehension of adult ESL students than the level of syntactic/semantic complexity. In another study, Johnson (1982) found that building vocabulary knowledge may not improve reading comprehension among advanced ESL students at the college level. An induced cultural schema was not as effective as knowledge obtained from real-life experiences in the target culture. Hudson (1982) has noted that induced schemata can compensate limited English language proficiency as a factor of reading comprehension, but an induced schema seems to be more useful at the lower levels of proficiency than at higher levels of language ability.

Specific aspects of background knowledge have been investigated in various recent studies. Carrell (1983) studied the effect of three components of background language: (1) *context*, the presence or absence of a title and picture page preceding the text, which inform the reader in advance of the context; (2) *transparency*, the presence or absence of specific, concrete lexical items within the text that provide textual clues to the content; and (3) *familiarity*, the presence or absence within the reader of prior knowledge or experience of the text content. Recalls were written in English by three groups of students, native speakers of English and two groups of ESL learners reading at two levels of proficiency. She found that among the ESL students, understanding and recall of a text were not dependent on background knowledge. Lee (1986) replicated Carrell's (1983) study among third-year college students in advanced Spanish classes. The students, all native English speakers, were asked to recall and write Spanish passages in English in order to determine Spanish reading comprehension abilities. The findings indicated that all three components of background knowledge play a role in the way learners read, comprehend, and recall Spanish texts.

Reading from a multidimensional perspective (Kaya-Carton & Carton, 1986) takes into account the interaction between reader characteristics (cognitive ability, linguistic knowledge, personal and cultural experiences) and the features of the text (syntax, semantic/pragmatic content, vocabulary, level of formality, literal vs. interpretive presentation, and text organization). Following this perspective, Bensoussan (1986) has noted that reading comprehension in a foreign language can be affected by such factors as vocabulary, familiarity with conventions of written text in the native and second language, awareness of cultural differences, and knowledge of the macro- and micro-level structures of a text. The study by Osman (1984) examines how prior knowledge and language proficiency in L1 and L2 affect the comprehension of English texts among Malaysian high school students. She found that both language proficiency in L2 and prior knowledge about the text were powerful predictors of text comprehension. It was not possible to identify one of the variables as the more important predictor of ESL reading since there is probably a "linguistic threshold" or ceiling in language proficiency necessary for a reader to successfully comprehend a text. Some research findings suggest that particular rhetorical patterns in English (comparison and contrast, problem and solution, and cause and effect) may be recalled more easily than others among nonnative readers in general. Nevertheless, there seems to be some difference among various language groups (e.g., Spanish, Arabic, and Asian), indicating influences from L1 rhetorical patterns and the lack of appropriate L2 textual schemata (Carrell, 1984).

Research studies examining the implication of the ACTFL's definition of reading proficiency in terms of text type, reading skill, and task-based performance (Lee, 1988) challenge a hierarchical model of reading that does not take into account how readers interact with different text types. Allen, Bernhardt, Berry, and Demel (1988), in their study of foreign language readers in French, German, and Spanish at the secondary school level, found that comprehension scores on the texts sampled from the typology did not follow the progression as anticipated. All text types (friendly letter, general-interest article, business letter, and newspaper article) were comprehended to the same degree. Only when both reader characteristics (proficiency level according to language) and language by text type were considered did the scores for each text type vary significantly. It seems that "readers may appear to be proficient on topics with which they have familiarity and nonproficient on topics with which they do not have familiarity" (Bernhardt, 1986, p. 26). It seems that text types by themselves do not explain the variation of reading abilities among L2 learners.

As noted earlier, Lee and Musumeci (1988) have questioned the validity of the ACTFL's hierarchy of reading skills and text types. Their study of college students enrolled in lower-division Italian language classes indicates that texts such as TV program guides and tables of contents from magazines were as difficult as newspaper editorials and such literary texts as novels and short stories. Reading skills such as decoding and classifying (type-two-level processes) were more difficult than skills involving skimming and scanning (type-one-level processes); inferring, guessing, and hypothesizing (type-three-level processes); and analyzing, verifying, and extending hypotheses (type-four-level processes). These findings point to the need to more closely examine actual reader performance on specific text types and explore the effects that linguistically based versus cognitively based reading skills have on task-based reading activities across a variety of text types.

The actual reading behaviors of L2 learners continue to be addressed by a number of researchers. Barnett (1988), for example, examined how real and perceived strategy use among college students affects the comprehension of French texts. Students who consider and remember "context" as they read understand more about the text than those students who make less use of this strategy. The use of context as a strategy is also associated with the perception of its effective use and results in better comprehension reading scores. Students can be taught to use this strategy, thereby improving the ability to read through context. Examples of some of the items used in the questionnaire to elicit perceived strategy use are presented in Figure 8.1.

* Strategies considered to be effective are marked with an asterisk.

1. When I read, I pay most attention to
   a. what individual words mean.
   *b. what the reading passage means.
   *c. what the form or grammatical function of the words are.
   d. what the structure of the passage is.

2. When I read French, I
   *a. read the whole passage once and then reread it.
   *b. read part of the passage, then reread that part before going on.
   c. reread only the difficult sections.
   *d. read straight through or reread, depending on the passage.
   e. read straight through the passage and do not reread.

3. I read a French reading passage because
   *a. I find the topic interesting or I want to find out how the story ends.
   b. I have questions to answer about it.
   c. it has been assigned.
   *d. I want to find out what the author has to say.
   e. I want to learn how to read in French.

4. When I begin reading a French passage, I
   a. don't usually consider how it relates to what I already know.
   *b. think about what I know about the topic or source of the passage.
   *c. think about what I know about the author's style or point of view.
   d. simply begin reading the text itself.

5. I read different French passages
   a. the same way because French passages are usually difficult.
   b. the same way because they're in French.
   *c. depending on what I need to learn from them.
   *d. depending on what kind of passages they are.

6. When I read in French, I find that I hypothesize about what might come next
   *a. often.
   *b. sometimes.
   c. hardly ever.
   d. never.

7. When I read in French, I
   a. can't tell what the structure of the reading passage is.
   *b. expect certain things because of the reading passage structure.
   c. read each paragraph by itself.
   *d. look for a logical structure.
   *e. try to relate the points or ideas mentioned together.

8. When a French reading passage has a title, I
   a. read the title but don't consider it as I read the passage.
   *b. read it first and imagine what the passage might be about.
   *c. think about what I already know and how it might relate to the title.
   d. read the title but don't think much about it.

9. When a French reading passage has illustrations with it, I
   *a. imagine what the reading passage might be about, considering what the illustrations are.
   b. look at the illustrations without relating them to the reading passage.
   c. look at the illustrations but don't think much about them.

FIGURE 8.1   Questionnaire for determining the use of context as a strategy

SOURCE: From "Reading Through Context: How Real and Perceived Strategy Use Affects L2 Comprehension" by Marva A. Barnett, 1988, *Modern Language Journal*, 72, pp. 161–162. Reprinted with permission.

*d. expect the reading passage to reflect what is in the illustrations.
*e. compare what is in the illustrations to what I read.
10. When I read in French, I think that
    a. all the words are important.
    *b. I can't skip some words and still understand.
    c. I don't know which words I can skip.
    d. it is a mistake to skip any words.
    e. I need to look in the dictionary for the words I don't know.
11. When I read in French, I
    a. feel uneasy when I don't know what most of the words mean.
    b. look up most of the words I don't know.
    c. want to know exactly what is in the passage.
    *d. am willing to guess what some words mean.
12. If I come to a word I don't know, I
    a. skip the word and come back to it later.
    *b. guess what the word might mean and go on.
    *c. guess what the word might mean and reread the sentence.
    *d. look the word up in a glossary or dictionary and reread the sentence.
    e. look up the word up in a glossary or dictionary and write the English meaning on the page.

FIGURE 8.1 (continued)

Chamot and Kupper (1989) found in their case study that effective learners of Spanish engaged in the following behaviors:

1. Read Spanish in ways similar to English (L1)
2. Searched for meaning by reading according to phrases (constituent groups) rather than single words
3. Used a number of cognitive strategies to aid comprehension (translation, summarizing, self-evaluation)
4. Employed self-monitoring procedures to minimize comprehension breakdowns
5. Utilized remediation strategies such as inferring, elaboration (relating new information from the passage to prior knowledge), and deduction during comprehension breakdowns

They suggest the use of retrospective interviews or think-aloud (explain as one reads) procedures as a means of identifying reading strategies during a group activity, thereby making learners aware of their own thinking processes and those of their classmates. For example, students could be asked to read a short story or perhaps a newspaper article that contains some new words. Then they have to answer questions based on the reading passage. A typical set of questions might address these concerns:

As you are reading, what do you do that helps you understand the meaning of the reading passage?

Describe your general reading approach (Chamot & Kupper, 1989, p. 23)

As you are reading, what do you do when you come to a new word?

What do you do that helps you answer the comprehension questions?

Do you ever read these *before* you read the passage? If so, why? (Chamot & Kupper, 1989, p. 23)

Kern (1989) makes the point that students can benefit from direct instruction on the use of specific strategies that can assist them in word recognition by inferring word meaning through the use of context, or synthesizing meaning from larger segments of texts. Carrell (1989) further states that strategy training and practice need to go beyond task-specific considerations and include instruction in metacognitive awareness. Students need to be made aware of what types of reading strategies are involved, why they should be learning them, where, when, and how they should be used in different reading situations, and how to evaluate or monitor the use of different strategies.

In summary, learners are actively involved in the reconstruction of meaning in written texts. The major findings of the studies reviewed suggest the following:

1. Proficiency levels influence the use of syntactic, semantic, and discourse information about a text.
2. Reading comprehension behaviors do not seem to be influenced by the native language.
3. Good readers in the native language tend to be good readers in a second language, although text difficulty can cause readers to revert to poor reading strategies.
4. Culturally familiar topics are easier to comprehend than culturally unfamiliar ones.
5. Background knowledge involves various aspects such as the use of visual clues, textual clues, and familiarity with text content.
6. Reading comprehension can be affected by numerous factors, including reading abilities in the native language, reader's cultural experiences, the type of text or genre, reader's knowledge about the topic, and the linguistic complexity of the text.
7. Reading proficiency involves the use of different types of cognitive strategies associated with particular types of texts.
8. Readers utilize different comprehension strategies, some of which can be taught in the classroom through strategy training.

TEACHING CONSIDERATIONS

Sequencing of reading activities can be approached from the perspective of *communicative tasks* (Nunan, 1989). Tasks such as filling out forms, using a timetable, locating information in a newspaper to find out about current movies in local theaters, and reading a short story in order to write a summary can be organized so as to give students the opportunity to develop different comprehension skills (skimming for gist, identifying the main points of the text, understanding information not explicitly stated in the text, recognizing grammatical cohesion devices between parts of a text). It should be noted that reading comprehension cannot be separated from the other language modalities—listening, speaking, and writing (Grellet, 1981). The development of reading competencies appears to interact with and influence both writing abilities and oral proficiency (Swaffar, 1988).

The teaching of reading on the basis of proficiency as the "organizing principle" (Higgs, 1984) implies ordering text types on the basis of performance levels (novice, intermediate, advanced, and superior) and descriptions in terms of language functions (identify main idea, understand descriptions and narrations of factual material, understand new vocabulary through contextual guessing strategies), content (weather, travel forms, health, money, literary texts), and degree of accuracy (misunderstanding specific details; inability to understand irony, satire or cultural illusions; having some difficulty in comprehending reading material that contains jargon, slang or unfamiliar dialect). Omaggio (1986) provides techniques and activities for each of the four reading levels corresponding to the ACTFL's (1986) proficiency specifications. The techniques that she considers appropriate for novice, intermediate, and advanced levels are listed in Table 8.1.

TABLE 8.1 Reading techniques appropriate for the novice, intermediate, and advanced levels

Novice	Intermediate	Advanced
Anticipation/prediction	Comprehension checks	Comprehension checks
Skimming	Guessing from context	Guessing from context
Gisting	Clue searching	Clue searching
Detecting functions of texts	Making inferences	Making inferences
Scanning	Scrambled stories	Cloze techniques
Extracting specific information	Extracting specific information	Reverse cloze
Contextual guessing	Skimming	Scrambled stories
Prereading activities	Scanning	Extracting specific information
Simple cloze (multiple-choice adaptations)	Paraphrasing	Skimming
Filling out forms	Gisting/resume	Scanning
	Note taking/outlining	Paraphrasing
	Passage completion	Gisting/resume
	Identifying sociolinguistic factors	Passage completion
	Understanding idioms	Identifying sociolinguistic factors
	Understanding discourse structures	Filling out forms
	Understanding link words and referents	Anticipation/prediction
		Identifying discourse structure
		Identifying link words and referents

SOURCE: From *Teaching Language in Context* (pp. 153–155) by Alice C. Omaggio, 1986, Boston: Heinle & Heinle. Reprinted with permission.

Some of the techniques in Table 8.1 involve reading for different purposes (skimming, scanning, intensive reading), developing various comprehension skills (contextual guessing, making inferences, identifying discourse structure, identifying sociolinguistic factors), and types of responses to written texts (fill-in of words deleted in a passage, arranging scrambled sentences, story, events, note taking, outlining, passage completion).

Phillips (1985) offers a five-stage plan for reading passages from textbooks or authentic material. The sequence approaches reading from a top-down perspective and enables students to develop various reading strategies in relation to other language areas. The sequence follows these stages:

1. *Prereading/preparation stage*: Students engage in a number of activities such as brainstorming, interpreting accompanying visuals, and predicting and anticipating text context based on the titles, headlines, or topic. Critical vocabulary can be presented or reviewed; cultural background necessary for understanding is explained and expectations about the topic might be highlighted to focus attention on the context.

2. *Skimming/scanning stage*: Students read the text for the first time in order to obtain a general idea before concentrating on details about content or features of language. The reading can be timed so that students will focus on the main idea or important points; they can then respond by answering general comprehension questions in English, selecting the main idea from multiple-choice items, underlining topic sentences in reading text, filling in charts for specific information, or relating text illustrations or titles to the content.

3. *Decoding/intensive reading stage*: Students focus on specific aspects of comprehension requiring bottom-up processes (recognizing grammatical relationships, understanding the use of discourse connectors, understanding word meaning through context or analysis). Techniques could include discussion questions, worksheets, word lists based on the text, and open-ended study questions.

4. *Comprehension stage*: Students are evaluated on their comprehension of the entire selection. A number of exercises can be used to assess the literal meaning, inferences, and opinions about the text. Formats such as true/false, multiple-choice, matching, completion, fill-ins, and summaries are appropriate.

5. *Transferable/integrative skill stage*: Students might engage in transfer exercises such as cognitive pattern recognition, word-family study, interpreting grammatical patterns, and contextual guessing to hypothesize, confirm, and predict. The reading selection can be used as a point of departure for speaking and writing activities. It can further lead to related readings or listening situations.

Papalia (1987, pp. 78–80) recognizes the need to approach reading activities in terms of a sequence that includes a prereading stage, reading comprehension exercises, and postreading activities. He also emphasizes the importance of giving students the opportunity to relate the text to their own lives, interests, and concerns. Texts can be used to promote interaction with the reader and between students. He offers a number of activities designed to increase student interaction with the text, the author, other students, and the teacher:

Interaction between Reader and Text:

1. Students draw a picture to illustrate what was just read or some aspect of it, such as the room where the action took place.
2. Students look for specific information, such as selecting a meal from a menu or identifying times of arrival and departure in airline or railway schedules.
3. Students read a passage and then list three important facts, ideas, or events contained in it.
4. Students read a specially constructed passage and correct sentences that contain wrong information. This is an opportunity to use some humorous sentences that play on similarities in the appearance of words. Students learn to pay careful attention as they read.
5. Students read a story with the ending deleted. They try to make up an ending consistent with the story.
6. Each student is given a comic strip with eight frames. In the first, third, fifth, and seventh frames the dialogue is provided, but in the second, fourth, sixth, and eighth frames it is missing. Students must create meaningful dialogue for these four frames, linking what was said in the preceding frame to the content of the succeeding frame. This activity integrates reading and writing with formulation of oral utterances.

Interaction between Reader and Reader over Text:

7. After reading a short descriptive paragraph about something or someone in which the name of the person or the object is not revealed, students in small groups try to guess who or what is being talked about or draw a picture of the person or object.
8. A transparency of the reading passage is projected. After rapid perusal to extract the general tenor, lines are highlighted segmentally and each is discussed for meaning, with the whole group contributing. The lines may be numbered to facilitate quick reference. It is essential to project the complete passage again at the end to draw together what has been extracted from the parts.
9. The first two or three sentences of a passage are shown on the overhead projector. Students then formulate questions to which they expect to find the answers in the completion of the passage. The questions are written on the board. Students finish reading the passage and discuss the answers to the questions.
10. After reading a passage, students supply a suitable title. This can be a

large-group activity, allowing students to discuss why they agree or disagree with the titles proposed.

11. Students read a story with the ending deleted. They try orally to make up an ending consistent with the story. Later they may write a summary of the story, adding their own endings. These versions may then be circulated and a vote taken on the most satisfactory ending. Students then compare this ending with that of the original author.

12. Students form their own questions based on a reading selection they have read and call on other students to answer their questions to check comprehension. This may be a competitive activity among small groups. Students are encouraged to challenge questions they feel distort the meaning. In this way a lively discussion often ensues.

13. Students work together to paraphrase a reading passage without changing the original meaning. This forces students to pay close attention to nuances of meaning and the author's intent.

14. Students in small groups read a series of provocative statements on a major public event, a common experience, or a subject of current interest and controversy. Discussion follows the reading, again integrating reading and oral communication.

15. Students work out, as a group, a summary of a passage they have read individually. The teacher should cue students where necessary. (Deciding on key words and testing these beforehand is helpful as a preliminary for elementary-level students). Groups read their summations to each other and discuss the validity of their interpretations.

16. Students in small groups rearrange a series of sentences into a logical paragraph. The sentences should parallel the kind of material read or at least deal with familiar subject matter. They may consist of a rearrangement of sentences from a passage to be read later. This task forces students to discuss concepts and come to certain conclusions by paying attention to elements of contextual cohesion.

17. Sheets are prepared containing questions related to a text being read, with a series of multiple-choice responses that require students to make value judgments as they rank the various alternatives. Small-group discussion follows. This activity demands close reading by students as they determine the precise meaning of the alternatives. It also integrates reading with oral communication.

18. Students in small groups are each provided with a card on which an incident is described, but with a different segment of vital information omitted from each card. Students discuss the information with each other until they have pieced together the full account of the incident or situation. This is a problem-solving activity that integrates reading and discussion. Students then write out the complete account of the incident as a small-group composition, thus integrating reading, oral discussion, and writing.

The need to develop a systematic approach to L2 reading based on research findings has been advocated by a number of investigators. Young (1989) is particularly concerned about teaching L2 reading from a strategies-oriented perspective, taking into account the transfer of reading strategies from L1 to L2, providing opportunities for strategy training, and utilizing authentic texts so that students can discover textual messages. Swaffar (1988) provides the following classroom applications based on an examination of current research:

1. Use authentic texts at all levels of language instruction for the sole purpose of training in gist comprehension or top-down processing. This will provide students the opportunity of using schema as a strategy.
2. Select L2 reading texts by taking into account students' backgrounds and interests.
3. Provide students with explicit strategy training (i.e., experiment with one classroom of intensive strategy practice and metacognitive awareness).
4. Utilize previewing activities to help establish the context and logical organization of a text.
5. Provide students with the opportunity to identify the episodic structure of the text (changes in scene or time, sequence developments, or shifts in perspective).
6. Ask students to reread texts from another point of view (e.g., burglar vs. police, child vs. adult) or another structural logic (e.g., problems and solution instead of comparison and contrast).
7. Allow students to take issue with textual ideas. They can provide their own opinions about textual facts and assertions after the initial reading, thereby bridging the gap between comprehension and production, especially in small-group practice.

The question of how to sequence reading tasks remains an important issue. The ACTFL guidelines for sequencing text types according to proficiency levels has been called into question by some researchers. Organizing reading activities on the basis of learning or communicative tasks is also problematic. Wallace (1992, p. 71) points out that a number of factors need to be kept in mind when selecting reading materials. A reading text should:

1. Serve as a vehicle for teaching specific language structure and vocabulary
2. Offer the opportunity to promote key reading strategies
3. Present content that is familiar and of interest to the learners
4. Correspond to the appropriate language level
5. Be authentic, naturally occurring in the target culture, and not specifically written for language teaching
6. Be exploitable in the classroom by leading to a broad range of language activities.

A communicative-based orientation might pay special attention to issues such as those represented by numbers 1, 4, 5, and 6. A more learner-centered approach must give more attention to the concerns raised by items 2 and 3. Teachers should examine the development of reading abilities in light of their basic curriculum framework (e.g., modular, cyclical, matrix, or story line). These models have been described in Chapter 4. Specific procedures for designing language curricula on the basis of learner needs and language outcomes are also presented in Chapter 4.

Using literary texts to develop reading skills offers a number of possibilities. Second language learners can be encouraged to read materials that take into account their preferences in terms of genres, topics, and periods. This would encourage reading for pleasure instead of relying on reading solely for language analysis. Some simple texts could be read with an interactive perspective, asking the reader to respond to the author, the content, or other students (Wallace, 1992).

Literary texts might be particularly useful in promoting cultural literacy. For example, literary works can:

1. Convey content in the form of sophisticated historical-cultural information
2. Increase students' cultural awareness, essential to understanding the contemporary social and cultural conditions of the speakers of that language
3. Help students "live" with the text by stepping out of themselves and interacting emotionally with the characters
4. Contribute to the development of grammar, vocabulary, and discourse elements through textual analysis (Mueller, Goutal, Hérot, & Chessid, 1992, pp. 57-71)

DESIGNING READING TASKS

Reading tasks may require learners to engage in top-down or bottom-up strategies with regard to different reading purposes. Spratt (1985) outlines various reading levels along with the corresponding learner activities (Table 8.2). The tasks vary from arranging jumbled sentences or paragraphs to discussions based on written texts.

The 10 reading tasks that follow in this chapter represent a broad range of written text types, learner behaviors, and cognitive strategies. Table 8.3 classifies each task according to genre, activity type, and cognitive process. The specific tasks can be adapted to other proficiency levels and languages.

Tasks B, C, D, and F in Table 8.3 focus on reading for specific information in a variety of texts. Tasks D, G, I, and J require the participation of various students to analyze the texts and propose a response. Task E involves text reconstruction by filling in the blanks, while task H requires going beyond the text to select an appropriate title. Task A is relatively simple in terms of cognitive demands since it entails classifying information, while tasks D, G, I, and J require numerous steps to

TABLE 8.2 Reading skills and classroom activities

Reading Level	Selected Activities
Understanding the relationship between sentences and clauses	1. Arrange jumbled sentences or paragraphs. 2. T circles the reference devices in a text and Ss work out what they refer to. 3. T gives Ss a passage in which the logical connectors are blanked out. Ss have to read the passage and work out what the connectors must be. 4. Prediction exercises (e.g., on an overhead projector). Ss read the first part of a text up to and including a logical connector. They then predict the next line, which is masked or covered for the remainder of the text.
Skimming for gist	1. The text is used simply as a springboard for discussion on a particular topic. 2. Ss read through a passage and then suggest a title for it. 3. Ss match different text titles to a series of short texts within a given time limit. 4. Ss read and list main points.
Scanning for specific information	1. Underline or circle the required information in a given time limit. 2. Answer questions focusing on specific information. 3. Complete forms to indicate specific information.
Reading for detail	1. Answer questions 2. Note taking on the order of events or emotions in a text. 3. Answer true/false questions. 4. Fill in information gaps in text.
Making inferences	1. True/false, multiple choice, or discussion questions on possible interpretations of the text.
Recognizing the organization of a text	1. Arrange jumbled paragraphs. 2. Discuss the function of particular paragraphs within a text.

SOURCE: Adapted from "Reading Skills" by Mary Spratt, in A. Matthews, M. Spratt, and L. Dangerfield (Eds.), *At the Chalkface: Practical Techniques in Language Teaching* (pp. 67–68), 1985, Andover, England: Thomas Nelson Publishing Services. Used with permission.

TABLE 8.3 Components of reading tasks

Text/Genre	Learning Objective	Reading Skill
A Description	List information by category	Identify information and classify
B Directory	Answer questions with details	Identify and relate specific information
C Advertisement	True/false answers	Recall details
D Letter	Transfer information to form	Analyze and compose orally
E Newspaper	Fill in blanks	Interpret
F Movie advertisement	Answer questions	Explain
G Travel brochure	Group decision	Analyze and solve
H Movie review	Select title for text	Synthesize and identify
I Story	Arrange scrambled story	Analyze, develop, and explain
J Letter	Read and prepare written response	Analyze, solve, and create text

complete. In addition, the tasks incorporate diverse textual features (genre, topic, linguistic elements). The procedures identify the situation and the conditions under which each task is accomplished.

It is important to remember that reading tasks need to be presented in the context of prereading and postreading activities. Prereading activities might require a question-and-answer sequence to determine the students' familiarity with the topic or linguistic knowledge. The teacher may need to introduce culturally relevant information or provide textual schemata so that students can understand the information structure of the genre. Postreading activities can give students the opportunity to relate the text to their own lives, interests, and concerns. Students can react to the text through oral or written communication. Furthermore, the text can lead to related readings or listening situations.

TASK A

Task:	Classify information according to categories
Genre:	Description
Topic:	Eating habits of French families
Function:	Obtain information from text and provide lists of items
Linguistic elements:	Foods; eating habits; table manners
Objective:	Students will read text and collect information according to classes.
Procedure:	The teacher presents a prereading activity to review food items, dinner table cultural scripts, and behaviors while eating. Teacher distributes a text about French eating habits. Students are given a form to fill out, with places to write (1) the types of food mentioned, (2) the times the various meals of the day are eaten, and (3) the table manners among the family members. Students read the text, write their responses, and then compare their answers. Afterwards the students express orally their opinions about eating in a typical French home.

TASK B

Task:	Scan for specific information
Genre:	Store directory
Topic:	Shopping in a department store
Function:	Obtain information to indicate location of specific items

Linguistic elements:	Question forms; vocabulary related to shopping and services offered in a department-type store
Objective:	Students will understand the location of products and services in a department store by answering questions.
Procedure:	Teacher discusses culturally relevant information about department-store organization. Then teacher distributes a "store directory" to students and reviews unknown words, illustrating with word map the interrelationship of store items and customer services.

Students then answer yes/no questions:

1. I want to buy a doll for my sister. Can I find one on the third floor? _____
2. I have to buy notebooks and pencils. Should I go to the basement? _____
3. I need to buy some towels. Do you sell towels on the first floor? _____
4. I want to buy house shoes for father. Are they on the fourth floor? _____
5. I should buy more coffee cups. Are they on the second floor? _____

Store Directory
Basement
> Books
>
> Luggage
>
> Men's wear
>
> Cameras
>
> Business machines and office supplies
>
> Personal telephones
>
> Videotape purchase and rentals
>
> Stationery, candles, and gift items
>
> Souvenirs
>
> Men's fragrances
>
> Men's hairstyling

First floor
> Handbags
>
> Wallets and accessories
>
> Women's shoes
>
> Hosiery

Women's fashions

Jewelry and watches

Lingerie

Cosmetics and women's fragrances

Second floor

Beauty salon

Women's fashions, designer shops

Fur salon

Women's coats

Women's swimwear

Bridal salon

Maternity

Third floor

Sporting goods and clothing

Records and audiocassettes

Fabric, patterns, sewing notions

Needlework and yarns

Toys

Boys' wear and girls' wear

Infants' wear and furniture

Teen fashions

Hair salon

Fourth floor

Interior decorating

Bedding, linens, and bath shop

Lamps and lighting fixtures

Clocks

Pictures, frames, and mirrors

Silver, china, and glassware

Gift wrap and bridal registry

Carpets and oriental rugs

Follow-up activities might include preparation of a shopping list, a role-playing situation between a customer and a shopper, or a comparison of department stores in the United States and another country.

Task B is adapted from Amemiya, 1988.

TASK C

Task:	Read for specific details
Genre:	Advertisement
Topic:	Buying on a credit plan; home entertainment equipment
Function:	Obtain information about specific details
Linguistic elements:	Language of advertisement; vocabulary associated with buying on credit; television and VCR equipment
Objective:	Students will comprehend specific details about a television offer by answering yes/no questions.
Procedure:	Teacher directs discussion about advertisement formats in U.S. newspapers.

Students predict structure and content of Spanish ads.

Teacher distributes copies of an advertisement from a Spanish newspaper.

Teacher reads the text to the students and answers questions about unknown words. The Spanish monetary system is reviewed.

Students answer yes/no questions and later discuss their answers.

Students are given an opportunity to prepare a similar text on a different product.

Sample yes/no questions:

		Sí	No
1.	¿Ud. puede pagar su televisor en un período de mas de dos años?	_____	_____
2.	¿Se ofrecen por lo menos siete marca de televisores?	_____	_____
3.	¿El Corte Inglés ofrece facilidades de pago?	_____	_____
4.	¿Los pagos mensuales serán menos de 5,000 pts?	_____	_____
5.	¿Por 7,000 pts. le venden a Ud. el video?	_____	_____

TASK D

Task:	Scan for specific information
Genre:	Letter
Topic:	Skiing at a winter resort
Function:	Obtain specific information about ski trip
Linguistic elements:	Reflexive verbs; vocabulary associated with skiing and staying in a cabin

Objectives: Students will complete a form to indicate an understanding of the results of a ski trip.

Procedure: In French, students discuss going on a skiing trip.

They list in chart form some of their major concerns about skiing at a Canadian resort.

Students are given a letter written by an advanced language student who went on a ski trip the previous year.

Students read the letter in pairs and note the following information:

1. Skiing opportunities
2. Extracurricular activities
3. Resort facilities

Sample letter:

[At a Canadian Ski Resort]

le 18 février 1992

Chers amis,

Nous venons d'arriver à Mt. Tremblant. Comme il fait froid ici! Il y a une station de ski à la montagne. Nous nous levons de bonne heure chaque jour parce qu'il y a beaucoup de choses à faire. Nous nous amusons bien. Nous faisons du ski, nous jouons au hockey. Ce soir nous allons au restaurant pour dîner. Nous ne pouvons pas attendre!

Cette excursion est formidable. Il y a des professeurs du lycée qui sont ici avec nous. Vous savez M. Danna et Mme. Davies? Ils sont ici et comme nous sommes surpris! Ils parlent français, tous les deux. Essayez d'accompagner le groupe l'année prochaine. Ces vacances sont vraiment formidables. Nous restons debout jusqu'au moment où il est tard—nous ne nous couchons pas à l'heure.

Amicalement,

Suzanne Benoit

Working in pairs, the students then determine if there are ample activities to merit a ski trip this year. They report their opinions orally to the class.

Task D is adapted from Cichacki, 1988.

TASK E

Task:	Fill in missing information in a text
Genre:	Newspaper article
Topic:	Sports and leisure activities
Function:	Obtain information from text at the sentence and paragraph levels
Linguistic elements:	Paragraph patterns; declarative grammatical structures; vocabulary about sport activities
Objective:	Students will indicate their understanding of a newspaper article about sports by completing the missing words in the passage.
Procedure:	Teacher directs discussion about sports and leisure activities. Students are asked to consider how they might organize information in a newspaper article about sports activities. Students read a short newspaper article in the target language. After a brief discussion about the topic, the students read a second copy of the text with words deleted. They fill in the missing blanks and read individual sentences orally to the class. The answers are compared. Synonyms and sentence connectors are highlighted in the discussion.

TASK F

Task:	Read text and visual for details
Genre:	Newspaper advertisement
Topic:	Movies
Function:	Obtain specific information and details regarding the showing of a movie
Linguistic elements:	Expressions of time; question forms
Objective:	Students will understand the specific details about an advertisement of a movie.
Procedure:	Teacher directs discussion about movie advertisements in Spanish newspapers.
	Teacher will distribute advertisements of movies in Spanish newspapers. Students will read and answer specific questions.

For example:

1. ¿Dónde se exhibe la película *La Selva Esmeralda*?
2. ¿Cuántas veces al día se exhibe la película?
3. ¿Quién es el director de la película?

4. ¿De qué se trata la película?

5. ¿Qué se puede hacer antes o después de ir al cine según el anuncio?

Later, each one will provide information to the class about the particular movie. Students will then listen to a radio ad about a movie and compare it to the format used in newspapers.

TASK G

Task:	Read and compare text to decide on a course of action
Genre:	Travel brochure
Topic:	Youth hostels in Vienna
Function:	Obtain information from various texts to decide on a course of action
Linguistic elements:	Model auxiliary verbs, personal pronouns, and words pertaining to travel; youth hostels; city surroundings
Objective:	Students will determine in which of the three youth hostels to stay in Vienna after considering the advantages and disadvantages based on the descriptions.
Procedure:	Teacher leads a discussion about youth hostels in Austria. Students contrast the advantages of staying in a youth hostel, in a hotel, or with a host family. Student groups will read the three youth hostel descriptions and then consider the advantages and disadvantages of staying in each. A decision is made by each group on which youth hostel to recommend. Each group makes a recommendation to the class and includes relevant supporting details.

An example from a brochure:

> Jugendherberge Steinberger: Unsere
> Jugendherberge liegt im Stadt Zentrum. Wir
> haben zwei und drei Zimmer Räume. Jedes
> Stockwerk hat zwei grosse Duschräume.
> Frühstück ist von 7:00 bis 8:00 Uhr und
> Abendessen von 6:00 bis 7:00. Kosten pro
> person für eine Nacht: 15.00 Schilling. Bitte
> melden Sie sich ein paar Wochen vorher an.

Task G is adapted from Buhr, 1988.

TASK H _____

Task:	Skim for gist and suggest a title for the text
Genre:	Movie review
Function:	Obtain information about the text and consider an appropriate title given to the topic
Linguistic elements:	Writing style in movie reviews written in German
Objective:	Students will suggest appropriate titles for movie reviews to reflect an understanding of the text.
Procedure:	Students discuss what they would include in a movie review for a recent movie seen by most of the class. They also predict how such a review would be written in a German newspaper. Teacher distributes movie reviews to the class and talks about the relationships between titles and content in movies. Students receive copies of movie reviews in German. After reading the reviews several times, each student proposed a title and explains the choice to the class. Students may also have opportunities to write their own reviews.

Task H is adapted from Jones, 1988.

TASK I _____

Task:	Arrange scrambled story and report orally to the class
Genre:	Story, brief narrative
Topic:	Can vary depending on teacher or students' interests
Function:	Obtain information from the different parts of the story to arrange in the appropriate order
Linguistic elements:	Logical and temporal connectors; reference devices
Objective:	Students will arrange the parts of the story in appropriate order, to reflect an understanding of the sequence of events.
Procedure:	Teacher solicits help from individual students to construct a story line based on a specific set of characters and circumstances. Teacher writes the group-constructed story on the chalkboard. Teacher distributes a story segmented into parts and placed on different note cards.
	Students working in pairs read all of the cards and decide on an appropriate sequence.
	Students read their reconstructed stories to the class and explain the reasons for the event structure.

TASK J

Task:	Read for specific details and prepare a written response
Genre:	Letter
Topic:	Lost luggage at the airport
Function:	Obtain and provide information requested about lost luggage
Linguistic elements:	Business letter style; vocabulary pertaining to lost luggage and procedures to reclaim from air carrier
Objective:	Students will show their understanding of the procedures for reporting missing luggage by completing the appropriate steps
Procedure:	Teacher directs discussion about lost luggage at an airport and reviews procedures for making a claim. Working in small groups, students prepare a claim for lost luggage. Students read a copy of the letter [opposite] Janice received from World Airways regarding lost luggage.

Students work in small groups, discuss the situation, and decide how Janice should respond to the airline company.

Each group prepares a letter of response to the company based on the directions.

Student groups will exchange their letters and read them to see if all of the information requirements have been met.

You are to write a letter of response for Janice, using the directions found in the letter from World Airways. Please use the same business-letter format. You may include any information of your own, but remember to use the information found in the letter you just read.

Task J is adapted from Herman, 1988.

WORLD AIRWAYS
555 OPEN ROAD SQUARE
CHICAGO, IL 21378

November 14, 1993

Ms. Janice Ribbon
17 Pine Hills Lane
Albany, NY 12204

Dear Ms. Ribbon:

This letter is in reply to your request for information concerning your luggage that has been reported missing as of November 7. Our records indicate that your suitcase was tagged at Honolulu Airport upon check-in for Flight #601 bound for N.Y.C. JFK Airport. It is a large brown-and-white suitcase with a lock.

In order to submit a formal claim, it is necessary for you to send us a photocopy of your luggage claim receipt and a detailed description of the suitcase and its content to our office by November 25, 1993. Generally, requests of this nature take approximately four to six weeks to yield results since the request must be entered on our computer tracking system nationally. In the meantime, you may call our local customer service representative at 1-800-666-4141 during regular office hours 8:30 A.M. to 4:30 P.M. Monday-Friday to make personal inquiries. Please refer to your order #994041965508 when sending correspondence or personal inquiries.

Sincerely,

N. Herman
Customer Service Center

LUGGAGE CLAIM

FLIGHT 601
DESTINATION JFK NYC
NUMBER   99 4041965508
DATE   November 7, 1993
TIME   2:45 P.M.

SUMMARY

Written texts can provide linguistic input, develop reading strategies, and present cultural content. Reading situations in a second language include a broad range of text types, from literary genres and informative materials to orientational forms and evaluative reports. Written texts have a number of features that affect the reader's ability to reconstruct meaning. Factors such as text structure, communicative functions, task demands, familiarity with the topic, the reader's linguistic knowledge, and learner strategies influence reading comprehension levels to varying degrees. The role of cultural schemata, text complexity, reading abilities in the native language, and the use of certain reading strategies have been shown to affect reading performance.

It is important to note that reading proficiency involves different types of cognitive strategies and that readers utilize various comprehension strategies, some of which can be practiced in the classroom. The development of reading proficiency is closely associated with other language skill areas, since reading competency appears to interact with and influence both writing and oral language abilities. Reading activities can be organized on the basis of communicative tasks, language proficiency levels, an interactive teaching perspective, and a strategy-oriented approach. Reading tasks may require learners to use both bottom-up and top-down strategies depending on the reading purpose. Reading tasks can range from relating words and sentences to visual stimuli and reacting to literary texts. Textual features, task complexity, and learner abilities should be taken into account in the planning of reading tasks. Sequencing of reading tasks should be guided by such concerns as the use of authentic texts, development of reading skills and strategies, presentation of cultural content, and integration with other language skill areas. More importantly, reading tasks should be planned in terms of instructional sequences involving both prereading and postreading activities.

ACTIVITIES

1. Prepare a list of typical reading tasks a learner could encounter in the following situations: train station, city street, doctor's office, and restaurant.
2. Obtain authentic reading materials (e.g., pamphlets, schedules, newspapers, menus) from a target culture and prepare comprehension questions that would require the reader to skim and scan the texts for particular information.
3. Based on the research findings noted in this chapter with respect to successful reading comprehension strategies in teaching and learning, prepare a list of suggestions for a beginning teacher.
4. Select a reading passage from a language textbook and describe the possible role that background knowledge and cultural schemata play in comprehension of the text.
5. Examine a few lessons in a language textbook and describe (1) the types of reading texts included, (2) the kinds of reading comprehension questions asked, and (3) use of culturally authentic reading texts.

6. Using the items from the questionnaire prepared by Barnett, prepare a list of questions that can be administered to a group of students to determine their use of various reading strategies.
7. Using the retrospective interview technique exemplified by Chamot and Kupper, interview two language learners to identify their use of particular reading strategies for specific texts.
8. Consider Omaggio's reading techniques and activities for the novice, intermediate, and advanced levels. Classify the techniques according to (1) reading for different purposes, (2) developing various comprehension skills, and (3) ways of responding to written texts. In what ways can this classification be useful in instructional planning?
9. Choose an authentic reading text and prepare a lesson incorporating Phillips' five-stage reading plan.
10. Discuss the significance of teaching reading from an interactive perspective, as suggested by Papalia.
11. Prepare a reading task based on an advertisement or a short narrative.
12. Analyze a reading task in terms of task requirements, topic, function, linguistic elements, and learner behaviors.

REFERENCES

Allen, E. D., Bernhardt, E. B., Berry, M. T., & Demel, M. (1988). Comprehension and text genre: An analysis of secondary school foreign language readers. *Modern Language Journal, 72*(2), 163-172.

Amemiya, Y. (1988). Materials prepared for a course. Albany: State University of New York, School of Education.

American Council on the Teaching of Foreign Languages (ACTFL). (1986). *ACTFL provisional proficiency guidelines.* Hastings-on-Hudson, NY: Author.

Anderson, R. C., Spiro, R. J., & Anderson, M. C. (1978). Schemata as scaffolding for the representation of information in connected discourse. *American Educational Research Journal, 15,* 433-440.

Barnett, M. A. (1988). Reading through context: How real and perceived strategy use affects L2 comprehension. *Modern Language Journal, 72*(2), 150-162.

Bensoussan, M. (1986). Beyond vocabulary: Pragmatic factors in reading comprehension culture, convention, coherence and cohesion. *Foreign Language Annals, 19,* 399-407.

Bernhardt, E. B. (1986). Proficient texts or proficient readers. *ADFL Bulletin, 18,* 25-28.

Block, E. (1986). The comprehension strategies of second language readers. *TESOL Quarterly, 20,* 462-495.

Buhr, M. (1988). Materials prepared for a course. Albany, State University of New York, School of Education.

Byrnes, H. (1985). Teaching toward proficiency: The receptive skills. In A. C. Omaggio (Ed.), *Proficiency, Curriculum, Articulation: The ties that bind* (pp. 77-106). Middlebury, VT: Northeast Conference.

Carrell, P. L. (1981). *The role of schemata in L2 comprehension.* Paper presented at the TESOL annual conference, Detroit.

Carrell, P. L. (1983). Three components of background knowledge in reading comprehension. *Language Learning, 33,* 183-208.

Carrell, P. L. (1984). The effects of rhetorical organization on ESL readers. *TESOL Quarterly*, *18*, 441-479.

Carrell, P. L. (1989). Metacognitive awareness and second language reading. *Modern Language Journal*, *73*(2), 121-134.

Carrell, P. L., & Carron, J. E. (1983). Schema theory and ESL reading pedagogy. *TESOL Quarterly*, *17*, 553-573.

Chamot, A. U., & Kupper, L. (1989). Learning strategies in foreign language instruction. *Foreign Language Annals*, *22*(1), 13-24.

Child, J. R. (1987). Language proficiency levels and the typology of texts. In H. Byrnes & M. Canale (Eds.), *Defining and developing proficiency: Guidelines, implementation, and concepts* (pp. 97-106). Lincolnwood, IL: National Textbook.

Cichacki, W. (1988). Materials prepared for a course. Albany: State University of New York, School of Education.

Clarke, M. A. (1980). The short-circuit hypothesis of ESL reading—or when language competence interferes with reading performance. *Modern Language Journal*, *64*, 203-209.

Clarke, M. A. (1979). Reading in Spanish and English. *Language Learning*, *20*, 121-150.

Cziko, G. A. (1978). Differences in first and second language reading. The use of syntactic, semantic, and discourse constraints. *Canadian Modern Language Review*, *34*, 473-487.

Cziko, G. A. (1980). Language competence and reading strategies: A comparison of L1 and L2 oral reading errors. *Language Learning*, *30*, 101-114.

Grellet, F. (1981). *Developing reading skills*. Cambridge, England: Cambridge University Press.

Hauptman, P. C. (1979). A comparison of first and second language reading strategies among English-speaking university students. *Interlanguage Studies Bulletin*, *4*, 173-201.

Herman, N. (1988). Materials prepared for a course. Albany: State University of New York, School of Education.

Higgs, T. V. (1984). *Teaching for proficiency: The organizing principle*. Lincolnwood, IL: National Textbook.

Hosenfeld, C. (1979). Cindy: A learner in today's foreign language classroom. In W. Born (Ed.), *The foreign language learner in today's classroom environment* (pp. 53-75). Middlebury, VT: Northeast Conference.

Hosenfeld, C., Arnold, V., Kirchoffer, J., Laciura, J., & Wilson, L. (1981). Second language reading: A curricular sequence for teaching reading strategies. *Foreign Language Annals*, *14*, 415-422.

Hudson, T. (1982). The effects of induced schemata on the "short circuit" in L2 reading: Nondecoding factors in L2 reading performance. *Language Learning*, *32*, 1-31.

Johnson, D. (1981). Effects on reading comprehension of language complexity and cultural background of a text. *TESOL Quarterly*, *15*, 169-183.

Johnson, D. (1982). Effects on reading comprehension of building background knowledge. *TESOL Quarterly*, *16*, 503-515.

Jones, D. (1988). Materials prepared for a course. Albany: State University of New York, School of Education.

Kaya-Carton, E., & Carton, A. S. (1986). Multidimensionality of foreign reading proficiency: Preliminary considerations in assessment. *Foreign Language Annals*, *19*, 95-102.

Kern, R. G. (1989). Second language reading strategy instruction: Its effects on comprehension and word inference ability. *The Modern Language Journal*, *73*(2), 135-149.

Lalas, J. W. (1982). The influence of prior experience in ESL reading. *Bilingual Journal*, *6*(1), 10-12.

Lee, J. F. (1986). The effects of three components of background knowledge on second language reading. *The Modern Language Journal, 70,* 343-350.

Lee, J. F. (1988). Toward a modification of the "proficiency" construct for reading in a foreign language. *Hispania, 71*(4), 941-953.

Lee, J. F., & Musumeci, D. (1988). On hierarchies of reading skills and text types. *Modern Language Journal, 72*(2), 173-187.

Mueller, M., Goutal, B., Hérot, C., & Chessid, I. (1992). A step toward cultural literacy: Language through literature. In W. Rivers (Ed.), *Teaching languages in college: Curriculum and content* (pp. 57-71). Lincolnwood, IL: National Textbook.

Nunan, D. (1984). Discourse processing by first language, second phase, and second language learners. Unpublished doctoral dissertation. Flinders University of South Australia.

Nunan, D. (1989). *Designing tasks for the communicative classroom.* Cambridge, England: Cambridge University Press.

Omaggio, A. C. (1986). *Teaching language in context.* Boston, MA: Heinle & Heinle.

Osman, S. (1984). Effects of prior knowledge on ESL reading. In B. W. Kim (Ed.), *Reading in Asia* (pp. 43-62). Seoul, Korea: Hanyang University.

Papalia, A. (1987). Interaction of reader and text. In W. M. Rivers (Ed.), *Interactive language teaching* (pp. 70-82). Cambridge, England: Cambridge University Press.

Phillips, J. K. (1985). Developing reading proficiency in a foreign language. In A. Papalia (Ed.), *A communicative syllabus* (pp. 37-41). Schenectady, NY: New York State Association of Foreign Language Teachers.

Spratt, M. (1985). Reading skills. In A. Mathews, M. Spratt, & L. Dangerfield (Eds.), *At the chalkface: Practical techniques in language teaching* (pp. 64-68). London: Edward Arnold.

Stanovich, K. (1980). Toward an interactive compensatory model of individual differences in the development of reading fluency. *Reading Research Quarterly, 16,* 32-71.

Stubbs, M. (1980). *Language and literacy: The sociolinguistics of reading and writing.* London: Routledge & Kegan Paul.

Swaffar, J. K. (1988). Readers, texts, and languages: The interactive process. *Modern Language Journal, 72*(2), 123-149.

Tannen, D. (1979). What's in a frame? Surface evidence for underlying expectations. In R. O. Freddle (Ed.), *New directions in discourse processing.* Norwood, NJ: Ablex.

Van Parreren, C. F., & Schouten-Van Parreren, M. C. (1981). Contextual guessing: A trainable reader strategy. *System, 9,* 235-241.

Wallace, C. (1992). *Reading.* Oxford: Oxford University Press.

Young, D. J. (1989). A systematic approach to foreign language reading instruction: What does the research suggest? *Hispania, 72*(3), 755-762.

chapter 9

Speaking for Communication and Interaction

Motor-perceptive skills involve perceiving, recalling, and articulating in the correct order sounds and structures of the language. This is the relatively superficial aspect of skill which is a bit like learning how to manipulate the controls of a car on a deserted piece of road far from the flow of normal traffic. It is the context-free kind of skill, the kind which has been recognized in language teaching for many years in the rationale of the audio-lingual approach to language teaching.

Interaction skills involve making decisions about communication, such as: what to say, how to say it, and whether to develop it, in accordance with one's intentions, while maintaining the desired relations with others. Note that our notions of what is right or wrong now depend on such things as what we have decided to say, how successful we have been so far, whether it is useful to continue the point, what our intentions are, and what sorts of relations we intend to establish or maintain with our interlocuters.

M. Bygate, 1987

Developing oral proficiency in a second-language involves a broad range of competencies associated with different conversational situations, topics, and rules for talking. Oral communication includes both transactional uses of language related to the exchange of information and interactional purposes connected with the social functions of speech. Conversations are governed by a number of discourse rules enabling speakers to shift topics, repair problems associated with miscommunication, and maintain interactional sequences. Research in oral language proficiency suggests that different conversational situations may require a particular sequence of communicative acts. Classroom interactional structures can greatly influence the degree to which teachers and students communicate and the type of discourse options that are available to students. Learners utilize a number of communication strategies that facilitate oral production plans. Teachers can help their students acquire a range of strategies useful for the execution of different communicative tasks. At the same time, oral language activities can be sequenced in a variety of ways to promote development of conversational skills.

This chapter examines the development of speaking abilities in terms of conversational situations. Some of the issues raised have to do with the following questions:

1. What are the issues associated with L2 oral language development?
2. What are the different types of conversational situations?
3. How is language used in conversational situations?
4. What are some of the research findings in the area of oral language abilities?
5. What considerations need to be taken into account in designing speaking activities?
6. What are some examples of speaking tasks?

SPEAKING IN L2 CLASSROOMS

The development of oral proficiency in the L2 is closely linked with listening abilities. As stated previously, language acquisition tends to progress in stages. Learners' verbal output usually consists of (1) rule-governed structures (e.g., systematic use of linguistic rules to form questions, to make negative assertions, and to give orders), (2) verbal routines (set phrases such as "See you later"; "Glad to meet you"), and (3) prefabricated patterns (units that have a slot or blank to be filled with a word, phrase, or sentence, as in "How do you say _____?").

L2 students might be exposed to spoken language that is *static* in nature, such as a description of a scene or object or a set of instructions to get to a location, to draw a picture, or to build a model. The spoken text might be *dynamic* in nature, such as telling a story or recounting an incident in which there are shifts of scene and time as well as changes in characters or persons in different epidoses. The spoken text could be *abstract* in nature, in which speakers express their ideas or beliefs regarding a topic that is not concrete (Brown & Yule, 1983). Students might be exposed to language samples in videotapes and movies that present dynamic uses of speech (greetings, farewells, question-and-answer sequences, verbal routines, and communication strategies) along with nonverbal behaviors (gestures, posture, facial expressions).

Spoken language abilities involve a certain amount of knowledge about the language (grammar, vocabulary, use of appropriate forms with functions) and skills for communicating the message (use of verbal formulas and speech adjustments: rephrasing, repetition, fillers, and hesitation devices). In interactive situations, students have to learn, among other things, how to negotiate meaning, how to introduce or change topics, and how to open and close conversations with different participants (Bygate, 1987).

Language teaching methods offer various frameworks for developing oral language skills. Littlewood (1981) organizes activities in terms of a precommunicative phase (structural practice of linguistic forms and their meanings) followed by a communicative phase (functional language use and social-interaction practice). An example of this approach is presented in Figure 1.1. Littlewood's division implies a graded sequence of communication activities, involving different learning objectives and speech outcomes. Rivers and Temperley (1978) distinguish three types of oral language activities: (1) oral practice for the learning of grammar, (2) structured interaction, and (3) autonomous interaction. Furthermore, there are two processes involved in learning to communicate: (1) skill-getting (knowledge of language forms, units, and functions; and pseudocommunication rehearsal) and (2) skill-using (spontaneous communication). The two processes, however, do not represent successive stages in language learning since even beginners have some of the skills necessary for performing basic functions (greetings, farewells, introductions, directives).

The development of "conversational competence" in a classroom context presents a number of challenges, since each speaker needs to have the opportunity to speak individually, and someone needs to listen and respond to the message. At the same time, learners have to be encouraged to communicate through a "reduced" language system. Learners also need be taught how to compensate for their gaps in L2 proficiency by using communication strategies (e.g., circumlocution, paraphrase, gestures). Moreover, students must be provided with models of successful interactional styles through the use of media (video and audiotapes, films, television programs), simulated conversations (role plays and sociodramas), and interactions with native speakers (Scarcella, 1990).

TYPES OF CONVERSATIONAL SITUATIONS

Oral communication occurs in a number of situations. Participants may interact with each other as friends or strangers, psychologically neutral or sympathetic persons, employer and employee, and teacher and student in such social settings as a friend's home, a train station, a doctor's office, a hallway in a building, or a city street. The purpose of the interaction could vary significantly, from getting the time of day from a stranger to asking a friend about plans for the weekend.

There are at least two major kinds of conversational interaction: transactional functions related to the exchange of information and interactional uses related to the social functions of language (Brown & Yule, 1983). *Transactional functions* include providing and obtaining information about facts, events, needs, opinions, attitudes, and feelings. For example, a policeman can give directions to a traveler, or a salesperson can explain to a customer the store's policy for exchanging merchandise. A person can write a letter to a bank explaining intentions to open a checking account, a child can ask a parent's opinion on buying a bicycle, or a teacher can inquire from the students their attitudes about other cultures. *Interactional uses* include the socializing functions of language, such as greetings, leave taking, introductions, thanking, and apologizing. These functions might serve to indicate the nature of social relationships or peer solidarity. During the course of interaction, participants might negotiate role relationships by suggesting, requesting, directing, advising, warning, convincing, or praising. Expressions such as "It would be a good idea to do your homework," "Let's go to the movies," "I want you to be in class when the bell rings, or else," and "That's a wonderful idea, Robert" all reflect different social concerns among the participants.

Conversations are also collaborative ventures. Speakers take turns at speaking during both transactional and interactional uses of language.

A: Excuse me. Could you tell me the time?

B: It's five minutes past two o'clock.

A: Thank you very much.

C: Hi, how are you doing, Lara?

D: I'm doing quite well, Bill.

C: See you later.

Some of the utterances used above are classified as *conversational routines*, or verbal routines. Apologies ("Excuse me"), requests ("Could you tell me the time?"), greetings ("Hi, how are you doing?"), acknowledgements ("Thank you very much"), and leave-taking expressions ("See you later") are just a few examples among thousands of conventionalized language expressions used in different discourse situations to make conversations sound natural and nativelike. Some examples of ways of expressing specific language functions in French, German, and Spanish are listed in Table 9.1. These expressions are based on interviews with native speakers and foreign language teachers.

Conversations are governed by a number of discourse rules. There are verbal strategies for getting someone's attention, initiating a topic, terminating and avoiding topics, and interrupting a speaker (Kramsch, 1981). Some examples of verbal strategies used for maintaining a conversation in French, German, and Spanish are listed in Table 9.2 (p. 237). These expressions, not necessarily parallel across languages, are based on interviews with native speakers and foreign language teachers.

Speakers are able to shift and avoid topics through both verbal and nonverbal signals. Participants also engage in repair strategies to correct problems of miscommunication. Repairs may involve self-repairs (paraphrases, restatements, confirmation checking) initiated by either participant, or other-initiated repairs (requests for clarification, repetition, or slower speech rate) usually negotiated by a second language speakers. Speaking situations call for various uses of language and verbal strategies necessary for maintaining a conversation. Specific ways of developing these skills and strategies are discussed later in this chapter.

TABLE 9.1   Examples of French, German and Spanish verbal routines

French	German	Spanish
Greeting		
Bonjour, (Monsieur/Madame/ Mademoiselle)	Guten Morgen, (Herr/Frau/Frl. + Name)	Buenos días ¿Cómo estás?
Comment ça va? Ça va bien?	Wie geht es Ihnen (dir)?	¡Hola!
Salut!	Prima!	
Leave Taking		
Bonsoir! Bonne journée	auf Wiedersehen	Adios
à demain, à bientôt, à tout à l'heure	Mach's gut	Hasta luego/pronto
à la prochaine	Bis später/dann!	Nos vemos/Te veo
Expressing Surprises		
Quelle surprise!	ach so!	¡Qué sorpresa!
Comment?	Gott!	¡Caramba!
Tu plaisantes, non?	Was ist denn los!	¡No me digas!
Asking for Information		
C'est à quelle page?	auf welcher Seite sind wir?	¿En qué página estamos?
Qu'èst-ce que nous faisons aujourd'hui?	Was sollen wir heute tun?	¿Qué hacemos hoy?
Comment écrit-on. . .	Wie buchstabiert man. . .?	¿Cómo se escribe?
Apologizing		
Je regrette	Es tut mir leid	Perdóneme
Excusez-moi	Es geht leider nicht	Discúlpeme
Pardonnez-moi	Entschuldigen Sie, bitte	Lo siento (mucho)
Warning		
Faites (fais) attention.	Achtung!	¡Ten/Tenga cuidado!
Attention!	Vorsicht!	¡Presta atención!
Prenez garde!	Passen Sie auf!	Te aviso que. . .
Je vous previens que. . .		

Based on Papalia (1983), pp. 13–48.

SPEAKING IN INTERACTIVE SITUATIONS

From a discourse perspective, development of successful oral communication involves thinking about language in terms of the components of communicative proficiency. According to Galloway (1987), this means considering the nature of the context where the communication takes place (familiar or unfamiliar situation, predictable or unpredictable discourse sequences), the content or range of topics ad-

TABLE 9.2 Examples of French, German and Spanish conversational verbal strategies

French	German	Spanish
Getting Attention		
Excusez/pardonnez-moi	Verzeihung	Perdóneme
Attendez	Entschuldigung!	¡Oigame!
Vous permettez	Einen Moment bitte!	Me permite
Redirecting the Topic		
Notez bien que	Mit anderen Worten	De otro modo. . .
ça n'est pas la question	Kurz und gut	En otras palabras
D'autre part	Wie gesagt	De tal modo
Adding an Argument		
Mais je veux dire que	Außerdem (möchte ich	además. . .
Dans ce cas	sagen. . .)	También. . .
C'est à dire que	Ebenso. . .	No olvide que. . .
	Vergessen Sie nicht / Vergiß	
	nicht / man darf nicht	
	vergessen	
Giving in		
Peut-être	Vielleicht	Sí, tienes razón
Je suis d'accord	Ich bin einverstanden	Lo que tu digas
Bon alors	Das kann (schon) sein	Bueno, estoy de acuerdo
Dissenting		
Je ne suis pas entièrement	Ich weiß nicht	Quizás
d'accord	Ich glaube nicht	No creo que. . .
Tu crois que	Echt?	Pues. . .
Vraiment?		
Fighting Back		
Non!	Falsch!	Tú no lo sabes todo
Absolument pas!	Das stimmt nicht	La verdad es que. . .
Avez-vous bientôt fini?	Das ist mir egal	A mí no me importa

Based on Papalia (1983), pp. 19–48.

dressed during the conversation (immediate, autobiographical, factual, concrete, to esoteric, abstract topics remote in time and place), and the uses of language to perform communicative tasks (patterns of lexical, syntactic, and discourse errors, management of topics and tasks, appropriate speech style, use of nonverbal cues).

Nunan (1989) notes that there are many aspects to effective oral communication. Some have to do with the linguistic aspects of language (phonology, intonation patterns, appropriate conversational formulae), and others relate to the interactional aspects of conversations (strategies for negotiating meaning, effective turn-taking procedures, and successful conversational listening skills). To a certain extent, this implies considering the discourse situations where language interaction takes place (top-down approach) and then proceeding to the communicative functions of language with specific sentences or verbal routines used to convey specific meanings. Richards (1985) argues that it is important to consider the way in which language use reflects underlying communicative needs. This can be seen in role-playing activities requiring the student to perform a communicative function in a specific interactional situation:

Situation A
Teacher to student: "You are visiting me, your sick friend, and want to find out how I am feeling. You also want to tell me about what is going on at school. You begin."

Situation B
Teacher to student: "You bought a compact disc yesterday and found out that it was defective. You bring it back to the store to exchange it. I am the salesperson you bought it from. I'll begin." (Hartzell, 1988, p. 4)

In both examples, the learner is provided with the basic elements of a conversation:

1. Situation (a friend's home, a record store)
2. Participants (a sick friend; a salesperson seen before)
3. Purpose (inquire about illness and inform about school affairs; inform about the condition of the record previously bought, and request to have it exchanged)

In one situation, the topic centers on illness and school life, while in the other the context has to do with types of defects in audio recordings and getting purchases exchanged in a store. The language forms and vocabulary needed for inquiring about health ("How are you feeling/doing?" "I hope you get better soon." "When are you coming back to school?" "Have you seen a doctor?" "Are you taking medication?") and informing about school life ("We have a lot of homework." "The teacher gave us a test yesterday." "We miss you at school.") may be less technical or of higher frequency than those required in explaining a defective compact disc ("I bought this CD yesterday, and it doesn't sound good. The recording has background noise, especially at the beginning, and I am not pleased with the quality.") and requesting merchandise exchange ("Could I exchange for another one?" "I want to get my money back." "What can I do?" "What is your exchange policy?").

Each conversational situation may require a particular sequence of rhetorical acts. Conversations typically start with an "opener" ("Hi. How are you?") and end with a "closing" expression ("Goodbye," "See you later," "Thanks."). Speech events such as apologies and complaints may consist of a number of acts following a basic pattern. Olshtain and Cohen (1983) characterize the structure of apologies in several languages as consisting of one or more formulas:

- An expression of apology ("I'm sorry," "I apologize," "Pardon me")
- An explanation or account of the situation ("I wasn't thinking.")
- An acknowledgement of responsibility. ("It was my fault.")
- An offer of repair ("Let me pay for the broken vase.")
- A promise of forbearance ("It won't happen again.")

Complaints in Spanish, Japanese, and English have a similar structure and consist of the same discourse components. According to Hatch (1983), most complaints consist of the following sequence of discourse elements:

1. Opener ("Hi.")
2. Orientation ("I'm your neighbor.")
3. Act statement ("You charged me too much.")
4. Justification ("I have paid the bill.")
5. Remedy ("Would you change my grade?")
6. Closing ("Thanks.")
7. Valuation ("I am glad this is over.")

Other discourse genres such as debates, descriptions, narratives, and instructions follow certain conventions. Most stories in English, for example, consist of a setting followed by a series of episodes. The setting includes statements in which time, place, and characters are introduced. Then each episode consists of a beginning, development, intentions, end, and a resolution (Van Dijk, 1982). This macrostructure makes the story coherent and easy to follow among listeners who have the story schema. Creating discourse that is coherent is a crucial aspect in the development of communicative competence in a second language. Discourse competence involves the mastery of how to combine grammatical forms and meaning to achieve a unified text in different genres such as narratives, descriptions, or arguments (Canale & Swain, 1980). This type of competence is anticipated among the ACTFL's advanced level speakers, who should be able to narrate and describe with paragraph-length discourse, and superior level students, who should be able to support opinions and hypothesize using nativelike discourse strategies. Developing interactive competence is a complex process since it entails language skills, topic familiarity, conversational abilities, and practice opportunities. Teachers can utilize insights from research and design learning tasks that take into account the various factors. These are discussed in later sections of this chapter.

RESEARCH IN ORAL LANGUAGE PROFICIENCY

The development of oral language abilities has attracted considerable attention during the past decade. Issues such as the role of speech situation and its influence on the form and meaning of linguistic structures, the discourse rules that L2 learners violate, and the structure of conversations among nonnative speakers are reflected in the work of Larsen-Freeman (1980) on discourse analysis in second language learning.

The focus on the uses of language (Hymes, 1972) in terms of discourse levels such as speech acts (minimal conversational units reflecting the speaker's intention, as apologizing, suggesting, requesting, greeting), speech events (genres with an internal structure, as in a narrative, debate, interview, lecture, discussion), and speech situations (contexts where speech events take place, as during a party, court trial, church service, classroom) enables both teachers and researchers to understand how language works during verbal interaction. The acquisition of conversational competence among adult ESL students reveals a developmental pattern, with "greeting" and "closing" among the first to be acquired, followed by "introductions," and then getting the speakers to clarify meaning (Scarcella, 1983). The case study by Schmidt (1983) of the development of communicative competence in a Japanese adult, Wes, who was learning English indicated that Wes's command of directives over a three-year period reflected a heavy reliance on a limited number of speech formulas ("Please take this suitcase"), many of which could not be employed productively outside their use as fixed expressions. Nevertheless, Wes made the greatest improvement in the development of interactional competence, following an extended routine, as in the case of ordering food at a restaurant. It should be noted that Wes was an exceptional learner, perhaps not comparable to other cases.

Concern for conversational competence in relation to how persons talk to each other (native interacting with nonnative speakers) both inside and outside the classroom has been given considerable attention in ESL research. Studies by Gaskill (1980), Carpenter (1983), and Brock, Crookes, Day, and Long (1986) illustrate the linguistic adjustments that native speakers (NS) make in the areas of speech rate, vocabulary, and syntax, to communicate with nonnative speakers (NNS), who, in turn, use a number of compensatory strategies (direct or indirect appeals for help, echoing or repeating a word or phrase to indicate instances of misunderstanding) when faced with communication problems (Ellis, 1985). This can be seen in cases where there is a request for repetition:

NNS(A): How did you spend there?
NNS(B): Hmm?
NNS(A): How *long* did you spend there? (Schwartz 1980, p. 146)

Repeating a word or phrase not understood:

NS: We're going mountaineering tomorrow.

NNS: Mountain . . . ee . . . ?

NS: Mountaineering. You know, to climb up the mountain. (Richards, 1990, p. 72)

The native speaker clarifies meaning by defining the word. In other situations, a request for a repair can be approached syntactically by highlighting the topic, as in the case of:

NS: Do you come from a big family?

NNS: Uhh?

NS: Your family. Is it big? Do you have lot of brothers and sisters? (Richards, 1990, p. 72)

Hatch (1978) has argued that language grows out of experience, and it is out of participating in conversations that one learns how to interact verbally; out of this interaction, syntactic forms develop. Sato (1986) found that conversations indeed facilitated interactional competence and favored the acquisition of such grammatical features as English adverbial terms (yet, now, tonight, on Thursday) and irregular verbs with specific past tense forms (e.g., gave, had, did).

Classroom interactional structures can influence the degree to which the teacher and students interact and the types of discourse options. The classroom has been examined from the perspectives of input and interactional structures (Gass & Madden, 1985), the development of conversational competence as a result of instructional activities and learning tasks (Day, 1986), types of language learning (incidental vs. intentional, metalinguistic awareness, and strategic competence) (Lantolf & Labarca, 1987), and the development of second language discourse (Fine, 1988).

Language learning under classroom conditions is a rapidly growing field within the broader concerns of second language acquisition (Faerch & Kasper, 1985). Long (1987, p. 97) notes that classroom-centered research that focuses on the teaching and learning processes can provide much needed information "to put modern teaching on a scientific footing." Chaudron (1988) offers a comprehensive review of classroom-based research on such topics as teacher-student interaction, teacher talk, learner behaviors, learning outcomes, and directions for study.

At a more practical level, Malamah-Thomas (1987) guides language teachers toward a more critical appraisal of classroom interaction by asking them to consider the nature of communication in the classroom, examine classroom language from various frameworks and teaching approaches, and explore their own classroom through a series of tasks designed to promote professional development and changes in teaching behaviors. Teachers can ask such questions as *who* speaks *what*, to *whom*, *when*, and *why*. *Who* can include the teacher, the teaching medium (text, audiovisual materials, role plays, sociodrama, native speakers) and student groups (pairs, small or large groups, and pupils-to-teachers). *What* comprises the types of teaching activities (drills, dialogues, speaking exercises, free conversation), the linguistic content (vocabulary, grammar, discourse, cultural information, and conversational strategies) and the language focus (listening, speaking, reading, and writing). *When* (day, time, and point in the lesson) and *why* (introduction of new linguistic content, practice, review, skill-getting phase, skill-using activity) reflect the pedagogic classroom code.

Van Lier (1982) has identified four major types of interactional situations in the classroom, which reflect different degrees of teacher- or group-controlled activities with respect to a particular topic and the linguistic and/or procedural rules that may vary with the activity. For example, students can engage in private conversations in pairs without the teacher's monitoring of the way the interaction is organized or the level of accuracy. In another situation, the teacher may assign the topic to a group, which may result in the students' working on a text, participating in a role-playing context, or taking part in a problem-solving situation. The teacher may direct the whole class on a topic, controlling and managing the course of the conversation as in a discussion of a text, structured role-plays, or communicative exercises illustrating a grammar point or vocabulary items. There is also the situation in which the teacher controls the interaction during a mechanical drill (pronunciation exercises, transformation or substitution drills) where students respond on cue without regard to a specific conversation topic.

Pica and Doughty (1988) have found, for example, that the nature of the learning task in group work appeared to be a particularly critical factor affecting the type of discourse patterns among pupils. This suggests that group-work activities need to be examined in relation to those tasks that require information exchange and those that center on the social uses of language.

The strategies that learners use in the process of planning and articulating their speech-production intentions have been described in terms of communication strategies, consisting of simplification strategies (e.g., "He hitting me" for "He is hitting me"), compensatory strategies (literal translations, paraphrase, word coinage, appeal for help, use of mime or gesture), and self-error correction or monitoring techniques (Ellis, 1985). Chamot and Kupper (1989) consider three major categories of learner strategies associated by speech production.

1. *Metacognitive or self-regulatory strategies*, which involve thinking about the learning process, planning for learning, monitoring the learning task, and evaluating how well one has learned
2. *Cognitive strategies*, which comprise techniques for interacting with the material to be learned, manipulating the material mentally or physically, or applying a specific technique to a learning task
3. *Social and affective strategies*, which entail interacting with another person to assist learning, or using effective control to assist a learning task

Introspective or think-aloud interviews might be arranged by teachers to determine which strategies are used by their students during oral langauge tasks. These procedures allow students to reflect on the different phases of a learning task, from planning to execution, and to develop an understanding of the range of strategies used by different students while performing similar language tasks. The speaking situations listed below illustrate some of the types of learning strategies that can be assessed by using oral interviews:

Student Oral Class Presentation

You have to give an oral presentation in Spanish to the class, such as a book report or an account of something you have done.

How do you prepare for the oral presentation?

What helps you to present the report well?

Role Playing Situation

Your teacher gives you a practical situation to perform in Spanish, such as ordering a meal in a Spanish restaurant, ordering a plane ticket, or asking for directions in Spanish.

Have you ever had to do a task like this? (If no, skip this question.)

Do you have any special tricks that help you prepare for the task before you actually have to do it?

Do you have any special tricks that help you complete the task using appropriate Spanish?

What do you do to help yourself speak? What do you do if the person to whom you're speaking does not understand you?

What do you do if you do not understand what the person says to you?

Communication in a Social Situation

You encounter a few native speakers of Spanish and have the opportunity to talk with them. You must listen to what they say, understand the meaning, and speak to them as intelligently and appropriately as possible.

How often have you had to do this? (If the answer is never, skip this section.)

What do you do that helps you understand the Spanish you hear?

What do you do that helps you remember new words or phrases?

What do you do that helps you to talk?

What do you do if you don't understand what the native speakers say?

What do you do if the native speakers don't understand you? (Chamot & Kupper, 1989, pp. 23-24)

In summary, the development of oral language abilities is greatly affected by interactional opportunities. The major findings of the studies reviewed suggest the following:

1. The acquisition of certain language functions seems to follow a developmental pattern, with fixed expressions acquired first, followed by informatives, and then by requests and other functions.

2. The acquisition of one aspect of communicative competence (e.g., inter-actional strategies) is not necessarily paralleled with the development of another aspect (e.g., grammatical accuracy).
3. Native speakers make linguistic adjustments when they communicate with nonnative speakers.
4. Nonnative speakers rely on a number of compensatory strategies when communication problems arise.
5. Interaction facilitates the development of conversational competence and the acquisition of certain grammatical features.
6. Classroom interactional structures affect the speaking opportunities and the type of language functions.
7. The type of learning task assigned to student groups can influence the interactional patterns and the uses of certain language functions.
8. Teachers can assist learners in identifying their communication strategies and providing opportunities for them to practice and expand the use of different strategies.

Still, there are a number of issues that remained unresolved. It is not clear at this point what specific aspects of conversational competence can be explicitly taught. The role of practice and the use of specific techniques, activities, and approaches might stimulate some students in different ways. Some students may fail to achieve high levels of conversational competence because achievement might ultimately be tied to speaker identity, reflected to an extent by motivational drive (Scarcella, 1999).

TEACHING CONSIDERATIONS

The sequencing of oral language activities on the basis of the ACTFL's (1986) proficiency guidelines implies ordering speaking situations in terms of performance descriptions relating language functions, content, and accuracy levels. Descriptions corresponding to the four major levels are as follows:

1. The *novice level* is characterized by an ability to communicate minimally with learned material.
2. The *intermediate level* is characterized by an ability to (a) create with the language by combining and recombining learned elements, although primarily in a reactive mode, (b) initiate, minimally sustain, and close basic communicative tasks in a simple way, and (c) ask and answer questions.
3. The *advanced level* is characterized by an ability to (a) converse in a clearly participatory fashion, (b) initiate, sustain, and bring to closure a wide variety of communicative tasks, including those that require increased ability to convey meaning with diverse language strategies because of a complication or an unforeseen turn of events, (c) satisfy the

requirements of school and work situations, and (d) narrate and describe with paragraph-length connected discourse.

4. The *superior level* is characterized by an ability to (a) participate effectively in most formal and informal conversations on practical, social, professional, and abstract topics, and (b) support opinions and hypothesize using nativelike discourse strategies.

Papalia (1983, pp. 50–52) suggests a number of basic techniques suitable for the novice level and appropriate for promoting communication from controlled to spontaneous language:

Adaptation and Variation of the Dialogue
Use the expressions that appeared in the dialogue to:

1. Greet a friend. _____
2. Take leave from a friend. _____
3. Tell a friend that you will see him or her later. _____
   _____
4. Ask a friend what's new. _____
5. Say to a friend "Until next time." _____

Guided Dialogue
Example: Use the previous dialogue as a guideline and prepare a conversation about the following situation. You meet Alicia in the corridor of your school.

1. Greet each other.
2. You ask how Carmen is.
3. Alicia replies that she is sick.
4. You say that you are sorry.
5. She says thank you.

Ask Questions
Make questions requiring these answers. Example:

1. ¿Cómo _____?
   Mi hermana está muy bien, gracias.
2. ¿A qué hora _____?
   Yo voy a la biblioteca a las cuatro.

What Will You Answer?
Provide an answer appropriate to the situation. Example:

1. You arrive at school and a friend greets you:
   Hi, what's up?
   You would answer: _____

What Do You Do?
Things to do. Provide students with a list of action verbs, then ask them to select from the given list of verbs five things that they do every day.

Guess What?
Select from the following list five activities that you wish to do today and write them in the space provided (e.g., go home, eat at 12:00 noon). Then pair off with a classmate who will ask you questions to guess which activities you have selected. Take turns with each other in asking questions and answer them in complete sentences. The person who guesses all five of the other's answers first wins the game. Example:

STUDENT A: Are you going to watch TV tonight?

STUDENT B: No, I don't think so.

STUDENT B: Are you going home after school?

STUDENT A: Yes, I will go.

Activities   *Things I Might Do Today*
To open the window   1. _____
To go home   2. _____
To use the telephone   3. _____
To watch TV   4. _____
To eat at 12:00 o'clock   5. _____
To listen to music on the radio
To study mathematics
To go to the library

Do you remember the activities that your classmate plans on doing today? List them below:

1. _____   3. _____
2. _____   4. _____

Express These Speech Acts
Use the word(s) below in a sentence of your own choosing.

Example: Seek information (qui) . . . Qui est-il?

1. Greet someone (allez) _____
2. Give thanks (beaucoup) _____
3. Express excitement (content[e]) _____
4. Seek an answer (où) _____
5. Express curiosity (qui) _____

Express Wants, Needs, and Desires
Complete the following open-ended sentences: Example:

I want . . . ; I need . . . ; I would like . . . ; When it's hot . . . ;
When it's cold . . . ; When I travel, I'll take with me . . . ; etc.

Show Emotion

Example: Develop a conversation in which you answer the phone and the caller informs you that you have won the lottery. Express surprise, then pleasure and satisfaction. You are now a rich person. Tell him or her what you would do with your money.

List and Inform

Example: Make a grocery list of items you need for a party.

List five sports that you like to play at a picnic.

Inform your teacher or classmates what you are planning to buy for a party.

Tell your classmates what sports you would like to play at a school picnic.

Predict

Example: Predict what your mother has written on her grocery list.

Predict what your best friend likes to order in a restaurant.

Predict tomorrow's weather.

Report Orally

Example: Prepare a dialogue for the following situation. You are new at school and must ask a student for help. Excuse yourself and ask a student if he or she knows Mr. Smith, the English teacher. The student answers that he or she knows him and that he is in room 112.

A: Perdone, ¿conoces al señor Smith?

B: _____

Interview

Example: Interview a classmate and report the information to other students. Possible topics: sports, food, likes, dislikes, travel, family, school subjects, hobbies, friends, work, etc.

Role Playing

Example: In pairs, prepare a dialogue for a situation like the following one:

Imagine that Carla would like to go the movies Friday evening with some of her friends. However, she has a cold, and her father does not want her to go out for her well-being. She needs to persuade or convince her father that her health will not become worse. (After each pair makes its presentation to the class, the class can vote and determine which student's arguments are the cleverest).

Engage in Conversation
Example: Your school's foreign exchange student has just arrived in town. Your best friend has met the student but you have not. You need to find out from your friend various details about the new student. You and your friend meet at the lunch room and talk about the foreign exchange student for a few minutes.

Describe
Example: Bring a picture to class. Describe it and answer questions asked by others.

Personalized Questions and Answers
Ask questions that emanated from the oral presentation in which students are asked to present information about themselves.

Communication activities can also be planned on the basis of topics and situations. Papalia (1983, pp. 53-57) provides examples of speaking activities for use with students at the novice and intermediate levels:

Family/Home Life
A. There are X members in your family. Briefly describe each one.
B. Imagine that a friend of yours from another country is coming to stay with you for a few days. You are going to introduce your friend to your family. Name the members of your family that you are going to introduce to your friend.
C. You have been given the job of making a list of family names and ages for a family portrait to be shown at school.
D. You are shopping in large department store and become separated from a member of your family. Give a description of the person to the security guard.
E. Describe your family. How many people live in your house? How old are your brothers and sisters? Do your parents work? What do they do?

House and Home
A. A friend is moving to his or her own apartment. What will he or she need to furnish it?
B. You have a blind friend who will be spending a weekend with you.

Describe the rooms (entrance, bedroom, living room, bathroom) your friend will need to be familiar with during his or her stay. Remember, your friend cannot see and he or she must know the location of specific objects.

C. Your family is moving to a new apartment or home. You have an opportunity to redecorate your room. What things would you buy and how would you decorate or arrange your room?

D. Draw and label a floor plan of your house, detailing each room and its furnishings. What changes would you like to make? Explain why.

E. Tell your classmates what chores you are responsible for around the house. What chores do you like or dislike? What changes would you recommend for other members of your household?

Transportation

A. You are planning a trip around the world. Tell the class some of the methods of transportation you are planning to use during your trip.

B. Your family just bought a car. Talk about some of the benefits and problems related to having a new car at home.

C. Describe your first flying experience. Where did you go? How long did it take? With whom did you go? Were there any surprising moments during the trip?

D. Provide each student with a map of one particular city (detailed). Have a student give specific directions from one location, and see if the entire class arrives at the same destination.

Sports

A. My favorite sport is _____ because _____ .

B. You are spending a year in France. What kind of sports will you play throughout the year?

C. Invent a story to explain why certain sports are played in certain seasons and not in others.

D. Name any five sports. For each one, name the object(s) that is (are) used in the sport (for example: tennis racquet, hockey puck, baseball bat). Then name the place where each sport is typically played (e.g., tennis court, hockey rink).

E. On a map of Spain, students will locate at least three resort areas and name the sports or activities for which they are noted.

F. Who has a better soccer team? Why? Describe a soccer game. What does the crowd do? How do the players behave?

Entertainment—Movies

A. What types of movies do you like to see most often (love, sad, mystery, science fiction, etc.)? How do your viewing habits reveal your personality?

B. Answer the following questions concerning attendance at movies:
1. What is the average price of a movie?
2. Do prices differ according to times of the day? Explain.
3. How frequently do people attend movies?
4. Is it an outing that requires dressy or casual clothing?
C. You have a friend from another country who has told you about TV where he lives. Tell all the different types of shows that you can think of that exist on TV where you live, so that he will get a complete picture.
D. How much television do you usually watch? Name several of your favorite programs, and describe the types of programs you usually prefer (documentaries, comedies, dramas, news, etc.).

Restaurants

A. You spent last night at a superb restaurant. What are some of the things that come to your mind?
B. What types of restaurant do you like to go to? Examples: cafeteria, coffee shop, sit-down dinner restaurant, take-out, or pancake house?
C. Your friends call and invite you to go with them to a certain restaurant. Tell how the restaurant looks, including "visibility" (dark or light) and seating. Also, describe any music that is played, as well as the way food is served (warm, cold, fresh, stale, snack, etc.).
D. You are at a world-famous restaurant in another country. Order a meal for yourself.
E. Imagine you and your friend are in a French restaurant. Create a dialogue that might take place, one of you being the customer, the other being the waiter.

Topic and situations at the advanced level require the ability to interact in a sustained manner and resolve problems with unforeseen complications. For example:

We are in school. I am your friend. You saw a movie last night and thought it was great. Tell me about it and try to convince me I should see it. (Hartzell, 1988, p. 4)

At this level, students should be able to produce paragraph-length discourse dealing with such topics as self, family, home life, interests, jobs, vacations, and future plans. They should be able to paraphrase; handle past, present, and future time with few inaccuracies of tense; and present argumentation as needed in problem-solving situations. At the superior level, students are expected to discuss more-abstract topics (e.g., politics, economics, mass media, moral issues), which require the ability to hypothesize, argue, and persuade as well as produce extended discourse beyond the paragraph stage (Bragger, 1985).

The structuring of speaking activities can also be approached from the perspective of communicative tasks (Nunan, 1989). Speaking tasks would encompass language functions (give personal details, ask and make statements about the likes of self and others, describe a sequence of events in a variety of tenses, give a short summary of the main points and supporting details of an aural presentation) and interactional structures (take part in short, contextualized dialogues; work in pairs or small groups to share information and solve a problem; work in groups to solve problems requiring the resolution of conflicting information). The use of conversational routines and strategies (formulae for greeting and leave-taking, use of discourse strategies to change topic or provide additional information, use of discourse strategies for "holding" the floor, disagreeing and using appropriate nonverbal behavior) would also be taken into account.

Communicative language teaching approaches focus on the uses of language (greetings, suggestions, apologies, directives, and informatives) within social context (a friend's home, the doctor's office, the train station). Students receive practice by interacting with their teacher and peers. Class activities are usually characterized by interactive situations where there is an information gap (one of the speakers knows something the listener does not know: "Where do you live?," "What are your plans for the summer?"). The speaker who wants to obtain this information needs to use the appropriate linguistic forms (grammatical structures, vocabulary) to convey the meaning to the listener. Based on the feedback received from the listener, the speaker may have to negotiate the meaning of the message by paraphrasing, restating, or using nonlinguistic resources.

Procedures for developing "communicative ability" among L2 learns in the ESL classroom have been formulated by Littlewood (1981). As noted in Chapter 1 (Figure 1.1), classroom activities are organized so that there are both precommunicative (part-whole language drills) and communicative activities (functional language use and social interaction practice). During the precommunicative phase, the focus initially is on the linguistic forms and structures of the target language, emphasizing acceptability and/or accuracy. Later, an attempt is made to relate the language forms to their potential functional meanings ("Shall we go. . . ." "Oh, no, I don't feel like. . . ." as ways of making and rejecting suggestions). During the communicative phase, the learner is placed initially in a "functional" situation, which requires various uses of language:

1. Sharing information with restricted cooperation (yes/no questions)
2. Sharing information with unrestricted cooperation (information-gap activities, discovering differences)
3. Sharing and processing information (discussing or evaluating information, pooling information to solve a problem)
4. Processing information (discussing and evaluating facts in order to solve a problem or reach a decision)

The last phase involves social interaction activities, which require the learner to pay close attention to the social as well as the functional meanings that language conveys. The communicative activities call for role-playing situations through cued dialogues, role-playing controlled through information, situations, goals, debate, and improvisation. Some of the activities call for language use in the context of the actual classroom situation, while others use simulation as a means of placing the learner in target culture situations. Thus, sequences of discourse activities range from the use of mechanical drills in the precommunicative phase to the practice of "authentic" language use in specific sociolinguistic situations included during the communicative phase.

The communicative language teaching perspective has been extended to the foreign language classroom by Omaggio (1986). She argues that it is possible to develop high levels of communicative abilities among learners by organizing classroom activities around the concept of language proficiency. The five hypotheses advocated as the basis for proficiency-oriented instruction are presented in Chapter 1.

The approach calls for a variety of activities such as information-gap tasks, problem-solving situations, games, simulations, and opportunities for students to articulate personal preferences, feelings, or attitudes (Nunan, 1989). Specific examples of activities used in promoting language interaction through information-gap, reasoning-gap (problem-solving tasks), and opinion-gap activities have been outlined by Prabhu (1987). Pattison (1987), for example, offers seven activity types designed to develop communication skills. These include the following exercises:

1. *Questions and answers*: activities designed to create an information gap by having learners make personal or secret choices from a list of items related to a topic (e.g., location of a person or object in a picture, display, or chart); learner attempts to discover their classmates' secret choices
2. *Dialogues and role-plays*: entirely scripted or wholly improvised, enabling the learners in pairs, for example, to engage in interviews, go shopping, play detectives or smugglers, and find their way home
3. *Matching activities*: learners match items or complete pairs or sets as in clock bingo, people and things, and split dialogues (matching phrases to complete a conversation)
4. *Communication strategies*: designed to promote the use of production strategies that include paraphrasing, asking for feedback, simplifying, using gestures, and borrowing or creating words
5. *Pictures and picture stories*: use of stimuli to elicit narration or description by having students spot the difference in a set of pictures, recall the details of a picture, or sequence a set of pictures to tell a story
6. *Puzzles and problems*: activities that require learners to make guesses or use their imagination in order to complete story endings, to draw on their general knowledge and personal experience on quiz games and on their powers of logical reasoning by reaching a solution for a problem that is to be resolved by a group (e.g., relating persons to home towns and vacation destinations)
7. *Discussions and decisions*: learners collect and share information so as to reach a conclusion on what to take on a holiday, decide on the best

order of the incidents in a story, or determine the most essential items needed for a stay on a desert island

Crookall and Oxford (1990) provide a comprehensive treatment of the role and application of simulation and gaming in language learning. They incorporate perspectives from numerous contributors and offer specific procedures for conducting and designing classroom simulations for such areas as learning strategies, testing, teacher training, and computers. They point out that role-plays are simulations, in that the participants represent and experience typical character types known in everyday life. Role-plays can be seen in relation to the specified roles that participants take on or act out, usually written, preestablished social situations guided by scenarios. (See the examples below for Students A and B using conversation cards.) Games do not usually represent any real-world human behavior, although they may be inspired by human activity such as playing chess, bingo, poker, and the Olympics. Games like password, charades, 20 questions, and "Simon Says" allow players the opportunity to practice individual language features (classifying words by topic or grammatical category, asking questions, giving orders).

The development of communication skills in the classroom can be greatly influenced by the types of oral language activities. Communicative tasks typically deal with transactional uses of language (e.g., convey or request information, negotiate meanings, or complete a problem-solving task) through pair or group work but seldom enable learners to use language for interactional purposes. Role-playing situations and simulations need to have a central place in the curriculum to ensure that learners can develop a range of conversational strategies for turn taking, topic control, repairs, routines, fluency, and styles of speaking (Richards, 1990). Students need to be made aware that it is not necessary to converse perfectly in the L2 in order to communicate and that conversational strategies can be used to overcome communication difficulties in the real world. Students also need to be given feedback on their abilities to convey meaning and accomplish communicative objectives (Scarcella, 1990). Simulations allow students to move from the classroom environment to the real world of human activity in a cultural setting. By engaging in face-to-face communication, participants learn to negotiate meaning, make decisions, and develop a broad range of conversational skills.

Conversation cards may serve as a relatively simple, direct means to assess and provide feedback to students on their ability to perform various communicative functions related to specific topics. Two students are provided with a pair of conversation cards, one being assigned the role of A and the other one B, as in the following example:

Student A
You are a 16-year-old student from Lynchburg, Virginia. There are three people in your family and you like to play baseball. You would like to get to know a Chilean foreign exchange student who has recently enrolled in your school. You ask him or her:

what his/her name is

how old he/she is

where he/she lives

how many people there are in his/her family

what the names of his/her family members are

what his/her hobbies are

Student B

You are a 17-year-old Chilean student. You live in Santiago and come from a big family (there are 8 people in it). You like to play tennis. You speak with another student in your school. You ask the other student:

what his/her name is

how old he/she is

where he/she lives

how many people there are in his/her family

what the names of his/her family are

what his/her hobbies are

(Gutiérrez, 1987, p. 916).

Students need to be given a few minutes to prepare their presentation based on information found in the cards. The conversations could be tape recorded and later scored on communicative criteria, for example:

1. The student provides biographical information.

| _____ | _____ | _____ | _____ | _____ |
| None | Little | Some | Much | All |

2. The student requests biographical information.

| _____ | _____ | _____ | _____ | _____ |
| None | Little | Some | Much | All |

Each language sample could be scored on the basis of analytical scales, taking into account such aspects as fluency, vocabulary, structure, and comprehensibility. Assign a score to each component. Omaggio (1983, p. 66) proposes a scoring scheme for interviews (asking questions) that takes into account the relative contribution of each component to the "global proficiency":

Aspect	_Points_	
Fluency (17%)	1 2 3 4 5 6	_____
Vocabulary (19%)	1 2 3 4 5 6 7 8	_____
Structure (16%)	1 2 3 4 5 6	_____
Comprehensibility (34%)	1 2 3 4 5 6 7 8 9 10 11 12	_____
Listening comprehension (14%)	1 2 3 4 5 6 7 8	_____
	Total	_____

She provides specific descriptions that correspond to the number of points possible for each of the five aspects of oral communication.

DESIGNING SPEAKING TASKS

Speaking situations encompass a broad spectrum of learner responses, ranging from replying in order to indicate the comprehension of a message to interacting with others in order to solve a problem. Speaking tasks can be grouped on the basis of communicative goals (exchange information with others; express a personal opinion or attitude; request information; use social formulas for greetings, apologies, farewells) and activity types (questions and answers, dialogues and role-plays, matching activities, picture descriptions, discussions and decisions). Specific tasks might require students to:

1. Reply to directions or questions
2. Give directions to others
3. Produce original sentences that correspond to particular structures or communicative expressions presented in class
4. Ask questions to others based on class activities
5. Describe the objects in a picture or chart
6. Tell a personal story or repeat a story read in class
7. Give an oral report on a prepared topic and answer questions related to the talk
8. Role-play specific situations from the target culture
9. Participate in language games and solve problems or puzzles
10. Participate in a debate, discussion, or forum in order to express a point of view regarding controversial topics
11. Interview native speakers and report the findings to the class
12. Dramatize stories or assume character roles from popular movies, plays, or television programs

The 10 speaking activities presented in Table 9.3 represent various examples of text types or genres, interactional patterns, learning objectives, and speaking tasks.

The question of how to sequence speaking tasks is a major issue. Tasks could be organized on the basis of some of the characteristics of spoken texts: static (descriptions, instructions), dynamic (a story, recounting of an incident), and abstract language (speaker's opinions, beliefs about a topic). Tasks could be graded in terms of proficiency levels, as in the case of the ACTFL speaking guidelines, which call for the use of particular teaching techniques, language functions, topics, and text types. A communicative-based approach tends to focus on the functional uses of language in different social situations. An interactive-based approach, on the other hand, emphasizes speaking abilities with regard to other language skill areas and in relation to learner needs or interests. In any event, students need multiple op-

TABLE 9.3 Components of speaking tasks

Text/Genre	Interactional Structure	Learning Objective	Speaking Skill
A Informative sequence	Individuals	Express food preferences	Perform a communicative function
B Dialog	Pairs	Answer questions and perform situation	Complete dialog based on information provided
C Interview/survey	Whole class	Asks questions to complete survey	Ask about likes/dislikes and report information
D Role-playing situation	Pairs	Create dialog based on cue cards	Create a conversation based on information provided
E Comic strip	Pairs	Prepare dialog to accompany a comic strip	Prepare an oral text that corresponds to visual materials
F Discourse sequence	Groups/pairs	Create dialog based on discourse chain	Create dialog based on functions requested
G Oral description	Individuals	Prepare oral description of a person so that listeners will guess the person's identity	Describe a person with specific details
H Picture description	Individuals/groups	Compare and contrast the features of two pictures	Describe the basic differences between two pictures
I Question/answer sequence	Whole class	Interview classmates to determine the particular traits	Determine through question/answer a person's traits
J Group consensus	Groups	Use group consensus to determine what gift item can be bought	Determine through discussion what can be purchased with a set amount of money

portunities to practice speaking skills for different genres, purposes, and situations. Moreover, speaking activities need to be integrated with other language areas, taking into account the communicative needs of learners.

Nearly all of the speaking tasks that follow involve interaction among students. Students are able to participate in a variety of situations, from simulations to group discussions. Written texts are involved with activities B, C, D, F, I, and J. Tasks C, H, and J make use of visual materials to serve as the stimuli for oral language. Task A is relatively simple since students are only required to provide an example, while task J incorporates various steps. Each task is based on a specific set of textual features (e.g., genre, topic, linguistic features), but it can be adapted to other proficiency levels and languages. The speaking tasks that follow also specify the topic, language functions, and the linguistic elements. The procedures outline the conditions under which each task is accomplished. It is important to note that some speaking tasks involve a skill-getting phase in order to provide students with the necessary linguistic information and skills required for interacting.

TASK A

Task:	Express a communicative function
Genre:	Informative sequence
Topic:	Lunch at a French restaurant
Function:	Inform others about what they would like for lunch
Linguistic elements:	*Je voudrais* (I would like); partitive; vocabulary items related to food and drink
Objective:	Students will express what they would like for lunch and will recognize what others have expressed.
Procedure:	Three members of the class state consecutively what they would like for lunch while classmates listen. After three have spoken, others report what each has said. The activity then continues with another group of three speakers. Example: *Je voudrais du fromage, du pain, et de la glace*. (I would like cheese, bread, and ice cream.) This activity may be varied by giving a list of unavailable items to some students, who play waiters. As customer-students place orders, waiter-students may respond using such lexical expressions as *Bien sûr* (certainly) or *Je suis désolé(e) mais il n'y en a pas* (I am sorry but there is none). Students may reverse roles and continue the activity.

Task A is adapted from Porter, 1987, p. 326.

TASK B

Task:	Complete dialogue based on information provided
Genre:	Dialogue
Topic:	Eating at a German restaurant
Function:	Answer questions about food preferences
Linguistic elements:	Question forms; vocabulary about food and drink items in a German restaurant
Objective:	Students will complete a cued dialogue and act out dialogue scene before the class.
Procedure:	Students receive copies of a German menu and an unfinished dialogue about a restaurant situation.

Working in pairs, the students formulate answers to the waiters' questions, using the menu as the text. Afterwards the student pairs act out their dialogues.

Sample dialogue:

Guten Tag, hier ist unsere Tageskarte. (Good day, here's our menu.)

Was für eine Spezialität möchten Sie? (What kind of an entree would you like?)

Wir haben verschiedene Salate. Möchten Sie sie probieren? Welcher? (We have different types of salads. Would you like to try them?) (Which one?)

Würden Sie unsere Suppe probieren? Welche? (Would you try our soup? Which one?)

Was für einen Nachtisch möchten Sie? (What kind of dessert would you like?)

Task B is adapted from Jones, 1988.

TASK C _____

Task:	Ask others about their likes and dislikes and report the information.
Genre:	Interview/survey
Topic:	Sports and pastimes
Function:	Obtain and provide information regarding sports and leisure activity preferences
Linguistic elements:	Question forms; verbs; *gustar* and *jugar*; vocabulary pertaining to sports and leisure activities
Objective:	Students will obtain information from others through brief interviews to determine individual preferences about sports and leisure activities. They will also report the findings to the class.
Procedure:	Each student prepares three or four questions to ask other classmates about sports and leisure preferences.
	Each student designs a survey sheet to report the results to the class.
	Students go around the class and ask others to indicate their preferences.

Students then report the findings of the survey to the class.

Sample survey form:

Nombre	¿Cuáles son tus deportes favoritos?	¿Cuando los practícas?	¿Dónde los practícas?
1.			
2.			
3.			
4.			
5.			

Task C is adapted from Bien, 1988.

TASK D

Task:	Create a conversation based on paired situation cards
Genre:	Role-playing situation
Topic:	Travel
Function:	Obtain and provide information
Linguistic elements:	Future tense; modal auxilary *werden*; present subjunctive; vocabulary related to travel arrangements and means of transportation
Objective:	Students will create simple conversations based on conversation cards.
Procedure:	Teacher distributes conversation cards to pairs of students. The students in each pair assume the roles and practice the situation. The roles can be reversed, and students can exchange their conversation cards with other groups.

Example 1:

A Du willst nach Hannover fahren. Kaufe eine Fahrkarte am Schalter.	**B** Wohin? Wann? Abfahrt; Ankunft; Kosten
(You want to travel to Hannover. Buy a ticket at the counter.)	(Where to? When, What time arrival, etc.)

ABFAHRT DER ZÜGE nach				
München	1	0	2	0
Lüneburg	1	7	5	5
Lüneburg	1	9	0	8
Kiel	1	9	1	0
Lübeck	0	8	4	5
Hannover	1	0	5	5
Köln	1	1	4	5
Bremen	1	1	0	3
Berlin	1	2	3	0
Dortmund	1	7	0	0

Example 2:

A	B
Ihr plant eine Reise nach England. Bucht eure Reise im Reisebüro.	Erklären sie die Reise : Zug durch Frankreich; Schiff; wann; Kosten

(You are planning a trip to England. Book it at the travel agency.)   (Explain the trip; train through France; boat; when; costs.)

Task D is adapted from Buhr, 1988.

TASK E

Task:	Prepare a dialogue to accompany visual materials
Genre:	Comic strip
Topic:	Family situation; wife preparing dinner for husband
Function:	Greetings; apologies; complaints; informatives
Linguistic elements:	Language forms that correspond to the functions
Objectives:	Students will prepare a dialogue between husband and wife regarding a dinner situation.
Procedure:	Teacher will distribute the comic strip to the students. The captions that correspond to each picture are removed so that students can create their own text. The students working in pairs create their own dialogues and then present them to the class. Students can ask questions to the pair who are presenting once the dialogue is read.

This procedure can be repeated by having students

bring their own comic strip to class and describe the visual content in the target language.

TASK F

Task:	Create a dialogue based on specific functions requested
Genre:	Discourse chain
Topic:	Meeting a new person
Function:	Obtain and provide information requested by discourse sequences
Linguistic elements:	Question-and-answer sequence; question forms; social formulas (greetings, introductions, farewells)
Objective:	Students will create dialogues based on a discourse chain and present them to the class.
Procedure:	Teacher establishes a situational context (e.g., meeting someone, an invitation, a job interview, making a reservation) for the discourse chain.

The participants, their roles, communicative purposes, and location are described.

The discourse chain can be represented on the chalkboard, overhead projector, or a handout. Students can work in groups, pairs, or with the whole class. The teacher may practice the chain with several students to provide a model to the class. Students can practice in groups and present their own dialogue or a parallel version of the one modeled in class.

Example of a discourse chain:
"Meeting someone new at school"

Richard	Sandra
Greet ──────────────────────────→	Greet
Introduce yourself ◄──────────────→	Reply and introduce yourself
Give impression about new school ◄──────→	Ask about experiences at previous school
Reply to questions and ask about sports and school ◄────→	Reply and ask about personal background
Reply and ask about the same ◄──────→	Reply and finish conversation politely
Reply ◄──────────────────────────→	Take leave
Farewell ◄───────	

Task F is adapted from Spratt, 1985, pp. 28–30.

TASK G

Task:	Describe a classmate or a famous person with sufficient detail so that others can identify the person
Genre:	Oral description
Topic:	Personality traits and physical characteristics
Function:	Provide information to others so that the person described can be identified
Linguistic elements:	Descriptive adjectives related to personality and physical characteristics
Objective:	Students will describe another person so that others will be able to guess the person's identity.
Procedure:	Teacher describes a famous person and students try to guess the identity based on clues about (1) personal appearance, (2) personality characteristics, and (3) background (age, sex, place of birth, nationality).
	Students are given time to select a person and prepare a description.
	Each student presents the description of the person to the class. Students may ask questions to get additional details.
	This procedure can be repeated with oral sketches of objects and places.

Task G is adapted from Pattison, 1987.

TASK H

Task:	Compare and contrast the features of two pictures
Genre:	Picture description
Topic:	At the doctor's office
Function:	Provide information to indicate the differences between two pictures
Linguistic elements:	Expressions of comparison and contrast; locatives; *Il y a* constructions; vocabulary related to doctor's office
Objective:	Students will describe the differences between two related pictures.
Procedure:	Teacher distributes sets of pictures to students.
	Teacher compares two pictures so that students can

review the necessary vocabulary and grammatical constructions.

Examples of expressions to describe basic differences:

Sur la première image . . . , mais sur la deuxième . . .

Il y a . . . sur la première image, mais sur la deuxième il n'y en a pas (il n'y a que) . . .

Celui/celle-ci est (a, fait, etc.) . . . mais l'autre/celui/celle-là . . .

Examples of expressions to compare and contrast:

Les deux sont (ont, font, etc.) . . .

Ils/elles sont, etc. . . . , tous les deux/toutes les deux.

Il y a un(e)/des . . . sur les deux images.

Il n'y a pas de . . . sur les deux images.

Ni l'un(e) ni l'autre est (a, fait, etc.) . . .

Ils/elles ne sont pas (n'ont pas, ne font pas, etc.) . . . , ni l'un(e) ni l'autre.

Students then prepare their descriptions working individually or in groups.

Task H is adapted from Pattison, 1987, p. 185.

TASK I

Task:	Match the person with the attributes
Genre:	Question-and-answer sequence
Topic:	Personal interests, belongings, activities
Function:	Obtain and provide information about personal qualities
Linguistic elements:	Question forms; verbs *tener, gustar*, etc.
Objective:	Students will determine through a question-and-answer process the person who has particular interests, experiences, and possessions.
Procedure:	Teachers and students prepare several cards on which they write in the target language some traits, interests, experience, or personal belonging.

Examples:

Tengo una motocicleta nueva

Me gusta comer comida mexicana

No me gusta ir al baile

Tengo un hermano mayor y dos
primos que viven en Miami

The cards are collected and redistributed to everyone. Each student sets out to find the person in the room who fulfills the characteristics on the cards he or she has drawn.

Task I is adapted from Ervin, 1988.

TASK J

Task:	Determine the items that can be bought with a set amount of money
Genre:	Group consensus
Topic:	Gift items for a father and child celebrating a birthday
Function:	Suggest; express agreement or disagreement; convince
Linguistic elements:	Language forms that correspond to the functions
Objective:	Students working in groups will determine through

Procedure:

discussion what gifts they can buy a father and his child using a $50 budget.

Teacher explains the situation to the class and distributes a handout that includes advertisements of possible gift items with the prices.

Students in each group of two or three consider individually the types of gift items and prepare a list of possible gifts for the father and the child.

The students then compare their individual lists and negotiate which item(s) they will buy for each family member. Each student justifies the choice of gifts and why others should agree.

Father		*Child*	
Items	Cost	Items	Cost
1.		1.	
2.		2.	
3.		3.	
————		————	

A final decision is reached by the group as to what to purchase for each family member. The group can then report to the class the choices they made.

Task J is adapted from Amemiya, 1988.

SUMMARY

Speaking situations can vary significantly due to the social setting, participants, topic, and communicative function. Conversational situations normally involve both transactional and social uses of language. Conversations are collaborative ventures, based on a number of rules for talking that speakers follow when introducing and changing topics, repairing miscommunication problems, and participating in discourse sequences. The development of oral language proficiency is influenced by interactional opportunities that, in turn, favor the acquisition of certain grammatical features and speech formulas. Native speakers make linguistic adjustments when interacting with nonnative speakers. Nonnative speakers, for their part, rely on compensatory strategies when communication problems arise. Conversational situations in the classroom need to be examined in terms of the discourse options made available to learners. Group and instructional tasks, along with strategy training, can affect students' oral production abilities. Teachers can assist learners in identifying their communication strategies and providing opportunities for practice.

Instructional activities based on proficiency levels take into account the role of topic, function, accuracy, and text type as essential categories for developing conversational abilities. Communicative teaching techniques involving games, simulations, problem-solving situations, and opinion-gap activities offer opportunities for learners to expand their conversational abilities. Speaking tasks range from asking or responding to a question to participating in a group discussion. Speaking activities might be organized in terms of communicative goals, genres, interactional structures, and task complexity. Some tasks require only one step to complete, while others require the student to respond with several actions. Students need to be given numerous speaking opportunities in order to develop their oral language abilities. At the same time, speaking tasks require opportunities to relate the various language subskills before using them appropriately in social interactional situations. Speaking activities should be integrated with other language modalities and should be sensitive to learner needs.

ACTIVITIES

1. Prepare a list of typical conversational tasks a learner would encounter in the following situations: train station, restaurant, department store, and bank.
2. Write a one-page dialogue in the target language with a fellow student, and then note the use of (1) verbal routines, (2) the types of questions and answers, and (3) the range of topics included.
3. Prepare a set of role-playing situations that require the participant to perform a specific communicative function within an interactional context, as in the examples provided by Hartzell.
4. Examine a few lessons from a language textbook and describe (1) the types of conversational situations included, (2) the kinds of speaking activities for students, and (3) the use of different discourse genres (informal conversations, instructions, descriptions, and narratives).
5. Based on the research findings noted in this chapter with respect to developing oral proficiency, prepare a list of do's and don't's for a beginning teacher.
6. Using the retrospective interview technique outlined by Chamot and Kupper, interview two language learners to identify how each approaches oral language tasks.
7. Develop a set of communicative tasks for a group of learners, taking into account language functions, content, and accuracy levels according to the ACTFL's proficiency guidelines.
8. Discuss the usefulness of Littlewood's procedures for developing communicative ability among ESL learners when applied to foreign language situations.
9. Observe a language classroom and make an inventory of (1) the kinds of oral language tasks, (2) the range of communicative functions attempted, and (3) the use of student-centered activities.
10. Prepare a set of conversation cards as recommended by Gutiérrez and then have two learners act out their roles. Tape record the conversation and score the performance of each learner, taking into account such issues as content, accuracy, comprehensibility, and fluency.
11. Prepare a speaking task based on a role-playing situation or a group discussion.

12. Analyze a speaking task in terms of the task requirements, topic, function, linguistic elements, and learner behaviors.

REFERENCES

Amemiya, Y. (1988). Materials prepared for a course. Albany, NY: State University of New York, School of Education.

American Council on the Teaching of Foreign Languages (ACTFL). (1986). *ACTFL provisional proficiency guidelines.* Hastings-on-Hudson, NY: ACTFL Materials Center.

Bien, M. (1988). Materials prepared for a course. Albany: State University of New York, School of Education.

Bragger, J. D. (1985). The development of oral proficiency. In A. C. Omaggio (Ed.), *Proficiency, curriculum, articulation: The ties that bind* (pp. 41-76). Middlebury, VT: Northeast Conference on the Teaching of Foreign Languages.

Brock, C., Crookes, G., Day, R. R., & Long, M. H. (1986). The differential effects of corrective feedback in native speaker-nonnative speaker conversation. In R. R. Day (Ed.), *Talking to learn: Conversation in second language acquisition* (pp. 229-236). Rowley, MA: Newbury House.

Brown, G., & Yule, G. (1983). *Discourse analysis.* Cambridge, England: Cambridge University Press.

Buhr, M. (1988). Materials prepared for a course. Albany: State University of New York, School of Education.

Bygate, M. (1987). *Speaking.* Oxford: Oxford University Press.

Canale, M., & Swain, M. (1980). Theoretical basis of communicative approaches to second language teaching and testing. *Applied Linguistics, 1,* 1-47.

Carpenter, C. (1983). "Foreigner talk" in university office-hour appointments. In N. Wolfson & E. Judd (Eds.), *Sociolinguistics and language acquisition* (pp. 184-194). Rowley, MA: Newbury House.

Chamot, A. U., & Kupper, L. (1989). Learning strategies in foreign language instruction. *Foreign Language Annals, 22*(1), 13-24.

Chaudron, C. (1988). *Second language classrooms.* Cambridge, England: Cambridge University Press.

Crookall, D., & Oxford, R. L. (1990). *Simulation, gaming, and language learning.* New York: Newbury House.

Day, R. R. (Ed.). (1986). *Talking to learn: Conversation in second language acquisition.* New York: Newbury House.

Ellis, R. (1985). *Understanding second language acquisition.* Oxford: Oxford University Press.

Ervin, G. (1988). Purposeful practice with the four-by-six card: Quick, convenient, and communicative. *Foreign Language Annals, 21*(4), 337-339.

Faerch, C., & Kasper, G. (1985). Introduction. *Studies in second language learning, 7*(2), 131-133.

Fine, J. (Ed.). (1988). *Second language discourse: A textbook of current research* (Vol. XXV). Norwood, NJ: Ablex.

Galloway, V. (1987). From defining to developing proficiency: A look at the decisions. In H. Byrnes & M. Canale (Eds.), *Defining and developing proficiency* (pp. 25-73). Lincolnwood, IL: National Textbook.

Gaskill, W. H. (1980). Correction in native speaker-nonnative speaker conversation. In D. Larsen-Freeman (Ed.), *Discourse analysis in second language research* (pp. 125-137). New York: Newbury House.

Gass, S. M., & Madden, C. G. (Eds.). (1985). *Input in second language acquisition*. New York: Newbury House.

Gutiérrez, J. R. (1987). Oral testing in high school classrooms: Some suggestions. *Hispania, 70*(4), 915-918.

Hartzell, R. E. (1988). Testing in the communicative curriculum. *Language Association Bulletin, 39*(4), 1-4.

Hatch, E. (1978). Discourse analysis and second language acquisition. In E. Hatch (Ed.), *Second language acquisition: A book of readings* (pp. 401-435). New York: Newbury House.

Hatch, E. (1983). Foreword. In N. Wolfson & E. Judd (Eds.), *Sociolinguistics and language acquisition* (pp. ix-xviii). New York: Newbury House.

Hymes, D. (1972). Models of the interaction of language and social life. In J. J. Gumperz & D. Hymes (Eds.), *Directions in sociolinguistics* (pp. 35-71). New York: Holt, Rinehart, & Winston.

Kramsch, C. J. (1981). *Discourse analysis and second language teaching.* Washington, DC: Center for Applied Linguistics.

Jones, D. (1988). Materials prepared for a course. Albany: State University of New York, School of Education.

Lantolf, J. P., & Labarca, A. (Eds.). (1987). *Research in second language learning: Focus on the classroom*. Norwood, NJ: Ablex.

Larsen-Freeman, D. (Ed.). (1980). *Discourse analysis in second language learning*. New York: Newbury House.

Littlewood, W. (1981). *Communicative language teaching: An introduction*. Cambridge, England: Cambridge University Press.

Long, M. H. (1987). The experimental classroom. In R. D. Lambert (Ed.), *The annals of the American Academy of Political and Social Science: Vol. 490. Foreign language instruction: A national agenda* (pp. 97-109). Newbury Park, CA: Sage Publications.

Malamah-Thomas, A. (1987). *Classroom interaction*. Oxford: Oxford University Press.

Nunan, D. (1989). *Designing tasks for the communicative classroom*. Cambridge, England: Cambridge University Press.

Olshtain, E., & Cohen, A. D. (1983). Apology: A speech-act set. In N. Wolfson & E. Judd (Eds.), *Sociolinguistics and language acquisition* (pp. 18-35). New York: Newbury House.

Omaggio, A. (1983). *Proficiency oriented classroom testing*. Washington, DC: Center for Applied Linguistics.

Omaggio, A. C. (1986). *Teaching language in context*. Boston: Heinle & Heinle.

Papalia, A. (1983). *Developing communicative proficiency and cultural understanding in secondary school language programs*. Schenectady, NY: New York State Association of Foreign Language Teachers.

Pattison, P. (1987). *Developing communication skills*. Cambridge, England: Cambridge University Press.

Pica, T., & Doughty, C. (1988). Variation in classroom interaction as a function of participation pattern and task. In J. Fine (Ed.), *Second language discourse: A textbook of current research: Vol. XXV. Advances in discourse processes* (pp. 41-55). Norwood, NJ: Ablex.

Porter, L. P. (1987). Using the ACTFL proficiency guidelines to achieve goals of exploratory language courses. *Foreign Language Annals, 20*(4), 323-330.

Prabhu, N. (1987). *Second language pedagogy: A perspective*. Oxford: Oxford University Press.

Richards, J. C. (1985). *The context of language teaching*. Cambridge, England: Cambridge University Press.

Richards, J. C. (1990). *The language teaching matrix*. Cambridge, England: Cambridge University Press.

Rivers, W., & Temperley, R. S. (1978). *A practical guide to the teaching of English*. New York: Oxford University Press.

Sato, C. J. (1986). Conversation and interlanguage: Rethinking the connection. In R. Day (Ed.), *Talking to learn: Conversation in second language acquisition* (pp. 23–45). New York: Newbury House.

Scarcella, R. C. (1983). Developmental trends in the acquisition of conversational competence by adult second language learners. In N. Wolfson, & E. Judd (Eds.), *Sociolinguistics and language acquisition* (pp. 175–183). New York: Newbury House.

Scarcella, R. C. (1990). Communication difficulties in second language production, development, and instruction. In R. C. Scarcella, E. S. Anderson, & S. D. Krashen (Eds.), *Developing communicative competence in a second language* (pp. 337–353). New York: Newbury House.

Schmidt, R. W. (1983). Interaction, acculturation, and the acquisition of communicative competence: A case study of an adult. In N. Wolfson & E. Judd (Eds.), *Sociolinguistics and language acquisition* (pp. 137–174). New York: Newbury House.

Schwartz, J. (1980). The negotiation for meaning: Repair in conversations between second language learners of English. In D. Larsen-Freeman (Ed.), *Discourse analysis in second language research* (pp. 138–153). New York: Newbury House.

Spratt, M. (1985). Discourse chains. In A. Matthews, M. Spratt, & L. Dangerfield (Eds.), *At the chalkface: Practical techniques in language teaching* (pp. 28–30). London: Edward Arnold.

Van Dijk, T. A. (1982). Episodes as units of discourse analysis. In D. Tannen (Ed.), *Analyzing discourse: Text and talk* (pp. 177–195). Washington, DC: Georgetown University Press.

Van Lier, L. A. (1982). *Analyzing interaction in second language classrooms*. Unpublished dissertation, University of Lancaster, England.

chapter 10

Writing for Different Purposes

A writer is unable to exploit all the devices available to a speaker: gesture, body movement, facial expression, pitch and tone of voice, stress, and hesitations. A speaker can backtrack, or clarify and revise ideas as listeners question or disagree. A writer has to compensate for all of these disadvantages.

Compared with speech, effective writing requires a number of things: a high degree of organization in the development of ideas and information; a high degree of accuracy so that there is no ambiguity of meaning; the use of complex grammatical devices for focus and emphasis; and a careful choice of vocabulary, grammatical patterns, and sentence structures to create a style which is appropriate to the subject matter and the eventual readers.

T. Hedge, 1988

Developing writing abilities in a second language involves a broad range of competencies and skills associated with linguistic, sociolinguistic, and connected-discourse structures. Written tasks can vary significantly, from filling out forms to the transmission of information and the imaginative uses of language. Written discourse comprises both content and different forms of organization depending on the type of genre: directions, reports, letters, and narratives. Writing can be seen as a generative process, not always based on a preestablished plan. Writers utilize different composing strategies, some of which result in more acceptable final written products. Research in written discourse has focused on such issues as error correction, composing strategies, and the role of the teacher in the composing process. Teachers can make students more aware of their composing strategies while writing for different purposes. Instructional activities can be sequenced according to various writing perspectives. Evaluation procedures can be used to highlight specific aspects of student compositions such as content, function, and accuracy considerations.

This chapter examines the development of writing abilities in terms of the communicative uses of language. Some of the issues raised have to do with the following questions:

1. What is the nature of writing in L2 classrooms?
2. What are the different types of writing situations?
3. How is language used during composing activities?
4. What are some of the research findings on the development of writing abilities?
5. What considerations need to be taken into account in designing writing activities?
6. What are some examples of writing tasks?

WRITING IN L2 CLASSROOMS

Writing in the L2 has tended to have a secondary position in relation to listening, speaking, and reading skills. Until recently, writing acts were used primarily as a means to practice linguistic structures or to express personal meaning. Writing to communicate different messages to different audiences represents a new direction for many language teachers.

Development of L2 writing abilities, as with oral language skills, requires an understanding of how the linguistic components (knowledge of vocabulary, grammar, orthography, genre structures) are combined to create a text. In written composition a writer has to make guesses about what the reader knows or does not know about the topic. Unlike speaking, the meaning of a written text cannot be negotiated in most situations. However, the writer can consult others in the process of composing a text (peers and teachers might offer feedback, and collaborative writing assignments in class can generate discussion and suggestions for improvement).

Many recommendations have been proposed to help L2 writers become better communicators. Scott (1992), for example, suggests that students should be taught to write from the beginning. Writing practice is important, but students should be given meaningful tasks that take into account purpose, content, language concerns, and audience. Correction and feedback should be seen as only one aspect of writing instruction.

In the area of ESL/EFL, Hedge (1988, pp. 7–12) offers seven assumptions for establishing a framework for writing tasks:

1. Classroom writing tasks should reflect the ultimate goal of enabling students to write whole texts that form connected, contextualized, and appropriate pieces of communication.
2. Students need opportunities to practice various forms and functions in

writing and within these to develop the different skills involved in producing written texts.

3. Classroom writing tasks need to be set up in ways that reflect the writing process in good writers. We need to encourage our students to go
   through a process of planning, organizing, composing, and revising.
4. When setting writing tasks, teachers need to vary the audience, identify
   who the readers are to be, and try to make every piece of writing fulfill
   some kind of communicative purpose, either real or simulated. When students understand the context they are much more likely to write effectively.
5. The process of marking, with its traditional focus on error-correction by
   the teacher, needs review and modification into a range of activities involving students as well as teachers, thus making revision an integral part
   of the process of writing.
6. Students need time in the classroom for writing. The teacher's task is to
   select or design activities that support them through the process of producing a piece of writing.
7. Collaborative writing in the classroom generates discussions and activities
   that encourage an effective process of writing.

As mentioned in Chapter 8, reading and writing abilities are closely intercon-
nected. Reading influences writing abilities, and writing in turn affects reading
skills (Carson, 1990). The exact nature of the interaction appears to be complex,
with certain aspects of each language modality being somewhat independent of
each other (Grabe, 1991). Nevertheless, the implication is that reading texts as a
writer can improve the writer's abilities to compose texts for readers. Students
might engage in the analysis of reading samples (final products) and explore how
they were written (the process). There is also a reciprocity condition between
speech and writing. Writers can create texts with the collaboration of others.
Through a collaborative learning process, student groups can negotiate meaning
through discussions, provide oral feedback, and act as the audience. Finally, writing
should be seen primarily as a social act, with the individual writer attempting to
communicate a message to a particular member or group of society (Bruffee,
1986).

TYPES OF WRITING SITUATIONS

Writing demands can also vary significantly, from filling out forms, to corresponding with acquaintances through personal letters and creating short stories and
poems. Britton, Burgess, Martin, McLeod, and Rosen (1975) have suggested a
scheme to describe writing by taking into account the role of the writer (spectator or participant in the composing process) and three major functions of written
language: expressive (personal writing similar to informal talk), transactional (information sharing, often intended for a specific audience and placing the writer as

a participant as he or she informs, directs, persuades), and poetic texts (literary works such as poems, short stories, plays in which the writer adopts the role of spectator by distancing self from the immediate context in order to tell the story or create the poem). Kaplan (1983) states that there are essentially four types of writing activities:

1. *Writing without composing* (filling blanks in writing exercises, completing forms, writing transcriptions or word lists)
2. *Writing for informational purposes* (note taking, reports, summarizing outlines)
3. *Writing for personal purposes* (journals, diaries, memos, notes)
4. *Writing for imaginative purposes* (stories, plays, poems)

Kaplan adds that while the list appears to be hierarchical, at this time it is difficult to establish order of acquisitions since writing involves control of at least four kinds of knowledge: aspects of language, writing conventions, subject or topic, and the intended audience. Kaplan's list of four basic types of writing activities might be seen in relation to proficiency levels (novice, intermediate, advanced, and superior). Writing without composing involves student responses at the word level (novice-high). Writing for informational purposes calls for sentence-level production (intermediate low to mid). Writing for personal purposes requires some composing behaviors at the paragraph level (intermediate mid and beyond). Writing for imaginative purposes involves poetic use of langauge at the text level, presumably at the advanced level. It is important to remember that students can compose poems at the word and sentence levels. By writing poems and reading them orally, students can review specific grammatical features (prepositions, verb tenses, subordinating conjunctions) and practice pronunciation accuracy. At the intermediate level, students can also be asked to create ministories and plays.

The texts listed in ACTFL (1986) proficiency levels for writing interrelate content, language functions, and accuracy levels in relation to performance behaviors established on the basis of a hierarchy, ranging from novice to the superior level, with nine specific generic descriptions. The descriptions for the three types of "novice" writers and the two levels of "advanced" students are presented here:

Novice: The novice level is characterized by an ability to produce isolated words and phrases.

Novice-low: able to form some letters in an alphabetic system. In languages whose writing systems use syllabaries or characters, writer is able to both copy and produce the basic strokes. Can produce romanization of isolated characters, where applicable.

Novice-mid: able to copy or transcribe familiar words or phrases and reproduce some memory. No practical communicative skills.

Novice-high: able to write simple fixed expressions, and limited memorized material and some recombination thereof. Can supply information on simple forms and documents. Can write names, numbers, dates, own nationality, and other simple autobiographical information, as well as some short phrases and simple lists, can write all the symbols in an alphabetical or syllabic system or 50-100 characters or compounds in a character writing system. Spelling and representation of symbols (letters, syllables, characters) may be partially correct. (pp. 15-24)

Advanced: The advanced level is characterized by an ability to write narrative and descriptions of a factual nature, of at least several paragraphs in length, on familiar topics.

Advanced: able to write routine social correspondence and join sentences in simple discourses of at least several paragraphs in length, on familiar topics. Can write simple social correspondence, taking notes, write cohesive summaries and resumes, as well as narratives and descriptions of a factual nature. Has sufficient writing vocabulary to express self simply with some circumlocution. May still make errors in punctuation, spelling, or the formation of nonalphabetic symbols. Good control of the morphology and the most frequently used syntactic structures, e.g., common word order patterns, coordination, subordination, but makes frequent errors in producing complex sentences. Uses a limited number of cohesive devices, such as pronouns, accurately. Writing may resemble literal translations from native language, but a sense of organization (rhetorical structure) is emerging. Writing is understandable to natives not used to the writing of nonnatives.

Advanced-plus: able to write about a variety of topics with significant precision and in detail. Can write most social and informal business correspondences. Can describe and narrate personal experiences fully but has difficulty supporting points of view in written discourse. Can write about the concrete aspects of topics relating to particular interests and special fields of competence. Often shows remarkable fluency and ease of expression, but under time constraints and pressure writing may be inaccurate. Generally strong in either grammar or vocabulary but not in both. Weakness and unevenness in one of the foregoing or in spelling or character writing formation may result in occasional miscommunication. Some misuse of vocabulary may still be evident. Style may still be obviously foreign. (pp. 15-24)

These trisectional descriptions of L2 writing proficiency according to content, function, and accuracy do not take into account the series of complicated mental operations that are required to produce written discourse. Clark and Clark (1977) have illustrated, for example, that a writer has to consider such aspects as (1) the meaning that is to be conveyed, (2) the genre of the text (a narrative, a description, an explanation), (3) the style of the prose (casual vs. formal, neutral vs. personal), (4) the purpose of the text (to inform, persuade, or invite), and (5) the amount of detail needed to accomplish the writer's intention. These writing processes cannot be inferred from the product description as reflected in the ACTFL guidelines.

Different types of *writing genres* (narratives, directions, reports, business letters) seem to follow specific patterns of organization and discourse structures. While there appear to be universal rhetorical patterns for organizing information according to such semantic structures as comparison and contrast, definition and classification, or analysis and synthesis, differences may exist between languages at the level of grammar, particularly in the manner in which available syntactic devices are used to convey meaning (Kaplan, 1972).

Aside from the physical appearance of the text (indentation, margins, scripts, punctuation), the *discourse structure* of a paragraph (e.g., topic sentence supported by examples or details) may vary from the dominant linearlike pattern in English, for instance, to a less linear arrangement or nonlinear organization in such languages as Arabic or Chinese (Kaplan, 1966). Ostler (1987) has observed that the English discourse written by Arabic speakers tends to contain elaborate parallel structures. This cultural preference appears to have some relationship to Koranic writing style. Kaplan (1966) has noted that English expository paragraphs usually begin with a topic sentence, each supported by details, examples, and illustrations. Each paragraph proceeds to develop the central idea, and each paragraph is interrelated to the others, resulting in an integrated whole. Arabic paragraphs tend to be developed on the basis of complex series of parallel constructions, involving, for instance, the repetition of ideas (synonymous parallelism), cause-and-effect relationships (synthetic parallelism), and contrasting ideas (antithetic parallelism). Chinese paragraphs are marked by a writing approach that is indirect. The development of the main idea is accomplished in terms of circles or gyres that turn around the topic and present it from a variety of perspectives. The topic is not addressed directly. Romance languages such as French or Spanish begin by addressing the topic directly, but digressions from the main topic are not unusual, nor are they culturally inappropriate. The discourse structures for English, Arabic, Chinese, French, and Spanish are depicted graphically in Figure 10.1.

FIGURE 10.1 Dominant discourse patterns in formal written style of major language groups

SOURCE: Adapted from Kaplan (1966), p. 15.

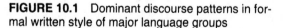

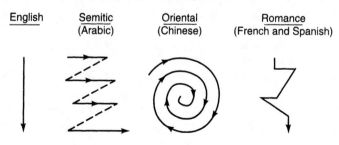

COMPOSING IN A SECOND LANGUAGE

Learning to write in a second language involves control of a number of aspects simultaneously. Bell and Burnaby (1984) argue that writing is an extremely complex activity, with the control of language both at the sentence level (grammatical structures, vocabulary, punctuation, spelling, and letter formation) and beyond the sentence rank (organizing and integrating information into cohesive and coherent paragraphs or texts). From a proficiency perspective, this involves various systems of knowledge and skills, including grammatical, sociolinguistic, and discourse competence (Canale, 1984) as well as the ability to use language in a context-reduced situation (Cummins, 1980; 1983).

The process of learning to write has been examined from the perspective of Krashen's (1984) theory of language acquisition, which makes a distinction between two independent processes: acquisition and learning. Acquisition is seen as an unconscious process that occurs during the comprehension of language input within a meaningful context that favors learning under appropriate affective conditions. Learning, on the other hand, is described as a conscious process that usually results from formal study or practice of grammar. From this perspective, writing competence is developed through sustained reading input and extensive composing practice. The most effective writing practice is that which places writing within a communicative perspective (writing to inform, persuade, describe personal experiences). Grammar teaching and error correction, therefore, should be limited to simple learnable rules.

Learning to write has also been seen as a developmental process. Emig (1981) has argued that writing skills emerge in predictable stages as children learn to separate and consolidate their speaking and writing abilities. Children move from expressive writing, which relies heavily on their oral language competence, to transactional writing that involves a greater concern for the reader-audience. The third stage, which not all writers attain, is poetic writing, in which the focus is the language itself (a poem, short story, or play) and the message the author-writer tries to convey through a particular genre.

The process by which writers arrive at their final product evolves through a series of stages as writers discover what they are trying to say. Zamel (1983) found that skilled ESL writers approached writing as a creative, generative process, not always based on clear, linear direction. For these students, writing involved integrating new ideas, revising those already recorded, and reconstructing the basic framework. Writing also required the ability to assess clarity of thought and logic as well as the capacity to distance oneself from the text in order to take into account the reader's point of view. Unskilled ESL writers, on the other hand, were less concerned with the creations of meaning and tended to view their writing as a series of linguistic elements—words, sentences, and paragraphs—that had to be organized in a linear fashion. Lapp (1984) compared the writing behaviors of skilled and unskilled ESL writers and documented significant differences during the prewriting phases as well as in the use of varied strategies between the two groups. Skilled writers spent a considerable amount of time thinking about the writing task. They organized their ideas and information, reviewed their writing at the sentence or paragraph level while attending to meaning, and made frequent revisions to clarify meaning or change the direction or focus of the text. Unskilled writers spent little time in planning, were concerned primarily with word choice and sentence formation, and used revisions for changes at the surface level, such as checking for accuracy in grammar, spelling, and punctuation.

Meaningful writing, according to Nystrand (1982, pp. 64–65), requires attending to a number of constraints that can affect the reader's reconstruction of meaning. These constraints include:

1. *Graphic constraints*: matters of orthography, legibility, punctuation, spacing, and layout
2. *Syntactic constraints*: sentence structure, homonym confusion, omission of punctuation marks, and in a few cases violations of prescribed usage
3. *Semantic constraints*: assumptions about what the reader brings to the text and the presentation of "new information" based on the reader's "given information"
4. *Textural constraints*: the use of cohesive devices (reference, substitution, ellipsis, and conjuction) that help to disambiguate or maintain text continuity
5. *Contextual restraints*: factors such as format, genre, mode, type, and title that are relevant to the text's situation

Writing in a second language entails the use of various language abilities and skills, including textual knowledge and communicative purpose. The composing process often involves a planning phase, followed by a drafting stage and a revising period. Skilled writers tend to approach writing as a generative process, while unskilled writers tend to be concerned more about the elements of language rather than the creation of meaning.

RESEARCH IN L2 WRITING

Writing abilities in a second language parallel, to a certain extent, the development of first language writing competence. The development of syntactic complexity (simple sentences joined first by coordination, then subordination, and finally clause reduction) seems to follow a pattern similar to that for first language learners (Gaies, 1980). As in L1 composition, the use of complex sentence structures in the L2 can be increased by providing students with sentence-combining exercises (Cooper & Morain, 1980). Learners also appear to be sensitive to the mode of discourse, producing more complex structures in argumentation than in narration (Dvorak, 1987). Another parallel is that L2 learners respond more positively to teacher feedback when the correction is related to content (Semke, 1980; Cardelle and Corno, 1981) rather than form (Hendrickson, 1980).

The concern for grammatical accuracy in written composition continues to be a topic of great concern. Semke's (1980) study of error treatment among first-year college German students suggests that teachers' feedback on content produces higher gains in writing fluency than requiring learners to correct and rewrite their own compositions. Lalande's study (1982) comparing the effect of two methods of error correction (rewriting compositions to incorporate error corrections provided by the teacher vs. self-correction of teacher-indicated error categories and rewriting compositions) shows that neither feedback on errors nor self-gains in grammatical accuracy were evident during the experimental period.

What learners actually do as they self-correct their written compositions indicates that students utilize a number of strategies to analyze and repair their language when they are informed of certain types of errors (Frantzen & Rissel, 1987). Learners, for instance, tend to correct their own errors according to a binary-option strategy; an error of type x needs a correction of y, where x and y are usually treated as instructional pairs (e.g., *ser/estar* in Spanish; *much/many* in English; *connaître/savoir* in French). Learners also seem to follow an "order of correctability," with individual correction rates being higher for simpler errors (article-and-adjective agreement) than complex rules (aspectual distinction that verb forms convey). Coombs (1986) notes that L2 writers in German are able to control the grammatical aspects of syntactic structures (word order and agreement) in writing before they are able to use them effectively in connected spoken-discourse situations.

The correction of composition errors may only produce a low correlation between knowledge of grammar and writing abilities. Approaching writing as a process may be potentially more beneficial to all students (Zamel, 1983). Assigning a letter grade, for example, can influence the length of compositions and the number and type of errors (Chastain, 1990). Substantial writing practice may encourage students to write longer compositions with fewer errors and a higher level of creativity (Smith, 1990). Chamot and Kupper (1989) report that the writing strategies of effective Spanish students yield important insights about the writing process. These students:

1. Followed the same processes used for writing in English: planning, composing, and reviewing
2. Focused on the writing task without being distracted
3. Tried to think and generate ideas in Spanish while writing
4. Stayed within their vocabulary range instead of looking for translation of English words and phrases, often substituting alternate words and phrases when intended forms could not be recalled
5. Concentrated on integrating new ideas rather than focusing on linguistic problems
6. Employed a number of cognitive strategies (deduction, substitution, and elaboration—relating parts of new information to each other)
7. Utilized metacognitive strategies such as planning and self-monitoring to check, verify, and correct the status of the written product in terms of a proposed writing plan

To identify some of the writing strategies students employ, Chamot and Kupper (1989) suggest the use of retrospective interviews or think-aloud (explain-as-you-read) procedures. Students might be asked, for example:

> Your teacher gives you the assignment of writing a few paragraphs in Spanish, perhaps on a personal topic or on a picture you are shown.
>
> Do you do anything before you start to write? What? How does this help you?
>
> As you are writing, what helps you to write better? Describe your general approach to writing in Spanish.
>
> Do you do anything after you have written? (Chamot & Kupper, 1989, p. 23)

This procedure can help make students aware of their own writing strategies as well as those of their classmates. Less successful students can be taught how to be more effective writers through strategy training (Oxford, 1990).

Case studies of successful L2 writers (Zamel, 1983; Lapp, 1984; Chamot & Kupper, 1989) reveal that learners are concerned about the creation of meaning and spend considerable time thinking about such aspects as purpose, audience, a writing plan, drafting, ways of revising, and the finished product (Raimes, 1985). Throughout this process, teachers need to act in ways that make it possible for learners to engage in effective composing behaviors. Hughey, Wormuth, Hartfiel, & Jacobs (1983) offer an extensive list of teacher behaviors considered essential in an ESL context:

1. Keep the writing task clear, simple, and straightforward.
2. Teach the writing process.
3. Analyze and diagnose a writing product.
4. Establish short-term and long-term goals for each student.
5. Balance classroom activities, providing some for individuals and some for groups.
6. Develop meaningful assignments.
7. Provide a real audience, one other than the teacher.
8. Make student papers available to students, allowing students to see their own work develop.
9. Move from the known to the unknown, utilizing the students' previous knowledge.
10. Provide writing activities that reinforce reading, listening, and speaking skills.
11. Provide heuristics for invention, purpose, and audience.
12. Outline clearly the goals for each writing assignment.
13. Teach the conventions of spelling, punctuation, and capitalization.
14. Teach the principles—rules, conventions, and guidelines of writing—as a means to develop thoughts, order ideas, and communicate these ideas in a significant way.

In summary, development of composing skills involves control of different kinds of knowledge, including aspects of languages, rhetorical structures, written conventions, content, and audience. Some of the major findings of the research studies reviewed suggest the following:

1. Writing abilities in the second language parallel developmental trends in the first language.
2. Learners appear to respond more positively to teacher feedback when error correction is related to content.
3. Learners engage in self-correction strategies if the errors are identified to them.
4. Error correction seems to correspond inversely to a hierarchy of difficulty (i.e., higher correction rates for simpler problems than complex rules).
5. Correction of composition errors may not produce gains in grammar or writing abilities.
6. Letter grades on compositions can influence the length of the product and error types.
7. Writing practice can encourage longer compositions, fewer errors, and greater creativity.
8. Teachers can assist learners in identifying their composing strategies and provide opportunities for them to practice and expand the use of different strategies.

TEACHING CONSIDERATIONS

Writing is an enormously complex skill, and students should be given the opportunity to approach written composition as a communicative activity (informing, requesting, expressing personal opinion, recording events). Dvorak (1986) suggests following a *developmental sequence* for early writing assignments. At the initial level of language learning, writing assignments would approximate speech: diaries, dialogues, letters, journals, and stories. This would encourage students to focus on meaning rather than form and would allow students to relate written language to their oral proficiency. The teacher could engage in a written "conversation" with the students, responding and reacting to topics of mutual interest. During this first stage, learners could also become familiar with the conventions of written language. Instead of having students engage in "guided composition" exercises (sentence and paragraph completions; cloze passages; paragraph rewriting to alter events, characters, and time), they could be provided with a writing context, for example:

Purpose: to provide information about activities during a typical day
Audience: a friend in a different school or city
Text type: an informal letter

For the next level, Dvorak recommends providing students with a greater range of writing purposes (description, explanation, persuasion) along with an awareness of discourse structure. At this point, students may benefit from reading and practicing with different types of rhetorical patterns (comparison and contrast, cause and effect, enumeration, episodes). Students also need to begin developing composing strategies for planning, drafting, and revising their texts. Attention should be given to issues related to grammatical accuracy, word choice, and the appropriate use of discourse connectors, since these aspects are essential for effective communication.

In the final, "language enrichment" phase, students learn to incorporate in their written compositions some of the qualities of oral language (voice, tone, and style). Here, students learn to use their writing skills in ways that are appropriate for specific purposes, audiences, and context. This stage may only be achieved by advanced undergraduate and graduate students who can assume the role of the reader and present different points of view effectively.

The development of writing abilities based on ACTFL (1986) guidelines involves selecting tasks for composing that correspond to the students' proficiency levels (novice, intermediate, advanced, and superior). The composing tasks might include a broad range of writing techniques (paragraph completion, descriptions with visuals, cloze passages, sentence combination, dictation, guided composition) that are related to specific language functions, topics, and accuracy levels. Magnan (1985), for example, offers a series of writing tasks for novice, intermediate, and advanced levels that incorporate the notions of content, functions of language, and accuracy levels.

NOVICE-LEVEL TASKS

Content: Items in Room

1. *Function: Identifying*
   Caroline's room. Give students a picture of a student's room containing lots of typical items (bed, stereo, desk, radio, books, typewriter, volleyball, etc.). Number the items. Have students write the names of the numbered items.
2. *Function: Listing*
   Shopping List: Have students study the above picture and make a shopping list for presents for Caroline. Students base the list on things that are not in Caroline's room.

Novice-level, Later-novice, and Novice and Intermediate-level Tasks are from "Teaching and Testing Proficiency in Writing: Skills to Transcend L2 Classrooms" by Sally Sieloff Magnan, in A. C. Omaggio (Ed.), *Proficiency, Curriculum, Articulation: The Ties That Bind* (pp. 125–127). Middlebury, VT: Northeast Conference on the Teaching of Foreign Language. Reprinted with permission.

3. *Function: Using memorized material*
   Using vocabulary studied and reviewed in the above exercises, students
   fill in the paragraph based on the picture.
   In Caroline's room there is _____ and even _____ .
   There aren't any _____ . Caroline even has _____ ,
   yet she doesn't have _____ . I think I'll get her _____
   for her birthday.

4. *Function: Beginning to create language*
   Telegram: Students write a telegram telling a friend (1) what Caroline
   has; (2) what she doesn't have; (3) what the friend should bring her as a
   gift.

5. *Function: Creating with language, under teacher direction*
   Students write a paragraph describing Caroline's room by answering the
   following questions:
   a. Does Caroline have a lot of things in her room?
   b. What furniture does she have?
   c. What furniture is missing?
   d. What things does she have for entertainment?
   e. What might she need?
   f. Would you like a room like Caroline's?

6. *Function: Describing in present time (the bridge to intermediate level)*
   Students write a paragraph from the following assignment. You are describing Caroline's room to a friend who wants to buy her a gift. Tell her
   what Caroline has and what she doesn't have. Suggest a good gift. In
   your paragraph use an introductory and final sentence and logical connective words like "also," "on the other hand," "yet," "however," and "therefore."

7. *Accuracy Check*
   Students answer a set of questions on their work. Are the points in the
   paragraph presented in a logical order? Does the introductory statement
   tell the reader the focus of the paragraph? Does the final sentence finish
   or summarize the paragraph? Are the lists given the appropriate length
   for your purpose? Are connectives logical and placed appropriately? Are
   spelling and punctuation accurate?

LATER-NOVICE TO INTERMEDIATE TASKS _____

Content: Daily Routine

1. *Function: Working with memorized material*
   Students make sentences by choosing one item from each of the three
   columns:

I	study		watch TV
you	work		listen to the radio
she	play		visit friends
he	shop		do homework

2. *Function: Working with memorized material to add cohesion to language*
Students combine elements to create paragraph-length discourse:

In the morning	I study		watch TV
Then	work		listen to the radio
At noon	play		visit friends
Later	shop		do homework

Then, students add another column of connective words, using two subjects:

In the morning	I study	On the other hand, my friend	watch TV
Then	work	while my friend	listen to the radio
At noon	play	and my friend	visit her parents
Later	shop	but my friend	do homework

3. *Function: Creating a cohesive description*
Students write a page on the following:
Describe your typical activities and those of your best friend on a normal Monday. Compare your activities with those of your friend. Be sure to include an introductory and final statements to focus your paragraph. Your introductory statement and final statements might answer these or similar questions: Do you work harder than your friend, or is it the other way around? Do you and your friend have different schedules? Do you and your friend get along well because your schedules are compatible?

4. *Accuracy check*
Students answer questions on their work. Is your writing organized, from a general introductory statement, through clear discussion of both yourself and your friend, to a summarizing or concluding statement? Do you make a comparison or contrast between yourself and your friend on each point? Do you provide appropriate examples? Do your subjects and verbs agree? Do your adjectives and nouns agree? Are your spelling and punctuation accurate?

USING NOVICE AND INTERMEDIATE-LEVEL TASKS TO PREPARE ADVANCED-LEVEL WRITING

1. *Function: listing*
   Students list things they did yesterday (partial sentences).
2. *Function: creating a series of statements to organize simple narration in the past*
   Students write a series of sentences that list what they did yesterday (use of preterite or passé composé).
3. *Function: building a paragraph that describes and narrates in the past*
   For each sentence students wrote listing what they did yesterday, they either add a clause or write an accompanying sentence to describe the situation as it was when they did each thing (use of imperfect). Then, students make their sentences into a paragraph by adding logical connective words and introductory and final statements (sequence suggested by Ozzello, 1983).
4. *Function: describing and narrating in the past*
   Students write a letter to a friend describing in some detail what they did last summer. They must describe the situation and circumstances surrounding the events as well as the events themselves.
5. *Accuracy check*
   Students answer a set of questions on their work. Does the paragraph describe the situation as well as tell the events? Are the things you did presented in a logical order? Are past tenses used appropriately (choice of tense, forms, punctuation accurate)?

Magnan (1985) points out that the novice-level tasks, for example, can be used as prewriting steps for composing activities at the next higher proficiency level. Students might be asked to revise or edit their texts to the accuracy standards of the next proficiency level. In addition, writing skills can be enhanced through class composition activities (each student produces a sentence related to the topic), small-group writing projects (collaboration among three to five students in the planning, drafting, and editing of a text), and community writing (interviews with native speakers outside the classroom for the purpose of producing informative reports for the class audience). These types of writing activities, along with individual writing assignments, make the composing process an interactive experience, enabling students to utilize language for both communicative and creative purposes by permitting use of factual language, fiction, humor, and fantasy (Russo, 1987).

To develop L2 writing competence from a process-centered approach, a number of instructional activities are possible during the different phases of composition. Richards (1990) provides numerous classroom activities designed to help students (1) develop their ideas to generate plans for writing during the rehearsal phase, (2) consider questions of audience, purpose, and form during the drafting and writing phase, and (3) attend to questions of grammar, cohesive markers, and confusing paragraphs during the editing and proofreading phases of writing. Examples of activities for each phase of the composing process are listed below:

Activities Related to the Rehearsing Phase

- *Journal*: Students explore ideas and record thoughts in a journal.
- *Brainstorming*: Students rapidly exchange information about the topic or about something they have selected to read.
- *Free association*: Put the topic on the board. Students quickly say whatever words come to mind when they see the topic word.
- *Values clarification*: Students compare attitudes toward a variety of specific problems and situations.
- *Clustering or word mapping*: The writer writes a topic in the middle of a page and organizes related words and concepts in clusters around the central concept.
- *Ranking activities*: Students rank a set of features according to priorities.
- *Quickwriting*: Students rank as much as they can in a given time (e.g., five minutes) on a topic, without worrying about the form of what they write.
- *Information-gathering activities*: Students are given assignments related to a theme or topic resources where related information can be found. These may include interviews, opinion surveys, field trips, experiments, and demonstrations. (pp. 112-114)

Activities of this type may lead to a summarizing session that prepares the students for the next phase in the writing process, in which they review their ideas and begin to focus on what they can use as a basis for writing:

Activities Related to the Drafting/Writing Phase

- *Strategic questioning*: Students examine a set of questions to help them focus, prioritize, and select ideas for writing. For example:

What do you really want to write about?

What is your goal?

What is your attitude toward this task? Why?

What have you learned about your topic?

What do you still need to find out?

What interests or surprises you about the topic?

What ideas seem to fit together?

What is the most important thing to know about the topic?

Who might want to read what you are going to write? (Lapp, 1984)

- *Time-focused writing*: Students write quickly within a specified time period on a topic they have selected during prewriting.

- *Elaboration exercise*: Students are given a sentence and collectively elaborate and develop it.
- *Reduction exercise*: Students are given a wordy and complex paragraph and break it down into simpler sentences.
- *Jumbled paragraph*: Students are given a jumbled paragraph and reorder the sentences.
- *Jumbled essay*: Students are given a jumbled set of paragraphs and reorder them to make an essay.
- *Writing thesis statements and topic sentences*: Students are given a statement from which to develop a thesis statement and a topic sentence.
- *Quickwriting*: Students quickwrite various sections of their composition: beginnings, central sections, conclusions.
- *Group drafting*: Students work jointly on drafting different sections of a composition. (Richards, 1990, pp. 112–114.)

Activities Relating to the Revising Phase

- *Peer feedback*: Students work in groups and read, criticize, and proofread their own writing.
- *Group-correction activities*: Students are given essays containing certain focused deletions (topic sentences, thesis statements, cohesive markers) and must supply the missing elements.
- *Rewriting exercises*: Awkward sentences or confusing paragraphs from student essays are distributed and rewritten by students
- *Revising heuristics*: Students examine a set of questions that prepare them for revision activities. Some examples from Whitlock (1984, p. 3.):

In composing your draft, what was the biggest problem you experienced?

If the teacher were to read your paper right now, what would be the first thing the teacher would say about it?

If the teacher were going to say something really nice about your draft, what would it be?

What would be some criticisms?

On the basis of the comments you've already received from your teacher, or your classmates, what changes do you intend to make when rewriting?

List three important details in your paper.

If you had something to add to this paper, what would it be?

If you had to cut something, what would it be?

- *Teacher feedback*: This may take place at several stages during the writing process, rather than at the end of the process, where it no longer serves any useful purpose. The teacher may comment on quick-writes, rough drafts, and peer feedback, for example.
- *Checklists*: Students may have short checklists, drawing their attention to specific features of sentence, paragraph, or text organization that they should attend to in revising. (Richards, 1990, pp. 112-114)

Responding to student writing is both a difficult and time-consuming task. Research on L2 writing has not shown consistently that error correction always has a positive effect on student writing. It appears that the teacher's feedback on the content of writing is more beneficial than error correction. Students seem to be more motivated when teachers respond to their writing as communication (meaning) instead of writing as form (word choice, sentences, paragraphing, mechanics, spelling). A process approach to writing provides students with many opportunities for peer and teacher feedback during the different composing phases. Teachers might interact with their students through dialogue journals, making marginal comments on students' writings and then in turn responding to the students' revisions (Stanton, 1983). They may also provide oral feedback to students' written drafts through the use of cassette tapes focusing on such aspects as organization, grammar, and mechanics (Turvey, 1984).

Assigning a grade to students' writing is a matter that should be differentiated from providing feedback. Grading may mean evaluating the overall quality of the work or the various features of a composition (grammar, vocabulary, mechanics, organization, context) through analytic scoring procedures. In holistic scoring, the entire text is evaluated as a whole with respect to predetermined performance criteria, as is the case with the ACTFL's (1986) proficiency guidelines noted previously.

Gaudiani (1981) advocates the evaluation of students' writing on the basis of analytical scorings, taking into account four separate components and assigning a grade to each: (1) grammar and vocabulary use, (2) stylistic technique, (3) organization of material, and (4) content. Each component is rated in terms of five levels of performance, allowing each level to be assigned point equivalents (A = 4, B = 3, C = 2, D = 1, F = 0).

1. Grammar/vocabulary:

    A = fluent with moments of elegance, few errors

    B = comprehensible, some errors

    C = substantial and significant errors

    D = one or more blocks to communication

    F = unintelligible

2. Stylistic technique:

A = skilled use of syntax in terms of content, variation in syntax

B = clear, appropriate, and sophisticated syntax

C = errors, but attempts at sophistication and appropriateness

D = errors and/or inappropriate syntax

F = garbled syntax

3. Organization:

A = well-organized paragraphs, use of clear topic and summary sentences, convincing, easy to follow

B = good evidence of structuring of paragraphs (perhaps an unwieldy use of patterns of organization)

C = some attempts at organization, but few topic, development, and summary sequences

D = hard to follow, organization undermines intelligibility

F = no evidence of planning in structure of paragraphs

4. Content:

A = significant, interesting, appropriate, well thought out, appropriate to assignment

B = generally good work, but facts may be unsupported, or repetitions or cliches may be apparent

C = careless development of data relevant to content

D = no effort to make content significant to composition

F = incoherent or wildly inappropriate content

(Gaudiani, 1981, p. 20)

This evaluation process can be used to highlight the specific strengths and weaknesses of individual student compositions by assigning a score to each component and adding the total points to ascertain an overall grade. For example, a well-organized, interesting, well thought out composition with numerous errors in grammar and repetitive sentence structures might be rated as follows:

Grammar/vocabulary	C = 2
Style	B = 3
Organization	B = 3
Content	A = 4

Perkins (1983) states that there are several advantages to analytical scoring, such as showing students the way grades were computed and providing them with specific feedback on the strengths and weaknesses on each writing task.

However, the various components of a composition may not contribute to the overall sum in the same degree. The grader's scoring scheme may be unreliable or arbitrary, and the scoring weights may need to be adjusted to reflect different types of texts (e.g., stories, letters, descriptions, directions, reports). Magnan (1985) expresses the need for multipart grades to assess, for example, function, context, and accuracy if one considers the ACTFL (1986) proficiency guidelines as the basis for teaching and evaluating writing skills. In approaching writing as a process, one might assign one grade for outlines and sketches during the prewriting phase, a second grade for drafts during the writing stage, and a third score for the final written product. All three grades could be averaged, yielding an overall grade for the assignment.

Writing can be approached from a developmental orientation with respect to the type of task: personal writing (dialogues, diaries, journals), transactional uses of language (explanations, instructions, persuasive texts), and composing for special purposes (essays, critiques, editorials). At the same time, one might organize writing tasks on the basis of ACTFL proficiency guidelines incorporating content, function, text type, and accuracy levels. Writing from a process-centered approach calls for the organization of instructional activities in terms of a prewriting (rehearsing) phase, a drafting or writing phase, and a revising stage. Error correction and grading policies do influence the way students engage in different writing tasks.

DESIGNING WRITING TASKS

Writing situations, like reading activities, encompass a broad range of skills associated with written language. Specific writing skills have been described in relation to five skill areas (Palmer, 1985, pp. 71-72):

1. *Graphical or visual skills*: conventions in spelling, punctuation, and capitalization; format of specific text types as in letters, memos, or shopping lists
2. *Grammatical abilities*: use of a variety of sentence patterns and constructions
3. *Expressive or stylistic skills*: use of appropriate writing skills or registers depending on the purpose and audience
4. *Rhetorical skills*: use of cohesive devices such as connectives, reference words, or lexical variety to link parts of a text into logically related sequences
5. *Organizational skills*: arrangement of information into paragraphs and text, taking into account the types of ideas and how they should be interrelated to produce a unified whole

Thus, writing tasks can focus on different levels or aspects of written language. Writing tasks, in turn, can be grouped on the basis of communicative goals (exchange information with others, describe, narrate, provide information requested, and write notes to oneself) and activity type (create sentences from words, describe a picture, complete a form, send a brief message, write a letter, or create a story). Specific student behaviors can vary greatly:

1. Label objects or articles in the classroom or a picture
2. Describe a picture
3. Answer specific questions
4. Complete a cloze passage
5. Take dictation from the teacher
6. Describe a daily or weekly routine
7. Fill out a form
8. Prepare autobiographical information, including likes and dislikes
9. Prepare a menu, advertisement, or poster
10. Report a specific incident with details and the sequence of events
11. Take notes from a lecture or slide presentation
12. Arrange a narrative sequence for a possible story
13. Write captions for a comic strip
14. Create a poem
15. Write a letter to a friend or a business firm
16. Keep a journal

The 10 tasks in Table 10.1 represent various types of genres, interactional situations, learning objectives, and writing skills.

TABLE 10.1 Components of writing tasks

Task/Genre	Interaction Structure	Learning Objective	Writing Skill
A Sentence	Individuals or pairs	Complete sentences	Rephrase
B List	Individuals	Prepare a list	Identify
C Note	Individuals or pairs	Write an invitation	Explain
D Paragraph	Groups	Fill in the blanks	Interpret
E Form	Individuals	Provide information	Describe
F Journal	Individuals	Write daily entries	Describe and compose
G Comic strip	Pairs	Create captions/text	Interpret and compose
H Message	Pairs	Sketch details requested	Analyze, solve, and compose
I Letter	Individuals and pairs	Introduce self to a pen pal	Classify and compose
J Story	Groups	Create story based on details provided	Analyze, synthesize, and compose

Writing tasks range from the sentence level to a story invented by the students. With the exception of task F, which makes use of visual stimuli, all other activities utilize written materials. Tasks F, G, H, I, and J entail actual composition, whereas tasks A, B, C, D, and E involve written responses to a specific set of cues. Tasks A and B are relatively simple, while tasks H, I, and J incorporate several steps. Each task consists of a distinctive group of textual features (genre, topic, linguistic elements), but it can be adapted to other proficiency levels and languages.

It is important to remember that most writing tasks need to be presented in the context of prewriting and postwriting activities. The writing process entails planning, organizing, composing, and revising. Some writing tasks might focus on one phase of the process, such as the prewriting stage.

TASK A

Task:	Create announcements from the words provided
Genre:	Newspaper ads
Topic:	School aids, electronic equipment, household appliances
Function:	Provide additional information based on words and model suggested
Linguistic elements:	Verbs *llamar, vender, comprar, buscar, necesitar* with *se* forms; vocabulary pertaining to school aids, electronic equipment, and appliances
Objective:	Students will write announcements based on words provided.
Procedure:	Students receive worksheet with slashed sentences. Students complete the exercise working individually and then read sentences aloud and compare the answers.

Example:

vender/televisor
Se vende un televisor SONY
Llamar a 345-8806 de 5 a 7 tarde.

1. buscar/computadora IBM
2. necesitar/enciclopedia Larousse
3. vender/radio GE
4. buscar/lavadora automática
5. necesitar/escritorio pequeño

This procedure could be used with students working in pairs. The students could also generate their own slashed sentences and exchange among each other.

TASK B

Task:	Prepare list of items that correspond to a topic
Genre:	Items in a list
Topic:	School materials
Function:	Provide information by listing materials needed for school
Linguistic elements:	Vocabulary items associated with school work and activities
Objective:	Students will prepare a list of items needed for school work and extracurricular activities.
Procedure:	Teacher distributes writing situations to students.

Example 1:
Tomorrow is the first day of school. Make a list of 10 items you want your mother to get for you when she goes shopping.

Things to buy:

_____

_____

Example 2:
School starts next week. You are planning to do some shopping with your friends. Make a list of places where you plan to shop and the things you plan to buy in each place.

Place	*Items to be purchased*
_____	_____
_____	_____

Task B is adapted from Hartzell, 1988.

TASK C

Task:	Write a note or a party invitation to a friend
Genre:	Note
Topic:	Party
Function:	Invitation
Linguistic elements:	Expressions of time and place; directions
Objective:	Students will write a note to a friend inviting him or her to a party and will include information about the occasion, place, time, and directions to the address.

Procedure:	Students will follow an outline prepared by the teacher:

You're invited to a _____ for _____ .

The address is _____ .

The party will start at _____ and end at _____ .

Directions to get to the house:

(Draw map if necessary)

Students will exchange their notes and indicate acceptance or nonacceptance of the invitation.

TASK D

Task:	Complete the blanks in a paragraph using the words and expressions provided
Genre:	Paragraph
Topic:	Greek myths
Function:	Provide information necessary to complete a story
Linguistic elements:	Parts of speech (nouns, verbs, adjectives); vocabulary pertaining to travel and incredible feats
Objective:	Working collectively, students will complete the blanks in a paragraph, selecting words and expressions from the lists provided.
Procedure:	Student groups receive paragraphs from the teacher.

First student (in each row of perhaps eight) fills out only the first line of the story. Second student fills out the second line.

A student from each row reads the finished story, and the different versions are compared by the class.

Using the words and expressions given below, complete the blanks of the following paragraph. Fill out only the first line of the story, fold the paper, and pass it on to the student sitting next to you.

- Hercule _____ un _____ . Il _____ très _____ .
  (être)   (nom)   (être)   (adjectif)
- Où est-il? _____ _____ _____ .
  (être) (préposition) (endroit)
- Ici, il y a des _____ et des _____ . Ici, c'est _____ .
  (nom)   (nom)   (adjectif)
- Hercule décide de partir en voyage.
  Il _____ _____ .
  (aller) (moyen de transport)
- Là, il y a des _____ et des _____ . Là, c'est _____ .
  (nom)   (nom)   (adjectif)

- Marie _____ un _____ . Elle _____ très _____ .
  (être)   (nom)   (être)   (adjectif)
- Un jour, Marie et Hercule décident de faire un voyage ensemble. Ils _____ _____ _____ . Là, ils _____ .
  (aller) (préposition) (endroit)   (verbe)
- C'est la fin de l'histoire. C'est une histoire _____ , n'est-ce pas?
  (adjectif)

Noms	Adjectifs	Endroits	Verbes	Moyens de transport
professeur	bête	bibliothèque	aller	à bicyclette
pingouin	tragique	hôpital	être	en avion
crocodile	comique	zoo	danser	en bateau
docteur	difficile	au pôle nord	marcher	en auto
vedette	élégant(e)	en France	rêver	dans un ballon
tigre	moche	au Mexique	parler	dans une fusée
soleil	immense	à l'université	explorer	_____
fleur	ridicule	sur Vénus	chanter	_____
livre	impossible	sur la lune	jouer	_____
jardin	ordinaire	sur la terre		_____
			_____	_____
_____	_____	_____	_____	_____

Task D is adapted from Birckbichler, 1982, pp. 64-65.

TASK E

Task:	Fill out forms with information requested
Genre:	Forms
Topic:	Health
Function:	Provide information about medical history
Linguistic elements:	Vocabulary items related to health issues; cultural points about ways to express weight and height in metric system and dates in European countries
Objective:	Students will fill out forms to provide the information requested.
Procedure:	Students fill out forms distributed by the teacher. Cultural points are discussed regarding ways of expressing weight, height, and dates in European countries, if necessary.

Health History Form

Name _____   Phone _____

Address _____

Weight _____ Height _____

Date of birth _____

Medical insurance _____ Policy number _____

Medical history

Have you had any broken bones? _____

Which ones? _____

Have you had a surgical operation? _____

When? _____

What childhood diseases have you had? _____

_____

Do you have any disorder of the following:

brain _____ stomach _____

mouth _____ heart _____

skin _____ lungs _____

ears _____ other _____

eyes _____

TASK F

Task:	Write a brief narrative based on visual materials
Genre:	Comic strip captions
Topic:	Family life, husband and wife, domestic tasks
Function:	Narrate the actions depicted in visual materials
Linguistic elements:	Adverbs of time; vocabulary items and expressions pertaining to home activities
Objective:	Students will write a brief narrative using temporal adverbs to describe the events depicted in the visual materials.
Procedure:	Teachers distribute comic strip to the students. The captions are deleted and the teacher reviews temporal expressions: "in the morning," "early in the day," "first," "then," "later," "at last," "finally," "at the end."
	Working in pairs, students write a brief narrative that includes temporal expressions and descriptions of the actions represented in comic strip.
	Later, students read their narratives to the class for comments and reactions.

TASK G

Task:	Write a list of memorable occasions or activities during a week
Genre:	Journal entries
Topic:	Important events during a one-week period
Function:	Record personal information
Linguistic elements:	Past tense forms and vocabulary as required
Objective:	Students will write entries in journal form for a one-week period.
Procedure:	Teacher distributes journal entry forms to students. Students are asked to include a memorable event or activity for each day of the week.

Das Jahr _____   Der Monat _____

Montag
⟶   Das Datum

Dienstag
⟶   _____

Mittwoch
⟶   _____

Donnerstag
⟶   _____

Freitag
⟶   _____

Samstag
⟶   _____

Sonntag
⟶   _____

One of the journal entries is to be used for developing a composition topic in class on the following week.

Task G is adapted from Buhr, 1989.

TASK H

Task:	Write a letter based on a given situation
Genre:	Brief messages
Topic:	Difficult circumstances: lost at sea, in a prison
Function:	Provide information about a difficult situation while being lost at sea or in a prison
Linguistic elements:	Forms of requests for help; locative constructions; vocabulary related to being shipwrecked on a desert island or being held in a prison
Objective:	Students will prepare brief messages to give information and request help from strangers or friends.
Procedure:	Working in pairs, students receive descriptions for the two situations and discuss their responses. Then each pair prepares two messages, which are exchanged with other students.
	The other students can respond to the messages by agreeing to help or explaining the reasons that make it impossible for them to provide any assistance.

Example (a):

Bouteille à la mer. Vous avez fait naufrage sur une île déserte. Heureusement, vous avez une bouteille et du papier. Composez le message que vous allez mettre dans la bouteille avant de la jeter à la mer.

(*Message in a bottle.* You have been shipwrecked on a desert island. Fortunately, you have a bottle and a piece of paper. Compose the message that you are going to put in the bottle before throwing it into the ocean.)

Example (b):

En prison. Imaginez que vous êtes en prison. Ecrivez une lettre à un(e) de vos ami(e)s pour lui décrire votre vie en prison. Vous êtes toujours en prison mais cette fois-ci vous écrivez au juge pour essayer de le persuader de votre innocence.

(*In prison.* Imagine that you are in prison. Write a letter to one of your friends describing your life in prison. You are still in prison but this time you are writing to the judge to try to persuade him that you are innocent.)

Task H is adapted from Jarvis, Bonin, Corbin, & Birckbichler, 1980; 1981.

TASK I

Task:	Write a letter of introduction to a pen pal in which you provide pertinent information about yourself
Genre:	Letter
Topic:	Personal background information, family, school, interests and hobbies
Function:	Provide information about self regarding personal characteristics, family, school life, interests, and hobbies
Linguistic elements:	Vocabulary pertaining to physical characteristics, family members, school life, likes and dislikes, hobbies
Objective:	Students will write a letter of introduction to a pen pal and include the pertinent information requested.
Procedure:	Teacher reads a pen pal letter to the class. Students note the information mentioned. Teacher tells students to consider different types of information for inclusion in their letters. Students classify the content in terms of such categories as:

1. Describe yourself.

_____
_____
_____

2. Say something about your family.

_____
_____
_____

3. Describe your school life.

_____
_____
_____

4. Mention your interests and future plans.

_____
_____
_____

5. Include details about your hobbies, likes, and dislikes.

_____
_____
_____

Students then write their first draft and exchange it with other students for corrections and/or comments. Students later prepare their final drafts after receiving feedback from the teacher.

TASK J

Task:	Create a story based on words and expressions from a student-selected topic
Genre:	Story
Topic:	Adventure or mystery
Function:	Narrate and describe with details the events in a story
Linguistic elements:	Words and expressions provided or generated by the students
Objective:	Students working in groups identify themes and a set of words and expressions; they write stories that will be exchanged.
Procedure:	Teacher asks students to think of topics for a story. Words and expressions are generated for the various themes. Students form small groups and decide on a topic for their short story, which will include the words and expressions written on the chalkboard. Each student is to contribute to the development of the story.

Example of words and expressions for a ghost story:

noche oscura	bruja	paralizados de miedo
luna	de repente	pánico
cementerio	fantasma	horror
tumbas	niños jugando	misterioso

A representative from each group reads its story to the rest of the class. Students can also exchange stories and correct them. Teacher might type corrected copies and distribute them in book form.

Task J is adapted from Birckbicher (1982), pp. 62–63.

SUMMARY

Writing situations can involve such activities as completing forms, taking notes, preparing descriptions and reports, sending letters, and composing poems and stories. The writing process entails control of different kinds of knowledge: language subskills, writing conventions, subject or topic, writing purpose, and intended audience. Development of writing proficiency is interrelated with growth in reading and speaking abilities. The ACTFL proficiency guidelines that relate content, function, accuracy, and text type do not take into account the complex mental operations required to produce written language. Writers have to consider such aspects as meaning, genre, style, purpose, and audience.

Research findings indicate that development of L2 writing abilities parallels, to a certain extent, writing maturational patterns in the L1. Skilled L2 writers tend to approach writing tasks as a creative, generative process, while unskilled writers view writing in terms of language elements (words, sentences, paragraphs) that have to be organized linearly into a text. Students appear to react more responsively when teacher feedback or error correction is directed at the content of a text rather than at language features. Writing practice as well as grading policies influence students' compositions. Teachers can assist students in identifying and expanding their composing strategies.

Instructional planning should take into account the ways different learners approach writing tasks. Writing activities can be structured along developmental, process-oriented, and proficiency-based models. A process-oriented approach would call for a prewriting phase, a drafting or writing stage, and a revising phase. Each phase would enable students to focus their attention on different aspects of written communication: content, organization, purpose, audience, and grammatical accuracy. Each writing task has a distinct group of textual features that in turn require the use of different kinds of language skills and composing strategies. Development of writing abilities places demands on class time and entails some reorganization of classroom routines so that students have opportunities to collaborate.

ACTIVITIES

1. Examine a few lessons from a language textbook and classify the writing activities according to Kaplan's four basic types of writing tasks.
2. Collect writing samples from students in first, second, third, etc., years of language study and rate the products according to ACTFL proficiency levels for writing. What other criteria do you suggest for rating writing samples?
3. Interview a language teacher to determine what criteria are used for evaluating students' written assignments. To what extent do the criteria take into account function, content, and accuracy issues?
4. List the major considerations involved in composing a letter, a poem, an invitation, and a description. To what extent are the issues similar or different?
5. Prepare a list of suggestions for beginning teachers on what to do when teaching writing, based on the research findings summarized in this chapter.
6. Interview two language learners to identify the use of particular composing strategies, based on the retrospective interview technique suggested by Chamot and Kupper.
7. Consider the list of effective teaching behaviors that Hughey et al. consider essential within an ESL context. Which behaviors are more appropriate than others for foreign language learners at different levels of proficiency?
8. Discuss the instructional implications resulting from sequencing writing activities developmentally, as recommended by Dvorak.
9. Discuss the instructional implications resulting from organizing writing tasks according to the ACTFL's guidelines incorporating content, functions, and accuracy levels.

10. Choose an authentic writing task and prepare a lesson that uses prewriting, writing, and postwriting activities along the lines suggested by Richards.
11. Prepare a writing task based on a form or comic strip.
12. Analyze a writing task in terms of task requirements, topic, function, linguistic elements, and learner behaviors.

REFERENCES

American Council on the Teaching of Foreign Languages (ACTFL). (1986). *ACTFL provisional proficiency guidelines*. Hastings-on-Hudson, NY: ACTFL Materials Center.

Bell, J., & Burnaby, B. (1984). *A handbook for ESL literacy*. Toronto: Ontario Institute for Studies in Education.

Birckbichler, D. W. (1982). *Creative activities for the second language classroom*. Washington, DC: Center for Applied Linguistics.

Britton, J., Burgess, T., Martin, N., McLeod, A., & Rosen, H. (1975). *The development of writing abilities* (11-18). London: Macmillan.

Bruffee, K. (1986). Social construction, language, and the authority of knowledge: A biographical essay. *College English, 48,* 773-790.

Buhr, M. (1989). Materials prepared for a course. Albany: State University of New York, School of Education.

Canale, M. (1984). A communicative approach to language proficiency assessment in a minority setting. In C. Rivera (Ed.), *Communicative competence approaches to language proficiency assessment: Research and application* (pp. 107-122). Avon, England: Multilingual Matters.

Cardelle, M., & Corno, L. (1981). Effects on second language learning of variations in written feedback on homework assignments. *TESOL Quarterly, 15,* 251-262.

Carson, J. E. (1990). Reading-writing connections: Toward a description for second language learners. In B. Kroll (Ed.), *Second language writing: Research insights for the classroom* (pp. 88-101). Cambridge, England: Cambridge University Press.

Chamot, A. U., & Kupper, L. (1989). Learner strategies in foreign language instruction. *Foreign Language Annals, 22*(1), 13-24.

Chastain, K. (1990). Characteristics of graded and ungraded compositions. *Modern Language Journal, 74*(1), 10-14.

Clark, H. H., & Clark, E. V. (1977). *Psychology and language*. New York: Harcourt Brace Jovanovich.

Coombs, V. M. (1986). Syntax and communicative strategies in intermediate German composition. *Modern Language Journal, 70,* 114-124.

Cooper, T., & Morain, G. (1980). A study of sentence-combining techniques for developing written and oral fluency in French. *French Review, 53,* 411-423.

Cummins, J. (1980). The cross-lingual dimensions of language proficiency: Implications for bilingual education and the optimal age issue. *TESOL Quartery, 14,* 175-187.

Cummins, J. (1983). Language proficiency and academic achievement. In J. W. Oller, Jr. (Ed.), *Issues in language testing research* (pp. 108-126). New York: Newbury House.

Dvorak, T. (1986). Writing in a foreign language. In B. H. Wing (Ed.), *Listening, reading, writing: Analysis and application* (pp. 145-167). Middlebury, VT: Northeast Conference on the Teaching of Foreign Languages.

Dvorak, T. R. (1987). Is written FL like oral FL? In B. Van Patten, T. R. Dvorak, & J. F. Lee (Eds.), *Foreign language learning: A research perspective* (pp. 79-91). Cambridge, MA: Newbury House.

Emig, J. (1981). Writing as a mode of learning. In G. Tate & E. P. J. Corbett (Eds.), *The writing teacher's sourcebook*. Oxford, England: Oxford University Press.

Frantzen, D., & Rissel, D. (1987). Learner self-correction of written compositions: What does it show us? In B. Van Patten, T. R. Dvorak, & J. F. Lee (Eds.), *Foreign language learning: A research perspective* (pp. 92-107). New York: Newbury House.

Gaies, S. J. (1980). T-unit analysis in second language research: Applications, problems, and limitations. *TESOL Quarterly, 14*, 53-60.

Gaudiani, C. (1981). *Teaching writing in a foreign language curriculum*. Washington, DC: Center for Applied Linguistics.

Grabe, W. (1991). Current developments in second language reading research. *TESOL Quarterly, 25*(3), 375-406.

Hartzell, R. E. (1988). Testing in a communicative curriculum. *Language Association Bulletin, 39*(4), 1-4.

Hedge, T. (1988). *Writing*. Oxford: Oxford University Press.

Hendrickson, J. M. (1980). The treatment of error in written work. *Modern Language Journal, 64*, 216-221.

Hughey, J. B., Wormuth, D., Hartfiel, F., & Jacobs, H. (1983). *Teaching ESL composition: Principles and techniques*. New York: Newbury House.

Jarvis, G. A., Bonin, T. M., Corbin, D. E., & Birckbichler, D. W. (1980). *Connaître et se connaître. A beginning reader* (2nd ed.). New York: Holt, Rinehart, & Winston.

Jarvis, G. A., Bonin, T. M., Corbin, D. E., & Birckbichler, D. W. (1981). *Vivent les différences* (2nd ed.). New York: Holt, Rinehart, & Winston.

Kaplan, R. B. (1966). Cultural thought patterns in intercultural education. *Language Learning, 16*, 1-20.

Kaplan, R. B. (1972). *The anatomy of rhetoric: Prolegomena to a functional theory of rhetoric*. Philadelphia: Center for Curriculum Development. (Distributed by Heinle & Heinle)

Kaplan, R. B. (1983). An introduction to the study of written texts: The "discourse compact." In R. B. Kaplan, A. d'Anglejan, J. R. Cowan, B. B. Kachru, & G. R. Tucker (Eds.), *Annual Review of Applied Linguistics: 1982* (pp. 138-151). New York: Newbury House.

Krashen, S. D. (1984). *Writing: Research, theory and applications*. Oxford: Pergamon.

Lalande, J. (1982). Reducing composition errors. *Modern Language Journal, 66*, 140-149.

Lapp, R. E. (1984). *The process approach to writing: Toward a curriculum for international students*. Unpublished master's thesis, University of Hawaii, Manoa.

Magnan, S. S. (1985). Teaching and testing proficiency in writing: Skills to transcend the second language classroom. In A. Omaggio (Ed.), *Proficiency, curriculum, articulation: The ties that bind* (pp. 109-136). Middlebury, VT: Northeast Conference.

Nystrand, M. (1982). An analysis of errors in written communication. In M. Nystrand (Ed.), *What writers know* (pp. 57-74). New York: Academic Press.

Ostler, S. E. (1987). English in parallels: A comparison of English and Arabic prose. In U. Connor and R. B. Kaplan (Eds.), *Writing across languages: Analysis of L2 text* (pp. 169-185). Reading, MA: Addison-Wesley.

Oxford, R. L. (1990). *Language learning strategies: What every teacher should know*. New York: Newbury House.

Ozzelo, Y. (1983, October). *Imparfait ou passé composé?* Paper presented at the fall meeting of the Wisconsin Association of Foreign Language Teachers, Madison.

Palmer, D. (1985). Writing skills. In A. Mathews, M. Spratt, & L. Dangerfield (Eds.), *At the chalkface: Practical techniques in language teaching* (pp. 69-72). London: Edward Arnold.

Perkins, K. (1983). On the use of composition scoring techniques, objective measures, and objectives tests to evaluate ESL writing ability. *TESOL Quartery, 17,* 651-671.

Raimes, A. (1985). What unskilled ESL students do as they write: A classroom study of composing. *TESOL Quarterly, 19*(2), 229-259.

Richards, J. C. (1990). *The language teaching matrix.* Cambridge, England: Cambridge University Press.

Russo, G. M. (1987). Writing: An interactive experience. In W. M. Rivers (Ed.), *Interactive language teaching* (pp. 83-92). Cambridge, England: Cambridge University Press.

Scott, V. M. (1992). Writing from the start: A task-oriented developmental writing program for foreign language students. In R. M. Terry (Ed.), *Dimension: Language '91 making a world of difference* (pp. 1-15). Valdosta, GA: Southern Conference on Language Teaching.

Semke, H. (1980). *The comparative effects of four methods of treating free-writing assignments on the second language skills and attitudes of students in college level first year German.* Unpublished doctoral dissertation, University of Minnesota.

Smith, K. L. (1990). Collaborative and interactive writing for increasing communication skills. *Hispania, 73*(1), 77-87.

Stanton, J. (1983) Dialogue journals: A new tool for teaching. Educational Resources Information Center (ERIC) Clearinghouse on Languages and Linguistics (CLL) *News Bulletin, 6,* 2.

Turvey, J. (1984). Our readers write. *English Journal, 73,* 91.

Whitlock, R. (1984). *Six writing exercises for helping students understand process.* Unpublished manuscript, University of Hawaii.

Zamel, V. (1983). The composing processes of advanced ESL students: Six case studies. *TESOL Quarterly, 17*(2), 165-187.

chapter 11

Language Testing for the Classroom

The proper relationship between teaching and testing is surely that of part-nership. It is true that there may be occasions when the teaching is good and appropriate and the testing is not; we are then likely to suffer from harmful backwash. But equally there may be occasions when teaching is poor or in-appropriate and when testing is able to exert a beneficial influence. We can-not expect testing only to follow teaching. What we should demand of it, however, is that it should be supportive of good teaching and, where neces-sary, exert a corrective influence on bad teaching. If testing always had a beneficial backwash on teaching, it would have a much better reputation amongst teachers.

A. Hughes, 1989

Testing language in the classroom context occupies a central role in instructional planning. Language can be compartmentalized according to different linguistic lev-els and performance skills associated with listening, speaking, reading, and writing. Distinctions can be made between linguistic accuracy and communicative uses of language. Communicative abilities can, in turn, be characterized according to vari-ous systems of knowledge and skills: grammatical, sociolinguistic, discourse, and strategic competence. Communicative language testing places a strong emphasis on actual use of language in a number of cultural situations. Specific test items can be constructed in the four language skill areas so that the students' linguistic com-petencies can be assessed and evaluated regularly. Guidelines for test construction are offered along with examples of tests in English, French, German, and Spanish developed by classroom teachers.

This chapter considers a number of issues related to language testing. The fol-lowing questions are addressed:

1. What are the major types of language tests?
2. What aspects are involved in communicative competence?
3. What issues need to be considered in communicative competence testing?
4. What are some ways of testing the four language areas?
5. What are some important considerations in formulating a testing plan?
6. What are some examples of language tests prepared by classroom teachers?

TYPES OF LANGUAGE TESTS

Dictation, translation exercises, comprehension questions based on reading assignments, paragraphs developed from topic sentences, fill-in-the-blank sentences, and role-playing situations are some of the methods used by teachers and researchers to test language abilities. These methods represent a number of important distinctions made in testing: discrete-point and integrative testing, direct and indirect testing, linguistic competence and communicative competence, and mastery testing and proficiency testing. Asking students to fill in blanks in sentences represents discrete-point language testing, since one of the elements of language (particular grammatical features) is assessed on an item-by-item basis. This activity may also be seen by some as a direct way to assess the mastery of grammatical features associated with linguistic competence (ability to produce and recognize structures that are grammatical). The development of paragraphs from topic sentences represents integrative use of language, since the writer has to combine many language elements (vocabulary, grammar, orthography) in order to complete the task. The writing sample is the most direct method to assess writing abilities, and it may also be seen as a means of assessing communicative competence, reflecting the writer's ability to perform a specific function such as describing, informing, or narrating.

All language tests represent samples of linguistic behavior that reflect the extent to which learners possesses certain knowledge or skills. Language tests tend to be used for three major purposes:

1. *Proficiency*: assessment of language abilities for the purpose of placement in a language course or level, admission to a program, and qualifications for a certificate or a particular job
2. *Diagnosis*: evaluation of particular areas of strength or weakness in language proficiency (determination of a student's linguistic knowledge and skills in different domains is usually conducted before a course of study is begun)
3. *Achievement*: measurement of the degree of mastery of linguistic skills relevant to a particular unit of instruction or syllabus (class progress tests, semester exams, end-of-unit tests)

Achievement tests as constructed by classroom teachers are usually scored on the basis of students' responses, which are evaluated in terms of specific criteria (right or wrong, acceptable or unacceptable) and performance levels. Items that test individual bits of linguistic knowledge (correct grammatical choices, multiple-choice comprehension questions, spelling errors) are associated with discrete-point testing. Language tasks that incorporate various aspects of language (grammar, fluency, vocabulary, accent) are scored on the basis of performance levels consisting of holistic ratings (high, middle, low, good, pass, weak, or poor) or analytic methods of scoring, the latter requiring a separate score for each linguistic area (e.g., grammar, vocabulary, mechanics, organization, and fluency, each with a range from 1 to 6). Tasks such as role-play, an interview, a summary, a picture description, or guided composition are examples of integrative testing. These tasks tend to involve more subjective judgment, and they may not be scored as consistently by raters as true or false or correct or incorrect items, which by contrast allow high levels of inter-rater agreement (reliability) because of objective criteria.

COMMUNICATIVE COMPETENCE PERSPECTIVES

Communicative competence is often characterized as an "integrated control" (Palmer, 1979) of language reflected in the speaker's ability to understand and use language appropriately to communicate in various situations. Testing of communicative competence tends to be associated with global ability (i.e., integrating the different elements of language: grammar, vocabulary) involved in performing communicative acts (giving directions, requesting permission, apologizing). In most instances, specific situations are described by the examiner and rating scales are used to evaluate how effectively the examinee performed the communicative act.

Definitions of communicative competence are often relatively broad, for example, ability to adapt the totality of one's communicative resources, both linguistic and functional (extralinguistic or paralinguistic), to a given situation (Legarreta, 1979). Attempts undertaken by communication experts (Wiemann & Backlaund, 1980) or applied linguists (Canale & Swain, 1980) to define the concept of communicative competence have only demonstrated the multiplicity of possible components. It seems that at least three distinct traditions of inquiry are merging in the communicative-competence field: (1) Psychologists and communication specialists view communicative competence primarily as the ability to understand, organize, and convey information (e.g., Flavell, Botkin, Fry, Wright, & Jarvis, 1968); (2) philosophers of language such as Austin (1962) and Searle (1969) approach communicative competence as the ability to perform speech acts efficiently; and (3) sociolinguists, often influenced by philosophers of language mentioned under (2) above, define communicative competence in terms of the appropriateness of language use in specific situations (Hymes, 1971; Shuy, 1979).

Communicative proficiency can be characterized in terms of various systems of knowledge and skills. Canale's (1984) framework includes four areas:

1. *Grammatical competence*: mastery of the language code (verbal or nonverbal), thus concerned with such features as lexical items, and rules of sentence formation, pronunciation, and literal meaning
2. *Sociolinguistic competence*: mastery of appropriate language use in different sociolinguistic contexts, with emphasis on appropriateness of meanings (e.g., attitudes, speech acts, and propositions) and appropriateness of forms (e.g., register, non-verbal expression, and intonation)
3. *Discourse competence*: mastery of how to combine and interpret forms and meanings to achieve a unified spoken or written text in different genres by using (a) cohesion devices to relate utterance forms (e.g., pronouns, transition words, and parallel structures) and (b) coherence rules to organize meanings (e.g., repetition, progression, consistency, and relevance of ideas)
4. *Strategic competence*: mastery of verbal and nonverbal strategies (a) to compensate for breakdowns in communication due to insufficient competence or to performance limitations (e.g., strategies such as use of dictionaries, paraphrase, and gestures) and (b) to enhance the effectiveness of communication (e.g., deliberately slow and soft speech for rhetorical effect) (p. 112)

This model incorporates the oral and written modalities of language within various communicative situations (e.g., writer to reader as friend or stranger; speaker to listener: student to teacher or teacher to teacher). At the same time, the linguistic component interacts with other systems of knowledge and skills (knowledge of the world, general perception strategies) as well as with a theory of human action involving personality factors and decision-making processes.

Other frameworks for depicting communicative competence have been proposed more recently. Faerch et al. (1984) argue that communicative competence consists of phonology/orthography, grammar vocabulary, pragmatics, discourse, communication strategies, and fluency. Bachman's (1990) model incorporates aspects from Canale and Swain but in a different formulation. To Bachman, for instance, language competence includes two major components: organizational competence, consisting of grammatical competence, and textual competence, which includes various language subskills. Pragmatic competence involves functional use of language (illocutionary competence) along with sociolinguistic competence. Strategic competence is a set of general abilities that utilize all of the elements of language competence in addition to the psychomotor skills used in the process of negotiating meaning. Chapter 2 discusses conceptions about communicative competence and language proficiency more extensively.

COMMUNICATIVE COMPETENCE TESTING

Measurement of communicative competence faces many problems, some of them related to the aforementioned vagueness of the concept or trait to be measured.

The measurement problems are compounded by the fact that the usual measurement of communicative competence is based on global assessment, using rating scales, while linguistic competence is generally measured in tests using the discrete-item method. As a result, the suggestion has been made that in many situations a presumed difference between measured linguistic and communicative competencies may reflect a difference in method of measurement rather than in the trait or constructs being measured (Carrigan & Upshur, 1978; Stevenson, 1979).

Morrow (1977), for example, suggests a "discrete feature" approach to testing communicative skills in order to isolate numerous variables that can have a bearing on a speech act. He suggests isolating the following aspects: setting, topic, function, modality, presupposition, role, formality, and status. Following is a sample that focuses on three sociolinguistic dimensions associated with a speech act:

Sample one:

Presentation: Oral (tape recorded or spoken)

Type: Identification

Present: *Excuse me, do you know where the nearest post office is, please?*

1. Setting   Where might one ask you that question?
                 A. In your house
                 B. In your office
                 C. In the street
                 D. In a restaurant

2. Topic   What is the person asking you about?
                 A. The price of stamps
                 B. The age of the post office
                 C. The location of the post office
                 D. The size of the post office

3. Function   Why is the person speaking to you?
                 A. To ask your advice
                 B. To thank you
                 C. To ask for information
                 D. To warn you

(Adapted from Morrow, 1977, p. 29)

One of the challenges in constructing communicative-competence tests is to resolve what has been referred to as the reliability-validity tension in language testing (Davies, 1978). Highly reliable discrete-item tests tend to present language out of context and lack the communicative situation, therefore having little face validity. Tests that elicit genuinely communicative types of responses have the validity but often depend for their reliability on inter-rater agreements based on rating scales rather than on right-or-wrong criteria.

Another area of concern is the accuracy-fluency distinction. Higgs and Clifford (1982) have proposed a trisectional view of communicative competence that includes statements about the linguistic functions a speaker is able to express, about the content (topic or areas) that can be discussed, and about the degree of accuracy in conveying the message. Thus, with respect to oral proficiency, pronunciation and the fluency/integrative factors relate directly to functions, while the sociolinguistic/cultural and vocabulary factors relate directly to context and content, and grammar predictably relates directly to accuracy (Lowe, 1985).

This view of communicative competence is reflected in the ACTFL's (1986) guidelines, which describe speaking, listening, reading, and writing proficiency in relation to function, context, and accuracy. Judgments of an individual's proficiency must take into account all three factors that are interrelated hierarchically.

One of the characteristics of communicative testing is the strong emphasis on actual use of language in real-life settings, usually based on the communicative needs of the learners. As a result of this, language tests are a collection of tasks at different levels (beginning, intermediate, and advanced) with respect to different language abilities (listening, speaking, reading, and writing) rather than one overall test of language proficiency. Communicative tests are necessarily integrative tests since the learner has to "bring together" the various elements of language—grammar, vocabulary, culture—involved in performing different communicative acts. Quantitative assessment procedures (right or wrong, yes or no) may be unsuitable in many cases since the performance of certain tasks or functions (giving directions orally, requesting information in a letter, reading a map or a timetable) may be best described with such criteria as accuracy, appropriateness, and flexibility. This requires the use of rating scales to assess relative proficiency on various dimensions, which constitute collectively an overall or global ability with respect to the performance of specific language tasks.

Canale and Swain (1980) point out that discrete-point tests may be more appropriate for assessing communicative competence, while integrative ones might be more suitable for assessing actual communicative performance. The distinction of *language knowledge* (receptive or interpretative knowledge of language) versus *language use* (productive or integrative use of language) may be meaningful in deciding the proportion of language tasks that can be assessed through pencil-and-paper tests and those that can be tested through actual performance of simulated communicative tasks (telephoning, ordering meals, applying for a job). Omaggio (1983) proposes a scheme for classifying test items that can vary both on a "naturalness" continuum and by the level of "discreteness" (Figure 11.1).

Traditional items on a grammar test would fall in quadrant A, since they usually focus on isolated sentences or phrases and are scored with a right-or-wrong criterion. A cloze passage, an example of a common reading task, calls for the use of appropriate words in the blanks provided in a written passage. Such a technique has an integrative format, which can be scored objectively (quadrant C). Slash sentences, sometimes called "dehydrated" sentences (John/home ⟶ "John went home," "John likes his home," "John lives in a comfortable home"), require students to create full and grammatical sentences. This activity is

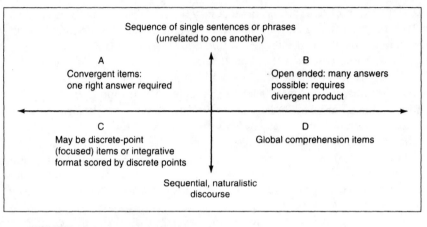

FIGURE 11.1 Locating test items

SOURCE: From *Proficiency-Oriented Classroom Testing* (Language in Education: Theory and Practice, vol. 52) (p. 10) by Alice C. Omaggio, 1983, Washington, DC: Center for Applied Linguistics. Reprinted with permission.

essentially open-ended, allowing a number of divergent answers (quadrant B). Items in quadrant D can include actual performance tasks (ordering a meal, playing the role of buyer or seller, filling out a form or report of an accident) as well as global/specific understanding of spoken or written texts (answering comprehension questions; writing a summary; recording specific information to fill in an incomplete chart, schedule, table, or special form).

TESTING THE FOUR LANGUAGE AREAS

Testing the four language skills within a communicative perspective involves an understanding of a number of concepts in language assessment:

- Knowledge tests and performance tests
- Discrete-point tests and global or integrated tests
- Single/unrelated sentences and sequential/naturalistic discourse

The evaluation of productive (speaking and writing) and receptive (listening and reading) language skills often involves the use of different assessment procedures. Receptive language skills can be evaluated through objective paper-and-pencil tests. Evaluation of authentic speaking and writing tasks may require use of qualitative procedures such as rating scales. This approach makes evaluation a much more subjective and time-consuming process. In order for a communicative test to meet the face-validity criterion, students need to feel that they are performing a "real" communicative act and that they are being evaluated on criteria (fluency, comprehensibility, amount or quality of language, effort to communicate) that indeed measure the degree of success in accomplishing the task.

In addition, testing one particular language skill usually involves another:

Stimulus Format	*Response Format*
Listen to a story	Write a summary
Listen to a conversation	Answer multiple-choice questions
Read a passage	Formulate questions
Read a story	Suggest a title
Teacher gives oral directions	Students carry out actions

Oral and written responses to a particular stimuli may involve a broad range of cognitive strategies, including the ability to distinguish, classify, order, combine, and synthesize. It is possible that on some communicative tasks, students may not perform successfully due to the cognitive demands of the test situation rather than as the result of a lack of language proficiency (Ramírez, 1984; 1986).

Each language skill can be approached at different levels. For example, a written text can be read for global comprehension (identifying the main idea or providing a title), for specific details and facts, or for understanding the use of particular grammatical cohesion devices (John/he/the student; moreover/in addition/finally). Students can name the objects in a picture, write a story based on a series of pictures, and then prepare a dialogue based on two of the persons in the pictures. These activities, of course, place language in different areas of Omaggio's (1983) framework involving the "naturalness" and "discreteness" continua. At the same time, each task usually requires a set of cognitive operations.

Listening Comprehension Formats

Selective Listening.   In selective listening, students listen to a passage and focus on specific lexical or grammatical features embedded in the selection. Students may write the number and types of verbs (Omaggio, 1983, p. 14). Students can listen to an announcement (train station, weather report) and answer questions about the content; format can range from multiple-choice to open-ended questions (Larson & Jones, 1984, p. 123).

Recording Specific Information.   Students listen to a passage and record specific semantic information. The student can take notes in the native language to follow a map or diagram; respond to comprehension questions; or fill in an incomplete chart, schedule, table, or other type of written form (Omaggio, 1983, pp. 14-15).

Gisting.   To get the gist, students might listen to a passage and then distill the critical information to a few words or sentences. This can indicate if the student has understood the general topic of the message and has been able to separate the key ideas from the other linguistic aspects (Larson & Jones, 1984, p. 123).

Comprehension Questions.   Students listen to a passage and answer comprehension questions using different formats (true or false, multiple choice, sentence completion). The questions may focus on different aspects of passage content (main idea, events, details, characters) and may call for making inferences from textually implicit information based on the topic or content (Omaggio, 1983, pp. 19-22).

Translation.   Students listen to a passage and then translate it orally or in writing. Students can take notes in English and then prepare a summary based on their notes (Larson & Jones, 1984, p. 123).

Making Decisions.   Students listen to a text or announcement (weather report, department store closing, directions to a certain location) and make decisions, selecting from the alternatives the most appropriate course of action (e.g., take an umbrella or not, after hearing a weather report) (Larson & Jones, 1984, p. 123).

Identifying Sociolinguistic Factors.   To identify sociolinguistic factors, a statement is read and students must decide if the language being used is formal or informal and appropriate or inappropriate for a particular situation. Or they must match the statement with another communicative expression that expresses the same function (Finocchiaro & Brumfit, 1983, pp. 192-193).

Reading Comprehension Formats

Many of the formats described for listening comprehension can be adapted to written texts. Students can read passages for selective comprehension, recording of specific semantic information, gisting purposes, and answering of comprehension questions.

Cloze Procedure.   Students complete prose passages utilizing a cloze procedure format in which every *n*th word (e.g., every fifth or seventh) has been deleted. The examinee must supply the missing words deleted from the original text. Scoring can be based on either "exact" or "appropriate" responses that are grammatical and contextually appropriate. The modified cloze procedure offers multiple choices at each blank, from which the testee selects the correct response.

Logical Continuation.   A paragraph-length context is provided followed by a series of multiple-choice options, one of which logically continues and completes the thought of the paragraph (Omaggio, 1983, p. 34).

Synthesis/Global Classification.   In synthesis/global classification, students read a passage and write an English (or second language) summary, choose a title, or classify the passage according to its purpose, function, topic, or situation (Omaggio, 1983, pp. 35-37).

Real-Life Reading Tasks. Students should be able to read authentic, real-life reading tasks in the target language. These tasks can include informative signs (telephone book, train/bus schedules, newspapers, menus, maps), simple messages (greeting cards, directions), simple narration of events, biographical information, and personal communication (letters, invitations). Advanced readers should be able to interpret both the physical and social aspects of culture in promotional brochures and read unedited texts such as essays, short stories, novels, poems, and legends. These reading tasks involve a number of cognitive processes: receiving, analyzing, interpreting, and evaluating the message. Test formats can range from indirect and direct procedures in multiple-choice formats to direct procedures requiring the testee to paraphrase, describe, or characterize what was read (Larson & Jones, 1984, pp. 131–132).

Written Composition Formats

Testing writing proficiency is similar in many respects to assessing speaking proficiency since both are productive skills. Students can write or speak on a topic, which can then be scored holistically (e.g., high/middle/low; acceptable or unacceptable; 1, 2, 3, 4) using trained raters. Writing, of course, is a slow process, involving reflection, monitoring, revision, and the act of handwriting itself (Magnan, 1985a, p. 119).

Most writing tasks among second language users can be classied into five major types (Larson & Jones, 1984, pp. 133–134): correspondence (friendly or business letters), providing essential information (e.g., to others), completing forms (visas, applications), taking notes (notes to self, lists of things to buy), and formal papers (e.g., written for courses in a foreign university). Specific formats for assessing writing proficiency in L2 are listed below. Some formats are more appropriate for one type of writing (information gap for completing forms) than another (topic/function development for correspondence).

Sentence Reconstruction. To reconstruct a sentence, students start with several words (e.g., girl/movies/tomorrow) and add any necessary function words, making any necessary morphological changes (Finocchiaro & Brumfit, 1983, p. 199).

Discourse Transformation. In discourse transformation, students rewrite a passage, changing specific grammatical features (use pronouns for any repeated nouns; change all verb tenses from present to past or future) (Omaggio, 1983, pp. 48–53).

Information Gaps. Students complete information gaps, for example a modified cloze passage with specific words omitted (e.g., parts of speech: verbs, adjectives, adverbs, prepositions). Students fill out a form or listen to a passage and complete an information sheet (characteristics of the speaker: age, sex, place of birth, occupation, likes) (Omaggio, 1984, pp. 44–48, 53–55).

Cued Writing.   Students write a text based on cues: sentences to describe a set of pictures (items in a room, activities on the street) or a paragraph to answer a set of questions given by the teacher (Magnan, 1985a, p. 125).

Topic/Function Development.   To be tested on topic or function development, students complete a set of writing tasks involving different functions or situations (make a shopping list, take an inventory of contents in a room, write an ad for a newspaper, send a telegram, write a party invitation or letter to a friend) (Magnan, 1985a, pp. 120-123).

Oral Skills Formats

Paired Interviews.   Students interview one another in pairs. One student asks the questions written on a card ("Ask your partner . . . what sports he or she likes.") while the second one answers according to his or her own preference. Students may then exchange roles while the teacher takes notes on the students' responses (Omaggio, 1984, pp. 67-68).

Situational Role-Playing.   Students are given a situation (e.g., train station, restaurant, airport) and are asked to role-play to inquire about specific bits of information (costs, types of service, arrival and departure times). One student can play one role (seller, agent, waiter) while the teacher or another student can play the role of a buyer or customer (Omaggio, 1984, pp. 70-71).

Individual Interviews.   The teacher sets up an appointment with each student for an individual oral interview. The teacher and/or the student can select a focus for the dialogue by choosing randomly from a set of conversation cards. The interview can be tape recorded for assessment or grading (Omaggio, 1983, pp. 70-71).

Monologues and Exchanges.   To perform monologues and exchanges for testing, students randomly select two or three topics from a set of topic cards previously discussed in class. Each card has a set of subtopics that can serve as a guide for student preparation of an impromptu monologue on one of the topics. The teacher can ask follow-up questions based on the information provided by the student. Students can later ask the teacher questions as a result of the exchange. Student performance can be rated with an instrument including such criteria as fluency, vocabulary, structure, and comprehensibility (Omaggio, 1983, pp. 62-69).

Additional techniques for oral language assessment are offered by Underhill (1987). These range from sentence repetition and transformation procedures to story retelling. He also outlines specific suggestions for evaluating oral skills and weighing language components.

CONSIDERATIONS FOR TESTING

Spratt (1985) summarizes the range of techniques available for testing linguistic abilities and skills. Table 11.1 outlines the language focus as well as subjective and objective methods for testing the specific language areas. Subjective techniques tend to involve language samples above the sentence level and are integrative by nature since the situations require grammar, vocabulary, fluency, and discourse considerations. Objective techniques, on the other hand, focus on recognition or pro-

TABLE 11.1   Subjective and objective methods of language testing

Testing Focus	Subjective Methods	Objective Methods
Listening	Open-ended question and answer Note taking Interviews	Blank filling Information transfer Multiple choice questions True/False questions Jumbled pictures
Speaking	Role plays Interviews Group discussions Describing pictures Information gap activities	Sentence repetition Sentence responses to cues
Reading comprehension	Open-ended comprehension questions and answers in the target language or mother tongue Summary writing Note taking	Information transfer Multiple choice questions True/False questions Jumbled sentences Jumbled paragraphs Cloze
Writing	Guided writing e.g., letter completion, re-writing, information transfer Free writing e.g., compositions, essays	Blank filling Sentence joining
Grammar	Open-ended sentence completion Re-writing	Expansion exercises Scrambled exercises Transformation exercises Mulitple choice questions
Functions	Giving appropriate responses Discourse chains Split dialogues	Matching Multiple choice questions Odd-man-out Listen and match
Vocabulary	Compositions and essays Paraphrasing	Crosswords Classification exercises Matching exercises Labelling

SOURCE: From "Achievement Tests: Aims, Content and Some Testing Techniques" (pp. 146–147) by Mary Spratt, in A. Matthews, M. Spratt & L. Dangerfield (Eds.), *At the Chalkface: Practical Techniques in Language Teaching*, 1985, Thomas Nelson Publishing Services, Andover, England: Reprinted with permission.

duction of a limited range of items that are restricted in both linguistic and situational contexts.

Subjective tests can provide more-valid information about students' communicative abilities with respect to different topics, functions, and language situations. Yet, it is not always easy to assess the responses in a reliable way. Proficiency descriptions based on analytical scales consisting of separate components (grammar, vocabulary, fluency, and comprehension) are often used to establish performance levels. The individual components are scored on a six-point scale, the ratings are then weighted, and the total is obtained to arrive at a performance level. The weighing of the individual components and the conversion tables have been established through research efforts. Figure 11.2 describes the criteria levels for oral ability assessment. Trained raters classify oral language samples according to five categories, assigning a score for each category, then each score is assigned a relative weight. The total of the weighted scores is converted to a five-point scale that corresponds to the five proficiency levels on the Foreign Service Institute (FSI) ratings.

Oral proficiency levels may also be established on the basis of holistic descriptions that combine functions, topics, and accuracy levels, as can be seen in the ACTFL oral proficiency scale presented in Chapter 1, Table 1.2. In the case of writing competence, Gaudiani (1981) has proposed analytical scoring for four components (grammar and vocabulary, stylistic technique, organization, and content) with five performance levels (0 to 4 points) for each area. The characteristics of the evaluation system are discussed in Chapter 10.

Selection of test formats for assessing the four language skill areas from a communicative approach needs to be considered from a number of perspectives. Factors such as the nature of the language skill or task (knowledge of grammatical forms; ability to greet, apologize, direct; comprehend an announcement, commercial, advertisement), the student's language ability, and the degree of "contextualization" (single or isolated items vs. sequential or naturalistic discourse) should be taken into account. Magnan (1985b) proposes a multisequence evaluation procedure that ensures systematic progress from tests measuring specific aspects of language through more expanded connected discourse. This type of test formats ranges from discrete-point approaches to integrative/functional uses of language in different situations. She outlines seven principles that need to be followed in order to establish a multisequence evaluation plan:

1. Test formats should be suited to the particular task. When isolated forms are being learned, discrete-point testing is most appropriate. When the focus of learning progresses to using learned forms in a limited, structured context, hybrid tests such as formats involving contextualized sentences and short paragraphs are appropriate. When highly integrative language use is the desired goal, testing should be open-ended and should approximate language use in sociolinguistically appropriate situations.

Accent
 1. Pronunciation frequently unintelligible.
 2. Frequent gross errors and a very heavy accent make understanding difficult, require frequent repetition.
 3. "Foreign accent" requires concentrated listening and mispronunciations lead to occasional misunderstanding and apparent errors in grammar or vocabulary.
 4. Marked "foreign accent" and occasional mispronunciations that do not interfere with understanding.
 5. No conspicuous mispronunciations, but would not be taken for a native speaker.
 6. Native pronunciation, with no trace of "foreign accent."

Grammar
 1. Grammar almost entirely inaccurate except in stock phases.
 2. Constant errors showing control of very few major patterns and frequently preventing communication.
 3. Frequent errors showing some major patterns uncontrolled and causing occasional irritation and misunderstanding.
 4. Occasional errors showing imperfect control of some patterns but no weakness that causes misunderstanding.
 5. Few errors, with no patterns of failure.
 6. No more than two errors during the interview.

Vocabulary
 1. Vocabulary inadequate for even the simplest conversation.
 2. Vocabulary limited to basic personal and survival areas (time, food, transportation, family, etc.).
 3. Choice of words sometimes innacurate; limitations of vocabulary prevent discussion of some common professional and social topics.
 4. Professional vocabulary adequate to discuss special interests; general vocabulary permits discussion of any nontechnical subject with some circumlocutions.
 5. Professional vocabulary broad and precise; general vocabulary adequate to cope with complex practical problems and varied social situations.
 6. Vocabulary apparently as accurate and extensive as that of an educated native speaker.

Fluency
 1. Speech is so halting and fragmentary that conversation is virtually impossible.
 2. Speech is very slow and uneven except for short or routine sentences.
 3. Speech is frequently hesitant and jerky; sentences may be left uncompleted.
 4. Speech is occasionally hesitant, with some unevenness caused by rephrasing and groping for words.
 5. Speech is effortless and smooth, but perceptibly nonnative in speed and evenness.
 6. Speech on all professional and general topics as effortless and smooth as a native speaker's.

Comprehension
 1. Understands too little for the simplest type of conversation.
 2. Understands only slow, very simple speech on common social and touristic topics; requires constant repetition and rephrasing.
 3. Understands careful, somewhat simplified speech directed to him or her, with considerable repetition or rephrasing.
 4. Understands quite well normal educated speech directed to him or her, but requires occasional repetition or rephrasing.
 5. Understands everything in normal educated conversation except for very colloquial or low frequency items or exceptionally rapid or slurred speech.
 6. Understands everything in both formal and colloquial speech to be expected of an educated native speaker (ETS, 1970, pp. 20–22).

(continued)

FIGURE 11.2   The FSI checklist of performance factors and descriptions

The FSI Weighting and Conversion Tables

FSI weighting table

Proficiency description	1	2	3	4	5	6	
Accent	0	1	2	2	3	4	____
Grammar	6	12	18	24	30	36	____
Vocabulary	4	8	12	16	20	24	____
Fluency	2	4	6	8	10	12	____
Comprehension	4	8	12	15	19	23	____
						Total:	____

FSI conversion table

Total score	Level	Total score	Level	Total score	Level
16–25	0+	43–52	2	73–82	3+
26–32	1	53–62	2+	83–92	4
33–42	1+	63–72	3	93–99	4+

The FSI Proficiency Ratings

Level 1: *Able to satisfy routine travel needs and minimum courtesy requirements.* Can ask and answer questions on topics very familiar to him or her; within the scope of his or her very limited language experience can understand simple questions and statements, allowing for slowed speech, repetition, or paraphrase; speaking vocabulary inadequate to express anything but the most elementary needs; errors in pronunciation and grammar are frequent, but can be understood by a native speaker used to dealing with foreigners attempting to speak his or her language. While elementary needs vary considerably from individual to individual, any person at level 1 should be able to order a simple meal, ask for shelter or lodging, ask and give simple directions, make purchases, and tell time.

Level 2: *Able to satisfy routine social demands and limited work requirements.* Can handle with confidence but not with facility most social situations including introductions and casual conversations about current events, as well as work, family, and autobiographical information; can handle limited work requirements, needing help in handling any complications or difficulties; can get the gist of most conversations on nontechnical subjects (i.e., topics that require no specialized knowledge) and has a speaking vocabulary sufficient to express himself or herself simply with some circumlocutions; accent, though often quite faulty, is intelligible; can usually handle elementary constructions quite accurately but does not have thorough or confident control of the grammar.

Level 3: *Able to speak the language with sufficient structural accuracy and vocabulary to participate effectively in most formal and informal conversations on practical, social, and professional topics.* Can discuss particular interests and special fields of competence with reasonable ease; comprehension is quite complete for a normal rate of speech; vocabulary is broad enough that he or she rarely has to grope for a word; accent may be obviously foreign; control of grammar good; errors never interfere with understanding and rarely disturb the native speaker.

Level 4: *Able to use the language fluently and accurately on all levels normally pertinent to professional needs.* Can understand and participate in any conversation within the range of his or her experience with a high degree of fluency and precision of vocabulary; would rarely be taken for a native speaker, but can respond appropriately even in unfamiliar situations; errors of pronunciation and grammar quite rare; can handle informal interpreting from and into the language.

Level 5: *Speaking proficiency equivalent to that of an educated native speaker.* Has complete fluency in the language such that his or her speech on all levels is fully accepted by educated native speakers in all of its features, including breadth of vocabulary and idiom, colloquialisms, and pertinent cultural references.

FIGURE 11.2   (continued)

SOURCE: *Manual for Peace Corps Language Testers*, Washington, DC: Peace Corps (1970), pp. 10–11, as reprinted in Oller, 1979, pp. 320–323.

2. The use of test formats should proceed along a continuum. At first, isolated forms should be tested, using discrete-point items for recognition and then for production; items should become progressively more open-ended and integrative in relation to more functional teaching objectives.

3. The continuum can be considered as having four key phases, in each of which a variety of test types would be found: (1) recognition phase, testing recognition and differentiation of isolated forms using discrete-point formats; (2) memory phase, testing active production of isolated forms or memorizing expressions using discrete-point formats; (3) contextualized phase, simultaneous testing of a variety of language forms and concepts as used in the context of sentences or short paragraphs; and (4) discourse phase, testing ability to use forms integratively to produce extended discourse.

4. This testing sequence implies teaching for recognition or passive knowledge before active usage. It naturally links reading to writing and listening to speaking. As this link suggests, multi-sequence evaluation can apply, with certain logical modifications, to all four skills, and ideally it should end in free integration of these skills.

5. Grading in each phase of the sequence should be in accordance with the nature of the tasks involved. Grading in the recognition and memory phases, therefore, can be quite objective since these phases are tested using discrete-point items. In grading items in the contextualized phase, we will need to consider more aspects, at least semantic content and grammatical form. In this phase, grading will still be mainly objective, with some subjective elements as necessary. In the discourse phase, where forms are used integratively to produce expanded discourse, we will want to consider function, content, and accuracy, including sociolinguistic as well as linguistic features. Another possible grouping would be grammatical competence, sociolinguistic competence, discourse competence and strategic competence, as suggested by Canale (1984). Since testing in the discourse phase involves a broad sampling of linguistic and nonlinguistic items, grading must be subjective to a great degree that is based on teachers' professional judgments in a more or less directive fashion.

6. The test sequence should be incorporated into the course syllabus so that the progression of the test sequence is respected. For example, verifications of short duration, perhaps five to ten minutes, should be used for the recognition and memory phases. Discrete-point formats are highly appropriate to the short duration of verifications, and, since discrete-point items are easy to correct, verifications can be given often. Quizzes of medium duration, fifteen to thirty minutes, should be used to recheck certain items of the memory phase and to test the contextualized phase. Quizzes would thus consist of a few discrete-

point items, mostly contextual items, such as personal questions to which a simple answer is appropriate, fill-in-the-blank paragraphs in a modified cloze format, and dehydrated sentences. Major tests of long duration, 40 to 60 minutes, would recheck a few items from the contextualized phase and concentrate on items in the discourse phase, such as dialogue completion and essay writing. Major tests would thus include a combination of both contextualized items and more open-ended items in which students are required to produce substantial chunks of discourse.

7. Teachers will want to proceed through the phases of the testing sequence at different rates and in different ways for students at different stages of instruction. For example, for beginning students most testing would be in the recognition and memory phases, working with single words or memorized material in a discrete-point format, with initial attempts into the contextualized phase. For intermediate students discrete-point items might be used initially to recheck learned material, and then testing would concentrate on the contextualized phase, with some fairly simple items in the discourse phase. For above-average students the memorized phase could be rechecked at home using self-graded exercises or in the language laboratory using audio tapes and/or computer-assisted instruction, so that classroom time could be reserved for selective testing in the contextualized phase and especially for thorough testing in the discourse phase. Within the confines of what is appropriate to their level of ability, students would repeat the testing sequence for each topic of the course syllabus, hence the term Multi-sequence evaluation. (Magnan, 1985b, pp. 123–125)

Testing oral proficiency within a communicative framework represents a number of challenges. One has to do with the selection of the format (interview, interaction with peers, situational role-playing, or response to visual or written stimuli). The other involves obtaining appropriate language samples that accurately reflect the examinee's abilities and that can be scored reliably. Hughes (1989) offers general advice on how to plan and conduct oral tests:

1. Make the oral test as long as is feasible. It is unlikely that much reliable information can be obtained in less than about 15 minutes, while 30 minutes can probably provide all the information necessary for most purposes. As part of a placement test, however, a 5- or 10-minute interview should be sufficient to prevent gross errors in assigning students to classes.

2. Include as wide a sample of specified content as is possible in the time available. Select what you regard as a representative sample of the specified content and *then* plan how you will elicit the neces-

sary behavior (this may well demand the use of more than one format).

3. Plan the test carefully. While one of the advantages of individual oral testing is the way in which procedures can be adapted in response to a candidate's performance, the tester should nevertheless have some pattern to follow. It is a mistake to begin, for example, an interview with no more than a general idea of the course that it might take.

4. Give the candidate as many "fresh starts" as possible. This means a number of things. First, if possible and if appropriate, more than one format should be used. Secondly, again if possible, it is desirable for candidates to interact with more than one tester. Thirdly, within a format there should be as many separate "items" as possible. Particularly if a candidate gets into difficulty, not too much time should be spent on one particular function or topic. At the same time, candidates should not be discouraged from making a second attempt to express what they want to say, possibly in different words.

5. Select interviewers carefully and train them. Successful interviewing is by no means easy, and not everyone has great aptitude for it. Interviewers need to be sympathetic and flexible characters, with a good command of the language themselves. But even the most apt need training. They can be given advice, shown video recordings of successful interviews, and can carry out interviews themselves, which can be recorded to form the basis for critical discussion.

6. Use a second tester for interviews. Because of the difficulty of conducting an interview and of keeping track of the candidate's performance, it is very helpful to have a second tester present. This person can not only give more attention to how the candidate is performing but also elicit performance which they think is necessary in order to come to a reliable judgement. One of the techniques suggested below needs the co-operation of a second tester.

7. Set only tasks and topics that would be expected to cause candidates no difficulty in their own language.

8. Carry out the interview in a quiet room with good acoustics.

9. Put candidates at their ease. Individual oral tests will always be particularly stressful for candidates. It is important to put them at their ease by being pleasant and reassuring throughout. It is especially important to make the initial stages of the test well within the capacities of all reasonable candidates. Interviews, for example, can begin with straightforward requests for personal (but not too personal) details, remarks about the weather, and so on.

   Testers should avoid constantly reminding candidates that they are being assessed. In particular they should not be seen to make notes on the candidates' performance during the interview or other activity. For the same reason, transitions between topics and between techniques should be made as natural as possible. The interview should be ended at a level at which the candidate clearly feels comfortable, thus leaving him or her with a sense of accomplishment.

10. Collect enough relevant information. If the purpose of the test is to determine whether a candidate can perform at a certain predetermined level, then, after an initial easy introduction, the test should be carried out at that level. If it becomes apparent that a candidate is clearly very weak and has no chance of reaching the criterion level, then an interview should be brought gently to a close, since nothing will be learned from subjecting her or him to a longer ordeal. Where, on the other hand, the purpose of the test is to see *what* level the candidate is at, in an interview the tester has to begin by guessing what this level is on the basis of early responses. The interview is then conducted at that level, either providing confirmatory evidence or revealing that the initial guess is inaccurate. In the latter case the level is shifted up or down until it becomes clear what the candidate's level is. A second tester, whose main role is to assess the candidate's performance, can elicit responses at a different level if it is suspected that the principal interviewer may be mistaken.

11. Do not talk too much. There is an unfortunate tendency for interviewers to talk too much, not giving enough talking time to candidates. Avoid the temptation to make lengthy or repeated explanations of something that the candidate has misunderstood. (Hughes, 1989, pp. 105–107)

EXAMPLES OF LANGUAGE TESTS

The appendix to this chapter presents examples of tests in English, French, German, and Spanish that are designed to assess listening, speaking, reading, and writing abilities within an exam period. The English test, prepared by Dangerfield (1985), is designed as an elementary-level achievement exam for EFL learners. The French, German, and Spanish tests were developed by teachers in the East Ramapo Central School District of New York. They illustrate different formats that can be used for assessing language skills and communicative competence. Some tasks place learners in specific cultural situations, while others entail resolving a problem. Many items approach the testing of oral/written communication in the form of discrete items perhaps because scoring problems are associated with global, divergent answers, and because the tests are final exams evaluating the mastery of content rather than language proficiency. The French exam, developed by Hurley, McHugh, and Tallis (1989), is an example of a seventh-grade final. The Spanish exam, prepared by Benger, Schumer, and Horowitz (1989), is intended for eighth graders. The German test, constructed by Hartzell (1989), is planned as a final exam for ninth graders.

All four tests were designed to assess the mastery of linguistic skills relevant to a particular unit of instruction. As achivement tests, they were designed for a group of learners who can complete the test during an exam period usually lasting two hours. All of the tests emphasize the assessment of language in context. Table 11.2 provides a comparison of the four language tests according to the different language modalities and assessment techniques. All four tests tend to emphasize objective procedures such as true or false, comprehension questions, matching, fill-in gaps, and listing the information requested. In the case of speaking skills, the English tests assesses them through writing a dialogue and using functional language in specific situations. The French test anticipates responses to linguistic cues (e.g., name: "My name is _____"; birthplace: "I was born in _____"), answers to questions, and functional language use in various conversational situations. The German test incorporates both informal assessment of oral language sampled three weeks before the examination as well as two speech functions (convincing and inviting) taken during the exam day. Writing abilities are assessed through both discrete-item testing (sentences, matching, picture descrip-

TABLE 11.2 Comparison of four language tests according to testing techniques

	Test			
	English	*French*	*German*	*Spanish*
Language area/technique listening				
True/false; Yes/no		X		X
Multiple-choice questions		X	X	
Matching		X	X	X
Answer questions	X		X	X
List information requested			X	
Listening/speaking				
Cued responses		X		
Answer questions		X		
Conversational situations		X	X	
Informal evaluation			X	
Reading				
Yes/no questions				X
Multiple-choice questions		X	X	X
Matching			X	X
List information requested				X
Fill in gaps			X	
Cloze (grammar)	X			
Writing				
Sentences/questions		X		X
Matching				X
Picture description			X	
Letter		X	X	X
Dialogue	X			
Conversational situation	X			
Paragraph	X			

tion) and integrative testing through the use of a letter or paragraph requiring the transmission of particular bits of information.

In terms of achievement tests, they all contain a mixture of formats designed to assess different aspects of language abilities. Although dictation is not included in any of the language exams, it offers the possibility of combining discrete grammar points and vocabulary in sequential, naturalistic discourse. Sentences dictated in a sequence form meaningful paragraph units (a description, a set of directions, a narrative passage), which, in turn, can be used to elicit particular student responses. Students might be asked to respond to the dictated text by answering comprehension questions, choosing an appropriate picture that matches a description, writing answers to a series of questions, and rearranging sentences presented in random order.

Concerns about time, scoring, and coverage of content are some of the practical issues that influence the methods used to test language learning. Deciding what to test and how to test it is not always an easy matter for the professional item writer or the classroom teacher. Omaggio (1983, pp. 80–82) offers a specific set of guidelines for designing test items that place linguistic elements and vocabulary in the context of language skill areas and text types. The steps are useful for the preparation of short quizzes, unit tests, and semester exams:

Step 1　Make an inventory of the material to be tested, listing the major grammatical features, vocabulary or lexical items, and cultural content to be examined on the test.

Step 2　Determine which language skill areas need to be emphasized on the test or quiz, choosing some of the formats noted above and also reported in Table 11.1 and Table 11.2.

Step 3　Prepare a testing grid in which the grammatical, lexical, and cultural content are listed (Step 1) in relation to the appropriate language skill areas and formats that need to be emphasized (Step 2) on this test.

Step 4　Create a context (a story, dialogue, or paragraph) that includes the features to be examined within each language skill area (Step 3). Reading passages, authentic materials, dialogues from the class, textbooks, and supplementary language books might all be consulted as possible models or used as edited versions.

Step 5　Establish a scoring system that will assign points for such aspects as grammatical accuracy, comprehension of meaning, communicative uses of languages, and appropriate word choice.

It might be useful to classify the different types of test items or formats in terms of Omaggio's (1983) framework, presented in Figure 11.1. A test or quiz needs to provide students with the opportunity to use language as sequential, naturalistic discourse. Discrete units of language (e.g., vocabulary items, grammatical features) are easier to test, but communicative tasks that allow for divergent answers engage students more in the testing process. The seven principles offered by Magnan (1985b) and noted previously may prove useful for establishing a systematic testing sequence. Teachers need to examine closely *what* they teach and *how* they test it. After all, communicative language testing is meaningful, and natural to the extent that there is communicative language teaching.

Examples of teacher-made tests are presented in the appendix at the end of this chapter (Figures 11.3–11.6). An elementary-level English test (Figure 11.3) is followed by a French exam (Figure 11.4), a Spanish exam (Figure 11.5), and a German exam (Figure 11.6).

SUMMARY

Language testing in the context of the classroom should be seen in relation to the particular curricular goals. There are many different types of testing techniques teachers can use to assess students' language learning and the extent to which instructional objectives are being accomplished. Language tests are typically classified according to the measurement purpose: proficiency, diagnosis, and achievement. Language abilities can be tested on the basis of discrete and/or integrative methods, linguistic and/or communicative competence, language modalities, and aspects of communicative competence. Communicative competence can be characterized in terms of various systems of knowledge and skills: grammatical, sociolinguistic, discourse, strategic, textual, and pragmatic. Some of the distinctions that are made with respect to communicative language testing point to the necessity of emphasizing the actual uses of language in specific cultural situations such as listening to a radio announcement, reading a newspaper to find out more about local events, and writing a personal letter to a friend.

There are numerous formats and tasks teachers can use to construct test items in the four language skill areas. Testing considerations need to take into account the language focus and subjective and objective methods for assessing different linguistic abilities and skills. Testing speaking skills represents a number of challenges involving the choice of methods, appropriate language samples, and scoring procedures. Magnan suggests the development of a multisequence testing plan, and Omaggio offers a useful framework for preparing test items. Specific tests in English, French, German, and Spanish illustrate the range of techniques used by classroom teachers in assessing student achievement in listening, speaking, reading, and writing. Many of the test items emphasize the assessment of language in context and the use of authentic materials.

ACTIVITIES

1. Obtain copies of tests prepared by language teachers and note what formats and procedures are used to assess different aspects of language proficiency.
2. What is your definition of communicative competence, given the various meanings associated with the concept?

3. Consider Canale's characterization of the four components of communicative proficiency. Suggest different test formats for assessing each component. Compare your results with those of other students.
4. Prepare a set of communicative test items that could be tested with a discrete-point approach, along the lines proposed by Morrow.
5. What are some of the problems associated with communicative testing on the basis of actual language use in real-life settings?
6. Prepare sample test items for a particular group of learners according to Omaggio's scheme, which includes convergent/divergent responses and single-sentence versus sequential-discourse considerations.
7. Review the test formats recommended for listening, speaking, reading, and writing abilities. Which formats are most appropriate for different proficiency levels?
8. What are some of the difficulties related to the assessment of oral language proficiency? What recommendations would you offer a beginning language teacher?
9. Review Magnan's multisequence evaluation plan and discuss it with a teacher. What are some of the problems that would be encountered in establishing such a testing plan?
10. With the help of other students, prepare a final exam using as models the English, French, German, and Spanish exams prepared by classroom teachers (Figures 11.3–11.6). What testing issues did the group consider in deciding *what* to test and *how* to test it?
11. Interview two second language learners and score the speech sample according to the FSI scale. What are some of the problems associated with using this type of scoring system?
12. Review a test prepared for a specific language classroom and classify the items according to Spratt's framework. Then classify the items according to Omaggio's scheme. What changes would you propose to make the test more communicative?

REFERENCES

American Council on the Teaching of Foreign Languages (ACTFL). (1986). *ACTFL provisional proficiency guidelines.* Hastings-on-Hudson, NY: ACTFL Materials Center.
Austin, J. (1962). *How to do things with words.* Oxford, England: Oxford University Press.
Bachman, L. F. (1990). *Fundamental considerations in language testing.* Oxford, England: Oxford University Press.
Benger, D., Schumer, V., & Horowitz, S. (1989). Examples of items from the Spanish 8 final exam. In A. G. Ramírez (Ed.), *From ideas to action: An agenda for the '90s* (pp. 106–115). Schenectady, NY: New York State Association of Foreign Language Teachers.
Canale, M. (1983). From communicative competence to communicative language pedagogy. In J. Richard & R. Schmidt (Eds.), *Language and communication* (pp. 2–28). New York: Longman.
Canale, M. (1984). A communicative approach to language proficiency assessment in a minority setting. In C. Rivera (Ed.), *Communicative competence approaches to language proficiency assessment: Research and application* (pp. 107–122). Avon, England: Multilingual Matters.
Canale, M., & Swain, M. (1980). Theoretical bases of communicative approaches to second language teaching and testing. *Applied Linguistics, 1*(2), 1–47.
Carrigan, A., & Upshur, I. A. (1978). *Test method and linguistic factors in foreign language tests.* Paper presented at the TESOL Convention, Mexico City.

Dangerfield, L. (1985). An elementary level achievement test. In A. Mathews, M. Spratt, & L. Dangerfield (Eds.), *At the chalkface: Practical techniques for language teaching* (pp. 164-168). London: Edward Arnold.

Davies, A. (1978). Language testing. *Language Teaching and Linguistics Abstracts, 11*, 145-159, 215-231.

Faerch, C., Haastrup, K., & Phillipson, R. (1984). *Learner language and language learning.* Copenhagen: Gyldendals Sprogbibliotek.

Finocchiaro, M., & Brumfit, C. (1983). *The functional-notional approach: From theory to practice.* Oxford, England: Oxford University Press.

Flavell, J. H., Botkin, P. T., Fry, C. L., Wright, J. W., & Jarvis, P. E. (1968). *The development of role taking and communication skills in children.* New York: John Wiley.

Gaudiani, C. (1981). Teaching writing in the FL curriculum. (*Language in Education Series: Theory and Practice, 43.*) Washington, DC: Center for Applied Linguistics.

Hartzell, R. (1989). Examples of items from the German intermediate 2 final exam. In A. G. Ramírez (Ed.), *From ideas to action: An agenda for the '90s* (pp. 116-123). Schenectady, NY: New York State Association of Foreign Language Teachers.

Higgs, T., & Clifford, R. T. (1982). The rush toward communication. In C. James (Ed.), *Curriculum, competence, and the foreign language teacher.* (ACTFL foreign language education series, Vol. 13, pp. 57-59.) Lincolnwood, IL: National Textbook.

Hughes, A. (1989). *Testing for language teachers.* Cambridge, England: Cambridge University Press.

Hurley, M., McHugh, W., & Tallis, S. (1989). Examples of items from the French 7 final exam. In A. G. Ramírez (Ed.), *From ideas to action: An agenda for the '90s* (pp. 99-105). Schenectady, NY: New York State Association of Foreign Language Teachers.

Hymes, D. (1971). Competence and performance in linguistic theory. In B. Huxley & E. Ingram (Eds.), *Language acquisition: Models and methods* (pp. 3-28). New York: Academic Press.

Larson, J. W., & Jones, R. L. (1984). Proficiency testing for the other language modalities. In T. V. Higgs (Ed.), *Teaching for proficiency: The organizing principle.* (ACTFL foreign language education series, pp. 113-138.) Lincolnwood, IL: National Textbook.

Legaretta, D. (1979). The effects of program models on language acquisition by Spanish speaking children. *TESOL Quarterly, 13*, 521-534.

Lowe, P., Jr. (1985). The ILR proficiency scale as a synthesizing research principle. The view from the mountain. In C. J. James (Ed.), *Foreign language proficiency in the classroom and beyond.* (ACTFL foreign language education series, pp. 9-53.) Lincolnwood, IL: National Textbook.

Magnan, S. S. (1985a). Teaching and testing proficiency in writing: Skills to transcend the second-language classroom. In A. C. Omaggio (Ed.), *Proficiency, curriculum, articulation: The ties that bind* (pp. 109-136). Middlebury, VT: Northeast Conference on the Teaching of Foreign Languages.

Magnan, S. S. (1985b). From achievement toward proficiency through multisequence evaluation. In C. J. James (Ed.), *Foreign language proficiency in the classroom and beyond.* (ACTFL foreign language education series, pp. 117-145.) Lincolnwood, IL: National Textbook.

Morrow, K. E. (1977). *Techniques of evaluation for a notional syllabus.* Reading, England: University of Reading, Center for Applied Studies.

Oller, J. W., Jr. (1979). *Language tests at school: A pragmatic approach.* London: Longman.

Omaggio, A. C. (1983). *Proficiency-oriented classroom testing.* (Language in education: Theory and practice, 52). Washington, DC: Center for Applied Linguistics.

Omaggio, A. C. (1984). The proficiency-oriented classroom. In T. V. Higgs (Ed.), *Teaching for proficiency: The organizing principle.* (ACTFL foreign language education series, pp. 43-84.) Lincolnwood, IL: National Textbook.

Omaggio, A. C. (1986). *Teaching language in context.* Boston, MA: Heinle & Heinle.

Palmer, A. (1979). Compartmentalized and integrated control: An assessment of some evidence for two kinds of competence and implications for the classroom. *Language Learning, 29,* 169-180.

Ramírez, A. G. (1984). Pupil characteristics and performance on linguistic and communicative language measures. In C. Rivera (Ed.), *Communicative competence approaches to language proficiency assessment: Research and application* (pp. 82-106). Clevedon, England: Multilingal Matters.

Ramírez, A. G. (1986). Language learning strategies used by adolescents studying French in New York schools. *Foreign Language Annals, 19*(2), 131-141.

Searle, J. (1969). *Speech acts.* Cambridge, England: Cambridge University Press.

Shuy, R. W. (1979). On the relevance of recent developments in sociolinguistics: The study of language learning and early education. *NABE Journal, 4,* 51-72.

Spratt, M. (1985). Achievement tests: Aims, content, and some testing techniques. In A. Matthews, M. Spratt, & L. Dangerfield (Eds.), *At the chalkface: Practical techniques for language teaching* (pp. 145-148). London: Edward Arnold.

Stevenson, D. K. (1979). *Beyond faith and face validity: The multitrait-multimethod matrix and the convergent and discriminant validity of oral proficiency tests.* Paper presented at the TESOL Convention, Boston.

Underhill, N. (1987). *Testing spoken language: A handbook of oral testing techniques.* Cambridge, England: Cambridge University Press.

Weimann, J. W., & Backlaund, P. (1980). Current theory and research in communicative competence. *Review of Educational Research, 50,* 185-200.

appendix: Sample Achievement Tests

Test

Part 1

Listening comprehension[1]　　　　　　　　*(20 marks: 10 mins*[2])

(a) You are going to listen to someone interviewing three people about their holidays.
(b) You will only hear the interviews twice.
(c) Look at your listening comprehension answer paper and, when listening, write in the appropriate information to complete the table. Usually only one or two words are necessary for each answer.

Listening comprehension answer paper

Question	Interview 1	Interview 2	Interview 3
Where?	Greece	Italy	Scotland
When?	1.	5.	Late July
How long?	2.	6.	1 ½ weeks
Accommodation	3.	Hotels/camping	9.
Method of travel	4.	7.	10.
Weather	Sunshine/ some rain	8.	Fine/some rain

Part 2

Grammar[3]　　　　　　　　*(30 marks: 15 mins)*

On your answer papers write the correct form of the verbs in brackets.

Example:　John ____(1)____ (like) coffee but he ____(2)____ not, like) tea.
Answers:　(1) likes　(2) doesn't like

　　Sue is on holiday in London and, after a few days, she goes to see a friend called Steve.

Sue:　Hello, Steve.
Steve:　Hello, Sue. Come in. I ____(1)____ (not, see) you for ages.

(continued)

FIGURE 11.3　An elementary level achievement test

SOURCE: From "An Elementary Level Achievement Test" by Les Dangerfield, in A. Matthews, M. Spratt, and L. Dangerfield (Eds.), *At the Chalkface: Practical Techniques in Language Teaching* (pp. 164–168) 1985, Andover, England: Thomas Nelson Publishing Services. Reprinted with permission.

329

Sue: Yes, right. I ____(2)____ (not, be) in London recently.

Steve: Well, what ____(3)____ (you, do) since you came here?

Sue: Erm, well, not a lot. On Monday, I ____(4)____ (go) to the Turner exhibition at the Royal Academy and on Tuesday I ____(5)____ (spend) the day with an aunt of mine.

Steve: ____(6)____ (you, like) the exhibition?

Sue: Yes, it was very impressive. ____(7)____ (you, see) it yet?

Steve: Yes, I ____(8)____ (see) it last week. Look, what ____(9)____ (you, do) this evening?

Sue: I ____(10)____ (not, plan) anything.

Steve: ____(11)____ (you, like) to go and see the Razor Blades in concert at the Roundhouse?

Sue: I ____(12)____ (never, hear) their music before. What are they like?

Steve: They're a new punk group. The pianist ____(13)____ (play) the piano with his toes and they ____(14)____ (play) their new song tonight. It's called 'I can't bear you'.

Sue: Well, actually, I ____(15)____ (not, like) punk music very much.

Steve: Oh, well, what about a meal then? . . .

Part 3   **Dialogue*⁴**   *(15 marks: 10 mins)*

Tom and Margaret are friends; they are trying to decide what to do this evening. Write their conversation, using the following guide.

Tom   *Margaret*

1. Ask for a suggestion

2. Suggest going to the cinema

3. Ask about the film

4. Give information about the film

5. Say no and give a reason

6. Suggest an alternative

7. Agree

8. Suggest a time and a place to meet

9. Agree and finish the conversation

Example: 1. Tom: What shall we do this evening?

Now you complete the dialogue.

Part 4   **Situations*⁵**   *(15 marks 10 mins)*

Write what you would say in the following situations.

Example: You are spending an evening with some friends. What do you say when you want to leave?

Answer: I'm sorry, but I must go now.

1. You don't know the word 'spiteful'. What do you ask your teacher?

2. What do you say when you introduce two friends to each other?

FIGURE 11.3 (continued)

3. You are going to have a birthday party. Invite a friend.
4. A friend is visiting you. You want to offer her a drink. What do you say?
5. You are on a train. You can't lift your suitcase into the luggage rack. How do you ask a stranger in the compartment to help you?

Part 5   **Writing***6   (20 marks: 15 mins)

Write three paragraphs for a tourist brochure about Oxford House using the following information.

Paragraph 1

Name	Oxford House
Type of building	a large country house
Location	near Reading (west of London)
Age	280 years

Paragraph 2

Number of floors	two
Ground floor	a museum of 18th century ceramics
First floor	a private house – seven bedrooms and two living rooms
Outside	large gardens, a farm, a lake

Paragraph 3 (the history of Oxford House)

1720-1800	the Edgerton family home
1800-1920	the Brown family home
1829→	the Richards family home
1955→	a ceramics museum on the ground floor
1990	an extension to the museum

.

Tapescript for Part 1, Listening Comprehension

Int = interviewer
A = first interviewee
B = second interviewee
C = third interviewee

Interview 1

Int: Excuse me, sir, I'm doing a survey about people's holidays. (Um) Do you mind if I ask you a few questions?
A: Not at all.
Int: Um. Have you had a holiday this year?

(continued)

A: Er, yes, yes I have.

Int: Where did you go?

A: Well, in actual fact I went to . . . Greece.

Int: Aha. And when did you go there?

A: Erm. It was in May, I think, yes in May.

Int: OK, and how long did you stay?

A: Just for 10 days.

Int: Uh. Where did you stay when you were there?

A: Well, we had a tent and used that most of the time.

Int: Um. And how did you get there?

A: We took a plane from Heathrow to Athens and then went to the coast by bus.

Int: OK. Fine. Erm. Was the weather good?

A: Yes. Most of the time it was brilliant sunshine. It was really lovely. We had a little rain, but not very much.

Int: OK. Good. Thank you very much, sir.

Interview 2

Int: Excuse me. I'm doing a survey about people's holidays. Do you mind if I ask you a few questions?

B: No, of course not.

Int: Have you had a holiday this year?

B: Yes.

Int: Erm. Where did you go?

B: To the north of Italy.

Int: Good. Right and er when did you go there?

B: In the month of . . . in August.

Int: Um. And er how did you get there?

B: I went by train to Milan and then hired a car.

Int: And how long did you stay?

B: Just a month.

Int: OK. When did you . . . Where did you stay when you went?

B: Oh! Lots of different places—hotels and camping most of the time. Er, I think that's . . . I think that's all.

Int: Right. Fine. And what was the weather like when you were there?

B: It was beautiful all the time.

Int: Good. Thank you very much.

B: OK. Bye bye.

Interview 3

Int: Excuse me, I'm doing a survey about people's holidays. Do you mind if I ask you a few questions?

C: Certainly.

Int: Erm. Have you had a holiday this year?

C: Yes, I went to Scotland.

Int: Um. Er. When did you go there?

C: I went there at the end of July.

Int: And how long did you stay?

C: About a week and a half it was, I think.

Int: Erm. How did you get there?

C: Er, car . . . We went by car.

Int: And where did you stay when you were there?

C: You mean what sort of hotel?

Int: Yes.

C: Well . . . stayed in, erm, farmhouses and places like that.

Int: And what was the weather like when you were there? Did you have a good time?

C: Erm. Well, we had some fine days, but it rained a bit, too.

FIGURE 11.3 (continued)

Name of Student _____

	Possible Score	Student's Score
I. LISTENING/SPEAKING		
A. Cues	10	_____
B. Responses	10	_____
C. Situations	10	_____
II. LISTENING COMPREHENSION		
A. Vrai ou Faux	5	_____
B. C'est Logique	5	_____
C. Des Conseils	5	_____
D. Un Ami Québecois	5	_____
E. Horoscopes	5	_____
F. Où est-ce qu'on va?	5	_____
III. WRITING		
A. Shopping List	5	_____
B. Note	5	_____
C. Interview	5	_____
D. Letter	5	_____
IV. READING		
A. Letter	5	_____
B. Projets pour la Semaine	5	_____
C. Advertisements	5	_____
D. Pen Pals	5	_____
	Final Mark	_____

LISTENING COMPREHENSION (30 points)

A. Vrai ou Faux

Directions: For each picture, you will hear a statement in French. If the statement is true according to what you see in the pictures, place a check next to *Vrai.* If the statement is NOT true, check *Faux.*

1. Alain et sa mère sont dans la cuisine où elle prépare les légumes pour le dîner. Ce soir on va avoir des carottes et Alain est content parce qu'il aime les carottes dans sa salade.

2. Marianne invite quelquefois des amis à la maison pour le dîner. Aujourd'hui elle va au supermarché parce qu'elle a besoin de beaucoup de choses. Maintenant elle achète de la viande.

3. Monsieur Lévèque va souvent à la pâtisserie pour acheter des desserts. Cet après-midi le voilà à table où il mange une belle tarte.

4. C'est le 17 juin et c'est le jour du grand march de tennis. Pierre adore les sports et joue bien et après un match il a toujours soif.

5. Sur la table il y a du fromage, de la viande, du lait, des oeufs, du jambon, du poulet, et des fruits.

B. C'EST LOGIQUE

Directions: You are going to hear five situations. Listen carefully to each situation and write the letter of the best answer on your answer sheet.

6. You are in a supermarket. You ask the grocer what kind of vegetables she has.

   You ask: Qu'est-ce que vous avez comme légumes?

   She answers: a. Nous avons un rôti délicieux.
   b. Nous avons des haricots et des pommes de terre.
   c. Nous avons des pommes et des poires.

7. You are in a restaurant and the waiter approaches your table. What could you expect him to say to you?

   a. Quel âge est-ce que vous avez?
   b. Qu'est-ce que vous désirez?
   c. Combien de légumes est-ce qu'il y a au supermarché?

8. It's a hot sunny day and you and your friends are deciding what to do.

   You ask: Qu'est-ce qu'on va faire?

   She answers: a. nager
   b. faire du ski
   c. aller à l'école

9. You are sitting around at a party and friends are talking about how they like to celebrate their birthdays. What could you expect them to say?

   a. Je voudrais aller à un restaurant.
   b. Je voudrais un examen.
   c. Mon frère a 18 ans.

10. While visiting her cousin in Marseille, France, Suzie needs to change some money. She says to her cousin Sophie: Je voudrais aller a la banque.

    Sophies says: a. D'accord. On va à l'école.
    b. C'est impossible. La banque est fermée aujourd'hui.
    c. D'accord. On va au match après l'école.

C. DES CONSEILS

Directions: Jean is asking his sister Annick for advice (conseils). Listen to the statements that Jean makes and decide if the advice is good or bad. If the advise is good, place a check next to *bon* and if it is bad place a check next to *mauvais.*

11. Jean: Je suis fatigué.
    Annick: Alors, reste à la maison.

(continued)

FIGURE 11.4 Examples of items from the French 7 final exam

SOURCES: Portions from *Et Vous?* Achievement Test (pp. 18–19), Austin, TX: Holt Rinehart and Winston, © 1983; reproduced with permission. Portions from Hurley, McHugh, and Tallis (1988).

12. Jean: Je voudrais regarder un programme à la télévision.
    Annick: Alors, consulte le téléguide.
13. Jean: J'ai besoin de faire mes devoirs.
    Annick: Alors, va à la bibliothèque après l'école.
14. Jean: J'ai très faim maintenant.
    Annick: Alors, va regarder dans le frigo.
15. Jean: Je voudrais voyager en France cet été.
    Annick: Alors, étudie l'anglais.

D. UN AMI QUÉBECOIS

Directions: A friend of yours has received the first cassette from his pen pal in Québec. He wants you to listen to it to make sure he has the right information. Listen carefully and put a check next to *Oui* if your friend has understood and a check next to *non* if he has not.

The students hear:

Bonjour! Je m'appelle Jean-Claude Duval. J'habite à Montréal avec ma famille. J'aime beaucoup les sports. Je travaille beaucoup à l'école mais j'adore les vacances et les week-ends à l montagne. J'y vais souvent avec mon père et mes deux frères pour faire du camping. A l'école j'étudie beaucoup. J'aime bien les sciences, mais je déteste mon professeur de sciences parce qu'il est sévère et embêtant.

16. His name is Jean-Claude.
17. He lives in Trois Rivières.
18. He is studying classical music.
19. He likes to go camping.
20. He likes science but not the teacher.

E. HOROSCOPES

Directions: A group of teenagers are visiting Madame Bonne Chance, a fortune teller at the carnival. She sees each one privately and tells them their horoscope for the week. Listen carefully and put a check next to *Oui* if each one has understood and a check next to *Non* for those who have not.

21. Bernard: Tu es très intelligent et sympa. Tu vas avoir une semaine difficile à l'école, mais tu vas passer un week-end formidable chez des copains.
    Bernard says: Je vais aller passer le week-end chez mes grands-parents.
22. Gilbert: Tu es très généreux et tu as beaucoup de patience. Jeudi va être ton jour de chance.
    Gilbert says: Jeudi, c'est mon jour de chance.

LISTENING COMPREHENSION (30 points)
A. VRAI OU FAUX

Directions: For each picture, you will hear a statement in French. If the statement is true according to what you see in the picture, place a check next to *Vrai*. If the statement is NOT true, check *Faux*.

1. _____ Vrai _____ Faux

3. _____ Vrai _____ Faux

4. _____ Vrai _____ Faux

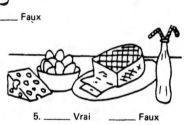

2. _____ Vrai _____ Faux

5. _____ Vrai _____ Faux

FIGURE 11.4 (continued)

334

B. C'EST LOGIQUE

Directions: You are going to hear five situations. Listen carefully to each situation and write the letter of the best answer on your answer sheet.

6. _____ A   7. _____ A   8. _____ A   9. _____ A   10. _____ A
_____ B   _____ B   _____ B   _____ B   _____ B
_____ C   _____ C   _____ C   _____ C   _____ C

C. DES CONSEILS

Directions: Jean is asking his sister Annick for advice (*conseils*). Listen to the statements that Jean makes and decide if the advice is good or bad. If the advice is good, place a check next to *bon* and if it is bad place a check next to *mauvais*.

11. _____ bon   12. _____ bon   13. _____ bon   14. _____ bon   15. _____ bon
_____ mauvais   _____ mauvais   _____ mauvais   _____ mauvais   _____ mauvais

D. UN AMI QUEBECOIS

Directions: A friend of yours has received the first cassette from his pen pal in Québec. He wants you to listen to it to make sure that he has the right information. Listen carefully and put a check next to *Oui* if your friend has understood and a check next to *Non* if he has not.

16. _____ Oui   17. _____ Oui   18. _____ Oui   19. _____ Oui   20. _____ Oui
_____ Non   _____ Non   _____ Non   _____ Non   _____ Non

E. HOROSCOPES

Directions: A group of teenagers are visiting Madame Bonne Chance, a fortune teller at the carnival. She sees each one privately and tells them their horoscope for the week. Listen carefully and put a check next to *Oui* if each one has understood and a check next to *Non* for those who have not.

21. _____ Oui   22. _____ Oui   23. _____ Oui   24. _____ Oui   25. _____ Oui
_____ Non   _____ Non   _____ Non   _____ Non   _____ Non

F. OU EST-CE QU'ON VA?

Directions: You are going to hear about five situations which require participants to go to a particular place in the town. Listen to each situation and identify the place in town where the people must go by writing the number of that place in the space on your answer sheet.

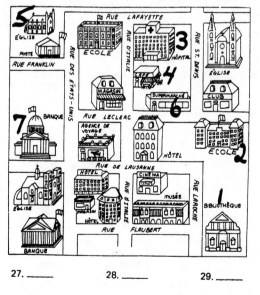

26. _____   27. _____   28. _____   29. _____   30. _____

(continued)

23. Chantal: Tu as beaucoup de charme et de patience. La semaine ne va pas être facile. Tes parents vont être très sévères et tes copains vont être embêtrants.

Chantal says: Je vais avoir beaucoup de problèmes.

24. Corinne: Tu aimes le théâtre et tu es toujours dynamique et très énergique. Mais attention! Ton énergie risque de fatiguer tout le monde.

Corinne says: Je suis très fatiguée et pas très énergique.

25. Christian: Tu es très logique et pratique. Tu vas avoir une excellente semaine! Tu vas aider un de tes copains dans une situation difficile.

Christian says: Je vais aider un ami avec des problèmes.

F. OÙ EST-CE QU'ON VA?

Directions: You are going to hear about five situations which require the participants to go to a particular place in the town. Listen to each situation and identify the place in town where the people must go by writing the number next to the place in the space on your answer sheet.

26. La grand-mère de Pierre est très malade et il voudrait la visiter. Où est-ce qu'il va?

27. Marc a besoin d'argent pour acheter une voiture de sport. Où est-ce qu'il va?

28. Marie et ses amies ont très faim et elles voudraient manger des sandwiches et peut-être des desserts. Où est-ce qu'elles vont?

29. Michel et sa famille vont faire un pique-nique à la campagne. Ils ont besoin de pain, de fromage, et de fruits. Où est-ce qu'ils vont?

30. Jeannette et Gigi sont des étudiantes très sérieuses et elles aiment étudier. Après l'école elles vont faire leurs devoirs pour la classe d'histoire. Où est-ce qu'elles vont?

WRITING (20 points)

A. You and your friend are planning a picnic. Make a shopping list of ten (10) food items that you want to bring.

_____

_____

B. You are passing notes in class talking about the teacher, the subject and the class. You do not want the teacher to understand what you are saying if the note is taken away. Write five (5) sentences in French telling what you think about the class.

_____

_____

C. You are working for the school newspaper and have been assigned to interview a French exchange student. In preparation for the interview, write down five (5) questions that you intend to ask.

_____

_____

D. Choose either Task 1 or Task 2. (You do not have to do both!!)

Task 1: You are writing a letter to a French pen pal. Talk about yourself, your family, your school, places you like to go, etc.

Task 2: Write to a pen pal telling five (5) things you plan to do this summer.

_____

_____

READING (20 points)

A. LETTER

Directions: Imagine that your friend, Corker, has received the letter shown below from a student in France. The problem is that Corker does not understand French, so he comes to you for help. Read the letter and then answer his questions (in English).

FIGURE 11.4 (continued)

Cher Corker,

    Je m'appelle Christine Tremoulet. J'ai quinze ans. Mon papa s'appelle Henri Tremoulet. Il a trente-huit ans. Ma mère s'appelle Suzy et elle a trente-six ans. Mon frère s'appelle Bernard. Il a douze ans. Il est très stupide. J'ai aussi une petite soeur qui s'appelle Marie-Claire.

    Nous habitons à Molignac, un petit village dans le sud-ouest de la France. C'est très joli!

    Qu'est-ce que tu aimes faire? J'aime danser et j'aime nager et j'aime faire des photos.

    Mon papa aime travailler à la maison les week-ends et ma mère aime prèparer de bons repas à la maison. Bernard aime faire du vélo et il aime jouer au football avec ses copains.

    Ecris-moi une petite lettre bientôt, s'il te plaît!

                    Ton amie française,

                        Christine

1. How old is Christine? _____
2. What are her parents' names? _____
3. Who is Marie-Claire? _____

4. Where do Christine and her family live? _____
5. What kinds of things does Christine like to do? ____
_____

B.   PROJETS POUR LA SEMAINE

    Directions: You and your friends are spending a week with families in Trois Rivières, Québec, and going to school with children. Before you arrived your host family set up a schedule of activities for the week. One of your friends calls you to find out what *you* are doing that week. (Answer the questions in English).

LUNDI	MARDI	MERCREDI	JEUDI	VENDREDI	SAMEDI	DIMANCHE
matin						
aller al' école	aller à l'école ètudier avec Marie	aller à l'hôpital faire un examen	aller à l'école faire du ski	aller à l'école étudier dans la bibliothèque	rester à la maison regarder la télé	aller à l'église
après-midi						
aller chez Marie jouer	rester après l'école jouer au football	étudier pour un examen aller au café	aller au parc travailler pour la mère de Marie	rester à la maison	jouer dans le parc	manger le déjeuner chez Alain
soir						
étudier	rester à la maison écouter la radio	aller au théâtre	aller chez des amis	aller au restaurant	aller au cinéma	

(continued)

1. Are you going to school every day that week (except for the weekend, or course)? _____
   _____

2. Are you and your host family going out for dinner? When? _____
   _____

3. When are you going to stay at home? _____

4. What are you doing Thursday afternoon? _____

5. They want you to go to the park with them on Saturday afternoon. Will you be able to do that?_____
   _____

C. ADVERTISEMENTS

Directions: You are spending a few days in Paris and are looking in the newspaper for something to do in the evening. Look at the advertisements and answer the following questions (in English).

cinéma dans la région

COUTAINVILLE
• LE DRAKKAR 2 •

Samedi 8 mai à 21 h 15
Dimanche 9 mai
à 15 h et 21 h 15
EN EXCLUSIVITÉ

LE CHEF D'ŒUVRE
DU CINÉMA COMIQUE

**JOUR
de FÊTE**

UN FILM DE
JACQUES TATI

concerts

Orchestre de Paris, dir. D. *Barenboim.* Samedi 26 février. 10h. *Maison de la Radio.* Entrée libre.

jazz pop folk rock

Pink Floyd, pop. Jeudi 3 mars. 20h.30. *Olympia.* Places: 25F. Jeunes: 15F.
Rock. Samedi 5 mars. 18.30. *Théâtre Fontaine.* Places: 20F et 15F.

1. When can you see a concert of classical music?
   _____

2. If you want to see Pink Floyd, how much will you have to pay to get in?
   _____

3. Where would you go to see a film?
   _____

4. Who is the producer of that film?
   _____

5. Where is the rock concert being held?
   _____

FIGURE II.4 (continued)

D. PEN PALS

Directions: Here are three letters taken from a teen magazine in which three teenagers who are looking for pen pals describe themselves. You are to choose the one with whom you would like to correspond and, in English, give 3 specific reasons why. Then you are to choose the one with whom you would NOT like to correspond and give 2 specific reasons why not.

Carstairs
le 17 juin

Salut!

Je m'appelle Lee Darren Keddie et j'habite à Carstairs. C'est une ville au Canada. Mon anniversaire, c'est le 5 janvier. J'ai quatorze ans. J'aime les sports, la musique, et les week-ends. Je n'aime pas l'école, mon frère Etienne, le groupe Police. Mon sport préféré, c'est le hockey, mais j'aime aussi le tennis et le ski. A l'école je n'aime pas les sciences parce que c'est difficile. J'aime manger, et je suis toujours content quand nos allons au restaurant pour un bon dîner.

Au revoir,
Lee

7 place Gaston-Paillhou
Tours 45678
France

Bonjour!

Je m'appelle Marie-Hélène Bergerault. J'habite 7 place Gaston-Paillhou à Tours en France. J'ai 13 ans. Mon anniversaire est le 2 avril, et mon signe du zodiaque est Bélier. J'ai un frère, Pascal, et une soeur qui s'appelle Emmanuelle. Les week-ends j'aime préparer les repas avec mon père. Nous mangeons des pâtisseries et des glaces.

Je déteste les sports, les films d'horreur et les examens. Mon chanteur préféré est Michael Jackson, le chanteur américain. J'aime beaucoup parler au téléphone avec mon amie et danser à la discothèque.

Au revoir,
Marie-Hélène

5 avenue Saint-Michel
Paris 25890
France

Mon cher ami,

Salut! Je m'appelle Christian Bailleul. J'habite 5 avenue Saint-Michel à Paris. J'ai 15 ans. Mon anniversaire est le 24 october. Je suis très grand pour mon âge.

Je déteste ma famille. Mes frères, mes soeurs, et mes parents sont tous embêtants, et ma grand-mère aussi! Je n'aime pas les sports. J'ai une guitare, mais je déteste la musique et je déteste chanter. Je ne vais jamais au cinéma avec mes amis parce que je n'ai pas d'amis. Mes classes ne sont pas intéressantes et je n'aime pas étudier.

J'aime manger mais pas le déjeuner à l'ecole où il y a toujours des carottes et des épinards. Pouah!!!!

Au revoir!
Christian

1. Tell which one of the three teenagers you would like to correspond with and give specific reasons why.

_____

_____

2. Tell which one of the three teenagers you would NOT like to have as a pen pal and give 2 specific reasons why.

_____

_____

WRITING

1. You are shopping for the Mexican family that you are living with. for the summer. Here are the items needed and a map to help you. Make a list of the stores you will be going to.

   Match item with store number depicted in a shopping map of the city illustrated.

   queso _____
   dulces _____
   helado _____
   aretes y anillos _____
   sandalias _____
   panecillos _____
   pollo _____
   aspirina _____
   pasteles _____
   dinero _____

2. Una Carta

   Choose one of the following topics and write a letter to a Spanish pen-pal.

   a) You have been corresponding with a Spanish teenager, and are comparing the differences in your daily routines. Write a letter describing a typical day in New York. Tell what time you get up, shower, get dressed, eat breakfast and leave for school. Mention the subjects you study and the length of your school day. Describe some after school activities. Tell when you eat dinner, study, do your homework, relax and go to bed.

   b) You are going to visit your Spanish pen-pal in Madrid this summer. Write a letter about your impending visit. Tell what means of transportation you plan on using, when you expect to arrive and how long you plan on staying. Tell your friend what you would like to do when you get there, what sports you know how to do well and would like to participate in. Ask your friend what the weather is like in the summer, what clothing you will need and what sports equipment you should bring.

   _____
   _____

3. Buen Viaje

   You are taking your family on a trip to Cancún, México, and must make a checklist since you have to pack for your three children, ages 7, 12, and 18. For your checklist, be sure to include: 1) a travel document, 2) clothing needed for a warm weather climate, 3) medication and cosmetics, 4) sports equipment. Include at least one item from each category for a total of ten items.

   1. _____
   2. _____
   3. _____
   4. _____
   5. _____
   6. _____
   7. _____
   8. _____
   9. _____
   10. _____

4. You are planning a trip to Acapulco and want to rent a villa. Write a letter to a real estate agent and describe the type of accommodations you want. Be sure to include location, proximity to town, number of rooms, facilities and price range. You may use the symbols below to help you decide what your priorities are.

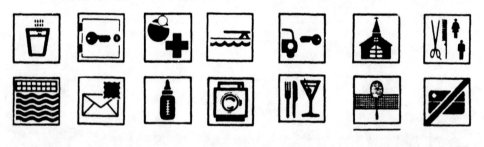

FIGURE 11.5 Examples of items from the Spanish 8 final exam

SOURCES: Pictures 1, 2, 3, and 5 on page 341 from *Practical Vocabulary Builder* (p. 12), Lincolnwood, IL: National Textbook, 1982; used with permission. Portions from *Y Tu?* Achievement Test (p. 21), Austin, TX: Holt Rinehart and Winston, © 1983; reproduced with permission. From *In Spain Workbook* (p. 17), 1987; reproduced with permission of Chancerel International, London, England. From *Mucho Gusto Workbook* (p. 87), St. Paul, MN: EMC Publishing, 1988; reproduced with permission. From Benger, Schumer, and Horowitz (1988).

Listening: Mark your answers for this section on the Scantron sheet.

Ir de compras:

A. While out shopping you overhear various people making comments. Listen to each of the following statements (A, B, C, D, E) and write the letter next to the scene in which the comment would probably have been spoken.

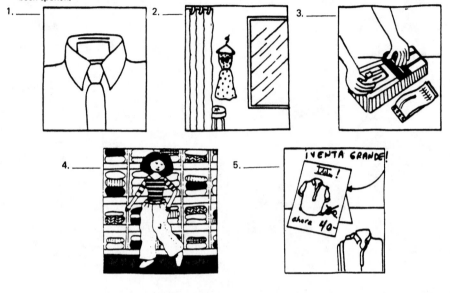

1. _____ 2. _____ 3. _____

4. _____ 5. _____

B. Flight Announcement — 6-10
   Listen to the following flight announcement and respond with Sí or No.

LISTENING (10 points) Preguntas Span. Beg. 2 6/88

C. 11. How much time does your friend spend in Mexico?
   a) 5 days   b) one week   c) 2 weeks

12. How did your friend travel to Mexico?
   a) by bus   b) by plane   c) by boat

13. How does Richard usually spend his mornings in Mexico?
   a) sleeping late   b) swimming or sight-seeing   c) shopping

14. Which activity *doesn't* Richard do at the beach?
   a) play volleyball   b) sunbathe   c) take walks

15. Each evening Richard has dinner
   a) at the hotel   b) at the same restaurant   c) at a different restaurant

16. What kind of collection does Richard have?
   a) postcards   b) hats   c) silver trinkets

17. Who is Elena?
   a) a new Mexican friend   b) Richard's mom   c) Richard's sister

(continued)

18. What does Elena like to do?
    a) shop for clothes   b) collect jewelery   c) write postcards

19. When Richard leaves Acapulco, where is he going next?
    a) to a hotel near the ocean   b) home   c) to a famous department store

20. How is the family traveling once they leave Acapulco?
    a) by plane   b) by bus   c) by boat

D. Asking for directions/Pidiendo direcciones:

You need directions to various places. Using the map provided listen to the directions given and choose the appropriate destination.

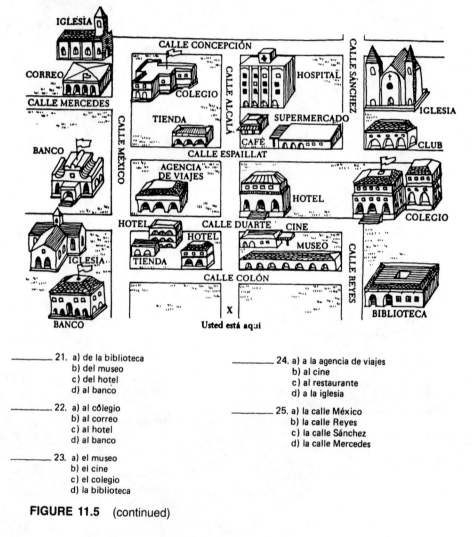

21. a) de la biblioteca
    b) del museo
    c) del hotel
    d) al banco

22. a) al cōlegio
    b) al correo
    c) al hotel
    d) al banco

23. a) el museo
    b) el cine
    c) el colegio
    d) la biblioteca

24. a) a la agencia de viajes
    b) al cine
    c) al restaurante
    d) a la iglesia

25. a) la calle México
    b) la calle Reyes
    c) la calle Sánchez
    d) la calle Mercedes

FIGURE 11.5   (continued)

E. Un Raton En La Casa (26-35)

Listen to the following story and follow the path of Pepe, a mouse that entered this house. You will then hear ten statements in English based on Pepe's tour of the house. Answer Sí (a) or No (b)

(continued)

READING

A. En el almacén:

As Ben entered the Corte Ingles in Madrid to do some shopping he found the following shopping directory. Look at the guide and complete Ben's list that will remind him which floor each department is on.

Planta	Departamento
7	Oportunidades, Cafetería, Restaurante, Buffet, Mesón
6	MUEBLES Y DECORACIÓN Dormitorios, Salones, Alfombras nacionales-orientales. Lámparas. Textiles del hogar
5	JUVENTUD Y DEPORTES: Confección joven El, confección joven Ella, Boutiques femeninas, Boutique masculino DEPORTES: Golf, Tenis, Caza, Pesca, Montaña
4	CONFECCIÓN SEÑORAS: Boutiques: Balenciaga, Dior, Balmain. Complementos, Zapatería Peluquería
3	CONFECCIÓN CABALLEROS Piel, Artículos viaje, Boutique, Complementos, Zapatería, Peluquería, Agencia de viajes, Cambio de moneda, Oficinas

Bebes: Toda confección para los bebes

Niños/Niñas (4 a 10 años) Confección, Complementos, Boutiques

CHICOS/CHICAS (11 a 14 años): Confección, complementos, Boutiques

JUGUETERÍA ZAPATERÍA: Señoras, Caballeros, joven, niños

1 HOGAR MENAJE: Artesanía, Accesorios Automovil, Cristales, Platería, Regalos, Vajillas, Lladros Cerámica

B COMPLEMENTOS: Bolsos, Cosméticos, Perfumería, Correo, Joyería, Librería, Medias, Papelería, Relojería, Sombreros, Discos, Recuerdos

S1 ALIMENTACIÓN: Supermercado, Licores, Vinos

IMAGEN Y SONIDO: Fotografía, Hi-Fi, Radio, TV, Videos, Video-Club

_____ a) sporting goods
_____ b) books and stationary
_____ c) women's clothes
_____ d) accessories
_____ e) men's clothes

_____ f) furniture
_____ g) toys
_____ h) food
_____ i) children's clothes
_____ J) hi-fi equipment

B.

Juan and Carmen are looking over the following ad in the newspaper trying to decide which film they want to see. Answer the following questions in English.

FIGURE 11.5 (continued)

CARTELERA

CINES

CINE VICTOR

(Aire acondicionado). Atención horario. 5, 30, 8, 15 y a las 10.45. El mayor acontecimiento de la temporada. 6. Nominaciones a los Oscars. «EL IMPERIO DEL SOL» Producida y dirigida por Steven Spielberg. Musica de John Williams. Con la grandiosidad del Sonido Dolby Stereo.Todos los publicos. 6 Nominaciones a los Oscars.

MULTICINES GRECO

(Cuatro salas). Sonido Dolby Stereo. Aire acondicionado. Los ultimos adelantos de Sonido. Butaca. Calidad. Espectacularidad. Cine para toda la familia. Horario: 4.15, 6.30, 8.30 y 10.45. Especial Semana Santa dibujos animados. Una extraordinaria pelicula de Walt Disney. «LOS RESCATADORES» Ultimos dias. Diario 4 tarde. Además. Viernes. sabado domingo. 11.30 de la mañanas y 4.30 tarde.

SALA 1: Una de las mais diverudas y deliciosas comedias. ¡Aplaudida y aclamada triunfalmente en el Mundo! Elegida una de las más fascinantes peliculas nominadas. 6 nomnaciones a los Oscars incluye: Mejor pelicula, mejor director, mejor actri/Cher. Ganadora de 2 Globos de Oro.«HECHIZO DE LUNA (Moonstruck). Con la maravilla del Sonido Dolby

Stereo. Dirigida por Norman Jewison Aclamada. «HECHIZO DE LUNA». Anticipese a los Oscars. «HECHIZO DE LUNA».

SALA 2: La deliciosa y divertida comedia del Invierno 88. Diane Keaton en «BABY TU VALES MUCHO». dirigida por Charles Shyer. ¡Menuda invitada! ¡Quiere quedarse para siempre! Una comedia dinámica y agresiva. Una película muy recomendable. El último gran éxito de Diane Keaton. «BABY TU VALES MUCHO». Una interpretación genial de Diane Keaton. Todos los públicos. Una deliciosa comedia para disfrutar.

SALA 3: Anticipese a los Oscars 87. 4 Nominaciones a los Globos de Oro ¡2° aniversario de Múlticines Greco! Michael Douglas y Glenn Close en «ATRACCION FATAL». Una película de Adrian Lyne. La mejor película de suspenso. Con la grandiosidad del Sonido Dolby Stereo. Seis Nominaciones al Oscar.

SALA 4: Grandioso y espectacular superacontecimiento. Richard Attenborough, laureado director de «Gandhi». Excitante y estremecedora película. «GRITA LIBERTAD». 7 Nominaciones a los Oscars. 7 Nominaciones de la Academia Cinematográfic Británica. Premio de la Asociación Cinematografica Alemana a la mejor película del Festival de Berlín. Panavisión y Sonido Dolby Stereo. Aviso horario: 5.30, 8.15, 10.45.

SALA X

La Rosa. 42.- A las 6.30, 8.30, 10.30 y sábados a las 12.15 noche, estreno de la apsionante y excitante producciónen Technicolor «POR NOGRAFICAMENTE TUYA». V.O. subtitulada. Intérpretes: Tracy Lords y Tanya Lawson. Mayores de 18 años.

MULTICINES OSCAR

Sonido Dolby Stereo. Aire acondicionado. Horario: 4.15, 6.30, 8.30 y 10.45. Especial Semana Santa dibujos animados. La última película de Walt Disney, «BASIL EL RATON SUPERDETECTIVE» . Sesiones diarias, 4 tarde. Viernes, sabados y domingos. 11.30 de la mañana. 4 tarde.

SALA 1: Fenomenal y formidable estreno. El último éxito triunfal de Barbra Streisand, Richard Dreyfus, Karl Malden. Barbra Streisand es «LOCA»«LOCA». Una película de Martin Ritt. Con la maravilla del Sonido Dolby Stereo. Maureen Stapleton-Eli Wallach. El último éxito de Barbra Streisand «LOCA» «LOCA». Barbra Streisand. Galardonada con dos Oscars.

SALA 2: El último éxito de Dudley Moore (Arthur), superdivertida y disparatada locura. Acontecimiento divertidísimo. «DE TAL PALO TAL ASTILLA...TAL PALO».Dudley Moore, Kirk Cameron. Dirigida por Rod Daniel. Con el nuevo sonido Dolby Stereo.

Answer the following questions in English:

1. How many theaters are available at the Multicines Greco complex? _____

2. How many showings are available daily for each of the films there? _____

3./4. Which complexes have special movies showing for children during Holy Week? _____

_____

5. Which theater has a special change of time for one of the films it is showing which is different from the times advertised for the rest of the complex? _____

6. Which movie couldn't they choose because they are underage?_____

7. Does the film "Los rescatadores" start at 4 on a Saturday afternoon? _____

8. Which film is advertised as showing there for its final days? _____

9. How many movies are advertised as comedies? _____

10. Are there special performances on weekends for the films showing in the Multicines? _____

(continued)

C. **Los quehaceres domésticos** (chores)

You are attending a summer school program in Guadalajara, Mexico and staying at a residence in which all student-guests must help with the daily chores. You look at the list of chores for the week to see who has been assigned which task. Look at the picture of what everyone is doing and fill in their names on the duty list.

Sábado

fregar los platos	Paco
poner la mesa	
hacer las camas	
barrer las habitaciones	
limpiar los cristales	
dar de comer al gato	
preparar la comida	
ir de compras	
ir a recoger el correo	
tirar la basura	

FIGURE 11.5 (continued)

JALTUR 85
ORIENTE ESMERALDA
INVIERNO
日本航空
VIAJE CON CREDITO
中国
U.S.D. $3,221.25
19 DIAS VISITANDO TOKIO, HONG KONG, BANGKOK, PEKIN OSAKA-KYOTO SINGAPUR
U.S.D. $2,184.00 VISITANDO JAPON, HONG KONG, MEDIA PENSION JAPON. 14 DIAS, ENERO 26, FEB. 23, MARZO 30.
SALIDAS,
Enero 17, Febrero 14, Marzo 28.

TRAVEL TRAVEL
Tels. 596-54-85 596-54-84 596-82-99
HOUSTON
THE WESTIN OAKS
280.00 USD. SITUADO EN GALERIA
PRECIO: POR PERSONA 2 NOCHES 3 DIAS
INCLUYE: Hospedaje en habitación doble, talonario de descuentos, impuestos hotel.

TRAVEL TRAVEL
Tels. 596-54-85 596-54-84 596-82-99
EN CANADA
SKI
9 DIAS 999.00 Dls.
MONT TREMBLANT (Que Bec)
VISITANDO NUEVA YORK
Tarifa aérea, hospedaje, impuesto del hotel, instrucción de ski a cualquier nivel, lifts durante 5 días.
CONSULTE A SU AGENTE DE VIAJES

MEDIO ORIENTE INCREIBLE

16 fabulosos días por
TIERRA SANTA, EGIPTO Y GRECIA
Sólo $1,999.00 U.S.D.*
Con extensión a
TURQUIA sólo 299.00 U.S.D.*

Consulte a su agente de viajes.
Pague en moneda nacional

Incluye tarifa aérea, hoteles de 1a. clase, traslados, visitas y media pensión.
Salidas todos los días.

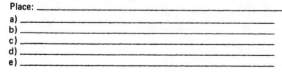

MERIDIANO VIAJES, S. A.

D. **Haciendo un viaje:**

You and your family want to go on vacation and are trying to decide where to go. You open to the travel and leisure section of the newspaper where you see adds to the following places.

Refer to the newspaper advertisement and answer the following questions in *English:*

1. Name the 5 possible travel locations identified in the ads.
   a) _____
   b) _____
   c) _____
   d) _____
   e) _____

2. Pick one of the locations and tell 5 things about each trip such as what the package deal may include, the cost, the length of stay, the departure dates available, etc. State first the vacation ad you choose to describe:

   Place: _____
   a) _____
   b) _____
   c) _____
   d) _____
   e) _____

(continued)

E. Read the following advertisement for Mexicana Airlines and answer the questions.

Bahías de Huatulco

Mexicana pone a su alcance un lugar mágico, lleno de encantos inexplorados, de playas aún vírgenes: Las Bahías de Huatulco.

Descubra la increíble belleza de nueve bahias rodeadas de vegetación . . . ¡casi el paraíso!

Mexicana lo pone en contacto con este paisaje espectacular. Gócelo a partir del 19 de diciembre y compruebe que a través de nuestra ventana ¡todo se ve mejor!

VUELO	FRECUENCIA	SALE DE MEXICO	LLEGA A HUATULCO	SALE DE HUATULCO	LLEGA A GUADALAJARA	SALE DE GUADALAJARA	LLEGA A LOS ANGELES
996	MAR., JUE., SAB.	8:05	9:10	9:40	11:15	11:50	13:00

VUELO	FRECUENCIA	SALE DE LOS ANGELES	LLEGA A GUADALAJARA	SALE DE GUADALAJARA	LLEGA A HUATULCO	SALE DE HUATULCO	LLEGA A MEXICO
997	MAR., JUE., SAB.	9:20	14:10	14:45	16:20	16:50	17:55

Compre con su agente de viajes, no le cuesta más

RESERVACIONES: 6-60-44-44

Asómate a la ventana de *mexicana* primera línea aérea de Latinoamérica

1. ¿A qué hora sale el vuelo de Los Angeles?
2. ¿Cuál es el número del vuelo que sale de México a las ocho y cinco?
3. ¿A qué hora llega vuelo número novecientos noventa y siete en Guadalajara?
4. ¿Puedes viajar los viernes?
5. ¿A qué hora sale el vuelo de México?

LISTENING STATEMENTS

D. Ask for directions

1. Siga derecho. Doble a la izquierda en la calle Colón. Siga una cuadra. Cruza la calle. Estás enfrente _____

2. Siga derecho tres cuadras. Doble a la izquierda en la calle Espaillat. Siga al fin de la cuadra. Doble a la derecha en la calle México y a la izquierda en la calle Mercedes. Llegas _____

3. Siga derecho en la calle Alcalá hasta la calle Duarte. Doble a la derecha. Siga por la calle hasta la calle Reyes. Allí encuentras _____

4. Siga derecho hasta la calle Duarte. Doble a la izquierda. El hotel está Frente _____

5. Siga derecho dos cuadras y doble a la derecha en la calle Espaillat. La próxima calle a la izquierda es _____

A. Ir de compras

a) ¿Qué tarjetas de crédito acepta Ud. aquí?
b) ¿Dónde están las cabinas de probarse? or ¿Me puedo probar este vestido?
c) Estos pantalones no me quedan bien.
d) Me gusta ir de compras aquí. ¡Hay muchas gangas!
e) Necesito talla cuarenta y uno en una camisa.

FIGURE 11.5 (continued)

B. Airline Announcement

Señores pasajeros, su atención, por favor. Aerolinea Aeroméxico anuncia la salida del vuelo cuatrocientos diez y seis de Cancún con destino a Nueva York. Tenga la bondad de ir a la puerta número tres a las quince y diez. El vuelo va a salir a las quince y media, y va a llegar en Nueva York a las veinte y uno menos cuarto. Pasajeros con niños o algún problema especial pueden abordar. por la puerta número tres ahora. Gracias. Aerolinea Aeromexico les desea un feliz viaje.

Sí o No

1. The flight will be leaving from Cancún at 5:30.
2. Passengers with small children or special needs may board first.
3. The flight number is 416.
4. Passengers must go to gate number 13.
5. Passengers may start boarding at 3:10.

C. Listening (10 points)

You receive a tape from your friend who is on vacation in Mexico. Listen to what your friend has to say.

Querido amigo,

Estoy aquí con mi familia en la ciudad de Acapulco. El avión llegó por la noche. Voy a pasar quince días de vacaciones en el Hotel Krystal. Hay muchas actividades aquí y todas son muy emocionantes.

Por a mañana juego al tenis con mi nuevo amigo, Miguel. Es mexicano y está aquí también para las vacaciones.

Por la tarde nado o visito a los puntos de interés. A veces voy a la piscina del hotel. Algunas veces mi familia y yo vamos a una playa magnífica lejos del hotel. Allí, tomamos el sol, jugamos en la arena o damos un paseo.

Por la noche, vamos a unos restaurantes diferentes. La comida mexicana es muy deliciosa.

Mañana, vamos a tomar el autobús a una plaza donde queremos comprar unos recuerdos de México.

Mi madre quiere unos pendientes de plata. Son muy populares. Prefiero unas tarjetas postales para mi colección. Mi padre colecciona sombreros. El va a comprar unos de paja.

Mi hermana Elena va a comprar las blusas de algodón. A ella, le gusta comprar la ropa nueva.

De Acapulco, mi familia y yo vamos a salir para casa. Queremos viajar en barco. Me gusta viajar en el océano.

Tu amigo,
Ricardo

E. Teachers will read the following:

Pepe, el ratón, entra en la cocina y se pone debajo de la nevera. Tiene frío y por eso se pone sobre la estufa. Tiene calor y se pone en el fregadero. Ahora entra en la sala y se pone a la derecha del televisor. Porque no puede mirar bien la televisión se pone entre el sillón y la mesita. A ese punto tiene sueño y va a la alcoba para dormir. Se pone al lado de la cómoda. Oye a alguien que entra en la alcoba y tiene miedo y se pone en el armario. Cuando la persona abre el armario el ratón corre detrás de la cama. Ahora va al cuarto de baño y se pone delante del espejo para mirarse y peinarse, pero el pobrecito Pepe se cae en el toilet y adiós ratón.

Answer Sí or No to the following statements based on the story you have just heard:

1. Pepe enters through the living room.
2. Pepe goes under the refrigerator.
3. He goes into the stove because he is cold.
4. He goes into the sink.
5. He goes to the left of the T.V.
6. Pepe wants to watch T.V. so he goes between the chair and the table.
7. Pepe goes into the dresser.
8. He becomes freightened and goes into the closet.
9. He goes in front of the bed.
10. He falls into the bath tub.

Name _____

PART I: Listening/Speaking (20 points)

  A. Informal evaluation of speaking done in class during three weeks before examination is given. (10 points)   _____

  B. Formal evaluation (10 points) Student interacts with teacher in two situations.   _____

    1. Situation 1   _____

    2. Situation 2   _____

Speaking Situations   Total _____

  1. Your friends are going to the movies this evening. You want to go, too. Convince me, your father, that I should give you permission to go along.

  2. I am your friend Fritz. We are in school. Invite me to come to your house this afternoon after school to watch T.V. and listen to records. You start.

PART II: Listening (20 points)

  1. *What do you do now?* (5 points, 1 each) Write the number of the correct answer in the blank.

    A. You are on the street in Hamburg. Someone walks up to you and says the following: * * * * * * * *

    Since you are a nice and helpful person, you _____.

      1. give directions.
      2. tell him to get lost.
      3. give him 5 Marks for a meal.
      4. call the police.

    B. You now see an elderly woman run out of an apartment building. She comes over to you and says the following: * * * * * * * *

    Since you are a nice and helpful person, you _____.

      1. help the old lady turn on the T.V.
      2. help her look for her dog.
      3. buy her a cup of coffee.
      4. help her look for her grandson.

    C. You are in school. An announcement is made over the P.A. just as school is dismissing for the day. This is what you hear: * * * * * * * *

    Now you will _____.

      1. sit and cry because you have no money.
      2. Take your permission slip home.
      3. sign your name on the student list.
      4. write a note to your parents.

    D. The telephone rings. You pick up the receiver and hear: * * * * * * * *

    Now you will _____.

      1. sit and cry because you don't like obscene phone calls.
      2. borrow 100 Marks from your parents.
      3. run to the store and rent a film.
      4. turn on the T.V.

    E. You are sitting in the subway station in Berlin waiting for the train. A woman sits down besides you and starts to talk. This is what you hear: * * * * * * * *

    Although you are not an expert, it is still very easy to pinpoint her problem. You will advise her not to

      1. eat so much candy and so many cookies.
      2. drink so much coffee and wine.
      3. eat so much cake and whipped cream.
      4. drink so much beer.

FIGURE 11.6 Examples of items from the German intermediate final exam

SOURCE: From *In Germany Workbook* (pp. 26, 36, 73), 1987; reproduced with permission of Chancerel International, London, England.

2. Das Liebesspiel. (5 points, one each)

You are listening to the ever popular game show – The Dating Game – Das Liebesspiel on the radio. Listen and see if you can guess which contestant might be the lucky winner. * * * * * * * *

Now, what do you think? Which of the three men will Miss Schönkopf pick? Circle the number. Which will pick if she

1. is a health food nut?	1	2	3
2. is fat?	1	2	3
3. thinks a romatic evening is watching T.V.?	1	2	3
4. likes to gaze at the stars?	1	2	3
5. enjoys talking about books and classical music?	1	2	3

3. Im Flugzeug. (10 points, one each)

You are in a Lufthansa airplane on your way to Germany. You hear an announcement. Your travelling companion knows no German. Jot down the information so you can tell him what it is all about. This is what you hear: * * * * * * * * *

Now write down the information for your travelling companion.

1. Altitude the plane is flying at. _____
2. Duration of the flight. _____
3. Why the flight will last that long. _____
4. How you will know if a storm develops. _____
5. Why you should not disturb the flight attendants. _____
6. How you will know if you are not in Frankfurt. _____
7. What four problems there are with the flight. _____
8. _____ 9. _____
10. _____

PART III: Reading (20 points)

A. Read the following items and fill in the blanks with the appropriate letters.
   (20 items, 1 point each = 20 points)

   1. You have collected these entrance tickets from your trips abroad and stuck them in your scrapbook as souvenirs. Write the correct letter in the blanks so you won't forget which is for which.

   This ticket gives you permission to take photos. _____
   This one is for a cave. _____
   This is for climbing a tower and for an exhibition. _____
   This one is for a romantic spa town. _____
   This one is for the theater. _____
   This one is from Switzerland. _____
   This one cannot be replaced. _____

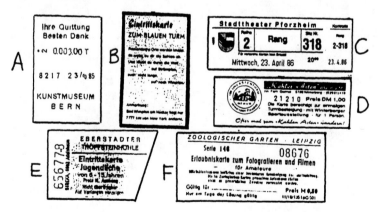

(continued)

2. You are an avid stamp collector and are therefore interested in advertisement _____

3. Auf Job-Suche!

Nikola has had enough of baby-sitting! She is now looking through the ads in the local paper to see if there is a job she could apply for. Read her comments and write the letter of each job she is not interested in.

Geht nicht. Ich bin erst 15. _____

Geht nicht. Ich möchte keine kleinen Kinder mehr um mich haben. _____

Geht nicht. Moderne Musick mag ich überhaupt nicht. _____

Geht nicht. Ich möchte zwei Wochen vor Weihnachten zu Hause verbringen. _____

Geht nicht. Hausarbeit halte ich einfach nicht aus. _____

Geht nicht. Tippen kann ich nicht. _____

Geht nicht. Haareschneiden habe ich nie gelernt. _____

Geht nicht. Ich habe keinen Führerschein. _____

Geht nicht bei meinem Heuschnupfen. Mit so vielen Blumen würde ich den ganzen Tag nur niesen! _____

Since there is only one job left, which number must she call to get further information. _____

FIGURE 11.6 (continued)

4. Der Zoo. What will it cost you, your 3 year old brother and your 2 parents to get into this zoo?

   a. DM 2,50
   b. DM 3,--
   c. DM 1,50
   d. DM 4,50

Write your answer here. _____

```
┌─────────────────────────────────────────────┐
│  ┌───────────────────────────────────────┐   │
│  │          EINTRITTSPREISE              │   │
│  └───────────────────────────────────────┘   │
│                                               │
│  ┌──────────────┐                             │
│  │ Tageskarten │                              │
│  └──────────────┘                             │
│                                               │
│  Erwachsene                          1.00 M   │
│  Kinder über 4 Jahre                  .50 M   │
│  Kinder unter 4 Jahren                frei    │
│                                               │
│  Schüler und Studenten                .50 M   │
│  Schwerbeschädigte und Rentner        .50 M   │
│                                               │
│  Besuch von Gruppen: ab 20 Pers.              │
│  Eintrittskarten nur an der Hauptkasse        │
│                                               │
│  Erwachsene                           .80 M   │
│  Kinder über 4 Jahre                  .40 M   │
│  Kindergarten und Schulen                     │
│  Kinder und Schüler                   .25 M   │
│  Berufs- Fach- und Hochschüler        .50 M   │
│  Begleitpersonen                      .80 M   │
│  je 10 Kinder usw Schüler: Begleiter  frei    │
│                                               │
│  Nutzen Sie die Vorteile einer Jahres- oder Monats Karte │
│  Verkauf im Geschäftszimmer                   │
│                                               │
│  ┌──────────────────────┐                     │
│  │ Foto- und Filmerlaubnis │                  │
│  └──────────────────────┘                     │
│                                               │
│  Für Amateure    Tageskarten          .50 M   │
│                  Monatskarten        1.00 M   │
│                  Jahreskarten        3.00 M   │
│                                               │
│  Für gewerbliche Zwecke, Veröffentlichungen und Blitzlichtaufnahmen │
│  Genehmigungen nur im Sekretariat.            │
└─────────────────────────────────────────────┘
```

Hier geht's rund

Ein Radrennen mit Tradition und Pfiff. Seit 76 Jahren drehen Amateure und Profis beim Berliner Sechs-Tage-Rennen ihre Runden. Auch heute noch pfeifen die Fans auch den Rängen den bekannten Sportpalast-Walzer, auch wenn das sportliche Spektakel heute über die Holzbahn der Deutschlandhalle geht.

An 17. Oktober beginnt das Rundenkarussell sich wieder zu drehen. Täglich ab 19 Uhr wird dem Besucher ein volles Programm geboten, das neben dem Radsport jede Menge Unterhaltung bietet, mit Berliner Bands, Bier, Bratwurst und Buletten.

Ein Volksfest mit Musik- und Showeinlagen. Übrigens: Die Wahl der "Miss Kurve" oder die "Golden Nacht" der Radsport-Prominez sollten Sie sich nicht entgehen lassen.

Infos: 030/3 03 81 (AMK Berlin). Karten von 10 bis 40 DM. U-Bahnhof Theodor-Heuss-Platz oder Kaiserdamm, S-Bahnhof Westkreuz. Busse 4, 10, 65, 69 und 94.

5. Aus der Zeitung. You will be interested in attending the event described in this article if you _____

   a. like to ride the merry-go-round.
   b. are interested in watching bicyclists compete in a race.
   c. want to spend 6 days running in a race.
   d. want to spend 10 Marks riding the subway.

(continued)

PART IV: Writing (20 points) (Tip: Use NO English. If you do not know a word or phrase, then write about something else).

A. *Brief an einen Brieffreund:* Write a letter to your friend, Heinz, in Germany. The school year will soon be over and vacation starts in a week. Tell him about this past year in school, how your classes were, some of the activities you participated in, about your friends and mention one problem in particular. Then tell him about your Summer vacation plans and how you could travel to Italy. You must include all of this information and use the proper German letter form.

B. *Geschichten:* Look at the four pictures below (A, B, C, D). Choose *ANY 2* and write a 5 sentence story in German about each of the two. The story may be in the present, past, or future or you may mix according to what you want to say. Be sure to write the letter of your choice before beginning. *REMEMBER — CHOOSE ONLY 2!!*

DO NOT DESCRIBE THE PICTURE!! WRITE A STORY!!

Write your stories here.

Story 1. Picture

_____

_____

Story 2. Picture _____

_____

_____

FIGURE 11.6 (continued)

1. **What do you do now?** (5 points, 1 each)

   A. You are on the street in Hamburg. Someone walks up to you and says: Entschuldigung. Ich bin hier fremd. Können Sie mir helfen? Ich muss heute abend unbedingt in Frankfurt sein. Ich will mit dem Zug dorthin, aber ich habe keine Ahnung, wo der Bahnhof ist. Er steht in der Goethestrasse, das weiss ich, aber wo ist diese Strasse? Sie soll ganz in der Nähe sein. Wissen Sie vielleicht?

   Since you are a nice and helpful person, you
      1. give directions.
      2. tell him to get lost.
      3. give him 5 Marks for a meal.
      4. call the police.

   B. You now see an elderly woman run out of an apartment building. She comes over to you and says: Hilfe! Hilfe! Mein kleiner Max ist weg. Ich kann ihn nicht finden. Vor ein paar Minuten war er in seinem Schlafzimmer und hat ferngesehen. Er ist erst 5 Jahre alt, und seine Lieblingssendung, weisst du, ist Sesamstrasse. Und jetzt ist er verschwunden. Er trägt eine blaue Hose und ein weisses Hemd. Sein Turnschuhe sind gelb. Hilfst du mir ihn suchen? Bitte, bitte?

   Since you are a nice and helpful person, you
      1. help the old lady turn on the T.V.
      2. help her look for her dog.
      3. buy her a cup of coffee.
      4. help her look for her grandson.

   C. You are in school. An announcement is made over the P.A. just as school is dismissing for the day. This is what you hear: Tja, Kinder. Guten Tag! Hier spricht der Schuldirektor. Vergesst nicht, Kinder, dass der Schulausflug ins Theater am Donnerstagabend stattfindet. Um 6.30 Uhr fahren die Schulbusse ab. Alle müssen schon um 6.00 Uhr vor der Schule sein. Morgen muss jeder die Erlaubnis mit Elternunterschrift zur Schule bringen. Und vergesst auch nicht, dass der Ausflug vollkommen kostenlos ist. Bis morgen, Tschüs!

   What do you do?
      1. sit and cry because you have no money.
      2. take your permission slip home.
      3. sign your name on the student list.
      4. write a note to your parents.

   D. The telephone rings. You pick up the receiver and hear: Guten Tag. Hier spricht Fräulein Puffendorf. Ich bin Angestellte im Videogeschäft Irrenhaus. Ich rufe deswegen an, weil Sie sich vor zwei Monaten eine Videocassette von unserem Geschäft ausgeliehen haben gegen eine Gebühr von zwei Mark pro Tag und die Cassette noch nicht zurückgebracht haben. Was ist los? Warum haben Sie die Cassette so lange behalten? Das dürfen Sie nicht! Sie müssen sie sofort zurückbringen und die Gebühr von zwei Mark pro Tag bezahlen. Wenn Sie bis morgen die Cassette nicht abgeliefert haben, rufe ich die Polizei an. Verstanden? Gut! Wiederhören.

   What do you do?
      1. Sit and cry because you don't like obscene phone calls.
      2. Borrow 100 Marks from your parents.
      3. Run to the store and rent a film.
      4. Turn on tHe T.V.

   E. You are sitting in the subway station in Berlin waiting for the train. A woman sits down beside you and starts to talk. This is what you hear: Ach, Gott im Himmel! Ich kann kaum atmen, nur schwer laufen. Weisst du warum? Ich bin zu dick. Ja, es ist wahr. Ich sehe nicht so dick aus, aber ich wiege fast 200 Kilos. Und ich kann nicht abnehmen. Ich bin immer auf Diät, aber ich nehme zu, nicht ab. Ich werde immer dicker. Ich verstehe es einfach nicht. Und meine Kleider passen mir nicht mehr. Ich muss neue kaufen. Was kann ich machen? Ich esse fast nichts. Zum Frühstück nur Kaffee, Orangensaft und ein Stück Schwarewalderkirschtorte mit Schlag. Zum 2. Frühstück nur Kaffee, drei Brötchen mit Wurst und Käse

(continued)

und zwei Stück Torte mit Schlag. Zum Mittagessen habe ich nur zwei Stück Kuchen, natürlich immer mit Schlag. Ohne Schlag kann ich nicht leben. Zum Kaffee am Nachmittag habe ich nur ein Stück Kuchen mit Schlag. Zum Abendessen esse ich gewöhnlich sehr leicht: fünf bis sechs belegte Brötchen, drei Glas Wein und ein paar Stück Torte. Und ich trinke Kaffee sehr gern mit Schlagsahne. Nun, was meinst du? Warum werde ich immer dicker und nicht schlanker?

Although you are not an expert, it is still very easy to pinpoint her problem. You will advise her:

1. not to eat so much candy and so many cookies.
2. not to drink so much coffee and wine.
3. not to eat so much cake and whipped cream.
4. not to drink so much beer.

2. Das Liebesspiel. (5 points, one each)

You are listening to the every popular game show — The Dating Game — Das Liebesspiel — on the radio. Listen and see if you can guess which contestant might be the lucky winner.

Guten Abend, meine Damen und Herren. Hier spricht Herr Holzkopf, der Leiter von dem aufregenden, spannenden und sehr beliebten Radioprogram, Das Liebesspiel. Wir haben heute abend als Spielerin das schöne, junge Fräulein Schönkopf. Sie hat die Gelegenheit und die Aufgabe, einen Mann von drei Männern zu wählen. Nun, wer wird Glück und wer wird Pech haben? Nr. 1, Nr. 2, oder Nr. 3? Nun, Fräulein Schönkopf. Die 1, Frage, bitte.

FS: Danke, Herr Holzkopf. Nun, ich möchte wissen, Nr. 1, was ist für Sie ein romantisches Abenteuer?

Nr. 1: Ooooo, Fräulein Schönkopf. Ich glaube, dass ein romantisches Abenteuer ein Abend ist, wo ich mit einem schönen Mädchen ein Fussballspiel im Fernsehen zusammen sehen und dabei ein paar Flaschen Bier trinken und Kartoffelchips naschen. Meinst du auch?

FS: Danke, Nr. 1. Und Nr. 2? Was ist Ihre Meinung zur selben Frage?

Nr. 2: Ah, guten Abend, schönes Fräulein. Für mich ist es nur romantisch, wenn zwei Leute zuerst in einem feinen, eleganten Restaurant sehr gut bei einer Flasche Champagner zu Abend essen und dann durch den dunklen Wald zusammen spazieren gehen und den Mond und die Sterne am Himmel betrachten. Möchten Sie es mal mit mir machen?

FS: Danke, Nr. 2. Und Nr. 3?

Nr. 3: Nun, sehen Sie, Fraulein Schönkopf. Ich bin sehr sportlich und glaube, dass romantisch bedeutet, eine Radtour machen. Ja. Es gibt nichts besseres als Radfahren, sagen wir 50 bis 75 Kilometer. Und dann ein Picknick haben und dabei nur frisches Gemüse und Obst essen: Salat, Spinat, Carotten, Pilze, Apfel, Bananen, u.s.w. Und zu trinken? Milch. Nur Milch. Ziegenmilch, wenn möglich.

FS: Hmmm. Danke. Und die 2. Frage? Was ist für Sie das ideale Mädchen Nr. 1?

Nr. 1: Für mich ist das ideale Mädchen ein Mädchen, das sich sehr für Sport interessiert. Sie muss sehr schön sein. Sie muss gut kochen können und sie muss gern essen und Bier trinken. Ich habe schlanke Mädchen nicht besonders gern. Eigentlich; wenn sie ein bisschen dick sind, umso besser. Ja, ich könnte sogar sagen: je dicker, desto schöner und idealer.

FS: Und Nr. 2?

Nr. 2: Das ideale Mädchen freut sich sehr über die Natur. Sie geht gern spazieren. Aber sie ist auch froh, wenn sie zu Hause bleiben kann und klassische Musik hört oder ein Buch liest. Schön oder nicht schön, das ist mir egal. Viel wichtiger ist es, dass sie eine interessante Persönlichkeit hat und gern über Politik und Kunst spricht. Aber, nicht dick, bitte, lieber schlank.

FS: Und Nr. 3?

Nr. 3: Das Mädchen, das ich kennenlernen möchte, ist sehr schlank und sportlich. Sie trinkt kein Alkohol und isst nur Gemüse und Obst — kein Fleisch. Sie ist auch sehr religiös und geht jede Woche in die Kirche. Sind Sie das Mädchen für mich?

FS: Danke, Nr. 1, Nr. 2, und Nr. 3. Sehr interessant.

FIGURE 11.6 (continued)

Now, what do you think? Which of the three men will Miss Schönkopf pick? (Circle the number.) Which will she pick if she

1. is a health food nut?
2. is fat?
3. thinks a romantic evening is watching T.V.?
4. she likes to gaze at the stars?
5. enjoys talking about books and classical music?

3. **Im Flugzeug.** (10 points, one each)

You are in a Lufthansa airplane on your way to Germany. You hear an announcement. Your travelling companion knows no German. Jot down the information so you can tell him what it is all about. This is all about. This is what you hear:

Guten Tag, meine Damen und Herren. Hier spricht der Pilot, Kapitän Fallschirm. Willkommen auf Flug Nr. 007. Wir sind, wie Sie hoffentlich schon wissen, auf dem Weg von New York City nach Frankfurt. Das Wetter hier oben über den Wolken ist herrlich. Wir erwarten eine ganz ruhige Reise. Die Reise dauert genau 23 Stunden. Sie soll nur 7 Stunden dauern, aber wir haben ein kleines Problem: zwei von den vier Motoren funktionieren nicht mehr. Sie sind aus — kaputt. Wir müssen deshalb etwas langsamer fliegen. Aber, haben Sie keine Angst, bitte. Die zwei anderen sind in bester Ordnung.

Wir fliegen in der Höhe von 30,000 Metern. Und wie gesagt, erwarten wir einen ruhigen Flug. Es ist aber möglich, dass es zwischen NYC und Frankfurt einen Sturm gibt. Wir können nicht genau wissen, denn unser Radarapparat funkioniert auch nicht. Wir werden erst wissen, dass wir mitten in einem Sturm sind, wenn wir Donner und Blitzen hören und sehen. Nun, meine Herrschaften, wenn ich Donner und Blitzen sage, meine ich nicht die zwei Rentiere vom St. Nikolaus. Ha ha! Ein kleiner Witz für Sie.

Na ja, und noch ein kleines Problem. Bitte, benutzen Sie die Toiletten nicht. Sie sind auch kaputt. Und bitte, stören Sie die Stewardesssen nicht. Sie sind sehr müde und wollen ihre Ruhe haben.

Der Film, den wir Ihnen in ein paar Minuten zeigen, ist ein sehr spannender Film. Er heisst Terroristen in der Luft. Der Film wurde vor einem Monat in diesem Flugzeug gedreht. Vielleicht haben Sie von dem Ereignis in der Zeitung gelesen.

Hoffentlich haben Sie alle etwas zu essen mitgebracht, denn wir haben an Bord nur genug Essen für die Stewardessen und die Piloten.

Also, ich wünsche Ihnen eine schöne Reise.

O ja, noch etwas. Wenn wir landen, hoffentlich in Frankfurt, müssen Sie durch die Zollkontrolle gehen. Wenn die Zollbeamten kein Deutsch sprechen, dann wissen Sie, dass Sie nicht in Frankfurt sind.

Now, write down the information for your travelling companion.

1. Altitude the plane is flying at.
2. Duration of the flight.
3. Why the flight will last that long.
4. How you will know if a storm develops.
5. Why you should not disturb the flight attendants.
6. How you will know if you are not in Frankfurt.
7. What 4 problems there are with the flight.
8.
9.
10.

chapter 12

Teaching for Learning

Guiding students to explore effective options for learning the language, using the language, and enjoying the language will demand that as teachers we are first and foremost aware not just of ways to present and test materials, but of ways to learn. This knowledge must begin by suspending our views of ourselves as teachers to reflect critically on ourselves as learners, for if we have no notion of the strategies we ourselves use and therefore no notion of the true complexity of a task, it will be difficult for us to construct tasks for learners, much less teach them the strategies they may use to plan and conduct these tasks. But while our efforts must begin with self-awareness, they must not end there.

V. Galloway and A. Labarca, 1990

Teachers play many roles in the classroom. These include such functions as planning learning activities, developing materials, managing and controlling pupil behavior, evaluating student learning, and acting as a counselor as well as language model. What distinguishes effective classroom practice from ineffective learning environments has attracted much attention in recent years. Research on effective classroom instruction offers language teachers the possibilities of examining their own instructional practices. Successful language teaching can also be seen in relation to the degree or extent to which teachers enable their students to develop their learning strategies. Language lessons and textbooks can be examined critically to determine the levels of effectiveness or the appropriateness of the content and tasks for different learner needs. By reflecting on their instructional beliefs and practices, teachers can begin to understand the learning consequences of their actions.

This chapter examines a number of issues related to effective teaching practices. The following questions are addressed:

1. What is known about effective teaching?
2. What concerns need to be taken into account to establish a successful learning environment?
3. How can teachers determine the ways their students learn?
4. What issues need to be considered in evaluating language lessons?
5. What issues need to be considered in evaluating textbooks?
6. How can teachers reflect on their classroom practices?
7. What are the major professional organizations that can support teachers in their professional development?

EFFECTIVE TEACHING PRACTICES

The question of what it means to be an effective teacher has attracted considerable attention over the past 15 years. Researchers have identified several key areas that influence students' learning outcomes. Blum (1984), in his review of the characteristics of effective schools, lists a number of features that distinguished successful classrooms from ineffective learning environments. Effective classroom instruction incorporates many of the following elements:

1. Instruction is guided by a preestablished curriculum.
2. Instructional objectives are clear and focused.
3. Instructional groupings are formed to accomplish specific learning outcomes.
4. Teachers hold high expectations for student learning.
5. Class time is used for learning.
6. Students are oriented to learn lesson content.
7. Students are retaught if they do not understand essential content.
8. Learning progress is monitored constantly.
9. Learning tasks and classroom routines are carefully articulated.
10. Standards for classroom behavior are high.
11. Teachers interact positively with their students.
12. Excellence is promoted through the use of incentives and rewards for students.

Kindsvatter, Wilen, and Ishler (1988) offer a self-evaluation checklist to help determine the extent to which teachers engage in effective teaching practices. The checklist, presented in Figure 12.1, incorporates four major areas within the domain of instructional effectiveness: time on task, context coverage, academic success, and student feedback.

Brophy and Good (1986) caution that complex instructional problems cannot be solved with simple lists of do's and don'ts. Teachers need to understand the dynamics of classroom interaction and the influence that instruction has on student learning. What teachers *say* and *do* in the classroom makes a difference in students' achievement. Teaching is a dynamic process, and the key to instructional

This rating sheet can be used to assess the extent to which the teacher is using effective teaching practices. It is designed for both supervisory use and self-examination.

Time-on-Task

Directions:

Circle the appropriate number reflecting what was observed during the lesson:
(1) Never (2) Seldom (3) Half the time (4) Most of the time (5) Always

	1	2	3	4	5
a. Teacher is aware of amount of time spent each period by students being actively involved.	1	2	3	4	5
b. Teacher actively monitors practice portion of lesson.	1	2	3	4	5
c. Teacher starts class promptly and uses time fully for learning activities.	1	2	3	4	5
d. Teacher is aware of verbal and nonverbal feedback that indicates students are off task.	1	2	3	4	5
e. Teacher organizes class procedures so that they can be accomplished quickly and efficiently.	1	2	3	4	5
f. Teacher uses a variety of practices to increase student participation.	1	2	3	4	5
g. Teacher studies those students who have difficulty staying on task to determine measures that can be taken to help them.	1	2	3	4	5

Appropriate Content Coverage

	1	2	3	4	5
a. Teacher knows the ability levels of the students.	1	2	3	4	5
b. Teacher knows the instruction level of materials being used.	1	2	3	4	5
c. Teacher is able to identify the skills and information needed to be successful with the content.	1	2	3	4	5
d. Teacher knows if students' prior learning is sufficient to learn new content.	1	2	3	4	5
e. Teachers' tests cover objectives taught.	1	2	3	4	5
f. Teacher is able to individualize content to fit students' differences in learning and cognitive development.	1	2	3	4	5

Performance Success

	1	2	3	4	5
a. Teacher plans learning tasks in which all students can encounter some success.	1	2	3	4	5
b. Teacher allows students time to become successful.	1	2	3	4	5
c. Teacher gives corrective feedback.	1	2	3	4	5
d. Teacher gives consistent rewards for success.	1	2	3	4	5
e. Teacher gives frequent progress reports obtained from tests and quizzes.	1	2	3	4	5

Feedback

	1	2	3	4	5
a. Teacher provides constant and immediate feedback on written work, oral discussion, and recitation.	1	2	3	4	5
b. Teacher encourages students to provide feedback.	1	2	3	4	5
c. Teacher lets students know what the standard of performance is, how student fared in trying to meet the standard, what corrective procedures are to be taken.	1	2	3	4	5
d. Teacher uses a variety of verbal and nonverbal behaviors for praise.	1	2	3	4	5

(continued)

FIGURE 12.1 Self-evaluation and checklist for effective teaching practices

SOURCE: From *Dynamics of Effective Teaching*, by Richard Kindsvatter, William Wilen, and Margaret Ishler. Copyright 1988 by Longman Publishing Group (pp. 186–187).

e. Teacher specifically references the student response being   1 2 3 4 5
   praised to the reasons why it is appropriate; inappropriate
   responses are handled similarly.
f. Teacher specifically references the student behavior being   1 2 3 4 5
   criticized to the reasons why it is inappropriate and what student needs to do to change it.
g. Teacher establishes a positive-feeling tone with criticized stu- 1 2 3 4 5
   dent later.
h. Teacher includes use of student ideas as a reinforcement   1 2 3 4 5
   technique.

FIGURE 12.1   (continued)

effectiveness is informed teacher decision making within a particular classroom in a specific educational setting. Kindsvatter et al. (1992, p. 307), advise that "in a real sense, aspiring teachers must reinvent the effective teacher based on their knowledge, beliefs, perceptions, personality, and interaction with students at various contexts."

Effective teaching in the context of second or foreign language classrooms also tends to support findings from generic teaching practices. McGroarty (1991) reports on the importance of direct instruction (content coverage), time on task, and grouping students for different interactional possibilities in the language classroom. It appears that effective teaching in L2 classrooms entails different proportions of teacher-directed and student-centered learning activities that need to be organized according to students' proficiency levels and ages (elementary school; university settings; novice, intermediate, and advanced levels).

CLASSROOM CLIMATE AND MANAGEMENT

In addition to the concerns associated with effective instructional practices, classroom teachers must establish a successful learning environment. The affective aspects of *classroom climate* include students' perceptions about learning, feelings generated by and about the teacher, and the learning routines, all of which contribute positively or negatively to the learning atmosphere. The classroom climate necessary for promoting functional language proficiency must encourage interaction, communication, and individual student contributions. Birckbichler (1982) offers an informal checklist (Figure 12.2) that teachers can use to evaluate their own classroom atmosphere and to determine in what ways they can increase communication-based learning activities.

Responses of *yes* to items 1, 2, 3, 4, and 5 in Figure 12.2 indicate your willingness to foster a climate of respect and trust, enabling students to express their personal opinions, feelings, and beliefs in different communicative situations. Responses of *no* or *unsure* to items 2 and 12 might imply a classroom policy that

1. Are students encouraged to express their own ideas, thoughts, and reactions without fear of embarrassment or ridicule?   yes____ no____ unsure____

2. Do you allow students to learn from their mistakes or errors?   yes____ no____ unsure____

3. Do you have a basic attitude of trust, respect, and confidence in all students' abilities to be responsible?   yes____ no____ unsure____

4. Is there open communication between you and your students so that students feel free to express themselves?   yes____ no____ unsure____

5. Do you respect the ideas of individual students even though they may differ from your own?   yes____ no____ unsure____

6. Do you consider the abilities of your students when preparing classroom activities so that adequate structure can be provided when necessary?   yes____ no____ unsure____

7. Do you encourage students to work together to complete certain tasks, thus avoiding excessive competition and hostility among the students?   yes____ no____ unsure____

8. Do you think that group work can facilitate creative behaviors and that students can work together responsibly in groups if adequately prepared?   yes____ no____ unsure____

9. Do you reward students who go beyond the demands of a particular activity and who subsequently make additional errors or fail?   yes____ no____ unsure____

10. Do you clearly explain how a task is to be evaluated so that students can be attentive to task demands rather than trying to guess your intentions?   yes____ no____ unsure____

11. Are you attentive to the needs and potential of individual students so that each can reach a reasonable level of success?   yes____ no____ unsure____

12. Do you believe that students should be given frequent opportunities to express their ideas without constant correction of grammatical and lexical mistakes?   yes____ no____ unsure____

FIGURE 12.2   Classroom climate teacher checklist

SOURCE: From *Creative Activities for the Second Language Classroom* (Language in Education: Theory and Practice, vol. 48) (pp. 10–11) by Diane W. Birckbichler, 1982, Wahington, DC: Center for Applied Linguistics. Reprinted with permission.

considers grammatical accuracy more important than communicative intent. Items 7 and 8 focus on the role that collaboration plays in learning, while item 11 draws attention to individual learning needs.

The California *Foreign Language Framework* (1989) outlines some of the features of a successful classroom environment. The characteristics include references to a supportive learning environment (13), attention to physical (7) and group activities (6), concern about the learner (1, 2, and 13), and effective instructional planning (4, 5, 8, 10, 16, and 17). Cultural and literary experiences (11 and 15) also contribute to the type of classroom climate (see Table 12.1).

Another role teachers play in the classroom is that of manager of instruction. A full discussion of *classroom management* is beyond the scope of this chapter, but management encompasses planning and organizing learning activities, classroom routines and procedures, and systems for handling disruption (Kauchak &

TABLE 12.1 Features of exemplary and less effective instruction

Exemplary instruction	Less effective instruction
1. Is student centered	1. Is teacher centered
2. Meets expectations and needs of students	2. Follows a set curriculum without regard to students' needs
3. Features much communicative activity	3. Focuses on drill and grammatical explanations
4. Provides for language comprehension before production is required	4. Often features student production of language before students can comprehend the language involved
5. Features a variety of activities, well-paced throughout instruction time	5. Features only one or two activities per instructional time period
6. Provides for grouping students in a variety of ways to maximize interaction	6. Focuses on whole-group activities
7. Includes physical movement during communicative interaction	7. Takes place where students must be quiet and passive and are not permitted to move around
8. Presents the target language through content in realistic contexts	8. Emphasizes studying about the target language and its mechanics
9. Uses the target language as the instructional medium	9. Uses the students' native language as the instructional medium (an undesirable practice, except in the case of classes in native-language development)
10. Uses a variety of materials, including those presented through the use of technology	10. Uses the textbook only
11. Guides student to experience and enjoy the best examples of the literature in the language	11. Presents literature as a translation exercise
12. Provides activities that encourage divergent thinking and negotiation	12. Emphasizes only one correct answer
13. Is supportive and nonthreatening in an environment conducive to employing the language	13. Emphasizes constant correction
14. Encourages students to also use the language outside the classroom	14. Leads students to view the language only as an academic subject
15. Includes content and activites for increasing students' awareness of cross-cultural, international, and global considerations	15. Adheres mainly to matters of language and structure rather than stressing the value of vital content
16. Takes place daily for at least one instructional hour	16. Takes place only a few days each week or each month for very short periods of time
17. Focuses evaluation on students' overall abilities to use the target language for communication	17. Focuses evaluation on short-term mastery of discrete elements of the language

SOURCE: From *Foreign Language Framework for California Public Schools, Kindergarten through Grade Twelve*, p. 42, copyright 1989, California Department of Education, P.O. Box 271, Sacramento, CA 95812-0271. Reprinted by permission.

Eggen, 1989). A number of important general tips are suggested below for second language teachers (Lewis & Hill, 1985):

1. Arrange the seating to correspond with the learning activities or tasks.
2. Stand up when you're directing the activity.
3. Look at the students.
4. Use your hands and body language to encourage and direct students.
5. Use pauses to punctuate what you say.
6. Vary your voice.
7. Keep your language to a minimum when students are doing something.
8. Don't comment on everything you're doing or planning to do.
9. Don't be afraid of silence.
10. Don't be afraid of noise.
11. Use pair work to increase student talking time—even if it seems chaotic sometimes.
12. Use group work to increase student talking time.
13. Be explicit.
14. Admit your ignorance.
15. Consult colleagues.
16. Consult students.
17. Demonstrate, rather than explain, new activities.
18. Exploit real events.
19. Use audiovisual materials.
20. Machinery will not solve all your problems.

More detailed explanations about classroom management and discipline can be found in such books as *Learning and Teaching* (Kauchak & Eggen, 1989) and *Dynamics of Effective Teaching* (Kindswatter et al., 1992).

TEACHING FOR LEARNING

Hosenfeld (1979) views teaching effectiveness in terms of the extent to which teachers enable the learners to follow their own path toward language mastery. Successful teaching implies successful learning. What the teacher does in the classroom is only part of the process in a learning-teaching framework. Successful learning may depend on how a teacher structures classroom activities and attends to learner strategies. The field of learner strategy research is an important area of second language acquisition. Books such as *Helping Learners Succeed: Activities for the Foreign Language Classroom* (Omaggio, 1981), *How to be a More Successful Language Learner* (Rubin & Thompson, 1993), *Learning Strategies in Second Language Acquisition* (O'Malley & Chamot, 1990), *Language Learning Strategies: What Every Teacher Should Know* (Oxford, 1990) indicate the serious attention being given by teachers and researchers to the learning process. The identification of specific learning strategies with respect to such areas as speaking, reading, and writing and the use of this information for strategy training for specific groups of learners is now considered an essential component of instruction. Oxford (1990) suggests that different strategy assessment options (observations, interviews, think-aloud procedures, note taking, diaries, and self-report surveys) can be used to obtain information about learning behaviors. An observation instrument developed by Omaggio (1981) for determining learner problems in different classroom tasks is shown in Figure 12.3. The instrument classifies learner problems in nine areas: (1) poor memory (items 1, 2, and 3), (2) lack of flexibility (4, 5, and 6),

Rank the student's characteristic behavior for 1 (never) to 5 (very frequently) for each of the questions below:

Does the student(s) . . .

	1	2	3	4	5
1. Have trouble remembering syntactic and/or semantic information in the foreign language?	1	2	3	4	5
2. Leave large gaps in dictations?	1	2	3	4	5
3. Write skimpy or inaccurate resumes of listening or reading passages in the foreign language?	1	2	3	4	5
4. Exhibit a lack of fluency when answering questions or speaking on a topic in the foreign language?	1	2	3	4	5
5. Have trouble with creative tasks?	1	2	3	4	5
6. Write skimpy or brief compositions in the foreign language?	1	2	3	4	5
7. Tend to answer questions impulsively, giving quick but often inaccurate answers?	1	2	3	4	5
8. Speak fluently, but make frequent and careless errors?	1	2	3	4	5
9. Guess randomly and inaccurately?	1	2	3	4	5
10. Reflect a long time over answers?	1	2	3	4	5
11. Write lengthy compositions riddled with errors?	1	2	3	4	5
12. Turn in written work that is disorganized and/or unsystematic?	1	2	3	4	5
13. Tend to get lost in detail when reading?	1	2	3	4	5
14. Read word-for-word and refuse to use contextual guessing techniques and inferencing skills?	1	2	3	4	5
15. Fail to correct errors that have been previously explained several times?	1	2	3	4	5
16. Fail to pay attention to the important details in a listening or reading task?	1	2	3	4	5
17. Get easily distracted by irrelevant words and structures?	1	2	3	4	5
18. Become easily frustrated when there are unknown elements in a task, making it "too complicated"?	1	2	3	4	5
19. Fail to make pertinent distinctions between syntactic or semantic categories, blurring similar words or structures?	1	2	3	4	5
20. Tend to be overly analytical, wanting to create a rule for every example?	1	2	3	4	5
21. Have difficulty making generalizations about the structure of the language?	1	2	3	4	5

FIGURE 12.3 Diagnostic inventory

SOURCE: From *Helping Learners Succeed: Activities for the Foreign Language Classroom* (Language in Education: Theory and Practice, vol. 36) (pp.12–13) by Alice C. Omaggio, 1981, Washington, DC Center for Applied Linguistics. Reprinted with permission.

(3) excessive impulsiveness (7, 8, 9, and 16), (4) excessive reflexiveness or caution (10), (5) lack of systematicness or organization (11, 12, 15, and 21), (6) field dependence (13, 14, and 17), (7) leveling/categorization (19), (8) sharpening or categorization too narrow (20), and (9) low tolerance for ambiguity (18). The instrument includes both aspects of style (typical modes of perceiving, thinking, remembering; problem-solving approaches) and learning strategies (reactions to a learning situation that are amenable to change). Results can be used as the basis for providing appropriate classroom activities to meet learner needs.

Oxford's (1990) framework for language learning strategies incorporates six broad categories: metacognitive, affective, social, memory, cognitive, and compensatory strategies. Each category, in turn, is composed of a number of specific behaviors most appropriate for certain learning tasks and language situations. Social strategies (e.g., asking questions, cooperating with peers and proficient users of L2) may be useful for getting language input and oral practice. Cognitive strategies such as reasoning, analyzing, and summarizing might be important for receiving and sending written message. Compensation strategies such as guessing meaning through cues, using mime or gesture, circumlocution, and production tricks can be used to overcome linguistic limitations (see Figure 12.4).

EVALUATING LANGUAGE LESSONS

The concept of the learning task has been central to the study of teaching effectiveness with respect to time on task, content coverage, and student achivement. In the second language classroom, communicative tasks can be evaluated on the basis of learning goals, the type of activities, learner roles, implementation procedures, level of difficulty or complexity, and assessment procedures. Nunan (1989) offers a set of criteria for evaluating the characteristics of a "good" language lesson in the context of ESL instruction. An effective communicative lesson incorporates the following features:

1. Derive the input from authentic sources.
2. Involve learners in problem-solving activities in which they are required to negotiate meaning.
3. Incorporate tasks that relate learners' real-life communicative needs.
4. Allow learners choice in what, how, and when to learn.
5. Allow learners to rehearse, in class, real-world language tasks.
6. Require learners and teachers to adopt a range of roles, and use language in a variety of settings in and out of the classrom.
7. Expose learners to the language as system.
8. Encourage learners to develop skills in learning how to learn.
9. Integrate the four macroskills: listening, speaking, reading, and writing.
10. Provide controlled practice in enabling microskills (e.g., vocabulary, and language structures needed to describe a room, house, or friend).
11. Involve learners in creative language use. (Based on Nunan, 1989, pp. 132)

Strategies for remembering, storing, and recalling information might include items like the following ones:

	Always	Often	Seldom	Never
1. When I learn new words or idioms, I repeat them aloud one or more times to remember them.	——	——	——	——
2. I review the same word in its different forms; for example, the different tenses of verbs.	——	——	——	——
3. I take notes of the language presented in class by the teacher.	——	——	——	——
4. When listening to tapes, I repeat aloud or to myself whatever is said on the tape.	——	——	——	——
5. I use word association such as synonyms or antonyms to make it easier to remember new words	——	——	——	——
6. I draw pictures or cartoons of words, phrases, or structures to help me remember them.	——	——	——	——
7. I find the meaning of a word by breaking it down into parts, such as the root word and prefixes.	——	——	——	——
8. I actually imagine the spelling of words in my head.	——	——	——	——
9. I remember new words or phrases by recalling their location in my notes, the page in the textbooks, or the teacher's notes on the board.	——	——	——	——
10. I connect the sound of a new word with a picture or image of the word in my mind to help me remember the word.	——	——	——	——
11. I keep lists of new words that I learn in class.	——	——	——	——

Strategies for lowering anxiety, encouraging self, and practice opportunities can be assessed with this type of item:

	Always	Often	Seldom	Never
1. I establish a regular schedule for language study.	——	——	——	——
2. I take risks when using the foreign language, such as speaking with a limited grammar and vocabulary.	——	——	——	——
3. I control my negative feelings or frustrations so that they will not interfere with language learning.	——	——	——	——
4. I write in the foreign language for my own pleasure, not just for class assignments.	——	——	——	——
5. I go to the language laboratory to listen to tape recordings on occasions other than those required as part of my course work.	——	——	——	——
6. I listen to the radio or watch movies or TV programs in the new language.	——	——	——	——
7. I read magazines, newspapers, and any other kind of materials that are not part of my regular class assignment.	——	——	——	——

(continued)

FIGURE 12.4 Language learning strategies

SOURCE: Adapted from *Language Learning Strategies: What Every Teacher Should Know* by Rebecca L. Oxford, 1990, New York: Newbury House Publishers. Used with permission.

8. I consciously make an effort to concentrate all of the time during the language class periods. ____ ____ ____ ____

9. I look for opportunities to use the foreign language with other students or teachers outside the classroom. ____ ____ ____ ____

10. I seek opportunities to socialize with native speakers of the foreign language. ____ ____ ____ ____

Communication strategies can be assessed with items that focus on considerations in producing oral and written discourse:

	Always	Often	Seldom	Never
1. When I don't understand all the words in a conversation, I use my knowledge of the topic being discussed to fill in what I don't know.	____	____	____	____
2. If I don't understand what someone else has said, I ask for repetition or explanation.	____	____	____	____
3. I work in small study groups to help improve my fluency in the foreign language.	____	____	____	____
4. When speaking or writing in the foreign language, I think first of what I want to say in my native language and then traslate it into the new language.	____	____	____	____
5. When writing in the foreign language, I always make sure that sentences are grammatical before I write them down.	____	____	____	____
6. When I speak or write, I correct myself when I notice that I have made a mistake.	____	____	____	____
7. When writing or speaking, I try to use only expressions that I know to be correct.	____	____	____	____
8. When conversing, I concentrate more on what I want to say than on how to say it correctly.	____	____	____	____
9. I proofread my writing in the foreign language carefully and then go back to correct my mistakes when I notice them.	____	____	____	____
10. When I fail to understand what others have said, I pretend to understand in order to keep the conversation going.	____	____	____	____
11. If I notice that someone has not understood me, I rephrase my ideas to communicate more effectively.	____	____	____	____
12. When I cannot express an idea in one way I look for an alternative form.	____	____	____	____
13. When I cannot think of a word or phrase during a conversation in the foreign language, I create words in my own language to keep the discussion going.	____	____	____	____
14. When I cannot express my ideas in the foreign language, I use gestures to make myself understood.	____	____	____	____
15. I direct conversations to topics that are familiar to me.	____	____	____	____

FIGURE 12.4 (continued)

1 = Does not apply
2 = Applies rarely
3 = Applies occasionally
4 = Applies frequently
5 = Applies all the time

	1	2	3	4	5
1. Students perform both real and simulated language functions.	1	2	3	4	5
2. Classroom interaction is in target language.	1	2	3	4	5
3. Vocabulary and grammatical structures are presented in context.	1	2	3	4	5
4. Exercises are placed on the context of specific situations.	1	2	3	4	5
5. The students have opportunities to produce original responses.	1	2	3	4	5
6. Students work in pairs, small groups, and large groups.	1	2	3	4	5
7. Students perform role-plays in different cultural situations.	1	2	3	4	5
8. Listening skills are exercised in their natural use (e.g., announcements, short presentations, radio/TV programs, songs).					
9. Speaking skills are exercised in their natural uses (e.g., questions and answers, conversation, reports, interviews).	1	2	3	4	5
10. Reading skills are exercised in their natural uses (e.g., news bulletins, print media, letters, literary texts).	1	2	3	4	5
11. Writing skills are exercised in their natural uses (e.g., forms, letters, notes, reports, creative writing).	1	2	3	4	5
12. Correction techniques do not interfere with communication.	1	2	3	4	5
13. Students learn ways to perform functions in new situations.	1	2	3	4	5
14. Students perform functions with different vocabulary and grammatical forms.	1	2	3	4	5
15. Evaluation procedure and grading policies reflect a communicative emphasis (e.g., integrative assessment).	1	2	3	4	5

FIGURE 12.5   Characteristics of effective communicative-based teaching

SOURCE: Adapted from Grittner (1981), and Muyskens (1984).

Items such as those in Figure 12.5 could be developed to determine the degree to which foreign language lessons include characteristics of effective communicative teaching.

EVALUATING TEXTBOOKS

Language textbooks expose students to particular aspects of the language and culture of the target group. Language lessons are usually arranged to provide learners with certain linguistic forms (vocabulary, grammatical structures, verb morphology) and communicative functions (greetings, leave taking, asking for directions, expressing personal interests) within the context of different social situations (shopping in a market, going on a trip, visiting a family). The extent to which textbooks follow a communicative orientation or emphasize a proficiency-based approach is not always apparent from skimming the first three chapters or reading the table of contents. The textbook plays a dominant role as the purveyor of content (Apple, 1982; Wexler, 1982). Textbooks need to be evaluated by teachers to determine, for example, the ways students are introduced to various aspects of language, the types of learning activities, the uses of authentic language in specific cultural situations, and the manner in which photographs and illustrations are integrated with topics or linguistic content.

Bragger (1985) suggests a series of questions that should be asked and answered in the process of evaluating the components of a textbook.

1. To what extent are the exercises, even simple, transformational ones, contextualized and personalized?
2. To what extent are the exercises organized to move from structured pattern practice (skill getting) to open-ended activities using the new structures interactively (skill using)? Is this final phase omitted all together? Are skill-using activities termed optional; do they occur only occasionally; do they appear to be in the text only as a token to satisfy teachers interested in real communication? Or are they an important and well-integrated part of the text?
3. Are the communicative activities structured in such a way that students must accomplish a specific task using learned functions in a variety of contexts?
4. Are communicative activies always teacher-centered, or is the responsibility frequently turned over to the students?
5. In these activities, is there only one right answer, or are students free to create with the language?
6. Are dialogues in the book and on the tape program written in authentic language, or are they grammatically and lexically contrived?
7. Is there enough vocabulary presented so that students are given the opportunity to express their own likes and dislikes, or is all the vocabulary generic? Since not every personality can be taken into consideration when texts are written, all texts will be somewhat limited in this respect. However, the teacher's guide or teacher's edition of the text should present supplementary vocabulary the instructor can make available to those who need or want it in order to express their own situations. This should also be followed by the types of activities that encourage expression of individual and personal thought.
8. To what extent are structures and vocabulary items (contexts and topics) recycled in the text? If they are not recycled on a regular basis, the task of the teacher clearly becomes more complicated. If certain vocabulary items are seen only once or twice, never to be encountered again, students are not likely to remember them or try to use them.
9. Is the vocabulary functional, modern and high-frequency? Is there a distinction made, even implicitly, between some vocabulary that should be active because it is high frequency in everyday conversation, and other

vocabulary that should be for recognition only because it is most frequently encountered in reading?

10. Is there a real attempt made to link structures with the contexts in which they are most frequently used? For example, are students made aware of the fact that direct and indirect object pronouns are frequently encountered in question-and-answer situations to avoid repetition of their corresponding nouns?

11. Are the sentences used in exercises likely to be heard or used in real life, or are they constructed just for the sake of grammar practice? For example, the sentence "The banana is between the house and the bicycle" may reinforce a place preposition, but in terms of meaning, it is a sentence that is useless in fulfilling any real task or need.

12. Are the communicative situations simulations of what is likely to happen in the target culture, or are they divorced from any reality that is likely to confront students in the target culture?

13. Are photographs and illustrations included in the text only for aesthetic reasons, or are students asked to work with them, to imagine themselves in the situation, or to simulate conversations among the people in the pictures, etc.? In order for photographs to be useful, they should not only represent famous monuments but also include people in their native environment accomplishing specific tasks. This does not mean that monuments, cities, etc., should be excluded from language textbooks, but we would suggest that such photographs are difficult to describe even in one's native language and should be kept to a minimum.

The answers to these questions can be helpful in curriculum planning and determining the degree to which teachers need to supplement the textbook with ancillary materials (cultural realia, audiotapes, print media, and language activities) to achieve course objectives.

REFLECTIVE TEACHING

Research on teacher thinking documents that teachers hold implicit theories about how their students learn, how teachers should teach their content area, and how they should act as professionals. Clark (1988) characterizes teachers' implicit theories as tending "to be eclectic aggregations of cause-effect propositions from many sources, rules of thumb [and] generalizations drawn from personal experience, beliefs, values, biases, and prejudices" (p. 6).

Thinking about what happens in classroom lessons, how to achieve instructional goals through alternative means, and where ideas or beliefs about teaching come from are some of the concerns associated with "reflective teaching" (Cruickshank, 1984; Zeichner, 1983), through which teachers' efficacy in the classroom can be improved. A reflective teacher, according to Zeichner and Liston

(1985), is one who assesses critically the origins, purposes, and consequences of his or her actions.

In the second language classroom reflective teaching may entail asking a number of "what" and "why" questions about teaching practices, reasons for language study, and explanations for students' success or failure. Some of the questions may go beyond the classroom and deal with issues such as the social context of learning, schools as institutions, and the disciplines of linguistics, psychology, and others that underlie language teaching (Bartlett, 1990). Ramírez (1988) developed a questionnaire to assess teachers' instructional beliefs about language teaching in New York schools. The first six items in the questionnaire were formulated to determine views about teaching and the general approach followed in language teaching. Teachers can indicate their philosophies about teaching and then reflect on why they hold these beliefs and follow certain classroom practices (see Figure 12.6).

The answers to the questions in Figure 12.6 can be used to introduce teachers to the idea of reflection in their day-to-day classroom activities as well as the social context of second language instruction.

Reflection also involves exploring the relationship between an individual's thoughts or beliefs about teaching and the actual behaviors in the classroom. Teachers, for instance, might believe that overt error correction does not have a strong impact on learners' grammatical accuracy, but classroom actions (e.g., the type of feedback given to student answers) may reveal a number of inconsistencies between notions about errors in language learning and what is done during the teaching process. Ramírez's (1988) questionnaire on the instructional beliefs of foreign language teachers allows for the assessment of attitudes toward 16 areas of teaching (error correction, learning strategies, testing, grammar and communication, use of authentic materials, etc.). The 32-item questionnaire consists of 16 pairs of items that can be compared to determine the extent to which teachers hold consistent attitudes toward different aspects of teaching practices. The items are listed in Figure 12.7. The questionnaire examines sixteen aspects of language teaching and learning. The areas include error correction (items 1 and 6), contextualization (2 and 12), testing (3 and 5), learner anxiety (4 and 9), cultural information (7 and 27), grammar instruction (8 and 26), language competence (10 and 20), learning principles (11 and 13), interactional activities (14 and 19), student characteristics (15 and 22), sequence of language skills (16 and 18), learner strategies (17 and 25), language drills (21 and 31), and language and the culture connection (23 and 30).

Some of the items are stated in the affirmative (*should* or *do*) and others in negative terms (*should not* or *do not*). This will influence the level of agreement or disagreement with each statement. A high degree of agreement (SA) with an affirmative statement might be expected to correspond with a high degree of disagreement (SD) with the parallel negative item. Levels of correspondence may vary depending on the particular aspects of teaching. On some items teachers may appear undecided or inconsistent, perhaps due to a "contesting" of some teaching actions. Contestation of teaching practice may lead to an appraisal period where one

What do you think? (Circle one)   *Why do you think so?* (Explain)

1. What do you feel is the *most important* reason for secondary students to learn a second language?
    a. To learn about other cultures
    b. To communicate with people who speak a different language
    c. To learn more about English and languages in general
    d. To meet educational requirements of high school or college
    e. To develop the mind

2. Who do you feel should study a second language in secondary schools?
    a. Any student who is interested
    b. All students (except those in special education)
    c. Students who plan on interacting with speakers of another language
    d. Students with adequate verbal aptitude or ability
    e. Students who are going to college

3. What do you think are the *most important* considerations that should be taken into account in assessing oral proficiency?
    a. Comprehensibility, amount of communication, fluency
    b. Grammar, vocabulary, functions of language
    c. Grammar, fluency, appropriateness
    d. Grammar, pronunciation, appropriateness
    e. Amount of information, creativity, comprehensibility

4. What do you think is the *most important* goal of teaching culture in the second language classroom
    a. To know how the target culture differs from the native culture and to be able to act appropriately in culturally relevant situations
    b. To know and appreciate the artistic and intellectual leaders and their works, the historical events, and the geography
    c. To be able to relate facts about the target group to underlying cultural patterns or themes
    d. The student should know how to gain an empathetic understanding of other cultures

5. What is your view on how second languages are learned in the classroom?
    a. Languages are learned by understanding the rules and the vocabulary and learning to apply them through practice in various situations.
    b. Learners are exposed to a great deal of language in context. They learn about particular topics and situations. They learn certain rules and vocabulary that are useful for these contexts and practice using these forms as they deal with the situations.
    c. Adults learn languages in about the same ways as children do. People communicate with the learner. In the beginning they supplement language with objects, gestures, or pictures, to help the learner understand. Gradually the learner is able to understand more and more and is also able to use the language more and more. The process occurs naturally in this situation.
    d. Correct habits are learned by listening to correct forms, repeating them, sometimes memorizing them, and practicing them in speaking and writing until they become automatic.

    What do you do?   *Why do you do this?*

6.   a. I provide a great deal of language for the students to hear and read. We talk about things they are interested in. In the beginning they are mostly listening or reading, but gradually they are able to respond in speaking or writing. Grammar is practiced in exercises in class or at home, but most of our time is spent in communication activities.
    b. I provide models of certain forms, vocabulary, and expressions. Students repeat them in various combinations until they are familiar. They practice combining new expressions and patterns with what they already know to gradually expand their ability to communicate.

(continued)

FIGURE 12.6   Language teaching philosophy and classroom practice

SOURCE: Adapted from Ramírez (1988), pp. 92–93.

    c. I explain rules, patterns, or vocabulary using examples in the language. Students practice using them in exercises, and then apply them in communication.
    d. I focus on particular structures and vocabulary while talking or providing readings to the students. Students practice these forms while talking to me or other students. After they have seen the materials to be learned, I often summarize the rules involved.
    e. Other

FIGURE 12.6 (continued)

searches for alternative courses of action. The appraisal cycle might be followed by acting out in the classroom the new consciousness about what and how to teach (Bartlett, 1990).

Self-observation appears to be an important consideration in teacher development. Questionnaires provide useful information about such concerns as attitudes toward language teaching and effective instructional behaviors. Nevertheless, they do not provide direct insights about how to teach thinking processes. Bailey (1990) recommends the use of diaries in teacher preparation. Diaries offer teachers the possibility of self-examination and introspection on a number of topics related to the teacher learning process. Porter, Goldstein, Leatherman, and Conrad (1990) argue for the use of journals with courses and seminars that are part of graduate training programs. The journals or logs allow students the possibility of connecting writing with learning. Writing in this case is both a communicative activity as well as a means to learn, generate, and explore ideas.

The use of teaching scripts or scenarios offers the opportunity for studying teachers' thinking processes with respect to specific learning situations. Teachers might be provided with information about the students' proficiency levels, the lesson learning objectives, and the language area that needs to be emphasized. The five situations listed below are examples of scenarios that require teachers to reflect on the kinds of classroom procedures or instructional activities that need to be followed in order to attain a stated learning objective.

Teaching Scripts

Directions: The following section presents some learning objectives you may encounter in the classroom. Read the situations, objectives, and directions and then describe the procedure you would follow in each case. Be sure to include what students would do. Don't worry about time or lesson or unit boundaries. Describe in order *all activities* or *kinds of tasks* needed to reach the stated objective. Use enough detail so that another fellow teacher could implement your plan from your description.

I. Grammar

Situation: Students are in the first half of the first year. They "know" present tense statements, questions, and commands, definite and indefinite articles, and subject pronouns. Assume any vocabulary you wish.

Objective: Limited active, productive control of direct object pronouns.

Directions: Describe all activities from initial exposure to limited active, productive control.

List your activities and testing procedure.

II. Speaking/listening

Situation: Students are in the first year. They know present tense statements, questions, and commands. They are just learning the names for places in a city, directions, etc.

Objective: Give and follow directions to various public buildings on a simplified city map.

Directions: Describe all activities in a combined sequence for both the listening and speaking parts of the objective.

List your activities and testing procedure.

III. Reading

Students are at the intermediate level. The theme of the unit is sports. The topic and some of the expressions may be unfamiliar to the students.

Objective: Read for comprehension of the central idea and main supporting details.

Directions: Describe all activities that relate to the objective, including any that may occur before or after the actual reading.

List your activities and testing procedure.

IV. Functions

Situation: Students are in middle school in the second year of language instruction. Assume any knowledge you wish.

Objectives: Be able to make suggestions regarding what food should be provided at a party.

Directions: List the language forms, phrases, or structures that you may decide to teach and describe the learning activities.

V. Vocabulary

Situation: Seventh grade students are about midway through the first year of language instruction. They have already learned colors, numbers, days, months, seasons, family members, and basic school-related language. They have also been instructed in making present tense statements, questions, and commands.

Objective: Students should display active, productive control of vocabulary items related to clothing as part of the new unit on shopping.

Directions: Describe all activities that would lead to the accomplishment of the objective above and how they would relate to the rest of the unit.

Scenarios such as the ones described above provide teachers with opportunities to reflect and explore their own teaching approaches with respect to specific aspects of language. Individual teachers' responses to these classroom situations could be written down or discussed with other teachers. Then the teaching scripts could be compared to actual classroom behaviors in an effort to examine relationships between intentions and actions. Similarly, the scripts could also be contrasted with the teacher's instructional beliefs (Figure 12.7).

These procedures involve teachers in the process of gathering and analyzing data about their own teaching. Furthermore, these activities emphasize an inquiry-based approach to learning and require teachers to reflect critically on *what* and *how* they teach (Richards & Nunan, 1990).

PROFESSIONAL DEVELOPMENT

There is much that language teachers need to know in order to provide effective instruction. According to Thonis (1991), teachers should at least be *able to do* the following:

1. Identify students' language abilities and needs.
2. Organize appropriate level of instruction.
3. Maintain an orderly, businesslike classroom.
4. Provide for a range of language abilities and learning differences.
5. Manage several groups within a single classroom.
6. Create interest and enthusiasm for learning.
7. Present appropriate lessons and guide practice.
8. Monitor student progress.

In addition, second language teachers need to *have knowledge* about a number of areas:

- Linguistic principles
- Theories of language acquisition
- First and second language differences
- Available materials and their advantages and disadvantages
- Teaching methods
- Assessment and testing techniques
- Rationale for foreign language study
- Curriculum design
- Instructional planning
- Second or foreign language profession

Read each statement and indicate your opinion by placing an "X" on the blank that corresponds to the appropriate letters.

SA = Strongly agree D = Disagree
A = Agree SD = Strongly disagree
U = Undecided

	SA	A	U	D	SD
1. Teachers should correct primarily those errors produced by students that affect grammar and pronunciation accuracy.	___	___	___	___	___
2. The development of language skills (listening, speaking, reading, and writing) should not necessarily be related to specific natural settings in which communication in the target language takes place (e.g., eating places, airports, advertisements, menus).	___	___	___	___	___
3. Language testing should focus on the students' ability to understand or convey information/meaning in specific communicative situations with particular concern for grammatical accuracy.	___	___	___	___	___
4. It is important for teachers to reduce the level of student anxiety in the classroom so that language learning can occur successfully.	___	___	___	___	___
5. Language testing should focus on the students' ability to understand or convey meaning in specific communicative situations with an emphasis on comprehensibility.	___	___	___	___	___
6. Teachers should correct primarily those errors produced by students that affect the communication of meaning/information.	___	___	___	___	___
7. Cultural information (e.g., geographic facts, famous persons, important landmarks, historical events) should be emphasized along with the development of language skills.	___	___	___	___	___
8. Teachers should present grammatical structures in the context of specific communicative situations/functions.	___	___	___	___	___
9. Successful language learning can take place in the classroom without the teacher being overly concerned about the level of student anxiety.	___	___	___	___	___
10. There should be concern for the development of linguistic accuracy (pronunciation and grammar) for all students from the beginning levels of language instruction.	___	___	___	___	___
11. Explanation of grammatical rules should provide the basis for most student language learning in the classroom.	___	___	___	___	___

(continued)

FIGURE 12.7 Instructional beliefs of foreign language teachers

SOURCE: From "Instructional Beliefs of New York Foreign Language Teachers" by Arnulfo G. Ramírez, in A. G. Ramírez (Ed.), *Spotlight on Teaching* (pp. 94–96), 1988. Schenectady, NY: New York State Association of Foreign Language Teachers. ©1988. Reprinted with permission.

12. The development of language skills (listening, speaking, reading, and writing) should emphasize the natural settings in which communication in the target language takes place (e.g., train station, street scenes, forms, schedules, maps)   ___   ___   ___   ___   ___

13. Memorization and repetition of specific grammatical forms and expressions should provide the basis for most student language learning in the classroom.   ___   ___   ___   ___   ___

14. Language activities should be designed to ensure that a considerable amount of time is devoted to teacher-pupil interaction.   ___   ___   ___   ___   ___

15. The amount of learning that takes place in the foreign language classroom depends more on the use of certain teaching techniques than on the characteristics of the student (e.g., intellectual abilities, study habits, attitudes, and age).   ___   ___   ___   ___   ___

16. Language skills (listening, speaking, reading, and writing) should be taught in a specific sequence.   ___   ___   ___   ___   ___

17. Students do not have to be taught explicit language learning strategies (e.g., use of contextual cues, mnemonics, monitoring) along with the different aspects of the target language (e.g., grammar, vocabulary, functions, reading).   ___   ___   ___   ___   ___

18. Language skills (listening, speaking, reading, and writing) do not have to be presented in a particular sequence.   ___   ___   ___   ___   ___

19. Students should have the opportunity to work in pairs and small/large groups on a daily basis.   ___   ___   ___   ___   ___

20. There should be concern for the development of communicative abilities (e.g., convey imformation/meaning, fluency, comprehensibility) for all students from the beginning levels of language instruction.   ___   ___   ___   ___   ___

21. Students should be encouraged to use language creatively, as opposed to exclusively manipulative or convergent practice, in the beginning levels of language study.   ___   ___   ___   ___   ___

22. The amount of learning that takes place in the foreign language classroom depends more on the characteristics of the student (e.g., intellectual abilities, study habits, attitudes, age) than on the use of certain teaching techniques.   ___   ___   ___   ___   ___

23. Patterns of cultural behavior in the target language do not have to be taught in relation to specific communicative situations.   ___   ___   ___   ___   ___

24. Authentic language materials (e.g., signs, advertisements, commercials, brochures, songs, etc.) from the target culture should be   ___   ___   ___   ___   ___

FIGURE 12.7   (continued)

included in the language classroom from the beginning levels of language instruction.

25. Students need to be taught explicit language learning strategies (e.g., use of contextual cues, mnemonics, monitoring) along with the different aspects of the target language (e.g., grammar, vocabulary, functions, reading).   ____   ____   ____   ____   ____

26. Teachers should present grammatical structures and vocabulary before students see the features of language used in specific communicative situations.   ____   ____   ____   ____   ____

27. Cultural information (e.g., geographic facts, famous person, important landmarks, historical events) should no be emphasized in a language classroom.   ____   ____   ____   ____   ____

28. Authentic language materials (e.g., signs, advertisements, commercials, brochures, songs, etc.) from the target culture should be included in the language classroom only when students can fully comprehend the language included in the materials.   ____   ____   ____   ____   ____

29. Teachers need to adapt and supplement language textbooks in order to achieve communicative proficiency among their students.   ____   ____   ____   ____   ____

30. Patterns of cultural behavior in the targe language should be taught only in relation to specific communicative situations.   ____   ____   ____   ____   ____

31. Students should be expected to engage primarily in manipulative or convergent language practice in the beginning levels of language study.   ____   ____   ____   ____   ____

32. Current textbooks provide a sufficient range of language activities necessary to achieve communicative proficiency.   ____   ____   ____   ____   ____

FIGURE 12.7 (continued)

Chastain (1988) states that all teachers, beginning or experienced, have an obligation to stay abreast of current developments in the field. One way of promoting professional development is to participate in professional organizations at the state, regional, or national levels. Professional language organizations serve the interests of teachers, administrators, researchers, and other persons concerned with issues in second or foreign language learning. Professional organizations and publications provide valuable information about current perspectives and future directions.

The American Council on the Teaching of Foreign Languages (ACTFL) is the national organization of second language teachers, including those in English as a second language and classics. ACTFL publishes the Foreign Language Education Series (FLES), which is dedicated especially to classroom teachers and curriculum specialists in the field of foreign language education. Appearing regularly and covering the field comprehensively, the books in the series provide an in-depth analysis and synthesis of important developments, as well as chart new directions and opportunities. ACTFL also publishes *Foreign Language Annals*, which appears four times a year and serves to advance all phases of the profession of foreign language teaching.

The National Federation of Modern Language Teachers Association (NFMLTA) publishes *The Modern Language Journal*, which appears four times a year and is devoted to methods, pedagogical research, and topics of interest to all language teachers. In Canada, the Ontario Modern Language Teachers' Association sponsors *The Canadian Modern Language Review*, which addresses issues in second language teaching and learning.

Specific language organizations formed to promote the study of a particular language or languages include:

American Association of Teachers of French (AATF), which publishes *The French Review*, a journal containing articles on literature, civilization, and teaching.

American Association of Teachers of German (AATG), with its *German Quarterly*, dedicated primarily to literature and literary analysis and occasional articles on teaching concerns. The journal *Die Unterrichtspraxis* does include numerous monographs on pedagogical issues.

American Association of Teachers of Italian (AATI), which publishes *Italica*, dedicated to literary analysis and reviews.

American Association of Teachers of Slavic and East European Languages (AATSEEL), with *The Slavic and East European Journal*, which includes articles on literature, language, and linguistics.

American Association of Teachers of Spanish and Portuguese (AATSP), with its journal *Hispania*, which contains articles on literature, linguistics, pedagogy, and topics related to developments in the Hispanic world.

Teachers of English to Speakers of Other Languages (TESOL), which publishes the *TESOL Quarterly*, an international journal concerned with the teaching of English as a second or foreign language and as a standard dialect.

In addition to the national organizations, there are regional language groups such as Northeast Conference on the Teaching of Foreign Languages, the Southern Conference on Language Teaching, the Central States Conference on the Teaching of Foreign Languages, and the Pacific Northwest Conference on Foreign Languages. The Northeast Conference publishes the proceedings of its annual regional meetings. Reports from some of the Central States regional meetings have also been published.

A current directory listing all of the addresses of the organizations cited above is published annually in the December issue of *Foreign Language Annals*. The directory also includes all of the state associations of foreign language supervisors, and selected newsletters and journals.

SUMMARY

What it means to be an effective teacher has been a major educational concern for many years. A number of features have been identified that distinguish successful classroom environments from unsuccessful learning contexts. Teaching is a dynamic process, and such issues as time-on-task, content coverage, student performance, and the type of feedback are important aspects of instructional effectiveness. The successful teacher must also be concerned with establishing a positive learning environment. This entails an understanding of the affective aspects of classroom climate such as students' attitudes about learning tasks, teachers' feedback to student contributions, management procedures, and teacher/student interactional patterns. Successful language instruction can also be viewed in terms of the extent to which teachers enable learners to follow their own path toward language mastery. Teachers can assist their students with the identification of successful learning strategies. Omaggio's diagnostic inventory and Oxford's framework for assessing learning strategies can provide teachers with valuable information on how their students learn.

Effective language teaching entails the ability to examine critically the elements of a lesson as well as the contents of a textbook with respect to instructional goals and learners' needs. Teachers, for example, can assess the extent to which their lessons include the elements of communicative-based instruction: the use of context, student-to-student interactions, natural uses of language, and an emphasis on original responses. Teachers can reflect on their classroom practices in order to evaluate the origins, purposes, and consequences of their actions. Exploration of beliefs about teaching and actual behaviors in the classroom can be approached through the use of self-report questionnaires, diaries or journals, and teaching scenarios. Teachers also need to stay abreast of current developments in the field by participating in the major language organizations that foster professional development.

ACTIVITIES

1. Review the list of effective classroom instructional features identified by Blum. Which of the characteristics included in this list correspond to the behaviors exhibited by your most outstanding high school language teacher?
2. Prepare a profile of an effective language teacher based on the Checklist for Effective Teaching Practices developed by Kindsvatter et al. (Figure 12.1). Compare your profile with those of other fellow students.
3. Consider Hosenfeld's view of teaching effectiveness. Prepare a profile of an effective teacher using this perspective.
4. Administer the Diagnostic Inventory (Figure 12.3) to a group of learners and summarize the results. According to the results of this questionnaire, what are the major problem areas for these learners?

5. Interview several language teachers to ascertain what they might do with the results of Oxford's language learning strategies inventory. How would you use the results of the questionnaire in planning instructional activities?
6. What do you think are the characteristics of a "good" language lesson? Compare your list with the features outlined by Nunan to describe an effective communicative lesson.
7. Evaluate a language textbook using the criteria proposed by Bragger. What changes would you recommend to the authors to improve the contents of the book?
8. Analyze your teaching philosophy and instructional beliefs by completing the questionnaires prepared by Ramírez. Discuss your answers with other students and defend your views.
9. Prepare a set of "teaching scripts" as outlined in this chapter, and ask several fellow students to prepare brief scenarios for accomplishing the specific teaching objectives. Compare the results and inquire about the role that instructional beliefs play in the use of specific teaching strategies.
10. Interview a group of language teachers to determine their views of an effective teacher and their beliefs about a successful language lesson.
11. Read an article from *Foreign Language Annals* or the *Modern Language Journal* and consider the possible implications for teaching.
12. Consider Thonis' list of abilities that second language teachers should be able to demonstrate. What other items would you add, and why?

REFERENCES

Apple, M. W. (1982). Curricular form and the logic of technical control. In M. W. Apple (Ed.), *Cultural and economic reproduction in education* (pp. 247-274). London: Routledge & Kegan Paul.

Bailey, K. M. (1990). The use of diary studies in teacher education programs. In J. C. Richards & D. Nunan (Eds.), *Second language teacher education* (pp. 215-226). Cambridge, England: Cambridge University Press.

Bartlett, L. (1990). Teacher development through reflective teaching. In J. C. Richards & D. Nunan (Eds.), *Second language teacher education* (pp. 202-214). Cambridge, England: Cambridge University Press.

Birckbichler, D. W. (1982). *Creative activities for the second language classroom.* (Language in education: Theory and practice, 48). Washington, DC: Center for Applied Linguistics.

Blum, R. E. (1984). *Effective schooling practices: A research synthesis.* Portland, OR: Northwest Regional Education Laboratory.

Bragger, J. D. (1985). Material development for the proficiency oriented classroom. In C. J. James (Ed.), *Foreign language proficiency in the classroom and beyond* (pp. 79-115). Lincolnwood, IL: National Textbook.

Brophy, J., & Good, T. (1986). Teacher behavior and student achievement. In M. Wittrock (Ed.), *Handbook of research on teaching* (3rd ed.) (pp. 328-375). New York: Macmillan.

Chastain, K. (1988). *Developing second language skills: Theory and practice* (3rd ed.). New York: Harcourt Brace Jovanovich.

Clark, C. M. (1988). Asking the right questions about teacher preparation: Contributions of research on teacher thinking. *Educational Researcher, 17*(2), 5-12.

Cruickshank, D. R. (1984). Helping teachers achieve wisdom. Unpublished manuscript, Ohio State University at Columbus, College of Education.

Foreign language framework for California public schools, K-12. (1989). Sacramento, CA: California State Department of Education.

Galloway, V., & Labarca, A. (1990). From student to learner: Style, process, and strategy. In D. W. Birckbichler (Ed.), *New perspectives and new directions in foreign language education* (pp. 111-158). Lincolnwood, IL: National Textbook.

Grittner, F. M. (1981). How to break out of the never-ending circle of retraining: A self-adjusting mechanism for the 1980s. In D. L. Lange & C. Linder (Eds.), *Proceedings of the National Conference on Professional Priorities* (pp. 72-77). Hasting-on-Hudson, NY: ACTFL Materials Center.

Hosenfeld, C. (1979). A learning-teaching view of second language instruction. *Foreign Language Annals, 12*(1), 51-54.

Kauchak, D., & Eggen, P. D. (1989). *Learning and teaching: Research based methods.* Boston, MA: Allyn & Bacon.

Kindsvatter, R., Wilen, W., & Ishler, M. (1988). *Dynamics of effective teaching.* White Plains, NY: Longman.

Kindsvatter, R., Wilen, W., & Ishler, M. (1992). *Dynamics of effective teaching* (2nd ed.) White Plains, NY: Longman.

Lewis, M., & Hill, J. (1985). *Practical techniques for language teaching.* Hove, England: Language Teaching Publications.

McGroarty, M. (1991). What do we know about effective second language teaching? In M. Groarty & C. Faltis (Eds.), *Languages in school and society: Policy and pedagogy* (pp. 107-116). Berlin: Mouton de Gruyter.

Muyskens, J. A. (1984). Preservice and inservice teacher training: Focus on proficiency. In T. V. Higgs (Ed.), *Teaching for proficiency: The organizing principle* (pp. 179-200). Lincolnwood, IL: National Textbook.

Nunan, D. (1989). *Designing tasks for the communicative classroom.* Cambridge, England: Cambridge University Press.

Omaggio, A. C. (1981). *Helping learners succeed: Activities for the foreign language classroom.* (Language in education: Theory and practice, 36). Washington, DC: Center for Applied Linguistics.

O'Malley, J. M., & Chamot, A. U. (1990). *Learning strategies in second language acquisition.* Cambridge, England: Cambridge University Press.

Oxford, R. L. (1990). *Language learning strategies: What every teacher should know.* New York: Newbury House.

Porter, P. A., Goldstein, L. M., Leatherman, J., & Conrad, S. (1990). An ongoing dialogue: Learning logs for teachers. In J. C. Richards & D. Nunan (Eds.), *Second language teacher education* (pp. 227-240). Cambridge, England: Cambridge University Press.

Ramírez, A. G. (1988). Instructional beliefs of New York foreign language teachers. In A. G. Ramírez (Ed.), *Spotlight on teaching* (pp. 91-100). Schenectady, NY: New York Association of Foreign Language Teachers.

Richards, J. C., & Nunan, D. (1990). *Second language teacher education.* Cambridge, England: Cambridge University Press.

Rubin, J., & Thompson, I. (1993). *How to be a more successful language learner.* Boston, MA: Heinle & Heinle.

Thonis, E. W. (1991). Competencies for teachers of language minority students. In M. McGroarty & C. Faltis (Eds.), *Languages in school and society: Policy and pedagogy* (pp. 281-292). Berlin: Mouton de Gruyter.

Wexler, P. (1982). Text and subject: A critical sociology of school knowledge. In M. W. Apple (Ed.), *Cultural and economic reproduction in education* (pp. 275-304). London: Routledge & Kegan Paul.

Zeichner, K. M. (1983). Alternative paradigms for teacher education. *Journal of Teacher Education, 34*, 3-9.

Zeichner, K. M., & Liston, D. P. (1985, January). An inquiry-oriented approach to student teaching. Paper presented at the Practicum Conference, Geelong, Australia.

Author Index

Subject Index

Acquisition processes. *See also* Language learning errors
developmental stages, 152
error types, 150
influencing factors, 149
learning strategies, 150
models, 149
natural route of development, 152
American Council on the Teaching of Foreign Languages (ACTFL), 11, 379-380
criteria for assessing speaking, 12, 244-245, 255
cultural proficiency guidelines, 67-68, 80
oral interview procedures, 50-52
proficiency guidelines, 41-43, 52, 54, 239, 309
reading comprehension, 202, 204, 207, 211, 215
speaking abilities, 244-245
writing abilities, 273-275, 281, 287, 289
Audio-lingual method, 117, 124, 129
Authentic materials, 26-30, 32
captioned visuals, 28
in cultural context, 77-79
periodicals, 30
print media, 29
television commercials, 28
types, 26

Background knowledge, 203-206. *See also* Scripts; Schemata
Bottom-up comprehension processes

listening comprehension strategies, 179-182, 186
reading comprehension strategies, 204

Classroom climate, 361-362
teacher checklist, 362
Classroom interactional patterns, 2-5
communicative characteristics, 7
criteria for promoting communication, 10
Classroom language, 3-5
Classroom management, 362, 364
Cognitive strategies, 159-160. *See also* Learner strategies; Learning strategies
Communication strategies
definition, 161
research findings, 162
strategies, 162-163, 175
Communicative abilities. *See also* Conversations
procedures for development, 251-252
Communicative-based instruction
reading, 216
Communicative-based teaching, 251
instructional sequences, 251-252
types of activities, 251-252
Communicative competence, 37, 54. *See also* Language proficiency
components, 38-42
conceptualizations, 306
as context-embedded communication, 38-39
as context-reduced communication, 38-39

390

The Selected Poetry and Prose of Shelley